Social Progress in Britain

Social Progress in Britain

Anthony F. Heath

with Elisabeth Garratt, Ridhi Kashyap, Yaojun Li, and Lindsay Richards

OXFORD
UNIVERSITY PRESS

Great Clarendon Street, Oxford, OX2 6DP,
United Kingdom

Oxford University Press is a department of the University of Oxford.
It furthers the University's objective of excellence in research, scholarship,
and education by publishing worldwide. Oxford is a registered trade mark of
Oxford University Press in the UK and in certain other countries

© Anthony F. Heath 2018

The moral rights of the authors have been asserted

First Edition published in 2018

All rights reserved. No part of this publication may be reproduced, stored in
a retrieval system, or transmitted, in any form or by any means, without the
prior permission in writing of Oxford University Press, or as expressly permitted
by law, by licence or under terms agreed with the appropriate reprographics
rights organization. Enquiries concerning reproduction outside the scope of the
above should be sent to the Rights Department, Oxford University Press, at the
address above

You must not circulate this work in any other form
and you must impose this same condition on any acquirer

Published in the United States of America by Oxford University Press
198 Madison Avenue, New York, NY 10016, United States of America

British Library Cataloguing in Publication Data
Data available

Library of Congress Control Number: 2018940557

ISBN 978-0-19-880548-9

Links to third party websites are provided by Oxford in good faith and
for information only. Oxford disclaims any responsibility for the materials
contained in any third party website referenced in this work.

For Jane

PREFACE

This book grew out of a set of briefing papers, published online by the Centre for Social Investigation of Nuffield College (http://csi.nuff.ox.ac.uk/), which trace social change in Britain over the decades since Sir William Beveridge published his celebrated 1942 report on *Social Insurance and Allied Services*. The Centre for Social Investigation was established by Nuffield College with the aims of addressing contemporary social issues of public interest and providing rigorous, non-partisan reports to policy-makers and the general public. The Centre's aims are closely aligned with the College charter which encourages 'the study by co-operation between academic and non-academic persons of social (including economic and political) problems'. CSI's work builds on a long tradition of research at Nuffield exploring social change, of which the most famous examples are perhaps David Butler and Donald Stokes' *Political Change in Britain*, John Goldthorpe's *Social Mobility and Class Structure in Modern Britain*, and Chelly Halsey's *Twentieth-Century British Social Trends*.

Nuffield College also has a long tradition of cooperation between 'academic and non-academic persons'. Indeed, William Beveridge himself was associated with Nuffield College during the war and in his preface to his 1944 book *Full Employment in a Free Society* he mentioned how he had benefited from the 'admirable series of conferences in connection with the College, organized originally by Mr G.D.H. Cole'. Nowadays, G. D. H. Cole is not a well-known figure, but he played a key role in Oxford and more particularly in Nuffield College social science. He initiated the Social Reconstruction Survey, which collected demographic, economic, and social data for evidence-based social reform. It was the forerunner of many notable national surveys conducted by members of the college, on which I have drawn liberally in this book.

Social Progress in Britain thus stands in a Nuffield College tradition of research which extends back to William Beveridge and G. D. H. Cole, and which is greatly indebted to the many practitioners of that tradition such as David Butler, John Goldthorpe, and Chelly Halsey, who all developed the tradition during the intervening years. In some ways, though, *Social Progress in Britain* is not a typical representative of the Nuffield tradition since, in writing it, I have entirely avoided sophisticated statistical analyses and have instead simply tried to piece together the (sometimes confusing and contradictory) evidence about what has happened in the fight against the five giant evils that Beveridge identified in 1942. More sophisticated analysis should certainly be undertaken in order to test rigorously the many conjectures which I advance about the underlying causes of social progress in Britain, or its lack. However, I decided to follow the advice which I always give my doctoral students—'a completed thesis is always better than the perfect but incomplete thesis'.

While I am named as the author of *Social Progress in Britain*, it is important to emphasize that it has been a collective effort involving all the members of CSI—Beth Garratt, James Laurence, Lindsay Richards, Valentina di Stasio, Noah Carl, and Wouter Zwysen—as well as many academic and non-academic members of the college community. CSI has also been very fortunate in having a supportive advisory board—Andrew Dilnot, Iqbal Wahhab, Stephen Aldridge, Paul Cleal, Richard Dick, Stephanie Flanders, Michael Kell, Bruno Paulson, Gemma Rosenblatt, Ray Shostak, and Stephen Timms—who have been generous with their time and advice.

I would also like to thank Bess Bukodi, Felix Busch, Jonathan Cribb, Duncan Gallie, Michael Goldacre, John Goldthorpe, Angus Hawkins, Bernie Hayes, John Jerrim, Ridhi Kashyap, Alice Lazzati, Yaojun Li, Colin Mills, Nan Dirk de Graaf, Marii Paskov, Max Roser, Reannan Rottier, Ricky Taylor, Nathan Thomas, Becky Tunstall, and Dingeman Wiertz for their practical help and advice as well as the team at Oxford University Press—Dominic Byatt, Elakkia Bharathi, Sarah Parker, Dawn Preston, and Olivia Wells—for their support and forbearance with my various whims. Needless to say, neither the college, the advisory board, the members of CSI, nor any of these friends or colleagues are responsible for the final content of the book. I have freely used my author's prerogative to ignore advice and therefore take full responsibility for the interpretations of the data and for all errors and omissions.

Anthony F. Heath

Nuffield College

CONTENTS

1. Beveridge's Five Giants and Other Challenges to Social Progress — 1
2. The Fight against Want: Material Prosperity, Inequality, and Poverty — 13
   with Elisabeth Garratt and Lindsay Richards
3. The Fight against Disease: Life Expectancy, Disease, and Lifestyle — 34
   with Ridhi Kashyap and Elisabeth Garratt
4. The Fight against Ignorance: Participation, Standards, and Non-Economic Outcomes — 61
   with Lindsay Richards
5. The Fight against Squalor: Overcrowding, Homelessness, and Affordability — 88
   with Elisabeth Garratt
6. The Fight against Idleness: Unemployment and Discouraged Workers — 114
   with Yaojun Li and Elisabeth Garratt
7. The Challenge of Inequality of Opportunity: Class, Gender, and Ethnic Inequalities — 139
   with Yaojun Li and Lindsay Richards
8. The Challenge of Social Corrosion: National Identity, Social Divisions, and Disengagement — 165
   with Lindsay Richards
9. Progress in Tackling Beveridge's Five Giants: The Successes and Limitations of Social Reform — 198

ENDNOTES — 213
INDEX — 247

1 Beveridge's Five Giants and Other Challenges to Social Progress

Introduction

Britain has seen huge social changes over the course of my lifetime. The world of the 1950s, when I grew up in a modest suburb of Liverpool, has vanished for ever. The material standard of living we enjoyed then would nowadays seem to be distinctly substandard. We didn't have a family car; I shared a bedroom with my older brother; and there was no television set, though we did have a telephone—a rather unfamiliar contraption which we were all too scared to use. Computers, and even pocket calculators, were unknown, but we did know our times tables. There never seemed to be quite enough to eat and we were all rather skinny. There was no problem of obesity in our family, but we didn't grow particularly tall. Today's younger generation tower over us.

However, we did go to church every Sunday (reluctantly, it must be admitted) and belonged to the Boy Scouts (less reluctantly). And we were in no doubt that we were expected to make the most of the educational opportunities which opened up if one passed the scholarship exam. This was the era of the tripartite system—grammar schools, technical schools, and the secondary moderns. We never met anyone from one of the other types of school. We didn't even meet anyone from the nearby Catholic grammar school. We never really met anyone who wasn't white British, Protestant, and lower middle class, though looking back, maybe the Scouts reached a wider range of young people. And all schools were single sex, so we met no girls. My mother did not go out to work, and as far as I knew nobody else's mother did either.

But we were very proud to be British. We were thrilled when it was an Englishman, Roger Bannister, who beat the Australians and the Swedes to run the first 4-minute mile, and to be honest a bit disappointed that it was a New Zealander and a Nepalese Sherpa who were the first to climb Everest, even though it was a British expedition. And I loved my globe of the world with all the countries coloured red, parts of the British Empire, which decorated so much more of the globe than the blue of the French empire. I avidly collected stamps from as many British colonies as I could. We never met foreigners or went on foreign holidays. There was no immigration that we were aware of, though we did have distant relatives who had emigrated to the USA before the war.

It is a vanished world—and not one to which I personally look back with any great nostalgia. I think my grandchildren have a much nicer time growing up today. But many people do seem to look back on the 1950s as a golden age of stability and national cohesion, and perhaps it was an age which did have some strengths which we have now lost.

In 1942 (which happens to be the year I was born), William Beveridge published his report with the rather dry title 'Social Insurance and Allied Services', which helped to shape the post-war welfare state and the Britain in which I grew up during the 1950s. His report reviewed the pre-war schemes of social insurance against the risks of unemployment, ill-health, widows, orphans, and old age pensions, blind person's assistance, and workmen's compensation (for death and incapacity due to industrial accidents). There was already an extensive patchwork of insurance schemes in place when Beveridge wrote his report, and he claimed that

the picture presented is impressive in two ways. First, it shows that provision for most of the many varieties of need...has already been made in Britain on a scale not surpassed and hardly rivalled in any other country of the world. In one respect only of the first importance, namely limitation of medical service...does Britain's achievement fall seriously short of what has been accomplished elsewhere.[1]

The Five Giants

Beveridge's key proposals were for bringing the patchwork of insurance schemes into a unified system of social security. It was the creation of the NHS in 1947 (spearheaded by Labour firebrand and left-winger Aneurin Bevan) which tackled the limitations of medical services, while it was Rab Butler's Education Act of 1944 which established the post-war system of education. To be fair, Beveridge saw his proposals as only one part of a comprehensive policy of social progress (his term). He acknowledged that: 'Social insurance fully developed may provide income security; it is an attack upon Want. But Want is only one of five giants on the road of reconstruction and in some ways the easiest to attack. The others are Disease, Ignorance, Squalor and Idleness.'[2] The central theme of this book is how successfully Britain has tackled these five giants.

Social progress has a wonderfully optimistic ring about it, especially when one considers when Beveridge was writing. The war was still far from won in 1942, and memories of the Great Depression and the absence of any real social progress throughout the interwar years must have been fresh in Beveridge's mind.

But Britain did indeed make a great deal of progress in tackling the five giants in the immediate post-war period. Material living standards rose and by the end of the 1950s Prime Minister Harold Macmillan could boast that 'You've never had it so good'. He actually appears to have said in a 1957 speech to Conservative supporters, 'Let us be frank about it: most of our people have never had it so good. Go around the country...and you'll see a state of prosperity such as we have never had in my lifetime—nor indeed ever in the history of this country.'[3]

Certainly, there were great strides in health and the fight against infectious diseases. The 1944 Education Act with its abolition of fees for state grammar school education was expected to deliver equality of opportunity, and I certainly benefited personally from the new educational opportunities which had not been available to my parents. The raising of the school-leaving age to 15 in 1947 extended the length of schooling. There were major house-building programmes and slum clearance (though we now wonder whether the enthusiastic slum clearance might actually have destroyed some cohesive communities). And there was full employment. The five giants looked well on the way to being vanquished. The Conservative party manifesto in 1959 could claim that

We have provided over two million new homes and almost two million new school places, a better health service and a modern pensions plan. We have now stabilised the cost of living while maintaining full employment...By raising living standards and by social reform we are succeeding in creating One Nation at home.[4]

Nevertheless, modern forms of Beveridge's five giants remain high on the list of government priorities—in 2015 none of the main party manifestos missed out economic growth, improved education, an effective health service, reduced levels of unemployment, and more home building to meet the housing shortage. The main headings in the Conservative party manifesto for 2015, for example, included An Economic Plan to Help You and Your Family, Jobs for All, The Best Schools and Hospitals for You and Your Family, Securing Your Home, and Your Neighbourhood.[5] Want, Disease, Ignorance, Squalor, and Idleness still appear to be threatening giants, ready to attack once again. Have we been running fast but not moving forward, as if on a treadmill in the gym?

So what progress have we actually made in Britain? Why haven't we vanquished Beveridge's five giants? Why do they continue to remain at the top of the political agenda? Are they evolving like viruses as fast as we learn to tackle them? Or is it a case that our aspirations rise as quickly as our incomes: we always want 10 per cent more than we currently have and our feelings of well-being never improve.

Moreover, I doubt if anyone would dare nowadays to repeat Beveridge's boast that provision in Britain 'has already been made on a scale not surpassed and hardly rivalled in any other country of the world'. It is sometimes suggested that we have in fact been falling behind—for example in our standards of education. It is certainly true that our international standing has never been quite the same since Churchill, Roosevelt, and Stalin met at Yalta in 1945 to settle the framework for the post-war world. But have we fallen behind domestically too, slipping down the international league table in our standards of health, education, housing, and prosperity?

The Challenges of Equality of Opportunity and Social Cohesion

In prioritizing Beveridge's giants have governments neglected other, perhaps equally important, challenges or lost some of the strengths we used to have in the 1950s? One set of social issues which Beveridge perfectly reasonably left out of his list of giants are those connected to inequality. In one sense, Beveridge was indeed concerned about the inequality in the life chances of the more disadvantaged sections of society, and in his subsequent book *Full Employment in a Free Society* he did indeed refer to the 'evil of inequality', so perhaps I can legitimately take it to be a sixth giant.[6] The proposals in his 1942 report were essentially aimed at mitigating the risks to which manual workers and their families were disproportionately exposed. At the time when he was writing his report, economic inequalities in Britain were declining, and they continued to decline until the late 1970s. Thereafter, as is well known, the trend reversed and inequalities increased quite sharply after 1980. Britain became one of the most unequal highly-developed Western countries. So we certainly need to be charting not just the average improvements in tackling Want, Disease, Ignorance, Squalor, and Idleness but also the spread around the average. The average may have increased, but those at the bottom of society may not have seen much progress themselves. In a sense the five giants may have simply become more selective in whom they pick on, picking on the weak and vulnerable.

We therefore need to ask whether the trend towards increasing economic inequality is paralleled in the other domains of health, education, housing, and risks of unemployment. Are we seeing a general polarization of society between the haves and the have nots? It would not be surprising if trends in economic inequality have parallels in housing. But what about in education and health?

Oxford economist Anthony Atkinson, who did more than anyone else to put economic inequality onto the academic and political agendas, has also suggested that increasing economic inequality may undermine the equality of opportunity which was at the heart of the post-war educational reforms.[7] For much of the post-war period the political consensus was that inequality of outcomes was more or less acceptable provided that there was a level playing field for the competitors. The prize of huge wage packets, like those of footballers or bankers, was not in itself objectionable provided that anyone with the requisite talent and motivation could have a reasonable chance of securing the prize, regardless of their social class origins or ethnic background.

But with rising inequality has come the fear that the playing field is no longer as level as it had been back in the 1950s when bright boys and girls from humble backgrounds could win their scholarships and go all the way to Oxford or Cambridge. Nowadays the rich and privileged may be better able to ensure their children's success, for example by moving to the catchment area of a successful secondary school, or paying for private coaching for the high-stakes examinations. And today's youngsters have no chance of the generous maintenance grants which gave myself and my middle-class contemporaries a decent standard of living while at college and allowed us to graduate debt-free at the end of our course.

Inequality of opportunity is not only morally objectionable and economically inefficient (because of the wasted talent). It may also have serious knock-on repercussions. One fear is that a highly unequal society dominated by inherited privilege may come to lack political legitimacy. For this (and other worthy reasons), recent British governments have been exercised by Britain's lack of social mobility and have established bodies such as the Social Mobility Commission. In his foreword to the commission's report *Time for Change: An Assessment of Government Policies on Social Mobility 1997–2017*,[8] Alan Milburn (the then chair of the commission) wrote,

These are volatile and uncertain times. When more and more people feel like they are losing out, social mobility matters more than ever before. Higher social mobility can be a rallying point to prove that modern capitalist economies like our own are capable of creating better, fairer and more inclusive societies... The policies of the past have brought some progress, but many are no longer fit for purpose in our changing world. The old agenda has not delivered enough social progress. New approaches are needed if Britain is to become a fairer and more equal country. It is time for a change.

I shall try to answer the question whether Britain has become a fairer and more inclusive society.

Another set of negative consequences may also follow from rising economic inequality. Economic inequality may be important not just in its own right but also because it may have negative social consequences, even for the materially advantaged. As Richard Wilkinson and Kate Pickett have cogently argued in *The Spirit Level: Why Equality Is Better for Everyone*, we may all become worse off as society becomes more unequal—the spillover effects of inequality may well include declining social trust and cohesion alongside increasing crime. Increasing economic inequality may thus mean that the benefits of economic progress are offset by social retreat: 'The evidence merely confirms the common intuition that inequality is divisive and socially corrosive', conclude Wilkinson and Pickett.[9]

These concerns raise the question of whether social cohesion has been declining in Britain. Are we, as the 1959 Conservative manifesto proudly asserted, creating One Nation at home? Or are we moving back to the situation described by Benjamin Disraeli (later to become Conservative prime minister) in his 1845 novel *Sybil: or, the Two Nations*:[10]

'[S]ay what you like, our Queen reigns over the greatest nation that ever existed.'

'Which nation?' asked the younger stranger, 'for she reigns over two.'

The stranger paused; Egremont was silent, but looked inquiringly.

'Yes,' resumed the younger stranger, after a moment's interval. 'Two nations; between whom there is no intercourse and no sympathy; who are as ignorant of each other's habits, thoughts, and feelings, as if they were dwellers in different zones, or inhabitants of different planets; who are formed by a different breeding, are fed by a different food, are ordered by different manners, and are not governed by the same laws.'

'you speak of...' said Egremont, hesitatingly.

'THE RICH AND THE POOR.'

Should we, then, move away from the rather individualistic approach of Beveridge to a more social approach? In prioritizing economic growth and prosperity, have we lost sight of other, perhaps equally or more important, aspects of society which Beveridge probably could take for granted? A later Conservative prime minister, Margaret Thatcher, famously once said there was 'no such thing as society'. Her remarks were perhaps taken out of context,[11] but there is a sense in which society, and the social relationships, unifying national identities and shared sentiments which make up a one-nation society, had no place in the ideology of Thatcherism. Whatever Margaret Thatcher's precise views on society, a subsequent Conservative prime minister, David Cameron, emphasized the importance of social, and not just economic, progress. In his speech at the 2015 Conservative party conference, he affirmed that 'A Greater Britain doesn't just need a stronger economy—it needs a stronger society.'

It is not entirely clear exactly what David Cameron meant by a 'stronger society', but a good place to start is by looking at the strength of the social relationships between people, their willingness to help each other, and the vigour of the voluntary sector. Harvard political scientist Robert Putnam, in his landmark study *Bowling Alone: The Collapse and Revival of American Community*, showed that there had been a post-war decline of civic community in the USA; there was, for example, declining membership in the Scouts or Church groups to which we had belonged in the 1950s. The vibrant civic life, based on active participation in a wide range of voluntary groups and associations which had so impressed nineteenth-century observers of US life such as Alexis de Toqueville in his 1835 study *Democracy in America*, seemed to be in worrying decline.[12] Putnam termed this web of social relationships 'social capital'. He also argued that social capital has wide-ranging spillover benefits not just for individuals but for society as a whole, leading to better government and a more smoothly functioning economy. Social capital may thus be good for all of us, even for those who don't join in. As Robert Putnam explains, 'If the crime rate in my neighborhood is lowered by neighbors keeping an eye on each other's homes, I benefit even if I personally spend most of my time on the road and never even nod to another resident on the street.'[13]

Incidentally, William Beveridge himself was one of the earliest British thinkers to use the term social capital in the modern sense. In his 1944 report on *Full Employment in a Free Society* he talked about the way in which migration on the part of the workless to seek jobs could undermine community social capital and by implication weaken the strength of society (paragraph 22). Subsequently, in 1948, Beveridge published a further study, *Voluntary Action: A Report of Methods of Social Advance*, in which he developed rather similar arguments. He argued that there was a need for non-state voluntary action in order to improve conditions of life both for the individual concerned and for his or her fellow citizens. He focussed on mutual aid (as exemplified by the British tradition of friendly societies) and philanthropy or social conscience:

the feeling which makes men who are materially comfortable, mentally uncomfortable so long as their neighbours are materially uncomfortable: to have social conscience is to be unwilling to make a separate peace with the giant social evils of Want, Disease, Squalor, Ignorance, Idleness, escaping into personal prosperity oneself, while leaving one's fellows in their clutches.[14]

In essence, Beveridge seems to have felt that material advance on its own is likely to prove a rather hollow success in the absence of social advance based on social conscience and concerns for one's fellow citizens. And I would agree with him.

Rising individual prosperity, then, might well have been accompanied by declining vibrancy of civic life and social capital. If we are to take the notion of social progress seriously, then surely we need to take account of the nature of the strength and resilience of our social relationships and sense of social cohesion.

Another set of social changes which Beveridge would not have thought to tackle are those arising from immigration. Britain was still a country of net emigration in the 1950s when I was growing up.[15] Inward migration (in contrast to the outward migration which I had been familiar with in my childhood) has probably helped to drive our economic prosperity, although economists do not unanimously agree. But it has surely led to overcrowding, especially in houses and schools, and the increased competition for jobs may well have fuelled a backlash from more disadvantaged sections of British society who face competition for jobs and housing from newly arrived migrants. In particular, the European Union's insistence on free movement between member states, and the surge in immigration from the European Union, became a key issue fuelling opposition to membership of the Union. The 2016 Brexit campaigns and referendum outcome highlighted these concerns and led many commentators to suggest that Britain had indeed divided into two nations or tribes with little sympathy for each other and with incompatible visions for the future of Britain. Academic analysis suggested that the underlying conditions which gave rise to Brexit were the growing inequality between the winners and losers of globalization, the rapid pace of immigration, and growing distrust of the political elite on the part of those who had been left behind.[16]

Even before Brexit, former prime ministers Tony Blair, Gordon Brown, and David Cameron all emphasized the need to strengthen British society in order to cope with these challenges. They particularly emphasized the importance of British values in unifying society and integrating minorities. Whatever the root causes, there is a sense that social cohesion, shared sentiments of British identity, and the sense of pride in being British which I so clearly remember from my childhood have all been in decline. Gordon Brown, in a speech when he was chancellor of the exchequer, started a debate on Britishness. He argued:

Now for years we didn't think we needed to debate or even think in depth about what it was to be a British citizen. But I think more and more people are recognising not just how important their national identity is to them but how important it is to our country.

A strong sense of being British helps unite and unify us; it builds stronger social cohesion among communities... it helps us deal with issues as varied as what Britain does in Europe; to issues of managed migration and how we better integrate ethnic minorities... Like you I'm very proud of being British; proud of British values, proud of what we contribute to the world. And like you I [want] to make sure that we consider today all that we can do to build an even stronger sense of national purpose which unifies us for the years to come.[17]

We should always be a bit sceptical of commentators when they allege that things are not what they were. Your scepticism should certainly be extended to my own personal impressions of how pride in Britain has declined since I was growing up. One of my favourite sayings (attributed to the US statistician and management consultant J. Edwards Deming) is, 'In God we trust, all others must bring data.' So in the following chapters we will attempt to bring data to bear on measuring social progress in Britain over the last half century.

What the Book Covers

I will start by documenting how much progress has been made in tackling Beveridge's five giants. The giants by no means exhaust the list of topics which I could potentially cover. There are many other social changes which have occurred in Britain over the last fifty or sixty years, such as secularization, divorce, single parenthood, and immigration. However, some of these other social changes cannot unambiguously be regarded as representing social progress or its opposite. Whether secularization is a good or a bad thing would, I suspect, be hotly contested, whereas there would be much more of a consensus that Want, Disease, Ignorance, and Squalor need to be tackled, and that may be why they figure in one guise or another in all the manifestos of our major political parties. Beveridge's five giants are all legitimate objectives of public policy, rather than private matters for individual decision. They are a good place to start. Other changes which I would have liked to include are those of crime and disorder and those related to the environment in which we live, especially issues of pollution.[18] I apologize for their omission.

In order to translate Beveridge's colourful terms into measurable concepts, I interpret the five giants as:

- Want = material progress, particularly with respect to household income;
- Disease = health and life expectancy;
- Ignorance = educational participation and standards;
- Squalor = housing conditions, especially overcrowding;
- Idleness = unemployment and enforced inactivity.

Contemporary social science evidence suggests that Beveridge was right to identify these as his giants. All five have been shown to be important causes of people's sense of well-being.[19] To be sure, material prosperity is an important source of well-being and may also indirectly provide access to better health, education, and housing. But even among people with the same level of material prosperity, the quality of one's health and housing, education, and whether one is unemployed or not all make major differences to one's feeling of well-being.

A long and healthy life is perhaps the most basic measure of social progress. What is the value of ever greater material prosperity if it were to come at the expense of premature death and a shortened lifespan? Indeed, one could argue that a long and healthy life is an even better measure of social progress than is any of the economic measures. Good health appears to be even more strongly related to one's feelings of well-being than is material prosperity.[20] There is also excellent long-term data on mortality which are of a distinctly higher quality and reliability than the data for measuring material progress.

Education is often seen to be primarily a means to equip people for the labour market, increasing the number of skilled recruits for employers and improving Britain's competitiveness. And education is indeed one of the major routes for an individual to secure higher income and progress up the social ladder. However, education has a wider range of benefits for the individual and the society than simply improving one's own or the national income. Education tends to promote self-confidence, tolerance, and trust in others and is linked with the adoption of healthy lifestyles. It can also be thought of as a major means for improving citizens' capabilities in coping not only with the economy but also with the many other challenges of modern life.[21]

There is convincing evidence too that housing quality has a range of consequences for one's well-being—for one's physical and mental health and marital relations, for example.[22] A substantial body of evidence shows that falling below the normal standards of housing is associated with poorer outcomes, even among people with similar income levels. Moreover, well-being is responsive to improvements in housing conditions, getting better when housing conditions improve and declining when household conditions worsen.[23]

Unemployment also has harmful effects over and above the loss of income involved. It affects one's longer-term economic prospects since time out of the labour market means that one's work skills are becoming rusty, while people who have kept their jobs are acquiring further job skills and experience. But job loss has a much wider range of non-economic consequences in addition to its longer-term financial implications. It affects one's psychological well-being and physical health as well as one's pocket. It is associated with increased risk of alcohol and drug problems, increased risk of suicide, and reduced civic engagement and social participation. It also has spillover consequences for other people such as one's family, increasing for example the risks of divorce, of domestic violence, and even mental health problems for one's partner.[24] My reading of the evidence suggests that we should take these wider social and psychological effects of unemployment very seriously indeed. I am sure Beveridge was right to see Idleness as a serious evil in its own right. Figure 1.1 suggests that it comes second only to health as a driver of life satisfaction.[25]

After investigating social progress in tackling Beveridge's five giants, I will then address the themes of inequality of opportunity and social cohesion. These are features of the society as a whole rather than of the individual members. They do not fit neatly into an accounting model of social progress which the five giants lend themselves to, but they may have major potential consequences for individual members. Social conflict and disorder, which in a sense are the opposites of cohesion, have major consequences for well-being, not least because of the defensive measures which one needs to take against it, as people who lived through the troubles in Northern Ireland will remember. Discrimination, which is one major source of inequality of opportunity, has been shown to have major consequences for individuals' mental health and well-being.[26] More generally, inequality of opportunity may generate feelings of relative deprivation and thus have the potential to be a source of wider discontent.[27]

Throughout the book my perspective will be that of the well-being of the citizens themselves. Governments frequently emphasize national progress— for example the rate of growth of GDP. Harold Macmillan's Conservative party manifesto back in 1959, for example, had very little to say about the living standards of ordinary people, despite the 'you've never had it so good'

Figure 1.1. Of the Five Giants, Disease and Idleness have the strongest influence on life satisfaction

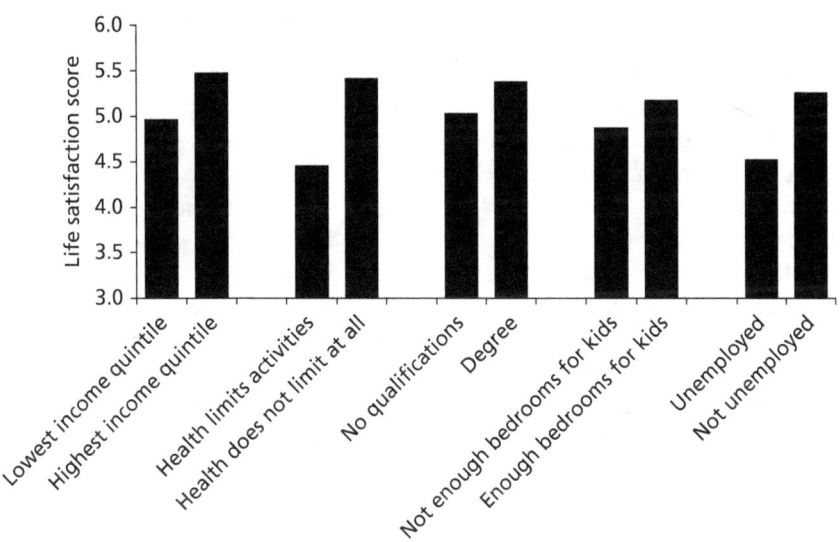

Note: life satisfaction measured on a 1–7 scale; all estimates adjusted for age
Source: Understanding Society, UK Household Longitudinal Study Wave 6 (2014–15)

slogan. Instead it catalogued the overall strength of the economy and the surplus of exports over imports, along with other national conditions like the strength of the armed forces. These are perfectly reasonable things for a government to tackle, and they may in turn lead to prosperity for the individual citizen. But as the Commission on the Measurement of Economic Performance and Social Progress recently noted, there is not necessarily a one-to-one relationship between them.[28] For example, a lot of Irish growth in the period of the so-called Celtic tiger actually ended up overseas as the growth had been fuelled by inwards investment, the profits on which returned to the foreign investors rather than to Irish citizens themselves. The approach I take in this book is intended to be broadly in line with that of the commission.[29]

In each chapter I will attempt to put the British experience in international context. Wherever possible I compare the key British trends with the ones in other large developed democracies, which I will term our peer countries. For these comparisons I have selected Canada, France, Germany, Italy, Japan, Sweden, and the USA. These are all highly developed countries (as measured for example by the United Nations Development Programme's Human Development Index) and most of them are large countries not too different in size from the UK.[30] To be sure, small Nordic countries like Norway and Finland regularly top international league tables such as the Human Development

Index. But I think that scale really makes a difference to many of the things that I will be covering in this book. I doubt if Britain could ever aspire to become a small cohesive country such as Finland, although it might make sense to compare Scotland or Wales with the smaller Nordic countries. However, because of the intrinsic interest of the Nordic model of welfare I have included Sweden, which is the largest of the Nordic countries. And I have also included the USA because of its intrinsic interest, although the much greater scale of the USA makes comparisons somewhat suspect. However, since one of the policy developments in Britain in the 1980s was to move Britain away from European models of welfare and towards the USA model, it makes sense to look for Anglo-American similarities in subsequent progress.

I must also be upfront: even for apparently straightforward matters such as mapping trends over time in freedom from want, there can be hideous problems of non-comparable data, changing definitions, and measurement error. Different sources often tell different stories. Rather than cherry-pick the data that suit my overall preconceptions, I will wherever possible compare results from different sources. This may well lead you to have less confidence in the robustness of economic and social science than I might like. But as Christopher Jencks once remarked, 'The methods we have used may involve considerable error. In self-defense, we can only say that the magnitude of these errors is almost certainly less than if we had simply consulted our prejudices, which seems to be the usual alternative.'[31]

Why are there more questions than answers, Grandad? was the title of one of my favourite children's books which I read countless times to my children.[32] Sandy's incessant questions frustrated Grandad, as he did not always have the answers. So he locked Sandy up in the attic filled with junk, ordering him to clean it all up. In the attic Sandy discovered a magic book with all the answers (and much more). Alas, this is not going to be a magic book with all the answers. Like Sandy, I have posed far more questions than can possibly be answered. As we will find as we go through the following chapters, some apparently simple questions cannot be answered confidently. We often lack reliable data, or worse still we find that different data tell us different stories.

So sometimes I shall become, instead of an inquisitive Sandy, an irritated grandad who is frustrated that, despite the importance of the questions, and the confident claims which politicians and commentators advance, we really cannot provide definitive answers. But to become clearer about the extent of our ignorance is perhaps, in itself, not an entirely useless exercise.

2 The Fight against Want

Material Prosperity, Inequality, and Poverty

with Elisabeth Garratt and Lindsay Richards

Introduction

'Want is one only of five giants on the road of reconstruction and in some ways the easiest to attack,' argued Sir William Beveridge in his 1942 report.[1] Want is a good place to start a review of social progress. While I have absolutely no desire to take a purely materialistic view of social progress, alleviation from Want is surely a precondition for achieving many other elements of social progress. Certainly, Want seems to be a major cause of many contemporary problems, driving populations whose food supplies have failed as a result of climate change, famine, or civil war to migrate—many of them to the El Dorado of the European Union where generous social insurance schemes like those proposed by Beveridge appear to have largely eliminated Want.

So my central question in this chapter is how successful has Britain been in tackling the giant of Want. Was it as easy as Beveridge had imagined? Did his social insurance proposals succeed in providing an effective safety net so that Want was no longer a problem? According to the social research of Seebohm Rowntree and his colleagues in York, poverty fell from 31.1 per cent of the wage-earning population in 1936 to a much more modest 2.8 per cent in 1951.[2] They claimed that much of the fall had been due to the reforms initiated by the Beveridge Report. Others were a bit sceptical as to whether Beveridge's social insurance schemes should take quite so much credit—they argued that post-war full employment and higher wages might have played a bigger part.[3] But there seemed to be agreement that 'social conditions are vastly better now than in pre-war days, although the remaining pockets of poverty, especially among the old, rule out any undue complacency'.[4] My question for this chapter is whether the giant of Want has continued to be kept at bay, or whether we have become unduly complacent.

There are several reasons why we might have been lulled into complacency. There was broad agreement between the main political parties throughout the 1950s and 1960s on the nature and scale of British welfare programmes. However, British welfare policy then changed direction after Margaret Thatcher became prime minister in 1979. Britain gradually moved away from the post-war settlement with its universal benefits towards a more US-style market approach in which welfare benefits became less generous relative to average earnings in employment and more restricted in coverage.[5] Incomes and earnings also became a great deal more unequal in the 1980s. The full unemployment of the 1950s was not maintained in the later decades of the twentieth century. Increasing immigration may also have exerted some downward pressure on wages, and more recently government austerity measures following the 2007/8 financial crash and the subsequent recession further curtailed government expenditure on benefits for working-age people.[6]

There are also indications that the giant of Want may be on the attack once again. There has been considerable publicity given to the rising use of foodbanks since the recession. Commentators have linked this to austerity measures.[7] There has also been a suggestion that diseases linked with poverty, such as rickets, which we had long thought to be a thing of the past in a developed country like Britain, have been making an unwelcome reappearance. So it is by no means implausible that Want has reappeared in contemporary Britain.

Debates about recent trends and the effect of austerity measures are, unsurprisingly, highly political. Before turning to these contentious issues, I will first set them in context with an overview of long-term trends in material prosperity since Beveridge's day. I will compare Britain's performance with that of other developed democracies—our peer countries. My questions are: how much has material prosperity improved in Britain? Have we fallen behind, or powered ahead of, other major developed countries? And how have the benefits of economic growth been distributed between rich and poor? Have we followed the US model with the rich gaining most of the benefits of growth, or have those at the bottom shared in the general improvement? And crucially, what have the implications been for keeping Want at bay? Has there been a resurgence of poverty since the financial crash and the subsequent recession? Let me warn you in advance, though, that we have more questions than convincing answers.

How Does Britain's Material Prosperity Compare with That in Peer Countries?

Let me start, then, with a review of the overall changes in Britain's material prosperity since Beveridge's day. I will set this in context by looking at the trends in Canada, France, Germany, Italy, Japan, Sweden, and the USA—which I refer to as our peer countries. Perhaps the most instructive comparisons are with France, Germany, and Italy, which are large post-industrial societies of a similar size as Britain (and with some similarities in historical and industrial legacies). Comparison with similar countries can potentially tell us, or at least give us a clue, whether British reforms like the move away from the post-war welfare state to a more US-style model and the deregulation of the labour market have increased risks of poverty in Britain. Alternatively, did the reforms increase the rate of economic growth and thus make it easier to eliminate poverty (which was almost certainly Margaret Thatcher's intention)?

I start in Figure 2.1 with the trends in GDP per head for the UK and the seven peer countries. GDP—gross domestic product—is a standard measure of a country's total economic output.[8] There are several important criticisms of GDP per head as a measure of material prosperity. I will come to these in a moment, but GDP has the advantage that it has been estimated over a long time span for all our peer countries. (This is because it can be derived from administrative data such as tax returns to government and does not rely on representative surveys of the population, which only started to become available in the 1960s.) The main data source I use here goes back to 1950. These figures have been adjusted so that they take account of inflation and also of differences in purchasing power between countries.[9] These adjustments are rather tricky issues, and the results obtained by different economists differ somewhat, but the broad picture is fairly clear.

Figure 2.1 shows that there was impressive improvement in material prosperity in all eight countries. In the case of the UK, GDP per head in 2014 was

Figure 2.1. Like Britain, all the peer countries became much richer between 1950 and 2014

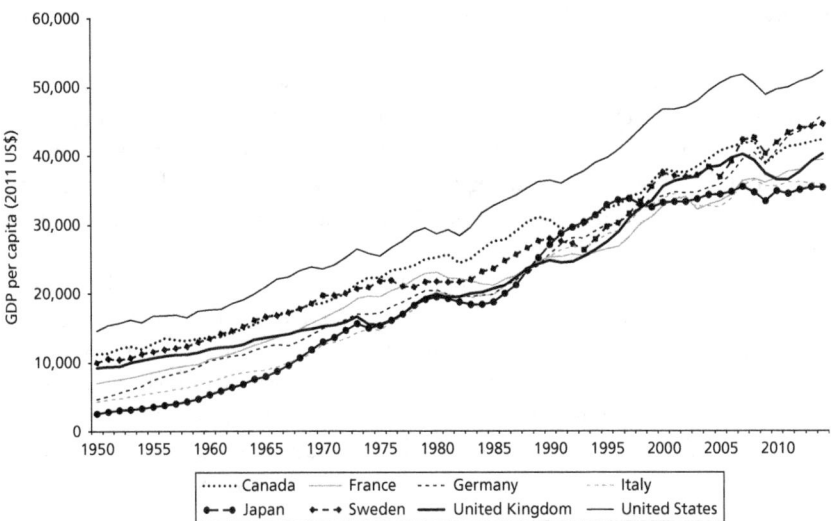

Source: Max Roser, 'Economic growth: I.4 GDP growth since 1950', Our World in Data, https://ourworldindata.org/economic-growth[10]

4.3 times what it had been in 1950. It is also clear that the USA was well in the lead throughout, about fifteen years ahead of second-placed Germany. That is, in 2014, Germany had reached the same level of GDP per head as the USA had reached fifteen years earlier in 1999. The UK was another four years behind and, at the back of this bunch of large developed countries, Japan brought up the rear twenty-six years behind the USA.

We can also see some pretty big downturns, more or less every decade (for example, mid-1970s, early 1980s, early 1990s) and of course the big dip after the financial crash of 2007/8 and the ensuing recession. It's been rather a bumpy ride. Different countries seem to have been more or less affected by the recession following the financial crash, but the most recent data from the World Bank suggest that, by 2016, all countries had regained the peak which they had achieved before the crash.[11] Britain has just about returned to its previous peak but in effect growth stalled after the crash. In contrast, Germany has performed much more impressively than Britain since the crash—quite possibly because Britain had an unbalanced economy at the time of the crash with too large a dependence on the financial services sector. Nonetheless, the big picture is pretty clear: all these countries were a lot richer in 2014 than they had been in 1950, and so all of them should have found it a much easier task to fight the giant of Want.

It also seems fairly clear that Britain was in the middle of the bunch both at the beginning and at the end of the period, more or less level pegging with France. The only reasonably clear change in ranking over the years is that of Germany, which made greater progress than most other countries. However, I should mention that one's choice of baseline year can make quite a big difference to one's conclusion. For example, Germany, Italy, and Japan (the principal defeated countries in the Second World War) took a considerable hit in the war years and by 1950 had not caught up with the position they had been in fifteen years earlier in 1935.[12] One could therefore argue that their positions in our baseline year of 1950 were misleadingly low. Sweden on the other hand remained neutral during the war and avoided the human and material costs which the other countries suffered. So perhaps Sweden's starting point in 1950 was misleadingly high.

What about Britain? Britain slipped behind in the first half of the period, and had fallen to the back of the bunch by 1980. However, Britain then began to make up some of the lost ground in the 1980s and 1990s and grew particularly fast in the decade leading up to the financial crash. Since then, Britain's progress has been unspectacular, though remaining in the middle of the bunch. Most economists would attribute Britain's improved progress since the 1980s to Margaret Thatcher's reforms, increasing competitiveness. On the other hand, the reforms may well have unbalanced the economy, making Britain too reliant on financial services and hence vulnerable to the financial crash of 2007/8.

The other major development after 1980 was the increase in inequality. As I mentioned earlier, there are several major issues with GDP and it is increasingly recognized as having limited usefulness for measuring economic progress.[13] Perhaps most important for the purpose of this book is that GDP per head ignores the issue of inequality around the average. If the rich become much richer, while the prosperity of the majority stagnates, then the average could increase even though the prosperity of the majority of people had not improved. Hence changes in GDP per head (which is essentially an average) can give a misleading impression of the material progress experienced by the bulk of the population. A better measure than the average is the median, a concept which I will try to explain in the next section.

In Figure 2.2 I show how income inequality changed over time in the eight peer countries. I use the Gini coefficient, named after the Italian statistician Corrado Gini, who first published the measure in 1912.[14] The Gini coefficient is the most widely used measure of income inequality, although there are lots of alternative measures. In essence it tells us how far the actual distribution of income (or wealth) in a country departs from perfect equality. Thus in a society where everyone receives the same income, the Gini coefficient would be 0.

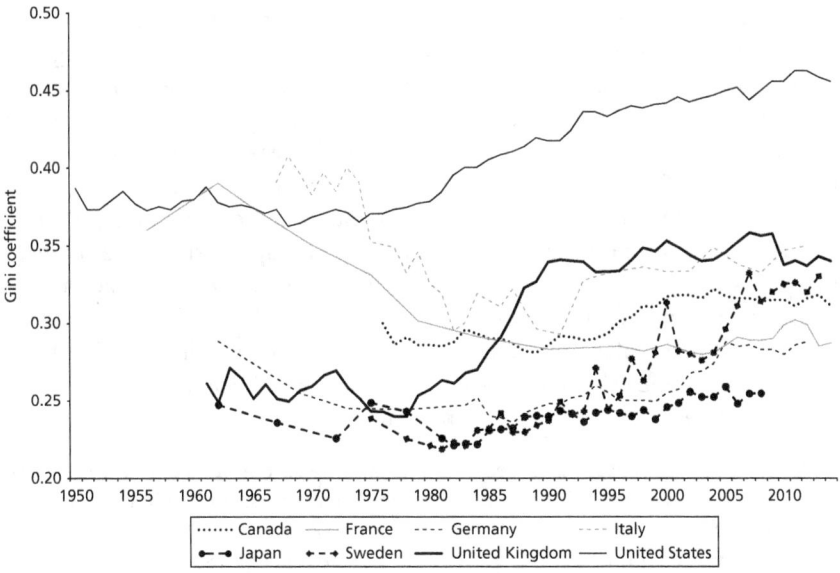

Figure 2.2. Income inequality increased particularly rapidly in the UK after 1979

Note: for the USA the Gini coefficient is based on gross equivalized household income whereas for the other countries it is based on equivalized household disposable income

Source: Anthony B. Atkinson and Salvatore Morelli, *Chartbook of Economic Inequality* (2016), www.chartbookofeconomicinequality.com

At the other extreme, if one person had all the income, and everyone else had none, the coefficient would be 1.[15]

As Figure 2.2 shows, the general trend in our peer countries, up until the 1970s, had been towards greater equality. There was then a reversal and income inequality began to rise. Of all eight countries, Britain showed the largest increase in inequality after 1980, going from being one of the most equal economies in the 1970s to one of the most unequal by the 1990s. Sweden also showed quite a large increase in inequality after 1990. In contrast, France saw declining inequality (albeit from a very high baseline) while Japan showed a much more modest increase than countries like Britain and the USA and was the most equal of the eight countries more or less throughout the period.

Why inequality increased in almost all of the peer countries, but especially rapidly in Britain, is not well understood even by professional economists. A range of explanations have been put forward, and there is probably some truth in all of them. One argument focusses on globalization, specifically on trade liberalization. Free trade with developing countries such as China, where labour is relatively plentiful, means that goods can be produced more cheaply in the developing countries than in the developed world. Manufacturing jobs thus get exported to China; there is declining demand for less-skilled manufacturing workers in Western countries; and wages of these less-skilled workers fall behind those of more highly skilled workers.

Globalization could also potentially explain the rocketing salaries of top executives and bankers, as the most skilled of these are now competing in a larger global marketplace and not just in the smaller marketplace of their own country. In addition to globalization, technical progress could be another explanation, as technical progress will tend to increase the demand for, and hence salaries of, the most highly qualified workers. In addition, the increasing employment of women in the labour market and their entry into higher-level jobs (which most of our peer countries apart from Japan experienced) means that there will be a new class of dual-career high-earning households with a larger combined household income.

None of these explanations really explains why inequality increased faster in Britain than in the other countries. It is likely that political choices may have made a difference. As economist Jonathan Cribb explains:

Changes in government tax and welfare policy may be part of the reason for increased inequality in net incomes (income after tax has been paid and including any welfare benefits). Before the election of the Conservative government in 1979, the top rate of income tax was 83% on earned and 98% on unearned income. Successive cuts to the top rates of tax during the 1980s directly boosted net incomes at the top of the income distribution, and increased the incentives to work for people earning very high salaries, which increased the very highest incomes relative to the rest of the population during the 1980s.[16]

Whatever the exact explanation, the key point for us is that the gains in material prosperity from economic growth were not shared equally but went disproportionately to the better-off. If we are interested in how prosperity has changed since Beveridge's day for those people who are most at risk of experiencing Want, then GDP per head may not be a good guide at all. The fourfold increase in GDP tells us that Britain was in a position to tackle Want. But it does not follow that Britain actually did.

How Has the Material Prosperity of Richer and Poorer Households in the UK Evolved?

In order to explore whether Want has indeed been kept at bay in Britain, I look first at the way in which household incomes have increased over time for richer and poorer sections of the population. In Figure 2.3 I therefore shift the focus from GDP per head to household income and how incomes have grown for poorer and for richer households. Unfortunately, unlike GDP, the available data only go back as far as 1961. This is because measures of household income are not available from the kinds of administrative sources that were used to provide estimates of GDP. Instead, they come from representative sample surveys of the population, which were not widely used by government

Figure 2.3. Real household income in the UK more than doubled between 1961 and 2015/16

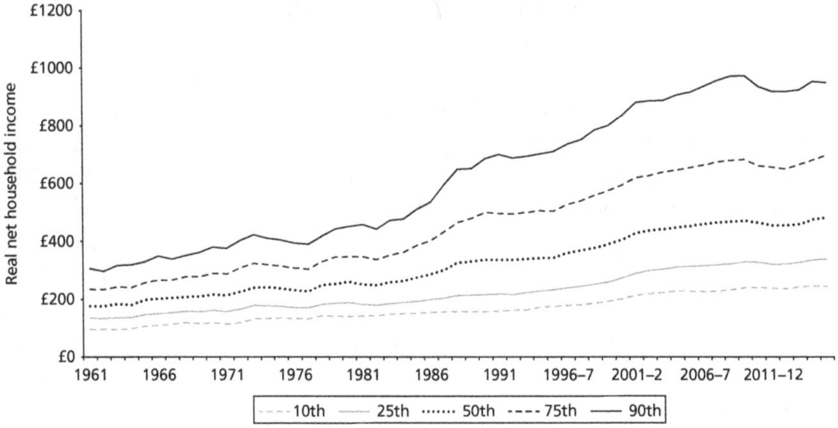

Note: expressed in 2015–16 prices, adjusted for inflation using a variant of the CPI that includes owner-occupied housing costs

Source: calculated by Jonathan Cribb of the Institute for Fiscal Studies using the Family Expenditure and Family Resources Surveys

(or academics) until the 1960s and 1970s. For the most part I focus on Britain since details for most of the peer countries are only available in this format for a much shorter period.[17]

Figure 2.3 shows how incomes (adjusted for inflation and for household size and composition) have changed for households at different points in the income distribution. Let me try to explain what these figures mean. I define a middle-income household as one that lies exactly at the middle, with half of households receiving more income, and half receiving less. This is technically termed the median income. Following the same logic, a household at the tenth percentile is towards the bottom of the distribution, with only 10 per cent of households receiving less income. These are the households who will be at most risk of Want. And it is the other way round for the ninetieth percentile— 90 per cent of households receive less income than a household at the ninetieth percentile and only 10 per cent receive more.

To give an idea of what this means in practice: a household with the median income in 2015 might be one containing two children and two adults with a combined income after tax (and including any benefits) of £34,500. A household with two adults and two children at the tenth percentile would have a combined income of £17,500, and a similar household at the ninetieth percentile would have a combined income of £68,900. A household at the ninety-ninth percentile—the top 1 per cent—would have an income of £171,500.[18]

Similarly to Figure 2.1, Figure 2.3 shows an impressive increase in material prosperity. In the case of a household at the middle of the income distribution—the median household—the increase was from £177 (measured in 2015/16 prices) to £482 per week over the fifty plus years from 1961 to 2015/16. This is a smaller increase than the increase in GDP per head over the same period, which increased by more than three times.

Part of the reason for the discrepancy between the GDP and household income figures is the rise in inequality. We can see that, up until 1980, there was steady although unspectacular growth for households at all the different income levels. In contrast, after 1980 the lines fan out, indicating different rates of growth for households at different income levels. As a result, over the period as a whole, for a well-off household at the ninetieth percentile the increase in their real income was over three times (rising from £307 to £950). In the case of households in the middle (the fiftieth percentile), income increased by two and two thirds (£177 to £482), but for less well-off households at the tenth percentile the increase was just over two and a half (£96 to £244).

This is of course just another way of saying that inequality increased over the period. Figure 2.2 shows clearly that the big increase in inequality was in the 1980s. Thus there was a rather steep rise in household income for those at the ninetieth percentile (and an even steeper rise for the ninety-fifth or ninety-ninth percentiles) between 1980 and 1990 whereas the gradient for households at the median or below was not all that different from what it had been before the 1980s.[19] The benefits of economic growth were thus shared rather unevenly between richer and poorer sections of society after 1980. Nevertheless, there were real gains over this period even for the most disadvantaged sections of society. In the USA, in contrast, there was virtually no progress at all after 1980 for households at the tenth percentile and by 2010 their real household income had slipped behind that of the tenth percentile in Canada, France, Germany, and Sweden and was only just ahead of the UK. (We do not have comparable data for Japan.)[20]

We should not, however, put all the blame on the growth of inequality. Another reason for the discrepancy between the growth in median household income and that of GDP per head is that average GDP per head is a calculation based on the number of *individuals* whereas median household income is based on the number of *households*. Over this period the number of households grew faster than the number of individuals.[21] This was due to a range of social changes, such as increasing divorce rates, divorcees being more likely to form a separate household (at least until they start living with a new partner). There was also an increase in the number of elderly people living alone. Since it is generally more expensive for two people to live apart than to live together, this shift towards more and smaller households can partly explain why the high growth in GDP per head did not translate into an equally high growth in median income per household.

Another point which we need to take into account is the increasing participation of women in the labour market. When I was growing up back in the 1950s, my mother did not go out to work, and it was quite rare for married women with school-age children to go out to work. The following decades, however, saw a huge increase in the proportion of married women with school-age children who go out to work (often part time). This will have increased household income quite considerably for these particular households. But a lot of that extra income will have gone straight out of the household budget in order to pay for childcare. In a sense, the spare cash available for the household to spend will not have increased nearly as much as their total monetary income. So it is not entirely clear that the actual increase in material prosperity was quite as large as these household income figures would imply.

Another way of putting the same point is to say that the value of the housewife's *unwaged* contribution to the household's prosperity is not taken into account by official estimates of household income, whereas the wages received by the paid childcare assistant will be included. In essence some activities such as childcare have become monetized—they have shifted from the non-market economy to the market economy. 'If you marry your housekeeper, national income falls' is a catchphrase which captures the essence of this argument (i.e., you used to pay her a wage when she was your housekeeper but no longer pay a wage once she is your wife). Since childcare costs are likely to be a larger proportion of the median household's expenditure than of the well-off household's, it is quite likely that the figures for the growth in median household income over the long term are unduly rosy.

There is one other important complication which I should mention—the rise of indebtedness. To be sure, household debt is not always a bad thing. Borrowing can smooth consumption over the life cycle, for example, by allowing young people to borrow against their future income (which is effectively what one does when one takes out a mortgage to buy a house). However, interest payments on the debt mean that the cash which the household has available for maintaining its material prosperity could be considerably less than the nominal household income shown in Figure 2.3. This provides another reason why the actual experience of Want may be somewhat different from the trends in income received before any outgoings like childcare costs and interest payments have been deducted.[22] Highly indebted households are also more vulnerable to economic shocks such as unemployment, a drop in income, or an increase in interest rates. Income, therefore, may not always be a good guide to the actual living standards of poorer households. It may well be better to construct measures of poverty based on consumption rather than income.[23]

Figures for levels of household indebtedness have been estimated by various bodies such as the Office for National Statistics and the Bank of England from 1988 onwards. The standard procedure is to show indebtedness as a multiple of total household income. In effect this measure tells us how long it would take a household to pay off their debt if they were to use the whole of their annual income on the debt repayment. This gives us a sense of the size of the burden on households.

Different sources estimate different levels of this debt to income ratio, but as we can see from Figure 2.4 they all show a similar picture of trends over time. The ratio of debt to income was just over 1 in 1988. It remained fairly steady up until 1999 but then increased sharply from 2000 onwards, peaking at 1.7 in 2007, just before the financial crash. Various reasons such as rising house prices, low interest rates, and increasing availability of credit have been put forward to explain this sharp rise. When the financial crisis hit in 2008, cut-backs in mortgage lending led the debt-to-income ratio to drop but it only fell back to about 1.5, still well above its level in the 1990s.

As one might expect, the increase in household indebtedness was not evenly spread across the population. Unsurprisingly, the ratio of debt to income tends to be higher among younger people and among those with lower incomes. Furthermore, detailed research by Marii Paskov has shown that low-income groups are particularly likely to have unsecured debt as opposed to secured debt in the form of mortgages (which are backed up by assets such as the house being bought).[24] Unsecured debt is a type of loan or credit that is

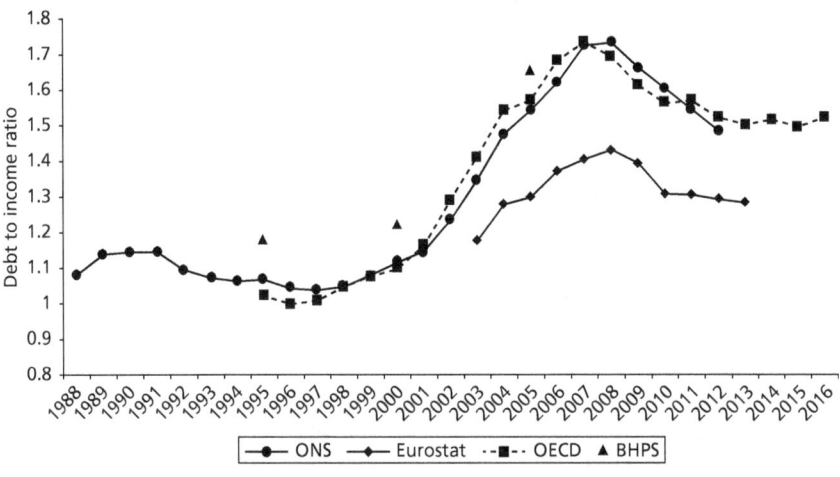

Figure 2.4. Household debt rose particularly rapidly in Britain during the 1990s

Source: Marii Paskov, 'Have we become more indebted?' CSI briefing note no. 16 (based on data from the Office for National Statistics, Eurostat, Organisation for Economic Co-operation and Development, and British Household Panel Study), http://csi.nuff.ox.ac.uk/wp-content/uploads/2015/11/CSI-16-Have-we-become-more-indebted.pdf

extended without a collateral requirement. It constitutes a smaller proportion of overall debt but it is generally more expensive with higher interest rates. Unlike secured debt, unsecured debt does not seem to have fallen back since the financial crash. Moreover, the growth in unsecured debt after the 1990s was particularly large for the poorest households.[25]

Unsecured indebtedness may increase living standards in the short term, but is unlikely to be sustainable in the longer run. The increase in indebtedness among poorer households may also lead to a disconnect between nominal income growth and actual experience of Want. Research by the Institute for Fiscal Studies, for example, has shown that families for whom unsecured debt such as credit cards is a heavy burden are much more likely to be materially deprived than others with the same household income.[26] There is no one-to-one relationship, therefore, between household income and level of material deprivation.

So What Has Actually Happened to Want and Poverty since Beveridge's Day?

This is not quite as easy a question to answer as Beveridge might have expected. For a start, it is not straightforward to know what is meant by Want or by terms such as poverty or material deprivation, which are more usual nowadays than Beveridge's quixotic term Want. As Professor Joad, a celebrity philosopher in the 1940s who became a household name through his contributions to the BBC radio programme *The Brains Trust* in my childhood, used to say, 'It all depends on what you mean by...' So what do we mean by Want?

There are basically two approaches to defining and measuring Want or material deprivation (and a huge number of detailed variants). The first approach, which is the one Beveridge seems to have had in mind, interpreted Want as lack of a basic *subsistence* level of living. We can think of this as a fixed and unchanging measure of destitution.[27] The second approach, which contemporary social reformers have emphasized, interprets poverty as a standard of living falling below the *minimum socially acceptable standard*, a standard which can change over time. This second approach lies behind contemporary notions such as the living wage.

Let's start with Beveridge's subsistence-level approach (an approach which does not seem to have been contentious in his day). He robustly declared:

During [the immediate pre-war years] impartial scientific authorities made social surveys of the conditions of life of a number of principal towns in Britain . . . They determined the proportions of the people in each town whose means were *below the standard assumed to be necessary for subsistence*, and they analysed the extent and causes of that deficiency. (My italics)[28]

One of the impartial scientific authorities on whom Beveridge relied was the Quaker businessman and social researcher Seebohm Rowntree. Rowntree's original approach, described in his book *Poverty* (published in 1901), defined a family as living in poverty if its total earnings were 'insufficient to obtain the minimum necessaries for the maintenance of merely physical efficiency'.[29] He was deliberately parsimonious in his estimates as he did not want to be accused of exaggerating the problem. He emphasized too that 'Expenditure needful for the development of the mental, moral, and social sides of human nature will not be taken into account at this stage of the enquiry.'[30] Drawing on the research of physiologists—one of whom conducted remarkably unethical experiments on prisoners, checking how their weight changed when they were given smaller rations and how much food would lead to an increase in their weight—Rowntree estimated how much protein, fat, and carbohydrate were needed for a working man, for a woman (eight tenths of the man's requirements), and for children. He even gave sample menus, which contained plenty of bread, milk and porridge, some cheese, but very little meat and no fresh fruit. He then worked out the cost of this subsistence-level diet, added on sums for rent, clothing, light, fuel, and soap. He derived the latter estimates from a survey of York, asking working people questions such as 'what in your opinion is the very lowest sum upon which a man can keep himself in clothing for a year?'

Rowntree then estimated the necessary expenditure each week for different sizes of family—21s 8d for a couple with three children, for example. From his 1899 survey of York he found that 1465 families, comprising 7230 persons, were living in poverty—15 per cent of the wage-earning class in York, and nearly 10 per cent of the whole population of York. When he repeated the exercise fifty years later in 1950 he found that the proportion below subsistence level had fallen to only 2.8 per cent of the wage-earning class in York. He attributed this largely to the success of Beveridge's reforms.[31]

The second approach to measuring poverty expands the necessities of life beyond food, clothing, heating, and rent. It adds on a range of items which are believed to be necessary for a socially acceptable standard of living. This approach goes beyond subsistence to include the 'mental, moral and social elements' that Rowntree had mentioned but excluded in his 1901 study. Following this kind of approach, more recent researchers such as Jonathan Bradshaw and his colleagues defined a minimum income standard as one which 'is rooted in social consensus about the goods and services that everyone in modern Britain should be able to afford'.[32] They argued that a minimum standard of living in Britain today 'includes, but is more than just, food, clothes, and shelter. It is about having what you need in order to have the opportunities and choices necessary to participate in society.'[33]

In this study by Jonathan Bradshaw and his colleagues, the mental, moral, and social aspects over and above subsistence requirements were judged by ordinary members of the public. They included: mobile phones and landlines, internet access (for secondary-school children), childcare (so that mothers could go to work), public transport (but not a car), money for social and cultural participation including meals out, going to the cinema, pubs, and also money for maintaining a healthy lifestyle, such as gym membership. It allowed for only a one-week budget holiday, but also included Christmas and birthday presents. These needs were based on what ordinary people themselves, after deliberation in focus groups, regarded as requisites for participating in society.

In my childhood my family would not have reached this minimum. At that time, we obviously did not have mobile phones (not yet invented) or internet access (ditto), and there would not have been many gyms (though there were tennis, golf, and rugby clubs), but it makes a lot of sense to add mobile phones and internet access today because they are part of the fabric of modern life: more and more essential functions are being carried out online, like job applications. Others, such as childcare or gym membership, reflect changing ways of life. When I was growing up, mothers were not expected to work and a minimum income standard for the 1950s would certainly not have included childcare costs. But it is entirely appropriate today, where there is a broad social acceptance that women should have the opportunity for paid employment.[34] On the other hand, some of the things we did have when I was growing up, such as a telephone landline, would not have been included in an equivalent study of minimum income standards in the 1950s. So my childhood circumstances would have been superior to a 1950s minimum, but below that of a 2010 minimum. As Britain has got richer, and also as ways of life have changed, so the minimum socially accepted standards have risen, too. The goal posts are continually shifting. The key point is that the socially acceptable standard of living is not fixed—it changes over time as society changes.

The first approach, then, takes a more or less constant yardstick of subsistence-level requirements. (Actually, even this constancy can be questioned—the specimen budgets which Rowntree gave in his 1901 book would certainly not be regarded as reaching minimum subsistence standards today since they did not include fresh fruit or vegetables—vitamins had not then been discovered.) The second approach allows that social needs will change over time and that, as a society becomes richer, what is needed in order to be a participating member of the society will rise too. Families with the kind of living standard my family had in the 1950s would nowadays feel left behind and left out, though at the time we were relatively well-off.

So taking this second approach, what we would really like to know is whether the increase in real household income for the poorest households has actually kept up with the changing socially acceptable standards. Unfortunately, the honest answer to this question is that we really do not know about long-term changes. We do not have the data from the 1950s, 1960s, or even 1970s about what were socially acceptable standards at those times. Possibly we could get older people like myself to reminisce and work out what would have been required in the 1960s, but I would not advise you to trust our memories.

There is one official measure of relative poverty that might conceivably give us a clue, but it should be treated with great caution. Thus it has become, for opaque reasons, standard for governments and international bodies to use the yardstick of 60 per cent of the median household income to define what is termed 'relative poverty'. To give a concrete example: in 2014/15 the median household income in Britain for a couple with two children under 14 was £688 per week. So the relative poverty yardstick amounted to 60 per cent of £688, that is to a household income of £398 per week.[35] Jonathan Bradshaw and colleagues' analysis suggested that this 60 per cent yardstick is rather lower than the minimum income standard derived from what members of the public thought was necessary in order to achieve a socially acceptable standard of living. Their minimum income standard varies for different types of household but is generally closer to 70 per cent than 60 per cent of the median.

But let us accept the official definition of 60 per cent of the median, and let us assume that the public's conception of what is a socially acceptable minimum has more or less tracked the growth in median household incomes. These are pretty heroic assumptions but they do allow us to report—though only from 1973 onwards—what proportion of households fell below the threshold. This is shown in Figure 2.5.

Figure 2.5 suggests that the proportion of households in relative poverty was fairly stable at around 13 per cent in the 1970s and early 1980s. It then climbed rather steeply in the latter half of the 1980s (which of course happened to be the era when inequality was increasing fastest), reaching 22 per cent in 1990. Since then it has been gradually declining but has not regained the levels seen in the 1970s. Thus in 2015/16, relative poverty remained at 16 per cent. In the long run, then, it seems that the numbers in relative poverty has remained higher after the 1980s than it was before. Incidentally, recent OECD data suggest that relative poverty in Britain is considerably higher than in Sweden, Germany, or France but lower than in the USA.[36]

Again, we need to take these figures with a pinch of salt. One of the oddities of the official measure of 60 per cent of the median income is that the numbers in relative poverty will be driven as much by what is happening to median income as they are by what has happened to the living standards of poorer households. For example, after the 2007/8 financial crash, economic growth initially fell sharply and wages (and median household income) fell. At first the value of state benefits (on which a lot of the poor depend) were maintained, and so the gap closed between people receiving benefits and the median household where wages were the major contributor to overall income.

Figure 2.5. Relative poverty in Britain was higher in 2015/16 than it had been in 1961

Source: proportion of households with less than 60 per cent of median household income, calculated by Jonathan Cribb of the Institute for Fiscal Studies using the Family Expenditure and Family Resources Surveys

So the numbers in relative poverty declined somewhat in the years after 2007/8, even though their actual real incomes hardly changed. To be sure, the public's standards of what constituted a minimum socially acceptable standard of living may also have fallen after 2007/8 in line with the fall in median incomes, but we do not have much hard evidence on this.[37]

Has There Been a Resurgence of Want in the Twenty-First Century?

Can we say anything about Want in the sense of falling below the basic subsistence level rather than in the relative, socially acceptable sense? There is no good reason to expect subsistence levels of poverty to follow the same path as relative poverty. Whereas we might expect the proportion experiencing the latter to remain more or less constant over time as socially acceptable standards rise (or fall) in line with general prosperity, we might in contrast expect the proportion who are destitute to fall in the long run as society gets richer. Seebohm Rowntree had claimed that it was already down to 2.8 per cent in his 1950 survey of York. Has it subsequently vanished altogether?

The Joseph Rowntree Foundation (which was established by Seebohm Rowntree's father Joseph in 1904) has recently carried out a study of the level of destitution in the UK in 2015.[38] They defined destitution as occurring if two of the following six essentials were missing: (1) *shelter* (slept rough for one or more nights); (2) *food* (had fewer than two meals a day for two or more days), (3) *heating* their home (been unable to do this for five or more days, (4) *lighting* their home (been unable to do this for five or more days), (5) *clothing and footwear* (appropriate for the weather), or (6) *basic toiletries* (soap, shampoo, toothpaste, toothbrush).[39] While the details differ, it is probably no accident that these six necessities are the same as the six included in Seebohm Rowntree's measure of subsistence-level poverty sixty-five years earlier.

The Joseph Rowntree researchers estimated that 668,000 households containing 1,250,000 people (of whom 312,000 were children) were destitute in the UK in 2015. This amounts to about 1.9 per cent of the UK population.[40] The Joseph Rowntree figures were based on a survey of people seeking help from voluntary agencies. It will therefore probably undercount destitution because some people will not have sought this help and others will have sought help from statutory agencies.

These 2015 estimates of destitution are only slightly lower than Seebohm Rowntree's 1950 estimate for York. We cannot legitimately compare the two sets of figures because of the completely different methodologies employed (even though the underlying concepts are pretty similar) and because of the different populations studied. Nevertheless it is pretty clear from the Joseph Rowntree research that destitution has not vanished, despite Britain's much greater prosperity at the beginning of the twenty-first century.

Although they did not compare their results with Seebohm Rowntree's, the authors of the Joseph Rowntree Report did attempt to answer the question of whether there had been any tendency for destitution to increase in recent years. They reviewed a range of data sources, such as the proportions on very low incomes, homelessness, and the use of foodbanks, but they were forced to admit that direct evidence on recent trends in destitution were lacking.[41] They concluded: 'The most plausible conclusion is therefore that destitution will have increased in the UK in recent years, but we cannot directly demonstrate this'.[42]

I think this is a fair conclusion. But let's have a quick look at the kind of data which is available. It is certainly true that the number of food parcels delivered by the Trussell Trust, the UK's largest foodbank network, increased hugely between 2008/9 and 2013/14. However, we also know that the Trussell Trust increased its network over this period, so some of the increase may have been due to increased supply rather than to increased demand. Nor do we know for sure whether the increased number of food parcels were consumed by the same people going back more and more often for parcels, or whether a larger number of people in total were making use of foodbanks.

Unfortunately, neither the government nor academics routinely collect data on food insecurity and the use of foodbanks. (The government really ought to do more to check on the scale of problems affecting vulnerable members of our society.) However, Figure 2.6 combines the various data sources which are available in order to provide an overview of trends in food insecurity and emergency food provision in recent years. As we can see, the number of food parcels distributed by the Trussell Trust and meals provided by FareShare increased more steeply than measures of how many people were missing meals or compromising food choices. This is in line with the interpretation that the rise in emergency food provision might in part reflect greater availability of this type of assistance. On the other hand, the survey data also suggest that there was an increase in food insecurity and not just increasing availability.[43]

There is also some circumstantial evidence in line with this interpretation. We know for example that food costs increased between 2002 and 2012 more rapidly than the rate of inflation, and that the increases were far greater for healthier food.[44] On average, the nutritional quality of the food people purchased declined after the financial crash.[45] Between 2007 and 2012, people spent more on food but bought less (although whether this reflects going without or being less wasteful cannot be determined). These changes were also larger in lower-income groups.[46] It therefore does seem plausible that poorer families might have been increasingly stretched to buy good food after the recession. We should certainly not dismiss the increasing-destitution hypothesis out of hand.

Figure 2.6. Food insecurity and the distribution of food parcels and meals increased in England after 2008

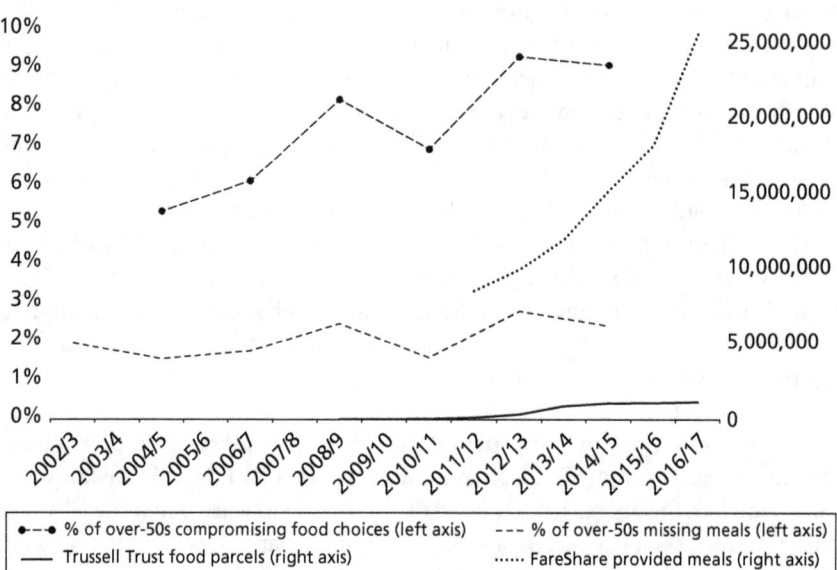

● ● % of over-50s compromising food choices (left axis) --- % of over-50s missing meals (left axis)
—— Trussell Trust food parcels (right axis)   ······ FareShare provided meals (right axis)

Source: Elizabeth Garratt, 'Food insecurity and foodbank use', CSI briefing note 28 (based on data from the Trussell Trust, FareShare, and English Longitudinal Study of Ageing) http://csi.nuff.ox.ac.uk/wp-content/uploads/2016/11/CSI-28-Food-insecurity-revised.pdf

A quite different source of data can be found in hospital admissions records on malnutrition. There is some short-run data on hospital admissions with a primary or secondary diagnosis of malnutrition. In England and Wales such admissions increased from 3899 in 2009–10 to 6686 in 2013–14, an increase of 72 per cent, while primary diagnoses of malnutrition increased by 28 per cent from 478 in 2009–10 to 612 in 2013–14.[47] Unsurprisingly, primary diagnoses of malnutrition were concentrated in more disadvantaged areas, and in December 2013 a group of doctors wrote to the *British Medical Journal*, warning of food insecurity as a public health emergency.[48] Low birth weight is another condition associated with poverty. In England and Wales, around 3 per cent of full-term live births were low birthweight (that is, less than 2500g) in 2015, more or less unchanged since 2006, although unfortunately we do not have longer-run data.[49]

We do, however, have much longer-term data on another condition associated with poverty and poor diet—namely, rickets. Rickets is a condition in children in which bones fail to develop properly due to a lack of vitamin D and calcium absorption. It was common in the nineteenth century but subsequently declined. Michael Goldacre and his colleagues have looked at hospital admissions records from 1963 to 2011 and found that there was a particularly marked increase after 1999, as Figure 2.7 shows.[50]

There is always the possibility with administrative data like hospital admissions that the increase may be due to changes in hospital admissions procedures or diagnoses. However, Michael Goldacre and his colleagues argue that, since rickets is a straightforward diagnosis, there is a good possibility that the true incidence had indeed risen.

The problem with this evidence is that the population was changing over this period, with increasing numbers of ethnic minorities resident in Britain. Children with darker skin tend to have higher rates of rickets in Britain, since they absorb less vitamin D from the available light. In fact, the increase in the size of the ethnic minority population started much earlier than in 1999 (and the recent increase in migration to Britain has been driven by migrants from European countries) so this is not a conclusive counter-argument. The increase could also be explained by children spending more time indoors, for example playing computer games. Once again, then, this is suggestive but not conclusive evidence.

Figure 2.7. The incidence of rickets remained around 1 per 100,000 children up until 1999 but increased sharply in the twenty-first century

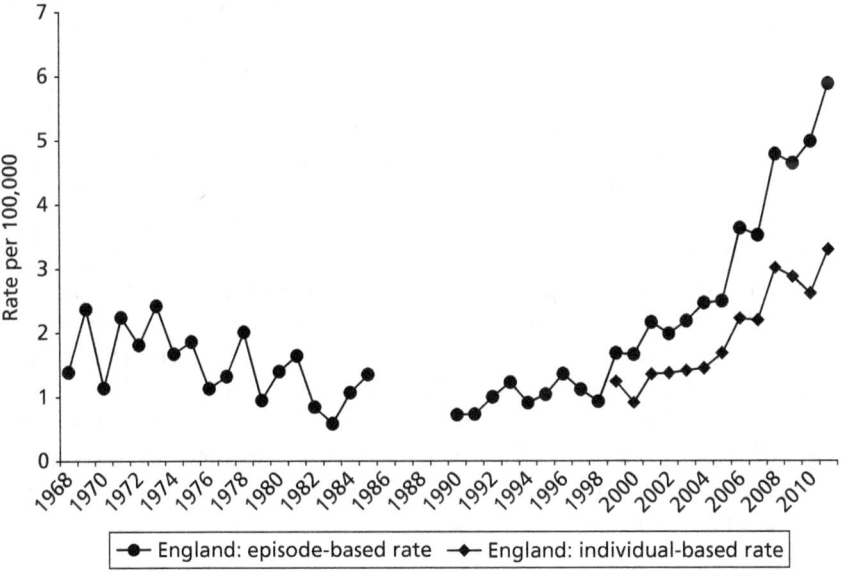

Source: derived from Michael Goldacre, Nick Hall, and David G. R. Yeates, 'Hospitalisation for children with rickets in England: A historical perspective', *The Lancet*, 383, no. 9917 (2014): 597–8, with permission from Elsevier (Licence number: 4217160155087).[51] DOI: http://dx.doi.org/10.1016/S0140-6736(14)60211-7

Conclusions

We can have no doubt that Britain, like other large Western democracies, became substantially richer in the post-war decades up until the financial crash of 2007/8. Even after the crash, both GDP per head and average household income were still much greater than they had been fifty years earlier. It has been a bit of a bumpy ride. Britain's growth was slightly slower than that of peer countries in the first couple of decades; it was around average in the 1980s and 1990s, and then surged in the 1990s and up until the financial crash of 2007/8. By the end of our period Britain was still somewhere in the middle of the pack of peer countries. We had dropped behind Germany (which had started off well behind) but Britain was still level pegging with France. This was not perhaps a spectacular performance overall but nevertheless it was one which should have made it possible to tackle the giant of Want.

However, the other great economic change which transformed the nature of the British economy was the rapid increase in economic inequality after Margaret Thatcher took office in 1979. Britain had been one of the most equal of our eight peer countries in the late 1970s, but by the 1990s it had become one of the most unequal (although still not as unequal as the USA).

Doubtless the architects of the 1980s reforms hoped that growth rates would increase and that living standards for all would increase as a result. While household incomes did indeed continue to rise throughout the 1980s and up until the 2007/8 crash, it was the higher-income groups who experienced an increased rate of progress. The poorest sections of society saw more modest increases in household income, and their rate of progress was largely unchanged from that of earlier decades. This should still have been sufficient to see a gradual decline in poverty in Britain but may well have been offset by increases in levels of personal debt, which increased faster for poor people than for the better-off.

Unfortunately, we cannot straightforwardly read off the experience of material deprivation from the income data. Measuring poverty and different forms of material deprivation is not at all straightforward, and we do not have good over-time data to discover what the trends have been. This is true whether we look at subsistence levels of poverty—having enough money to eat a healthy diet, to keep warm and clothed—or at access to a socially acceptable standard of living. It would be foolish to pretend that we can reach any definitive conclusion about long-run trends in either of these two conceptions of poverty.

However, the balance of the evidence does suggest that economic progress for the poorest families stalled in the twenty-first century or possibly even went into reverse. Even if we do not place any weight on the data on the rising use of foodbanks, and the rise of rickets and malnutrition, recent research by the Institute for Fiscal Studies indicates that the proportion of children living in material deprivation barely changed between 2004/5 and 2014/15.[52]

These scattered pieces of evidence are far from providing definitive proof, then, that destitution is increasing, but they do suggest that this is an hypothesis which cannot be dismissed out of hand. It should be taken seriously. One often hears people (especially spokesmen for lobbying groups) argue that there is no proof for a particular empirical claim. In my youth tobacco companies were guilty of this kind of thing, arguing that there was no proof that smoking caused lung cancer. And the companies were right at that time, since strong causal evidence had not yet been established. Nowadays few people who have studied the issue would deny that there is indeed a causal link between smoking and lung cancer. But even before the causal link had been established, there was plenty of evidence suggesting that the possibility of a causal link should be taken very seriously, not dismissed out of hand.

I would argue, then, that there are some cases where we can be sure 'beyond all reasonable doubt' that the claim is soundly based. There will be a larger number of cases where the evidence (often because no one has yet collected the relevant data) is not sufficiently strong to lead to a 'beyond all reasonable doubt' conclusion, but is still strong enough to say that the claim needs to be taken seriously and should not be dismissed out of hand. I suggest that increasing destitution during the twenty-first century falls into this category—not yet proven, but needs to be taken very seriously.

Given the uncertainty about the data and the trends over time, it would be hazardous to be dogmatic about the reasons why material progress has stalled. One obvious possibility is that the 2007/8 financial crash, and the austerity measures which followed, were partly to blame. Government policy after 2010 protected the real value of state pensions but reduced that of benefits for working-age people. In line with this, the available evidence suggests that it is younger single people who are most at risk of various forms of poverty. This contrasts with the situation in 1950, as shown by Seebohm Rowntree's survey of York, when it was the elderly who were most at risk.

In my experience of social research one rarely finds a single unique explanation which can answer our central question. I am deeply suspicious of one-liners and sound-bite explanations. We always need to entertain the possibility of an alternative explanation—something that medics term a 'differential diagnosis'. Potential differential diagnoses are low wages in the lower-skilled labour market, the deteriorating competitive position of poorly qualified workers in the job market, and the difficulty of finding any kind of work for the increasing number of people coming out of prison or leaving care. While austerity measures may eventually be reversed, once Britain's finances are on a sounder footing, these alternative problems may be harder to reverse. I do not think that we can be entirely optimistic that the (un)steady march of material progress will shortly be resumed—at least as far as the most vulnerable members of British society are concerned.

3 The Fight against Disease

Life Expectancy, Disease, and Lifestyle

with Ridhi Kashyap and Elisabeth Garratt

Introduction

Disease was the second of Beveridge's five giants. Considerable progress had already been made earlier in the century before he published his report. Successful interventions such as mass vaccination programmes, better sanitation systems, water supplies, and food safety standards had all worked together to substantially reduce infant mortality and the burden from infectious, water-, and food-borne illnesses. Progress at tackling infectious diseases and in extending years of life had been one of the great success stories of the first half of the twentieth century. And the discovery of antibiotics just before the war gave promise of tackling further diseases such as pneumonia and tuberculosis which were still major killers when I was young. I can remember from my childhood an uncle who had lost a lung to TB and had spent months in isolation hospital. Isolation hospitals are thankfully now a thing of the past. By 1960, the impact of infectious diseases had been dramatically reduced to the levels that are similar to those found today.

To be sure, Beveridge had singled out health care as the one area where provision in Britain fell behind that of other developed countries, but the establishment of the National Health Service, with its universal provision of free health care at the point of delivery, gave great promise of further progress and of reducing health inequalities between richer and poorer sections of society.

These medical and health-care improvements, and the continued progress in reducing infant mortality, mean that in the twenty-first century the vast majority of Britons can expect to live well into old age. Other diseases such as cancer and dementia now pose major challenges, and there are concerns that, among the elderly, advances in life expectancy may have come at the expense of quality of life, with increasing numbers of elderly people suffering from dementia (and other disabilities) in their later years.

The focus has thus shifted away from infectious diseases, which would have been uppermost in Beveridge's mind, to the so-called diseases of affluence, such as heart disease. There are concerns that, as a society gets richer, unhealthy lifestyles and problems of obesity and excessive drinking may be storing up trouble and may undermine future progress in advancing life expectancy. The incidence of a number of diseases for which lifestyle factors such as obesity and alcohol are risk factors appear to be on the rise. Increasing social inequality has also been linked to a wide variety of health problems.

So my main questions in this chapter are whether progress has been stalling and whether growing economic inequality has generated greater health inequalities too, holding back the health and life expectancy of poorer sections of the population. I also ask how Britain's progress compares with that of our peer countries. In particular, how successful has the NHS been in closing the gap with other countries?

I will begin the chapter by looking at trends in life expectancy both in Britain and in our seven peer countries. Life expectancy, leaving aside for the moment the issue of the elderly's quality of life, is perhaps the most basic measure of social progress. What is the value of ever greater material prosperity if it were to come at the expense of premature death and a shortened lifespan? Indeed, one could argue that a long and healthy life is an even better measure of social progress than are any of the economic measures. There is also excellent long-term data on mortality, at least for our large Western countries. These data are of a distinctly higher quality and reliability than the economic data which I examined in Chapter 2 or the educational data which I will examine in Chapter 4. Registration of deaths became compulsory in England and Wales early in the nineteenth century and ever since 1841 Britain has had accurate and comprehensive data on mortality.[1] Moreover, there are no technical issues akin to the difficulty of estimating purchasing power parity when trying to compare countries' material standards of living. Mortality means the same everywhere and at all times. We can actually trust the demographic data.

As I will show, Britain has made considerable progress in increasing length of life in the years since the war, and continues to do so. However, several other peer countries (apart from the USA) made even more progress. Britain slipped towards the back of the bunch. I will therefore explore some of the reasons for this relatively poor performance, focussing on lifestyle choices such as smoking, exercise, eating, and drinking. I will finally turn to the issues of social inequality and the performance of the NHS.

How Do British Trends in Life Expectancy Compare with Those in Peer Countries?

Let me start, as in Chapter 2, by setting Britain's progress in perspective by comparing improvements over time in the eight peer countries. I will focus on life expectancy at birth, which is the most usual and readily available measure (although not without its problems). Basically, life expectancy at birth tells us how long someone born in a particular year might expect to live. The measure is based, however, on a rather important assumption, namely that currently prevailing mortality rates at different ages will continue unchanged in the future. I will look at some alternative measures later to check the robustness of the conclusions.

Just as in the case of material progress, as measured by GDP per head, there was major progress between 1950 and 2015 in extending length of life. In all eight countries life expectancy increased by well over ten years (Figure 3.1). But in other respects there are major differences between progress in material prosperity and in life expectancy. First, in the case of life expectancy, we don't see the fluctuations every decade or so as a result of the periodic boom and bust which characterized economic growth. Life expectancy shows on the whole a steadier pattern of improvement, at least over these sixty-five years. If we had gone back earlier in the twentieth century, we would have found some big fluctuations during the two world wars and the flu epidemic after the First World War. British citizens like myself have been fortunate to have lived through relatively settled times without any major catastrophes. Russia, for example, experienced a catastrophic increase in mortality after the collapse of

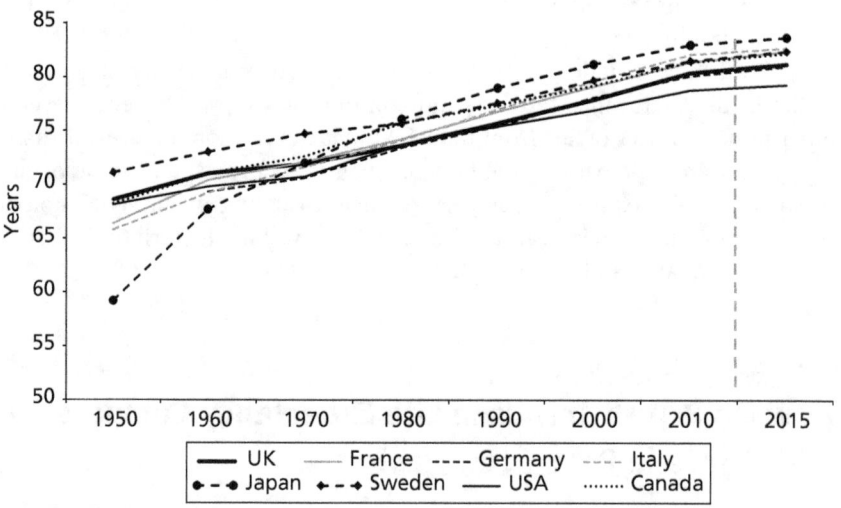

Figure 3.1. Life expectancy at birth increased by over ten years in all eight peer countries between 1950 and 2015

Note: estimates for Germany before 1990 refer to West Germany
Source: Human Mortality Database (1951–2013); World Health Organization (2015)

the Soviet Union and the economic shock therapy which followed, life expectancy falling by over five years between 1989 and 1994.

More remarkably, however, Figure 3.1 shows that in 2015 the rank order of the eight countries with respect to life expectancy was completely different from their rank order with respect to material prosperity. Italy and Japan brought up the rear in the case of material prosperity, but in the case of life expectancy these two countries are in the lead, while it is the USA which brings up the rear. Like the other countries, the USA has seen life expectancy increase by over ten years, but the US rate of progress has been much slower than in the other seven countries and in 2015 it was lagging behind by nearly two years. US life expectancy in 2015 was 79—a figure which Japan had reached twenty-five years earlier. Higher national levels of GDP per head do not seem to translate straightforwardly into longer life for the country's citizens.

Britain, too, has tended to slip behind. In 1950 Sweden, the UK, Canada, and the USA were in the lead, but France and Japan had caught up with Britain by 1970, and Italy had caught up as well by 1980. Since then Italy, France, and Japan have moved further ahead—in 2015 Italians had more than one year's greater life expectancy than Britons while the Japanese had more than two years' greater life expectancy. Thus Japan and Italy moved from the back of the pack to the front, while Britain, and even more so the USA, slipped to the back.[2] In 1950, the rank order of countries in terms of life expectancy was quite similar to their rank order for GDP per head—USA towards the front and Japan bringing up the rear. In contrast their improvements over the last sixty years seem unrelated to their improvements in GDP.

The differences are now quite small, smaller than they were in 1950. But it should dent British (and US) complacency. Leaving aside the catching up of Italy and Japan, which may reflect special features of their social conditions in the first half of the twentieth century and their wartime experiences, maybe Britain has something to learn from France. Britain is not doing as well as it could. Perhaps British governments have focussed too much on economic growth and not enough on health and social progress.

The poor performance of the USA in improving longevity has naturally worried Americans. In 2008 the American National Research Council set up a panel of social scientists to investigate.[3] They focussed on a shortlist of potential culprits for US underperformance—unhealthy lifestyles (such as cigarette smoking, obesity, and lack of exercise), lack of social integration, socio-economic inequalities, and an inefficient health-care system. They concluded that the very high levels of smoking in the USA in the 1950s were a major part of the story. They suspected that increasing levels of obesity and lack of exercise might also be part of the story but they were not sure how conclusive the evidence was. However, while there was plenty of evidence that social support and social integration promote longer life expectancy, they found no evidence that Americans had fallen behind other countries in these respects.

The panel was less sure about the role of socio-economic inequalities in explaining the poor US performance in prolonging its citizens' lifespans. To be sure, there is a socio-economic gradient in health and mortality (which is reflected in similar gradients in smoking and obesity). It is also likely, but less certain, that socio-economic inequalities have increased at a faster rate in the USA than in most European countries. The US panel concluded: 'These trends are consistent with the view that rising socioeconomic disparities contributed to the deteriorating longevity position of the United States, but data on trends in inequality are too scattered to permit a firm conclusion about their role.'[4] The panel also had some interesting things to say about the US health-care system.

It is quite likely that some of the same factors which the US panel identified—smoking, obesity, lack of exercise, and growing socio-economic inequalities—played a role in explaining British underperformance, too. I will explore these later in the chapter. First, however, I want to take a closer look at the trends in Britain so that we can check the findings of Figure 3.1 against alternative measures.

British Trends in Infant Mortality, Modal Age of Death, and Healthy Longevity

The standard demographic measure of life expectancy requires some strong assumptions. Basically, it tells us how long people of a particular age could expect to live if they were to experience the same mortality risks in the future as are currently prevailing for people of that age. In other words, the calculation assumes that the future will resemble the recent past. This is not a bad assumption, but we do know that, even in Britain, mortality rates have been declining at all ages due to medical advances. So it's a fair bet that the further we peer into the future, the less accurate this assumption will be. For example, at my current age of 74 my projected remaining life expectancy, based on prevailing death rates of people of my age and older in 2017, is another twelve years of life. (This of course is an average around which there will be a lot of variation depending on things like one's social class, drinking habits, lifestyle choices, and luck.) But if mortality rates decline in the future as they have done in the past, the estimate of another twelve years of life for a 74 year old could prove to be an underestimate.

In order to avoid making these assumptions about the future, demographers also look at hard facts about past and current mortality rates. Some of the most persuasive hard facts are those on infant mortality. Reductions in infant and child mortality account for a substantial proportion (one fifth) of the

Figure 3.2. Infant mortality showed a major decline in all peer countries, although the UK's relative position slipped

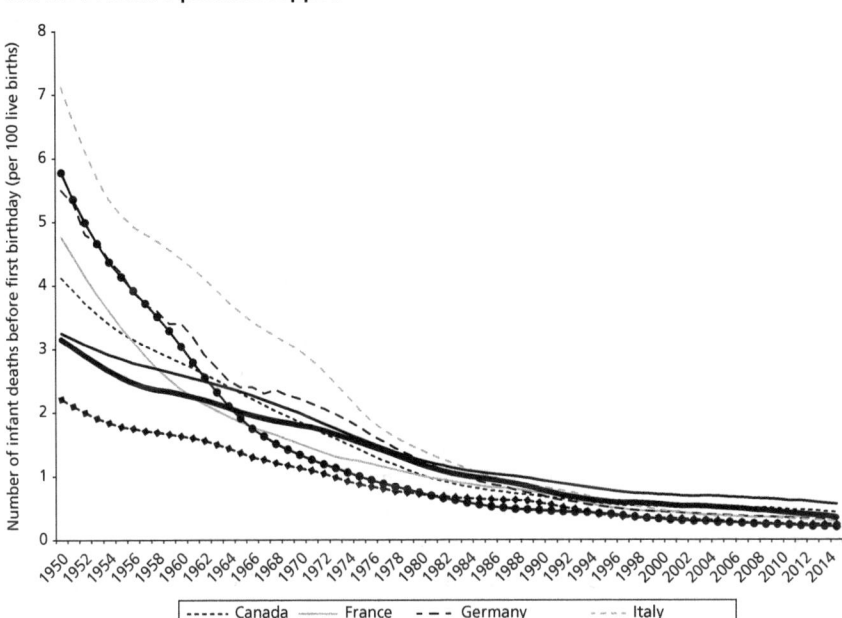

Note: break in data for Germany in 1967
Source: Max Roser, 'Child mortality', Our World in Data, https://ourworldindata.org/

British improvement in life expectancy in the post-war period. Figure 3.2 shows a major decline in infant mortality (that is, deaths before the first birthday) in all eight peer countries. In the case of the UK, just over 3 out of every 100 babies did not survive until their first birthday in 1950. By 2015, this figure had fallen to just over 3 per 1000.

So there was real progress in tackling infant mortality, although the rate of improvement gradually slowed. This is hardly surprising, since infant mortality rates had become so low in these large developed democracies. The main explanations for the long-term decline in infant mortality include the control of infectious diseases, higher birth weights, and improved health care. These reflected technical advances, improving nutrition, and improved access to health care with the newly created NHS after the war. But in 2015 the infant mortality rate was even lower in Germany (3.1 per 1000), Italy (2.9 per 1000), Japan (2.0 per 1000), and Sweden (2.4 per 1000) than in the UK, confirming the story told by Figure 3.1. International differences in infant mortality therefore mirror closely those in life expectancy—the UK was a relatively good performer in 1950, but it had slipped back by 2015.

As well as the decline in infant mortality, substantial reductions in mortality also took place at older ages. One third of the progress made after 1950 in extending length of life was made by progress at ages over 65. In Figure 3.3 I show the most common age at death (technically called the modal age at death), for deaths occurring after the age of 10.

Figure 3.3 shows a substantial improvement since 1950 with the most common age at death rising from around 82 years of age for women and 76 for men in 1950 to 90 for women and 88 for men in 2015—a major increase overall but also a substantial narrowing of the gender gap.[5] The trends are not as smooth as the Figure 3.1 trends in life expectancy at birth. This is because the modal age at death in any particular year will reflect mortality among older people; this could be higher or lower if there is a particularly harsh or mild winter or a more or less effective flu vaccine. In contrast, the estimates for life expectancy combine mortality rates for people of the full range of ages. In the case of modal age at death, therefore, one should focus on the longer-term trends rather than the short-term variations.

These trends in infant mortality and the modal age at death suggest that mortality has been postponed for most of the population to older ages. However, a key question is whether the longer lifespans are also healthy lifespans—does reduced mortality from disease imply that Britons are living those extra years

Figure 3.3. Modal age at death in the UK rose by eight years for women and twelve years for men between 1950 and 2015

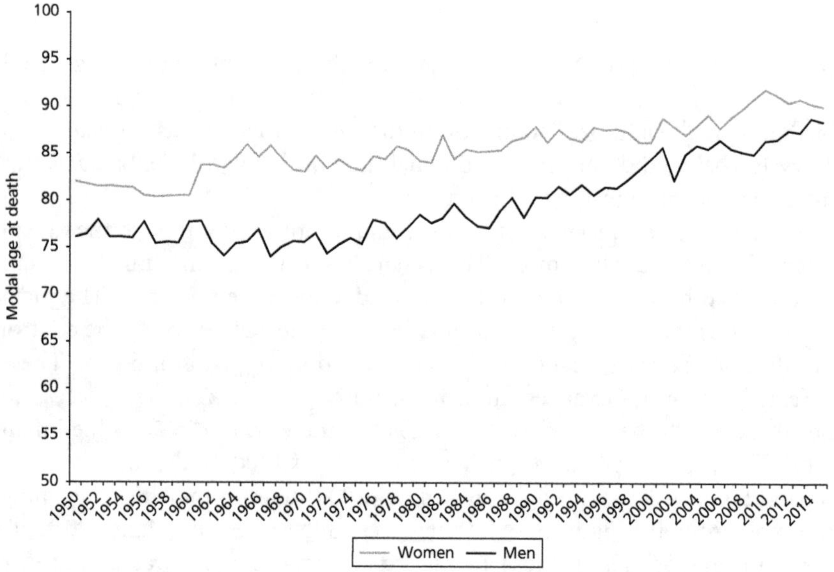

Source: Office for National Statistics[6]

gained healthily? One measure which adds a quality dimension to the standard measure of life expectancy is disability-free life expectancy.[7] To measure this, demographers use people's answers about their health and disability in nationally representative surveys in order to adjust the estimates of life expectancy. For example, someone who contracted polio as a child in the 1950s may report spending the rest of their life with a disability—a paralysed arm, perhaps. Someone who suffered a stroke in their seventies may report spending their remaining years confined to a wheelchair. In such cases their disability-free lifespan will be a lot shorter than their overall lifespan.

The surveys which enable us to calculate disability-free life expectancy are only available for the most recent period so I cannot show long-term trends. Figure 3.4 shows estimates both of life expectancy and of disability-free life expectancy for men and women in Great Britain over the period from 2000/2 to 2013/15. (In order to obtain more reliable estimates the results from adjacent years are pooled.) Unfortunately, even for this short period, the data are not as robust as one would like. One needs to interpret the results with caution.

Figure 3.4. Disability-free life expectancy in Britain increased during the twenty-first century, although more so for men than for women

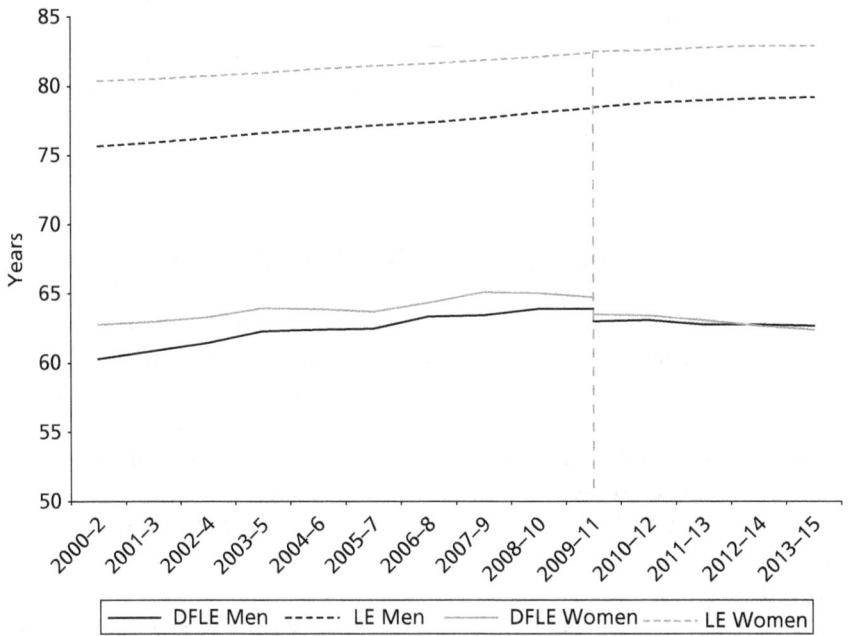

Note: the vertical break indicates the change in the data source; DFLE: disability-free life expectancy; LE: life expectancy

Source: General Lifestyle Survey (2000–2/2009–11); Annual Population Survey (2009–11/2013–15)

As we might expect, Figure 3.4 shows that disability-free lifespans are much shorter than overall life expectancy—in 2000/2 there were about fifteen years less for men and seventeen less for women.[8] The trends for the decade between 2000/2 to 2009/11 suggest that disability-free life expectancy increased over this period. Among men it increased by 3.6 years while among women the increase was a somewhat smaller 1.9 years.

The Office for National Statistics then moved to using a different source of data, which I indicate by a vertical line in Figure 3.4.[9] The new source suggests a slightly lower level of disability-free life expectancy than the older source had done, but more importantly, the new source suggests that the trends after 2009/11 were less positive. Crucially, estimates from 2009–11 onward indicate that disability-free life expectancy remained stable for men but fell for women. In 2009–11 a newborn baby girl in the UK would expect to live 63.5 years on average without disability. For 2013–15, this figure had fallen to 62.4 years. Since overall life expectancy continued to increase over this period, it follows that, in the most recent few years, both women and men were spending an increasing proportion of their lives with a disability.

Why might this have happened? One possibility is that improvements in tackling conditions such as heart disease and strokes allowed higher survival rates than were possible in previous years. One's chances of surviving a stroke, for example, were higher in 2015 than they were a decade earlier, but the increased survival rate also means that more people will survive to live with a disability. Survival from a stroke, for example, might leave survivors needing to use a wheelchair for their remaining lifespan. Less death from the disease does not necessarily imply less disability in the population.

Death Rates from Some Common Causes of Death

Beveridge termed his giant Disease, not mortality or life expectancy, so I feel that I should at least look at the diseases which have been the major causes of death in post-war Britain. I distinguish just some broad categories of disease—ischaemic heart disease (often termed coronary artery disease), of which the most familiar form is a heart attack; cerebrovascular disease, of which the most common form is a stroke; cancers (technically malignant neoplasm), among which I distinguish breast cancer and smoking-related cancers such as lung cancer; and finally, dementias, of which there are a number including the familiar Alzheimer's disease.

In Figure 3.5 I show trends over time since 1979 (which is the earliest that our source, the Global Burden of Disease Study, allows us to start) in age-standardized death rates. As one can see, there was a steep decline in deaths from heart disease, especially among men.[10] Women in general experienced

Figure 3.5. There were large decreases in deaths from heart disease between 1979 and 2013 in the UK, especially among men

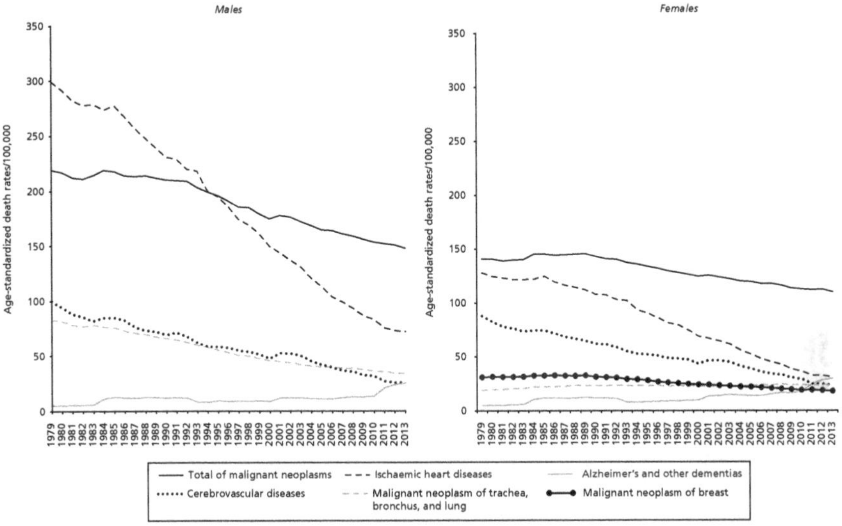

[Chart: Age-standardized death rates/100,000 for Males and Females, 1979–2013, showing Total of malignant neoplasms, Cerebrovascular diseases, Ischaemic heart diseases, Malignant neoplasm of trachea, bronchus, and lung, Alzheimer's and other dementias, Malignant neoplasm of breast]

Source: Global Burden of Disease Study, http://thelancet.com/gbd

lower levels of mortality from heart disease compared with men, but declines in mortality from these diseases also occurred among women, outpacing the reductions in other major causes of death.

In contrast, although reductions in cancer mortality also took place for both men and women, the rates of improvement were slower than for heart disease.[11] As a result, the contribution of cancers to mortality increased after the 1950s. The trends, moreover, varied for different types of cancer. Since the 1950s, lung cancer remained the most common cancer-related cause of death for men, and towards the end of the twentieth century came to rival breast cancer as the most common cancer-related cause of death among women.

Until recently mortality resulting from breast cancer was the most common cause of death from cancer among women. Mortality from breast cancer increased until 1988 after which it started to decline. In 2013, breast cancer accounted for 16 per cent of cancer mortality among women, down from 22 per cent in the mid-1980s. The availability of better treatment combined with the introduction of better screening were important developments in helping improve survival outcomes for breast cancer. Nevertheless, breast cancer mortality as well as mortality from cancers more generally was higher in the UK than in comparable European countries. A survival deficit for cancer in the UK compared to peer countries has been noted by several experts, and I will look at this further in the final section of the chapter.[12]

In contrast to the declining mortality from cardiovascular diseases and cancers, mortality from Alzheimer's and other dementia-related illnesses rose among both men and women. In part, this was due to declining mortality at younger ages, leaving more people surviving into old age. However, the contribution to overall death rates from dementias remains very low, although of course it has a major impact on quality of life (and on the cost of care) for the elderly.

Healthy Lifestyles? Smoking, Drinking, Obesity, and Exercise

So far I have been able to tell a fairly positive story—the evidence shows that life expectancy, infant mortality, modal age of death, and disability-free life expectancy have all improved, although more slowly in recent years. However, Britain—like the USA—made slower progress than several other rich countries and tended to fall behind. What is going on—and what might Britain need to do to catch up?

Since the British experience is quite similar to the US experience, it makes sense to look at the same list of suspects that the US panel did—smoking, obesity, lack of exercise, social inequalities, and health care. From the US list I have dropped social integration—partly because the US study found that this was not a major factor and partly because we shall be looking at social integration in its own right in Chapter 8. I have also added alcohol to the list, as it is another important aspect of a healthy lifestyle. Liver disease, of which alcohol consumption is a primary cause, has become the third most common cause of what demographers call premature deaths (ischaemic heart disease and self-harm being the most common causes of premature death).[13]

Smoking, obesity, lack of exercise, and excessive drinking can all be thought of as linked, more or less closely, to lifestyle choices. They are thus very different from previous causes of mortality such as those related to malnutrition and infectious diseases—these were all things that happened to one rather than things that one chose for oneself. The diseases which result from these lifestyle choices have sometimes been termed diseases of affluence—it is much easier to become overweight or to drink too much in a wealthy society where food and drink are cheap and in plentiful supply. While I am sure a full explanation would need to be much more complex, one can see why increasing prosperity might be related to new health challenges that a poorer country might not have to face in the same way.

SMOKING

Smoking is now known to be a major cause of lung cancer and also of other so-called degenerative diseases such as heart disease. British epidemiologist Richard Doll was the first to produce evidence that smoking might be a cause of lung cancer. In 1950, with Austin Bradford Hill, Doll undertook a study of lung cancer patients in twenty London hospitals. He suspected that lung cancer was due to the new material tarmac used for surfacing roads, or perhaps to fumes from the increasing number of motor cars. However, he rapidly discovered that tobacco smoking was the only factor that the patients had in common. Doll himself stopped smoking as a result of his findings, published in the *British Medical Journal* in 1950, which concluded 'The risk of developing the disease increases in proportion to the amount smoked. It may be 50 times as great among those who smoke 25 or more cigarettes a day as among non-smokers.'[14]

The initial reception of Richard Doll's ideas were quite mixed, with vigorous criticism from the eminent statistician R. A. Fisher who objected that correlation does not prove causation. (Fisher was quite right about proof, but a correlation is consistent with a causal hypothesis and failure to *prove* causation is no excuse for ignoring the *possibility* of causation.) The tobacco industry came forward with a range of criticisms of the research, and the government dragged its feet. Four years later, however, a larger study which followed up 40,000 doctors over a twenty-year period strengthened Richard Doll and Bradford Hill's original thesis, and the government subsequently issued advice that smoking and lung cancer rates were related.[15]

The health risks of smoking are now indisputable. Approximately half of lifelong smokers are expected to die as a consequence of smoking, losing on average twenty years of life.[16] In the early 1950s the USA had particularly high rates of smoking and it is likely that this had major consequences for limiting Americans' lifespans over ensuing decades, explaining in part why life expectancy in the USA dropped behind that of other rich countries. Historical evidence from cigarette and tobacco sales confirms that Britain too had one of the highest rates of consumption of manufactured cigarettes in 1950 (an average of six cigarettes a day for every adult), second only to the USA (nine cigarettes a day), and much higher than in any of the other countries apart from Canada. France (two and a half) and Italy (just under two) had levels of cigarette smoking less than half the British rate.[17] The good news is that smoking in Britain declined steadily after the 1970s—quite possibly because of public health campaigns and growing awareness in Britain of the risks associated with smoking. The decline brought the proportion of daily smokers in Britain down to levels lower than those in France, Germany, and Italy (although it became lower still in Canada, Sweden, and the USA).

Smoking basically takes a long time to show up in mortality statistics. High levels of smoking in the 1940s showed up in mortality from lung cancer and

Figure 3.6. Smoking-related mortality peaked around 1980 among British men but peaked nearly thirty years later among British women

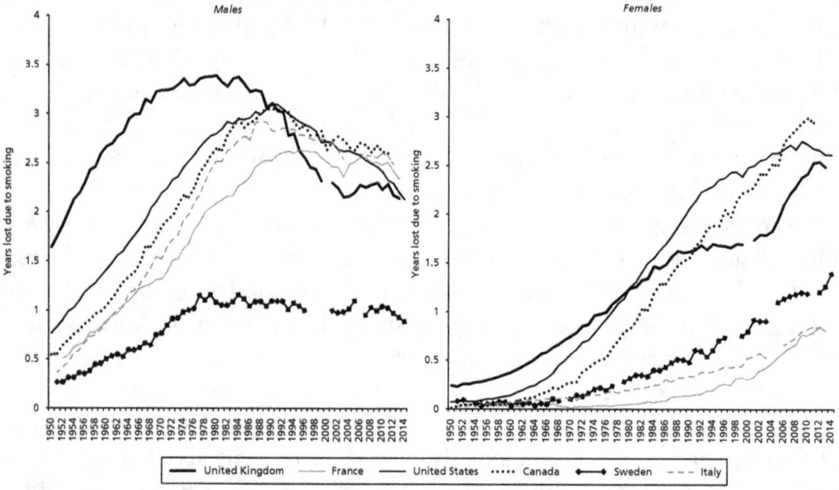

Source: Human Mortality Database; World Health Organization[18]

heart disease around twenty to thirty years later. We can see this in Figure 3.6, which highlights the number of years in life expectancy lost due to smoking in the UK and in five of the countries in the post-war period.[19] Men in the UK were among the earliest to experience the harmful effects of smoking on their life expectancy as they were among the first to have taken up smoking in the early decades of the twentieth century, particularly during the First World War. In the case of men, smoking-related mortality peaked by 1980 and started declining thereafter. After the 1990s the peer countries experienced a greater smoking-related mortality burden among men than the UK did.

Women took up smoking later than men in Britain, with smoking becoming popular among women during the Second World War. Even when women did take up smoking, they generally smoked less than men and also used brands of cigarettes with less tar that were on average less harmful.[20] This shows up in the mortality statistics where the female peak is a lot lower than the male peak. Moreover, the peak of smoking-related mortality among women occurred around thirty years later than the peak among men. This is an important part of the explanation for the narrowing gap between male and female life expectancy in Britain.

OBESITY

Obesity is perhaps the paradigm example of a condition which becomes more prevalent as a society gets richer and as food becomes cheap and plentiful. Technically, obesity is defined as occurring when a person's body mass index (often referred to simply as BMI) exceeds 30. This is equivalent to someone with my height of 5 feet 9 inches (a pretty average height) weighing 14.5 stone (203 pounds)—which happens to be four stone more than my actual weight and a lot more than the average for people of my height.

The links between obesity and mortality are not quite as clear-cut as they are in the case of smoking, but obesity is linked to a range of conditions such as diabetes, high blood pressure, heart disease, gallstones, and some cancers (colorectal cancer, breast cancer, endometrial cancer, and cancers of the kidney, pancreas, liver, and gallbladder) which all tend to increase the risk of premature death.[21] Like smoking, the effects of obesity are dose-dependent—the more obese one is, the higher the risk of premature death. One estimate suggests that a body mass index of 30 will likely lead to a 20-year-old white American man living one year less than if he had had a BMI like mine of 21. If his BMI increased to 32, he would be expected to lose two years of life; if his BMI increased to 36 he would lose nearly four years of life, and if it increased to 44 he would lose nearly eight years of life.[22] Obesity almost certainly has implications for the risk of disability, too.[23] It may well be that the principal impact of obesity is on disability-free life expectancy rather than on life expectancy itself.[24]

At any rate, Britain has seen a major increase in obesity. Just under 10 per cent of adults had a BMI of 30 or above in 1975, but in 2014 the proportion had risen to around 25 per cent. As we can see from Figure 3.7 the upward trend seems to have slowed down a little in recent years. All the same, a quarter of adults losing at least one year of life each amounts to an awful lot of lost years.

Britain, like the USA (and Canada) saw larger increases in the numbers overweight or obese than did Japan and other large European countries.[25] As a result USA is well ahead in terms of obesity, followed by Canada and the UK. France, Germany, and Italy all saw big increases in obesity too, but they remain some way behind Britain. The only country not to have seen a major epidemic of obesity is Japan, where obesity rates remain very low—far lower indeed than British levels of obesity forty years ago.

However, I doubt whether the high level of obesity in Britain can explain why Britain currently remains behind our European neighbours in life expectancy. The differences are relatively small, and are also fairly recent, and the impact of obesity on mortality is likely to be somewhat delayed, as in the case of smoking. The more worrying question is whether Britain's current obesity epidemic will have long-term consequences for disability and mortality. Obesity is perhaps the major new challenge for the future—and the worry is that it will lead Britain to fall further behind European countries, cancelling out the progress which Britain made on smoking.

Figure 3.7. The UK, like the USA and Canada, saw large increases in adult obesity between 1975 and 2014

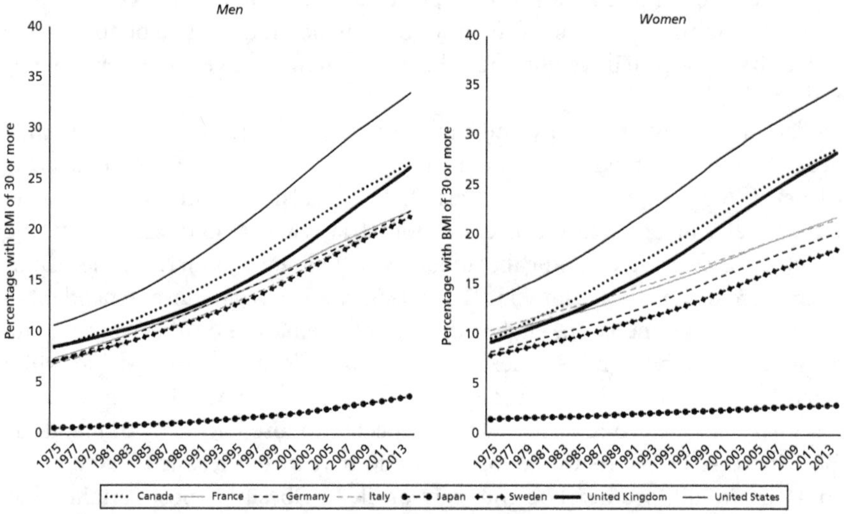

Source: Non-communicable Disease Risk Factor Collaboration[26]

LIFESTYLES: EXERCISE AND DIET

Taking exercise and eating a healthy diet are continually being emphasized by health professionals as important preventive measures for avoiding heart disease and degenerative diseases. Exercise is proving increasingly important for a wide range of illnesses, particularly cardiovascular diseases. It also appears to have wider consequences and is probably protective against neurodegenerative diseases such as dementia, as well as for psychological conditions such as depression.[27] So while lack of exercise is closely linked with being overweight, lack of exercise may well have wider implications for health than does obesity on its own.

We do not have decent long-term trend data about levels of physical exercise in Britain, although there is some recent evidence that increasing numbers of people may be taking recommended levels of exercise.[28] My guess is that people are indeed taking more leisure exercise than they used to. When I was a student, I was a keen middle-distance runner and used to compete regularly in local cross-country races and half-marathons. At that time the only competitors were other club runners, so a field of a few hundred would be a large one. But the most recent half-marathon which I ran (last year) had over 6000 runners, most of them fun runners like me running rather slowly, not the serious competitors of my youth.

The increase in leisure exercise, however, may have been cancelled out by declining levels of exercise going to and from work. In my youth in the 1950s, my father used to cycle to work every day and most of his fellow workers did, too. Today, cars have taken over from bicycles, and despite some government efforts to promote cycling, there seems to be little change in practice (Figure 3.8).[29] There is a growing body of evidence that cycling has major health benefits and is associated with lower rates of cardiovascular disease, type 2 diabetes, cancer, and mortality. Rigorous randomized experiments have confirmed that these findings are likely to be causal, not coincidental.[30]

We do not have good measures of international differences in levels of physical exercise; not many surveys have included relevant measures. When they have done so, they have measured exercise in different ways in different countries, making it almost impossible to establish how our eight peer countries compare. The best available evidence suggests that England (and the USA) are about the same as, or even above, the average for leisure exercise.[31] However, rates of cycling in the UK are very low compared with European countries: according to a recent survey by the European Commission, only 4 per cent of adults in the UK cycle daily. This is one of the lowest proportions in the whole of Europe. In contrast four in ten people in the Netherlands, and three in ten respondents in Denmark and Finland cycle daily.[32]

Figure 3.8. Vehicle miles by bicycle fell greatly in Great Britain whereas vehicle miles by car or taxi increased

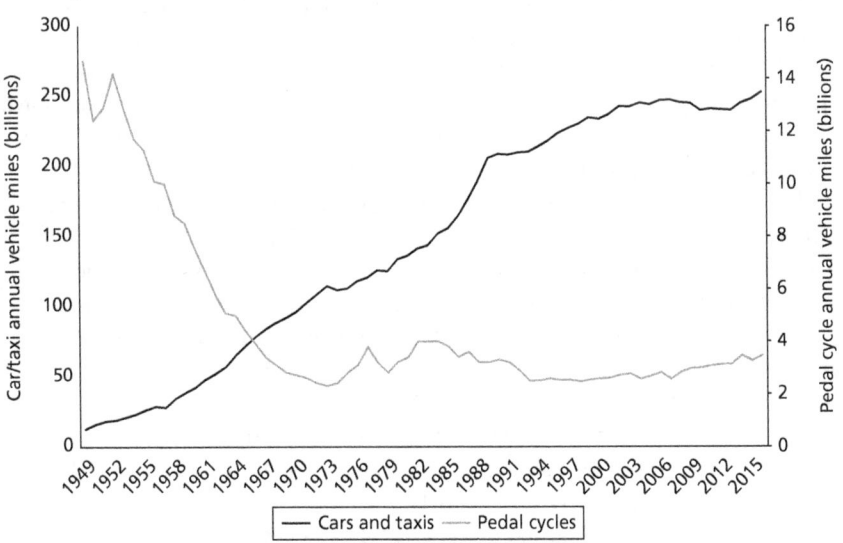

Source: Department for Transport Statistics[33]

So it is not clear that increases in leisure exercise have compensated for the decline in work-related exercise such as cycling to work. As a regular commuting cyclist, I am not surprised—it's terribly dangerous for cyclists on British roads whereas sensible cycle lanes are much more widespread in the Netherlands and Germany. My guess is that, in the absence of serious government investment, Britain is likely to remain well behind Europe, at least as regards cycling.

ALCOHOL

Drinking alcohol is associated with a range of negative health outcomes including heart disease, several cancers, diabetes, diseases of the liver and pancreas, and intentional and unintentional injuries.[34] Unsurprisingly, the risk of liver cirrhosis—a major cause of alcohol-related mortality—increases with higher levels of alcohol consumption.[35] As I mentioned earlier, cirrhosis is an increasingly common cause of death in Britain, so increasing consumption of alcohol represents another potential challenge to lengthening lifespans.

We do not have good survey data on drinking patterns. When answering questions in surveys about their drinking habits people almost certainly underestimate the amount they drink. (This is probably due to what survey methodologists term 'social desirability bias'.) However, the British Beer and Pub association has produced intriguing long-term data on sales of alcohol, going back to the beginning of the twentieth century. This is not perfect but the overall pattern is probably broadly accurate. There was a big decline during the first third of the twentieth century, a stable phase mid-century, a big increase in the last decades of the century (almost returning to the levels of the early 1900s), before starting to drop once more. The decline in the first half of the century may have been a result of government using the licensing laws to make access more restricted. The Defence of the Realm Act, passed in 1914 immediately after the declaration of the First World War, restricted licensing hours in order to limit alcohol consumption, the government believing that high levels of drinking could interfere with the war effort. Taxes on alcohol were also sharply increased.

In the more recent period it seems that changing price levels can partly explain the increasing consumption of alcohol, and the subsequent reduction after 2007. Figure 3.9 shows a measure of alcohol affordability in England (developed by the Office for National Statistics)[36] alongside sales of alcohol, measured by litres of pure alcohol and adjusted for population size. Incidentally, 1 litre of 100 per cent alcohol is equivalent to 54 pints of beer, 12.5 bottles of wine, or 125 single servings of spirits.

Figure 3.9 strongly suggests that changing price levels can explain some of the recent changes in consumption. Alcohol became increasingly affordable between 1983 and 2007 and alcohol sales increased over the same period. The

Figure 3.9. Alcohol consumption in the UK broadly reflects affordability

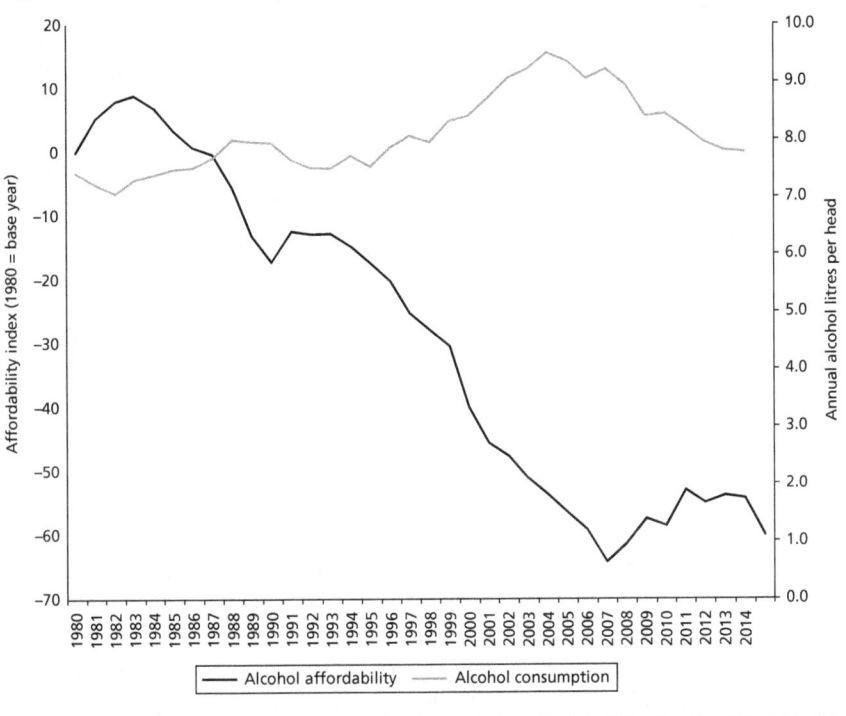

Source: alcohol consumption: British Beer and Pub Association, Statistical Handbook 2015, table B8. Affordability: Statistics on Alcohol, England 2015, https://www.gov.uk/government/statistics/statistics-on-alcohol-england-2016. Copyright © 2016, reused with the permission of NHS Digital. All rights reserved

trend in affordability then went into reverse after 2007 while consumption declined. Over the 1980–2015 period as a whole, then, levels of alcohol sales seem to mirror the affordability of alcohol, although I find it puzzling that sales started to decline in 2005 shortly before, rather than after, alcohol started to become less affordable. So price is probably not the only thing that matters.

However, although overall levels of consumption appear to be declining, it is not clear whether this has yet had any measurable impact on life expectancy in England. Alcohol-related hospital admissions and treatment for alcohol dependency continued to rise in England after 2007.[37] Alcohol-related death rates rose steadily throughout the 1990s, reaching a peak around 2008. Since then the number of deaths attributable to alcohol have been fairly stable in England, although they declined quite dramatically in Scotland, which had previously had mortality rates from alcohol that were more than double those of England.[38]

The contrast in the trends for consumption of alcohol and mortality may of course be because, as with smoking, excessive drinking has delayed effects on health and mortality. The decline in alcohol consumption in England started only recently, and current rates of hospital admissions and deaths probably reflect earlier patterns of alcohol consumption.

However, I should point out that Britain is not all that unusual in its level of drinking. Compared with the rest of Europe, data from the Organisation for Economic Co-operation and Development (OECD) suggest that UK levels of consumption have been catching up with European levels but are still below those of France and Germany.[39] It is unlikely, then, that alcohol consumption and consequent alcohol-related deaths can explain why Britain's record on life expectancy has been worse than those of European countries like France and Germany. Rising consumption of alcohol in the last two decades of the twentieth century will not have helped Britain's record, but Britain is not such an outlier in terms of alcohol as it was with respect to smoking or obesity.

Socio-Economic Inequality

There is a great deal of evidence that there are major socio-economic differences in many of the diseases which I have discussed so far in this chapter. In contemporary Britain it tends to be people in more disadvantaged economic positions (people who are workless or in low-skilled or insecure employment) and those with lower levels of education who are more likely to smoke or be overweight, and who are less likely to have healthy diets or take regular exercise. (Interestingly, alcohol consumption is an exception.) There are also clear differences between highly educated and less well-educated groups in infant mortality and in life expectancy.[40]

Medical researchers such as Michael Marmot sometimes term social and economic disadvantage 'the causes of the causes'.[41] In other words, excessive smoking, overeating, and failure to take sufficient exercise or an adequate diet should not be seen solely as matters of individual choice, for which the individuals could be blamed. Instead they may reflect or be a consequence of the disadvantaged social positions in which people have ended up. We are still some way from fully understanding quite why disadvantaged social positions have these effects, but it is likely to involve more than purely material poverty. While issues of cost may partly explain poor diets—junk food being notoriously cheaper—time pressures, stress, and lack of empowerment may be relevant, too. As I will show in Chapter 4, there is quite a strong link between empowerment and education, and this could well be relevant to health inequalities as well.

Notwithstanding the varied and complex causes of health inequalities, the worry is that the growth of economic inequality will have exacerbated these health inequalities and, in turn, may have slowed down Britain's progress in improving health and life expectancy. The key issue here is that an unequal society may have lower life expectancy than a similar but more equal society at the same level of development. Furthermore, a society which becomes more unequal over time may show less progress in reducing mortality than one where the level of inequality has remained unchanged. Why might this be the case? One possible answer comes from the economic principle of diminishing marginal returns: improving the situation of poor people (for example, by improving their access to high-quality health care) can bring them bigger health gains than the same investment in improving the lot of people who already have excellent access to health care. An additional line of argument suggests that there may be psychological damage as a result of being lower in the status and power hierarchy, although this is more controversial.[42] These arguments could be relevant to the British case because, as Chapter 2 showed, Britain experienced a much bigger increase in inequality in the 1980s than did peer countries.

There are some reasonably good data on changing patterns of social class inequalities in infant mortality and in life expectancy. Interestingly, the trends are rather different for the two outcomes, which suggests that they may have rather different explanations. Let me start with infant mortality.

In Figure 3.10 I show the results of a study conducted by Roderick Floud and his colleagues. They investigated social class differences in infant mortality, using a classification originally developed in 1911 by T. H. C. Stevenson, a medical statistician in the General Register Office. Stevenson set out to investigate social differences in infant mortality. He felt that culture was more important than income or wealth for understanding mortality differences and so he developed a classification of occupations, arranging them in order of their 'standing within the community', with professionals at the top and unskilled manual workers at the bottom.

In line with Figure 3.3, which showed the overall trend in infant mortality, Figure 3.10 shows that infant mortality declined sharply before the war, continued to decline although at a slower rate after the war, and declined more slowly still in the final decade of the twentieth century as infant mortality became more and more rare. Moreover, as the overall rate declined, so too did the gaps between the social classes. In the early 1930s, infant mortality was 80 per 1000 live births in the unskilled manual class compared with only 32 per 1000 among professionals, a gap of 48 per 1000. By the mid-1990s these rates had fallen to 7.2 and 4.5 per 1000, respectively, a much smaller gap of less than 3 per 1000.

This pattern of declining gaps between the social classes is not surprising when infant mortality falls so low. As the overall rate reaches what one could term the floor (the minimum possible level), there becomes less scope for advantaged classes to make additional improvements, and hence more scope for disadvantaged classes to catch up. So it is all the more surprising that, in the final decade of the twentieth century, the gap actually widened slightly,

Figure 3.10. Social class inequalities in infant mortality in England and Wales shrank until the 1990s but subsequently showed little change

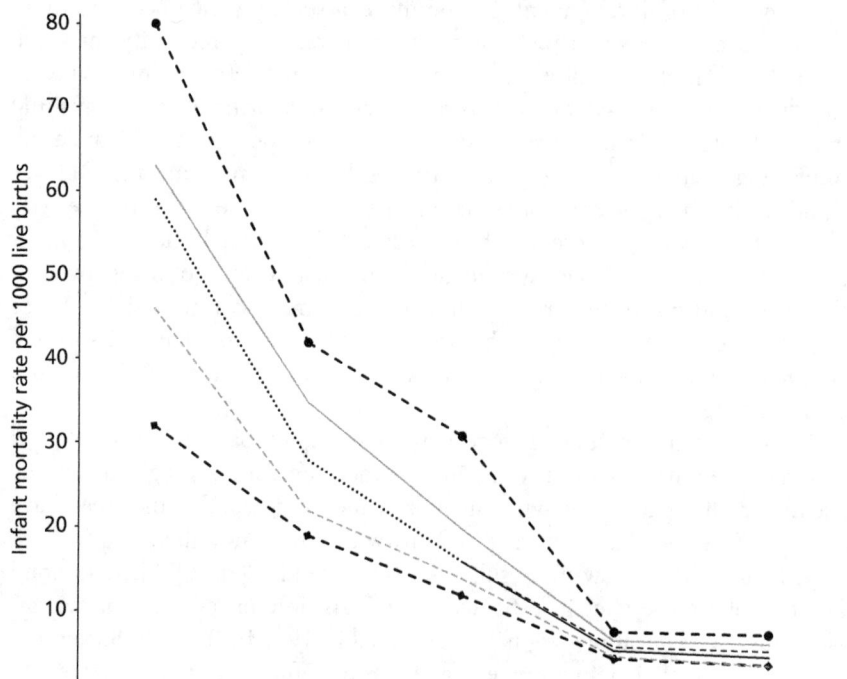

Note: after 1970–2, the 'skilled' group splits into two different groups: 'skilled manual' and 'skilled non-manual'

Source: Max Roser, 'Child mortality', Our World in Data, https://ourworldindata.org/[43]

with the professionals making more progress in improving their infant mortality than the unskilled workers.

The classification developed by Stevenson was finally abandoned in 2001 by the Office for National Statistics. A new classification was introduced (the National Statistics Socio-Economic Classification), which is not strictly comparable with Stevenson's so I have not attempted to add it to Figure 3.10. However, the Office for National Statistics has published some statistics for the twenty-first century using the new system. These show that there has been little change in the size of the gaps between the social classes, despite continuing decline in the overall infant mortality rate. In short, social class inequalities in infant mortality have become very small, but no longer appear to be narrowing.

Turning to the other end of life, the Office for National Statistics has also published estimates of social class inequalities in life expectancy among people aged 65 (that is, how much longer someone who had reached the age of 65 could expect to live given prevailing mortality rates). These statistics use the new socio-economic classification, so are not precisely comparable with the infant mortality statistics. Moreover, the ONS statistics only go back as far as the 1980s.

Figure 3.11 shows that, although life expectancy at age 65 in England and Wales increased for all social classes between 1982/6 and 2007/11, the gaps between the most and least advantaged social classes tended if anything to widen. Thus, in the early 1980s, 65-year-old men with higher professional and managerial occupations could have expected to live an extra 15.3 years. By the late 2000s this had increased by five years to an extra 20.3 years. Men in routine occupations also saw an increase over this period, but it was smaller and the gap between the two classes widened from 2.4 years to 3.9 years. The picture is not quite so clear for women, however. Higher-professional women made less progress than did their male peers and the gap between higher-professional and routine women stayed more or less unchanged.

A natural question to ask is whether the increasing class inequality in male life expectancy is in any way connected to the increasing income inequality

Figure 3.11. Social class differences in life expectancy among men at age sixty-five widened gradually in England and Wales between 1982–6 and 2007–11

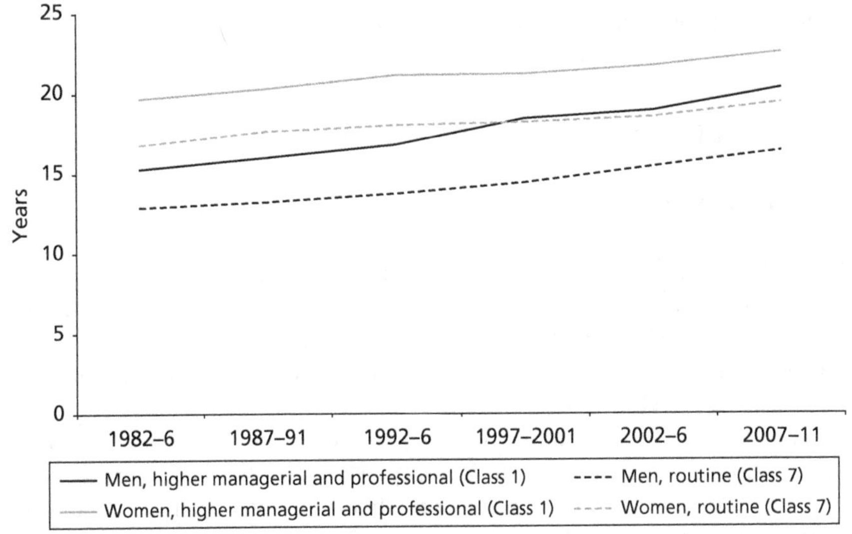

Source: Office for National Statistics Longitudinal Study[44]

which I reported in Chapter 2. To answer this, we would need to look at trends before the 1980s. If class inequalities in life expectancy paralleled changes in income inequality, declining up until the early 1980s and thereafter widening, it would be reasonable to think that the two might be connected. Is this what we find in practice?

Unfortunately, I cannot give a definite answer. For the period before the 1980s we do not have comparable data to that used by the Office for National Statistics in Figure 3.11. However, data sources using alternative methods suggest that the trend towards increasing class inequalities is a long-standing one. Ray Fitzpatrick and Tarani Chandola, for example, have shown that social class inequalities in mortality rates actually increased between the 1970s and the 1980s, and the Marmot review using methods more similar to those used by the Office for National Statistics also reached the same conclusion.[45]

While we cannot be 100 per cent sure, the most plausible interpretation is that increasing inequality in male life expectancy is not directly linked with the post-1980 increase in income inequality. Theoretically, too, this makes sense. A recurring theme throughout this chapter has been that trends in health and life expectancy are not straightforward reflections of trends in material prosperity. I suspect that T. H. C. Stevenson was right when he suggested in 1911 that mortality had more to do with culture than with income and wealth. My interpretation is that recent changes in health and longevity have had more to do with lifestyle than with material constraints. The higher professional and managerial classes have tended to be leaders in cutting back on smoking, for example. They may well also be the leaders in adopting other aspects of healthy lifestyles. This could explain why class inequalities have widened.[46] Economic inequality is important, but it is not the only form of inequality that exists in modern Britain.

Health Care

No discussion of disease and life expectancy should be without at least a brief consideration of our health-care system. The National Health Service was established in 1948 and was intended to provide a universal health service that was free at the point of use, replacing inconsistent paid-for care and employment-based insurance schemes that excluded many women and children. With some exceptions—notably for dental and optical services and prescription charges in England—seventy years later the NHS continues to operate according to this founding principle. However, there is mounting concern that the NHS, and especially its funding, is in crisis. How well does the NHS perform compared with health-care systems in similar countries?

Can Britain's lagging performance in life expectancy be blamed in any way on the lack of funding or other failings of the NHS?

This is another huge and complex topic in its own right so I am just going to look at one important health-care outcome where there is good evidence which enables us to compare the performance of the British health-care system with that of other countries—namely cancer survival rates. There is considerable evidence that cancer survival rates are considerably lower in the UK than in the seven peer countries. The OECD provide data on five-year survival rates for breast cancer, cervical cancer, and colorectal cancer. In Figure 3.12 I show the data for breast cancer, since this is such a major cause of death.

The data are rather patchy, but two conclusions stand out. First, breast cancer survival rates improved steadily in Britain from 72.5 per cent in 1995/2000 to 81.1 per cent just over a decade later. Second, survival rates have also improved in the other countries for which we have the data, and the UK's survival rate of 81.1 per cent is still lower than the figures for any of the other seven countries for any of the years for which data are available. This is not an impressive performance. The OECD also provides evidence on survival rates

Figure 3.12. Breast cancer survival rates improved in the UK between 1995–2000 and 2008–13, although lagging behind those of peer countries

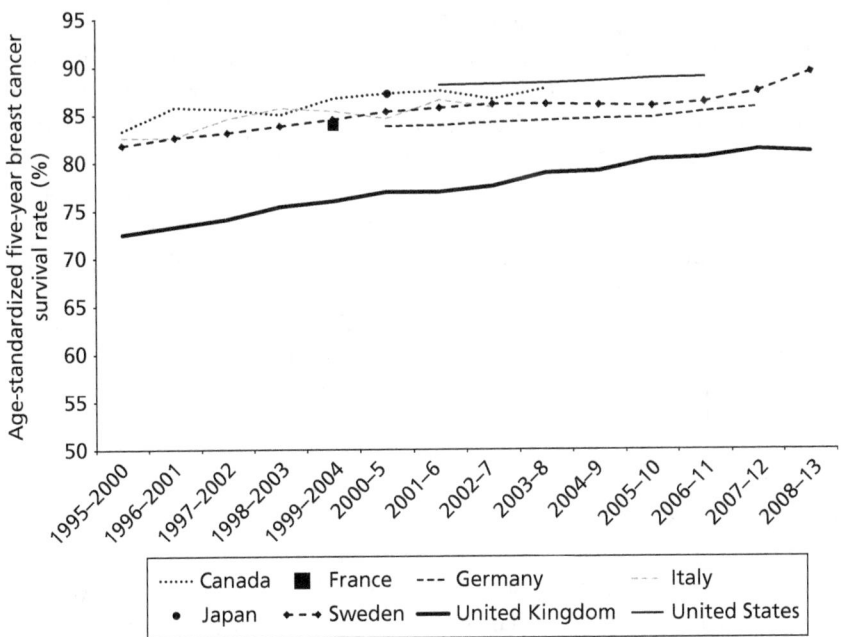

Note: data for females aged fifteen and older
Source: OECD Health Statistics 2016

from some other cancers, and Britain lags behind on these, too. To be sure, cancer survival rates are only one among many possible health outcomes that one could in theory investigate, so I should not attempt to generalize. Moreover, there are technical reasons why the results for Britain might not be strictly comparable with those for other countries.[47] One has to be cautious when comparing administrative data from different countries because of their different institutional arrangements and recording systems. It is possible, but unproven, that cancer survival rates in Britain are not quite as bad as Figure 3.12 suggests. Nevertheless, I think one should take very seriously the possibility that Britain is not doing nearly as well as peer countries.

The lower survival rates in Britain have been attributed to factors such as varied access to treatments across the UK, shortage of manpower, and delayed diagnosis.[48] Concerns about this gap resulted in the development of the NHS cancer plan in 2000.[49] The plan recommended reduction in diagnostic delay as a key priority, since much of excess cancer-related mortality in the UK happens early on after diagnosis. There appear to have been some improvements in one-year survival after the introduction of the NHS cancer plan,[50] and Figure 3.12 suggests that perhaps the gap with the peer countries has been narrowing. But Britain is still clearly well behind.

How far Britain's poor performance can be attributed to lack of resources for the NHS is unclear. It is true that the UK spends less on health care both per person and as a proportion of GDP than all the peer countries apart from Italy.[51] In 2015, for example, the UK spent 9.8 per cent of GDP on health care. Italy spent only 9.1 per cent whereas most of the other countries spent between 10 and 11 per cent, while the USA spent a whopping 16.9 per cent of GDP on health care (much of this being privately rather than publicly funded).[52]

However, the expenditure figures suggest that money cannot be the whole story. Despite its lower expenditure, Italy's survival rates are better than British ones. And while the USA does have relatively good survival rates, they are not markedly better than those of countries like Japan and Canada, whose spending is much closer to British levels. I am sure that more money for the NHS is essential, but I suspect that it will not be sufficient on its own to close the gap in cancer survival rates.

Conclusions

Progress in extending healthy lives may well be an even more important criterion of social progress than is increasing material prosperity. What is the value of ever greater material prosperity if it were to come at the expense of premature death and a shortened lifespan? The basic data on mortality are also more reliable and trustworthy than the economic data. I think government should give at least as much attention to health and longevity as they do to material progress.

There can be no doubt that Britain made huge strides in health and life expectancy during the second half of the twentieth century. This progress resulted from reductions in infant mortality and control of infectious diseases, while since the 1970s reductions in mortality from heart disease and cancers played an important role, too. Progress continued into the twenty-first century, although it begins to look as though disability-free life expectancy may be flatlining, or even going into reverse among women.

There is also clear evidence that many other advanced democracies made greater progress than Britain did. The USA made the least progress of all and slipped right to the back of our group of eight peer countries. But Britain has been overtaken by France, Italy, and Japan and is now towards the back of the bunch. So in these respects Britain's performance in promoting long and healthy lives has not been as strong as its economic performance.

While technical advances (for example, control of infectious diseases, treatment of cardiovascular disease and cancer) have been of major importance in extending length of life, lifestyles clearly play an important role—perhaps an increasing role as society gets richer. This is most evident in the case of smoking. Immediately after the war, Britain along with the USA had one of the highest rates of (male) smoking of all eight peer countries. Smoking subsequently declined, especially as the evidence linking smoking with lung cancer became more convincing and public health campaigns reinforced the message of the scientists. However, the major effects of the post-war smoking epidemic only showed up in the mortality statistics several decades later—smoking-related mortality peaked around 1980 among men in Britain, and has since been declining. British women took up smoking rather later than men, so the peak in smoking-related mortality for women has only just been reached. This can then explain (at least in part) why the male/female gap in life expectancy has been closing and also why Britain made slower progress than other countries where smoking had not been so prevalent after the war. Now that British men and women's rates of smoking have fallen and are no longer higher than those of other European countries, we might expect to see Britain making relatively better progress than it did before.

Unfortunately, other lifestyle choices may be working in the opposite direction. Important among these is obesity and lack of exercise. British rates of obesity have climbed—not as much as in the USA and Canada but rather more than in European peer countries and much more than in Japan. It is not entirely clear as yet what the implications will be for life expectancy but obesity is a new and threatening giant, and a major challenge for the future.

Two other major challenges are health inequalities and low cancer survival rates in Britain. Over the decades since the Second World War, absolute social class inequalities in infant mortality reduced strikingly. Infant mortality fell for all social classes, and did so particularly for the more disadvantaged classes up until 2000. Since then, however, the available evidence suggests that class inequalities in infant mortality have not reduced any further. Similarly, among older people, disadvantaged social classes do not appear to be catching up with respect to life expectancy, despite the general increase in length of life. If anything, the gaps have been widening among men—possibly because it has been the professional and managerial classes who have been earlier adopters of healthy lifestyles than more disadvantaged classes.

Finally, while Britain has a national health service that compares favourably with other countries, particularly the USA, with respect to equity, access, and efficiency, there are some aspects of health care where Britain trails behind peer countries. As we saw, breast cancer survival rates are particularly poor in Britain. This is indeed the first clear example where Britain is at the bottom of the class of the eight large democracies. Moreover, I think it is unlikely that this is simply a matter of lack of expenditure, since other countries such as Italy and Canada which spend similar amounts on health care have substantially better survival rates. The problem in Britain seems to be due to late diagnosis of cancer. This may well reflect the organization of health care—perhaps the length of time it takes to see a GP and then to be referred on and be seen in hospital.

The story is a complex one, but perhaps one of the crucial take-home messages is that progress in health and longevity does not straightforwardly parallel progress in material prosperity. Among our eight peer countries, rates of progress in improving material prosperity have no obvious link with progress in improving health and longevity. True, some rich countries saw smoking epidemics after the war, and some are seeing obesity epidemics in the twenty-first century. But other rich countries such as Japan have avoided these epidemics. The amount spent on health care seems to be largely unrelated to cancer survival rates. Increasing income inequality in Britain does not seem to translate straightforwardly into increasing social class inequalities in either infant mortality or mortality among older adults. I suspect that T. H. C. Stevenson's desire in 1911 to go beyond income and wealth in order to understand health inequalities remains as relevant today as it was one hundred years ago.

4 The Fight against Ignorance

Participation, Standards, and Non-Economic Outcomes

with Lindsay Richards

Introduction

Ignorance was the third of Beveridge's five giants. A contemporary commentator today would probably use a term such as underachievement or low standards rather than ignorance, but I rather like Beveridge's homely term. It encourages us to think about the content of education and not just about test scores or certificates.

Politicians and commentators have tended to emphasize education's role as a preparation for the world of work. Education is sometimes seen to be primarily a means to equip people for the labour market, increasing the number of skilled recruits for employers and improving Britain's economic competitiveness. In 1976, Labour prime minister James Callaghan started a 'great debate' about the role of education in contemporary life. While he recognized the wider purposes of education, his emphasis was more on the need to equip young people for the changing requirements of a modern economy.

> For many years the accent was simply on fitting a so-called inferior group of children with just enough learning to earn their living in the factory. Labour has attacked that attitude consistently, during 60 or 70 years and throughout my childhood... [But] in today's world, higher standards are demanded than were required yesterday and there are simply fewer jobs for those without skill. Therefore we demand more from our schools than did our grandparents.[1]

Ignorance may thus be a giant who is continually evolving. What counts as ignorance in the twenty-first century is likely to be rather different from Beveridge's idea of ignorance in the mid-twentieth century.

At any rate, Jim Callaghan was certainly correct in claiming that the skill requirements of the late twentieth-century economy were very different from those sixty or seventy years earlier. And he was also right to recognize that education has a wider range of benefits for the individual and the society than simply improving one's own or the national income. Education contributes to social progress in its own right, and not just in its role as the handmaiden of the economy. Education tends to promote self-confidence, tolerance, and trust in others and is linked with the adoption of healthy lifestyles, civic engagement, and fulfilling potential more generally. It can be thought of as a major means for improving citizens' capabilities in coping not only with the economic but also with the many other challenges of modern life.[2] A highly educated, well-informed citizenry will have the self-confidence and skills needed to challenge corruption, hold politicians to account, and make democracy work. Education can empower and emancipate as well as enrich.

There is evidence from around the world that education can empower subordinate groups. Closing the gender gap in education has helped women in developing countries to wrest control over their bodies from authoritarian husbands, leading to lower family sizes and increasing women's participation in the labour market and in politics.[3] The spread of education to the whole population can be seen as part of a democratic agenda, not just an economic or materialistic one. Equalizing education might also help to equalize healthy lifestyles and reduce inequalities in lifespans.

It is for these kinds of wider reasons that the United Nations Development Programme includes educational participation as one of the three components of its Human Development Index, alongside GDP per head and life expectancy. A country scores higher on the index when the average lifespan is longer, GDP per head is higher, and enrollment in education (at primary, secondary, and tertiary levels) is higher.[4] The inclusion of education alongside lifespans and material prosperity reflects the importance attached to education as a source of human flourishing in its own right, not just as a route to material prosperity.

Whatever their precise objectives, economic or humanitarian, British governments have certainly given education a great deal of attention ever since Beveridge's day. First came the revolutionary 1944 Education Act which enshrined the principle of free secondary education for all. The minimum school-leaving age was increased several times in the post-war period, and there was a parallel expansion in higher education. New universities were founded in the 1960s following the 1963 Robbins Report, which had recommended the immediate expansion of higher education in order 'to meet competitive pressures in the modern world'.[5] Then came the 1992 reform which transformed the former polytechnics into universities. In 2001 Tony Blair's Labour government set the aspiration of 50 per cent of young people attending university.[6] Other notable reforms were the shift, starting in 1965, from a selective system of education to a comprehensive system of secondary schooling. More recently there have been numerous government reforms designed to increase parental choice and to raise educational standards, especially of the lowest-performing schools.

So public education has witnessed a transformation as dramatic as those in material prosperity and life expectancy which were covered in Chapters 2 and 3.

When I was growing up in the 1950s we had the so-called tripartite system with grammar schools, technical schools, and secondary modern schools. So called, because alongside these three types of state-funded schools there was a fourth type: private schools. To get into a grammar school you had to pass the '11-plus' entrance exam. This was primarily based on tests of reading, arithmetic, and reasoning taken at the age of 11. Around 20–25 per cent of children passed the exam each year and went to a grammar school, and at grammar schools there was a clear route upwards to university. You had first to pass your GCE Ordinary Level exams, taken around the age of 15 or 16, and then Advanced Level examinations two years later. And if you were suitably ambitious (as my family were) you could stay on for a further year in order to prepare for the entrance examinations to Oxford or Cambridge.

For the other 75 per cent of the school population who did not go to a grammar school, the normal route was to leave school as soon as one reached the minimum leaving age—in my time 15—the great majority leaving school without any formal qualifications at all. Echoing Jim Callaghan's remarks which I cited at the start of the chapter, children at the secondary modern schools would not be entered for the Ordinary Level examinations (which were designed for more academically able students). Many would leave school at the earliest opportunity, before the summer term when the exams were taken. But there were at least plenty of factory jobs for them to go to in the 1950s.

Sixty years on, the experience of education is very different for the 75 per cent. Instead of attending the lower-ranking secondary modern and technical schools, nowadays they typically attend a co-educational mixed-ability comprehensive school or one of the smorgasbord of academies, faith schools, and free schools that recent governments have introduced. Many more of them will now join the top 25 per cent in continuing with their education beyond the minimum school-leaving age and will obtain some kind of school certificate. Nowadays it is a tiny minority (less than 10 per cent) who do not obtain any certificate at all. The educational experience has not changed much for the social elite who attend private schools, or the educational elite who attend the smallish number of grammar schools which survived government reforms. But these social and academic elites have been joined by very large numbers of young people who would have been effectively excluded from upper secondary or higher education in my youth.

So in my lifetime upper secondary and higher education have gone from being the preserve of a small minority, largely from elite backgrounds, to a mass system open to a much wider range of young people.

But the formal official statistics may give an unduly rosy picture of educational progress. There are critics who argue that the standard of qualifications like the GCE Ordinary and Advanced Levels that I took in the 1950s has been dumbed down, and that educational standards are falling, not rising.[7] According to these critics the increase in the number of young people gaining certificates may represent paper rather than real educational progress. There may indeed be some truth in this—the kind of exam which one sets for the cleverest 10 per cent of the age group needs to be rather different from one which will be attempted by 90 per cent. Similar arguments could be applied to university degrees, too. It may be difficult in practice to expand without changing standards. In short, there is a great deal of debate about what the official figures really mean. Does reality match up to the rhetoric?

In the next section I will look in more detail at some of the key official statistics, and why we might need to be a bit sceptical of them. In the section afterwards I will turn to independent, non-governmental statistics to see what light they shed on the question of rising or falling educational progress. Independent evidence from international bodies such as the Organisation for Economic Co-operation and Development (usually known by its initials—OECD) will also enable us to assess how British educational standards (in the sense of students' test scores) compare with those in peer countries. I will then look for evidence on some of the wider benefits of education such as empowerment. Important issues of equality of opportunity within the educational system, which have been major concerns of policy-makers and academics, I have reserved for detailed treatment in Chapter 7.

How Much Did Participation in Upper Secondary and Tertiary Education Change over Time?

Before getting on to the vexed questions of standards, I will begin with the somewhat more straightforward issue of the increase in participation in upper secondary and higher education. While there may be heated debates about exactly what young people are learning in school, it does not seem unreasonable to follow the United Nations Human Development Index and to take the spread of educational opportunities to a larger proportion of young people as one indicator of social progress. Going to school or college does not guarantee the diminution of ignorance or the increase of capabilities, but it is not a bad place to start.

There are long-run series of official statistics in Britain showing how many young people stay on at school (or in further education), and how many go on to higher education and university. In Britain, as in other developed countries, there are statutory rules specifying how long young people must stay in school. In Beveridge's day it was age 14. The school-leaving age was then successively increased from 14 to 15 in 1947, then to 16 in 1973/4, and most recently, although only in England, to 17 in 2013 and to 18 in 2015. However, these most recent increases merely require young people to continue in some form of education or training, not necessarily school-based or even full time.[8]

To begin with, I look at the proportion of young people staying on at school after their sixteenth birthday. In my day, this was roughly equivalent to entering the sixth form. Nowadays this will correspond to school year 12, in which young people in England, Wales, and Northern Ireland start preparing for A Level exams or other advanced technical qualifications. Education researchers often term this the transition from lower secondary to upper secondary education. Scotland, I should emphasize has long had its own distinct educational system with a different examination structure, and is not included in Figure 4.1.[9] However, the Scottish trends have tended to be fairly similar to those in England.[10]

For most of the post-war period the end of compulsory schooling represented a crucial transition for young people (which is why government collected these statistics). Young people who left before the age of 16 would move straight into the labour market, entering relatively low-skilled manual jobs, or would take apprenticeships which gave access to skilled manual work (and for the lucky few career progression to supervisory or managerial positions). Staying on at school in contrast gave the possibility of preparing for white-collar jobs and was essential for moving on to higher education and the professions.

Figure 4.1 reports the results, for boys and girls, from the official statistics provided by the Department for Education (and its various reincarnations). It covers the period from 1947 to 2015, albeit with numerous changes of definition and coverage. The vertical lines on the graph indicate when the Department for Education changed the way it measured staying-on rates. For example, in the early years the department reported the ages of young people in England and Wales when they left maintained secondary schools. However, from 1961 to 1979 the department published figures for pupils in the United Kingdom as a whole; they included all schools, including private schools; they did not look at the age when pupils left school but their age on 1 January of the school year. So the dip in 1961/2 is due to the changes in what the department published and does not reflect a real drop in the proportion of young people staying on at school. There were similar major breaks in the statistics in 1980, 1996, 2000, 2009, and 2012.[11] It is all rather messy. This kind of thing is quite common in administrative data—that is data collected by government through its various administrative procedures. Procedures are often changed (sometimes for good administrative reason) and so figures for different periods are rarely strictly comparable.[12]

Irritating though these changes are to a historian of British education, there can be no reasonable doubt that a much larger proportion of the age group was staying on into upper secondary school or college in 2015 than had been the case sixty years earlier. At the beginning of the series, in 1947, around 78 per cent of boys (school leavers) left school at age 15 or younger, as did 79 per cent of girls. So just over a fifth stayed on—and most of these would have been in

Figure 4.1. The proportion of young people in England still in full-time education at age sixteen showed a large increase between 1947 and 2015

Source: Department for Education, 'Participation in education, training and employment by 16–18 year olds in England, SFR22/2016, and previous years', https://www.gov.uk/government/statistics/participation-in-education-training-and-employment-2015

grammar or private schools. At the end of the series in 2015 the figures were completely the other way round. Eighty-five per cent of boys and 90 per cent of girls were still in full-time education at age 16. So fewer than a fifth had exited from education.

Some of this increase occurred in 1974 after the minimum statutory school-leaving age was raised to 16, with a twelve-point jump from 36 to 48 per cent.[13] There was another big increase in the early 1990s, when the proportion increased by another nineteen points from 51 (for boys) to 70 per cent in 1994. This increase perhaps had more to do with the deteriorating labour market condition for young people in the 1990s slump than with educational reforms. There was another big increase after the 2007/8 financial crash. So educational reforms have probably played some part, but the changing labour market for young people has probably been even more important in recent decades. (I will look at changing labour market conditions for young people in Chapter 6.)

The other striking change is that girls lagged slightly behind boys at the beginning of the period, had caught up with them around 1973, and moved clearly ahead in the twenty-first century. It is not entirely clear why this was the case. Perhaps it reflected the changing labour market options facing young men and women. Or perhaps boys, especially working-class boys, were more likely to find the atmosphere of the classroom uncongenial and were more attracted to the world of work, as for example was suggested by Paul Willis in his classic study *Learning to Labour*, which explored the link between the lads' anti-school subculture and the masculine culture of manual work.[14]

Figure 4.2. University enrolments in the UK increased greatly between 1954 and 2016, women moving well ahead of men

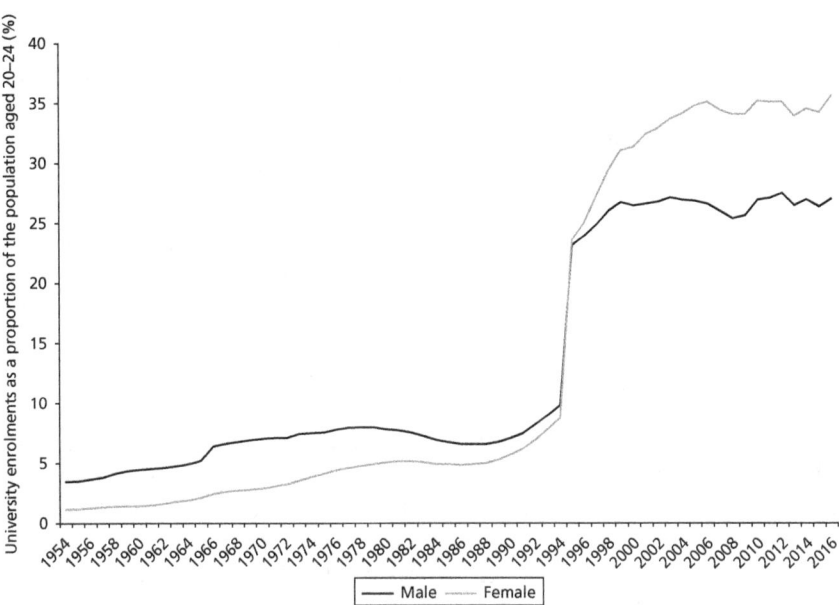

Note: the data are for full-time study and include degrees both of undergraduate and post-graduate nature. Data are for the United Kingdom

Source: calculated by Dingeman Wiertz of Nuffield College, Oxford based on Higher Education Statistics Agency and Office for National Statistics, Population Estimate, data

We find a similar enormous increase if we look at participation in higher education. The huge leap in 1994 is partly nominal, reflecting the reclassification of polytechnics as universities in 1992. This abruptly led students, who would have been studying previously in these institutions, as being counted as attending university. However, I don't think that the change was solely a nominal one—there was also a shift at this time towards longer, degree-level courses as in the cases of teaching and nursing qualifications, which had previously been taught in polytechnics.

The other striking change in Figure 4.2 is that women overtook men, the gender differential changing even more than in the case of staying on at school. In my day, in the early 1960s, twice as many young men as young women attended university. In contrast, in the twenty-first century, young women were ten points ahead of young men. Some of this change may have reflected the move, for example, of teacher training from shorter vocational to longer degree-level courses. But there were also real changes over time in access to traditional university degree courses. I can still remember, as a very junior academic, voting in favour of the admission of women to Churchill

College, Cambridge, the first of the all-male undergraduate colleges in Cambridge to open its doors to women—a move that was rapidly followed (because it was so successful academically) by all the other men-only Oxford and Cambridge colleges. There was real progress in the 1970s, at least in Oxford and Cambridge, in increasing opportunities for women in higher education.

These increased opportunities for access to upper secondary schooling and to university can be found in all our peer countries. In Figure 4.3 I show the trends from 1950 to 2010 (the latest year available at the time of writing) in the percentages of young people completing a university degree in the eight peer countries. These figures have been estimated by economists Robert Barro and Yong-Wha Lee, drawing on census and survey data from the different countries and distinguishing between different age groups. In the figure I show Barro and Lee's estimates of the percentage of 25–29 year olds who had completed a degree at each time point. The estimates are not exactly comparable with those in Figure 4.2 (which were based on administrative data and dealt only with enrolments, not completions). I also have some reservations about the reliability of Barro and Lee's estimates, but they are the best available data for the period.[15] They are definitely not of the same quality as the estimates of life expectancy which we looked at in Chapter 3, but they are in my judgement just about adequate for broad-brush comparisons of Britain with its peer countries.

Figure 4.3. All peer countries saw large increases in university education between 1950 and 2010

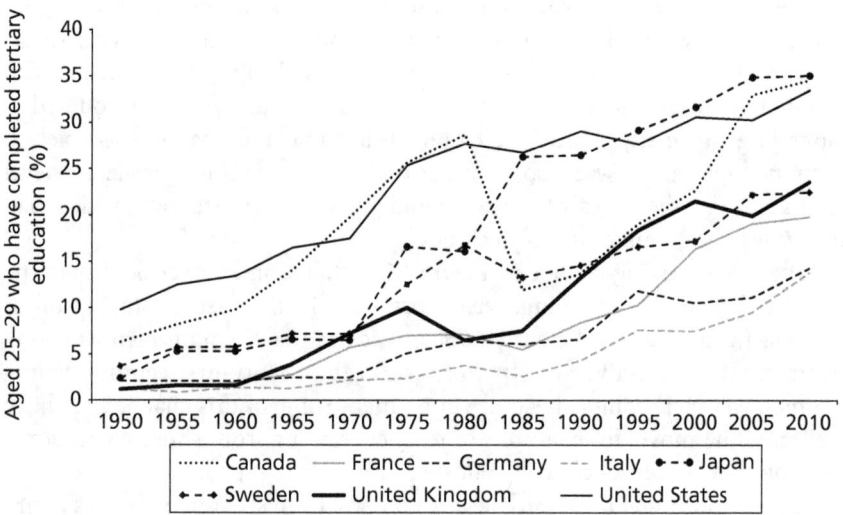

Source: calculated from the Barro-Lee dataset[16]

What Figure 4.3 shows is that all our peer countries experienced large increases in university graduation rates over the period from 1950 to 2010. In 1950 graduation rates were below 10 per cent of the age group in every country, and below 5 per cent in most countries. The USA and Canada were well in the lead in 1950, and remained at the front of the pack right up until 2010, at which date around a third of the age group in these countries was graduating with a degree. The USA and Canada were, however, narrowly overtaken by Japan, which had started well behind.

Britain actually compares quite well. It started at the back of the pack alongside Italy and France, but had clearly moved ahead of them by 2010, and had also moved ahead of Germany and Sweden. Barro and Lee's estimates for Britain over this period are reasonably close to those from the official British statistics, more or less tracking them though at a somewhat lower level. (This makes good sense since Figure 4.2 looked at enrolment rates whereas Figure 4.3 looks at graduation rates.) So I am inclined to accept the story that, on this measure, Britain has progressed relatively well, even if still lagging behind the world leaders. It is an encouraging story of progress.

Did Progress in Academic Achievement Parallel Progress in Participation?

Enrolment rates are relatively uncontroversial, the main problems being technical ones about the reliability and comparability of the measures over time and across countries. I don't think that anyone can seriously doubt that many more young people are now staying on at school and going on to university today than fifty years ago. Examination results, however, raise both measurement issues and more fundamental issues about their meaning. So let me now bite this particular bullet.

Britain is unusual among developed societies in having high stakes examinations taken at age 15 or 16—these exams were called School Certificate before the war, General Certificate of Education at Ordinary Level in my day, and General Certificate of Secondary Education since 1988. In other countries such as France and Germany, the high-stakes exams like the French *baccalauréat* and the German *Abitur* come right at the end of the school career and are taken at ages 17/18. Other countries such as Canada and the USA also have certificates for the completion of upper secondary school, but these are not such high-stakes ones as the *baccalauréat* and *Abitur*. Moreover, these other countries tend to maintain a much broader curriculum until the end of upper secondary schooling than do England, Wales, and Northern Ireland. Scotland has a broader curriculum, but England, Wales, and Northern Ireland are completely out of step with most other major developed countries in this respect.

Because countries' examination systems are so different, it does not make much sense to compare how many students in the peer countries pass these secondary school examinations. I will come back to international comparisons of test scores shortly, but first let's take a look at the trends over time in England in students' acquisition of Ordinary Level and GCSE. These have been the primary focus of government interventions and targets for schools, and have been the subject of considerable public debate and controversy.

In Figure 4.4 I show the official statistics for the percentages obtaining five or more GCSEs, or their equivalents, from 1955 to 2013. The government introduced a series of radical changes to the methodology of GCSE statistics from 2014 and the figures for later years are not remotely comparable with those for the years up to 2013.[17] Even so, the chart has a thicket of vertical lines indicating changes in the measures used before 2013: there were important changes in the certificates open to young people, the marking systems, the government's definition of what counted as five good passes, and the territorial coverage of the statistics.[18]

At any rate, regardless of whether we take the older, pre-2014 or the later post-2014 yardstick, we find a dramatic story of increasing certification of young people. When the series started in 1955, 11 per cent of boys and the same percentage of girls leaving school in England and Wales had passed

Figure 4.4. The percentage of students in England and Wales obtaining five or more GCSEs (or equivalent) increased dramatically between 1955 and 2013

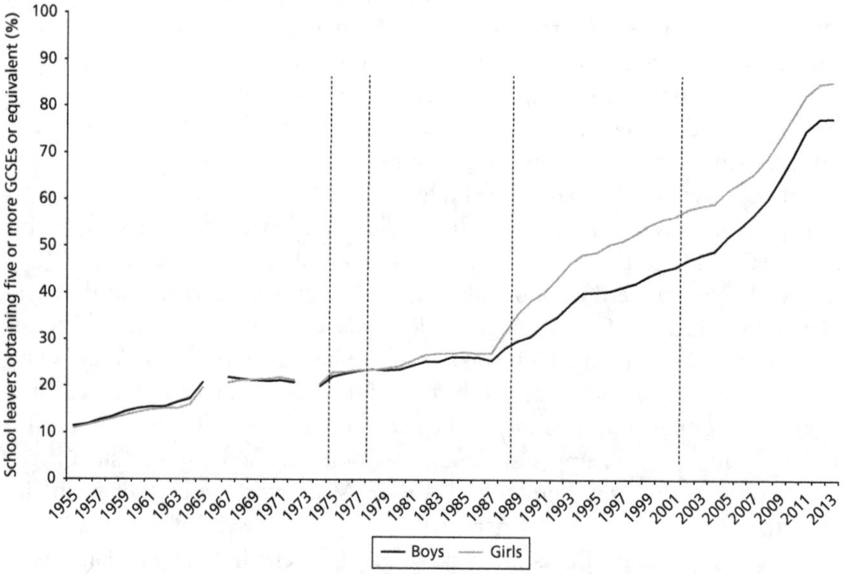

Source: Department for Education, education and training statistics for the United Kingdom, and previous DfE statistics

five or more subjects at GCE Ordinary Level. These students would mainly have been at grammar schools. In contrast, in 2014/15 59 per cent of boys and 71 per cent of girls in England achieved five or more passes at GCSE with grades A*–C at the end of Key Stage 4 (equivalent to the end of the period of compulsory education before the most recent increases in the school-leaving age). Moreover, 97 per cent of boys and 99 per cent of girls obtained a pass in at least one subject. So the change was as dramatic as that in the case of staying on at school. And as with staying on at school, girls ended up well ahead of boys.

Major questions, however, can be raised about the extent to which this certification revolution represents genuine educational progress. Some critics have raised questions about the possibility of grade inflation—the exams, it is alleged, may be getting easier to pass.[19] Other critics have suggested that the introduction (in 1992) of league tables and targets for schools, based on numbers of pupils attaining five or more passes at GCSE, encouraged schools to play the system, to teach to the test, and to manipulate entries for weaker students, for example by entering students for notionally equivalent but perhaps easier-to-pass technical qualifications.

Some years ago the economist Charles Goodhart put forward what has since become known as Goodhart's law: 'When a measure becomes a target, it ceases to be a good measure.'[20] The key idea was that targets will lead people—in this case teachers and headteachers—to modify their behaviour, and so the measure will no longer be measuring what it did before. While it could be argued that 'teaching to the test' may be a good thing if it leads students to have a better grasp of the subject matter, gaming the system by entering students for formally equivalent but less useful qualifications is likely to hinder rather than help students. A report by Alison Wolf for the government in 2013 argued that the system of vocational qualifications provided perverse incentives for students to be steered into notching up strings of qualifications which were of little help to them in finding work or moving on to higher education.[21] Goodhart's law most certainly applied in this case.

So while it is surely true that many more young people now leave school with formal certificates to their name, it is probable that the actual gains in their learning have been somewhat less than the nominal ones. We really do not know from the official statistics how much progress was made in the fight against the giant of Ignorance.

I find it a bit shocking that we really cannot say with any certainty whether young people's learning and competencies have increased over time. Education has been subject to repeated reforms and government interventions, and yet government has not thought it worthwhile to invest in rigorous independent measures to evaluate whether the reforms have had their intended effects. It is not surprising that many critics are highly sceptical and raise concerns about dumbing down and grade inflation.

Sammy Rashid and Greg Brooks have attempted to fill the gap left by government and have compiled, from a range of different sources, trends in literacy from 1948 onwards. These give us an alternative assessment of how much progress there has been in one basic educational skill. Like the official statistics, the series suffers from numerous changes in the measures used (and has other weaknesses, too), but the great advantage is that the sources were attempting to directly measure children's skills rather than their paper qualifications. And since these measures were never used as government targets, they are not vitiated by Goodhart's law.

Between 1948 and 1988 Rashid and Brooks found three overlapping, nationally representative surveys of reading among year 11 pupils (aged 15/16) in England (and sometimes including Wales).[22] There was then a break, but from 1993 to 2009 there was a new series of vocabulary tests (one key aspect of reading) administered to nationally representative samples of year 11 students in England. These sources show a fairly clear improvement between 1948 and 1960/1, although some scholars have suggested that there had been a decline during the Second World War and that the apparent improvement was actually more of a return to the pre-war situation.[23] There was then a long period of stagnation, or of stability if one wants to use a more positive term, from the 1960s up until 1988—a remarkable phenomenon in its own right since this was a period of major educational reform (comprehensive reorganization, raising of the school-leaving age, the introduction of CSEs and the increasing use of modern progressive methods of teaching). Finally there was gradual and modest improvement from the late 1990s until 2009, the latest date for which results are publicly available. The story told by these literacy tests, then, is of glacial improvement over time, rather at odds with the avalanche of qualifications shown in Figure 4.4.

Rashid and Brooks point out that their results are at odds with results of official tests at Key Stage 3. These were national tests introduced by the government which used to be taken at the end of year 9. Schools' results on the tests were published in league tables and schools which did badly came under intense scrutiny from parents and bodies like Ofsted (the Office for Standards in Education, Children's Services, and Skills). Schools had powerful incentives to appear to be doing well on these tests. Indeed, the tests showed a huge improvement between 1995 and 2007. The percentage attaining or exceeding level 5 (defined officially as the 'level expected') increased by nineteen points from 55 per cent in 1995 to 74 per cent in 2007. Statistical analysis by the Curriculum and Qualifications Authority suggested that marking standards had not changed between 1996 and 2001, and that the improvement was genuine. But even if marking standards had remained the same, it is still quite likely that, once performance at Key Stage 3 had become an official target, teachers started using various manoeuvres for improving measured performance in the league tables. Goodhart's law means that we really cannot trust official statistics when they are the basis of targets. In a magisterial inaugural lecture titled 'Improving education, the triumph of hope over experience' Robert Coe concluded,

> Despite the apparently plausible and widespread belief to the contrary, the evidence that levels of attainment in schools in England have systematically improved over the last 30 years is unconvincing. Much of what is claimed as school improvement is illusory, and many of the most commonly advocated strategies for improvement are not robustly proven to work...Overall, an honest and critical appraisal of our experience of trying to improve education is that, despite the best intentions and huge investment, we have failed—so far—to achieve it.[24]

All the same, even if progress on the literacy tests reported by Sammy Rashid and Greg Brooks was much less than the progress shown by government tests at Key Stage 3, the improvement in the literacy tests is itself an important story. It clearly refutes pessimistic claims that standards of literacy among young people had declined. Maybe young people's skills are not improving as fast as we would like, but they are certainly not in decline. According to the literacy tests, the giant of Ignorance may not have been vanquished, but he is slowly being pushed back.

How Do Educational Standards in Britain Compare with Those of Peer Countries?

There are a number of international studies using standardized tests to measure students' (and adults') performance in literacy, numeracy, and science. These studies provide us with independent measures of performance in most or all of our peer countries. Moreover, they are not vitiated by Goodhart's law, since their results have never been used as targets for schools or teachers—although governments are increasingly paying attention to the results of these studies and they are beginning to influence the education policies of some countries. These international studies aim to use state-of-the-art measures of literacy, numeracy, and understanding of science and have a higher degree of reliability and validity than do national measures such as GCSEs or test scores at Key Stage 3. Unfortunately, however, they are not a panacea. Just as with the British official statistics, there have been changes in methodology over time; questions have been raised about the quality of the data from Britain; and most of the studies cover only a decade or so, preventing us from studying long-term trends. Still, these are a somewhat different set of weaknesses from those inherent in British official statistics, so at the very least they provide an important alternative perspective.

From our point of view, the most interesting of these international studies is a series sponsored by the International Educational Association for the Evaluation of Educational Achievement measuring young people's scores in mathematics and science. This series has the longest history. The first of the studies (unsurprisingly named the First International Mathematics Study) was conducted in 1964 among samples of 13-year-old students in six of our peer countries. This was followed by the second study, conducted in the early 1980s among a slightly different set of six countries. These were followed by a further series of studies conducted in 1995, 1999, 2003, 2007, 2011, and most recently 2015. There was also a parallel series of studies of science, conducted among 14-year-old students (in roughly similar years).[25]

One major problem with this series is that different metrics were used in the first, second, and subsequent studies. This means that we cannot compare how absolute standards changed between 1964, 1980–2, and 1995, although we can do so from 1995 onwards. All we can do with the two earliest studies is to compare the ranking of the different countries. As Figure 4.5 shows, this is itself of considerable interest.[26]

Figure 4.5 shows remarkable stability over time in the performance of the countries covered. Japan is always at the top, in both science and maths, while Canada was also a consistently high performer throughout. In contrast, Italy was consistently a lower performer, with Sweden and the USA relatively poor performers in maths, too. England actually does relatively well. In 1964 it was clearly ahead of Sweden and the USA in maths, though well behind Japan. Fifty years later, the rank ordering of countries was not all that different, with England clearly ahead of Italy and Sweden, still well behind Japan but fairly close to the USA. These differences between countries therefore have very long and deep roots.

In science, the story is similar, although in more recent years England has been one of the better performers whereas it does not appear to have been especially strong in the two earliest rounds of the science studies. Possibly England has improved its relative standing at science over time (though it is not at all clear to me why this should have been the case in science but not in maths).

As I emphasized earlier, we cannot use the first two rounds of the maths and science studies to tell us whether English students have made progress in absolute terms. We can only talk about its ranking relative to other countries. But since 1995 the studies have employed comparable metrics and so in principle one could detect changes in absolute levels of performance. In practice, however, there seems to have been rather little change over the twenty-year period. There are hints that maths scores in England may have improved, but the science scores suggest trendless fluctuation.

This is more or less in line with the conclusions from Sammy Rashid and Greg Brooks' study of the literacy data in England. There is little or no support for the critics who claim that standards in England have been falling over time.

Figure 4.5. Independent international tests show that the maths and science performance of year 9 students in England scarcely changed between 1995 and 2011

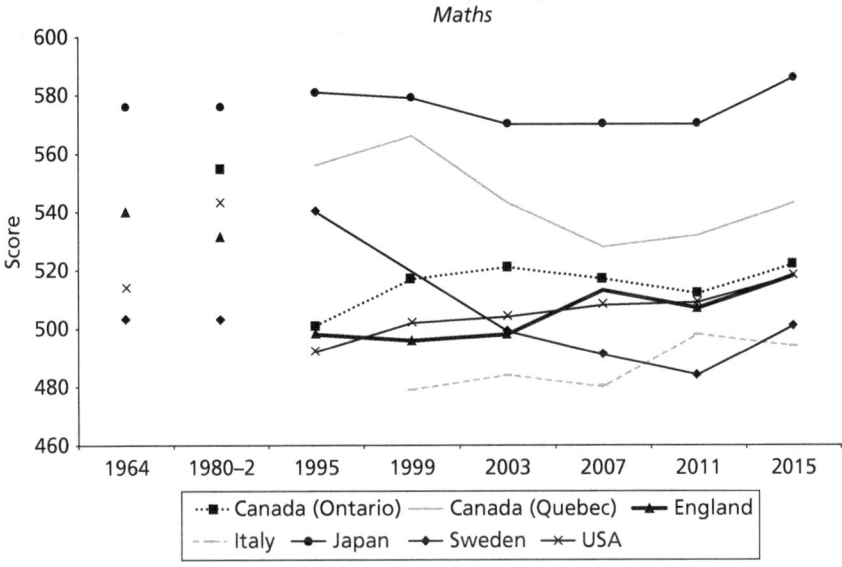

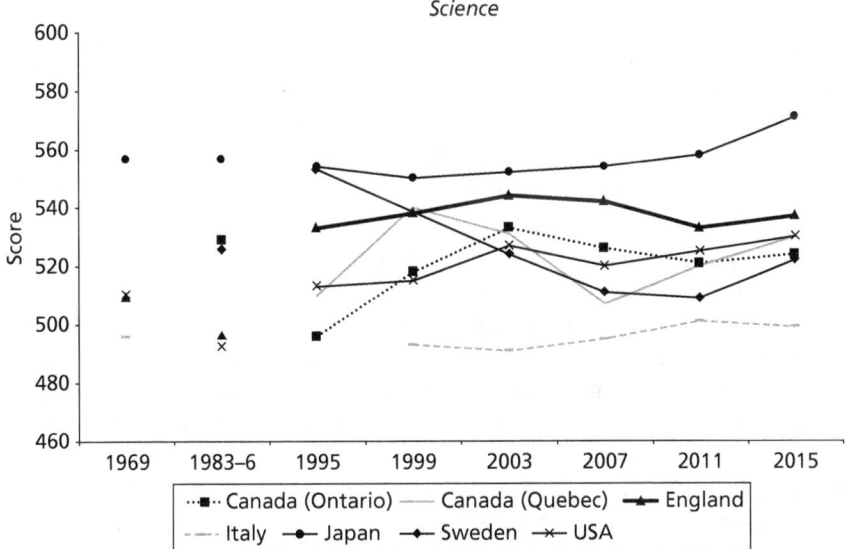

Source: calculated from the first, second, and subsequent international maths and science studies (FIMS, SIMS80, TIMSS)[27]

But if there has been any progress, it has been glacially slow. It really does not look as though all the educational reforms that England and Wales endured in the last twenty years have really done much to drive up average standards.

The OECD has also undertaken the Programme for International Student Assessment—usually known for short as PISA. PISA covers literacy as well as numeracy and science and is taken by young people in year 11 (aged 15–16). It is similar to the International Educational Association's series in that it uses independent standardized tests and provides a rigorous independent assessment of students' skills using measures which are genuinely comparable between countries. It has the additional advantage for us that it covers all eight of our peer countries.

PISA has been well publicized and their results have been the subject of considerable controversy in Britain. Unfortunately, PISA only started in 2000, so we cannot look at long-term trends in young people's skills. Even more unfortunately from our point of view, in the first two rounds of PISA the British data were held not to have reached the technical standards required for inclusion.[28] This was due to low response rates—and having carried out research in English schools I can confirm that schools are not keen to give up classroom time for purely academic research. Pressure to achieve in league tables and the like put schools in a difficult situation. So we only have reliable data for Britain from 2006.

Figure 4.6 shows the trends for all eight peer countries. There are some strange blips from one round to another, but the overall picture is pretty clear. Just as in the International Educational Association's studies, Japan is well in the lead. Canada is consistently a high performer, too, closely followed by Germany. Britain is then in the middle of the pack, alongside France and the USA, but ahead of Sweden, which is once again shown to be a surprisingly poor performer, and also ahead of Italy. Britain does a bit worse perhaps on reading than on maths (where the USA is a notably poor performer), but is clearly rather stronger when it comes to science.

There are some year-to-year fluctuations, to which one should probably not pay too much attention. I suspect that some of the blips, as with Japan's poor performance in reading in 2006, are a result of measurement error rather than a reflection of real change. Overall, the trends for the other seven countries have been fairly stable between 2000 and 2015, while Britain's position has been pretty stable since 2006. Exactly as with the International Educational Association's studies, countries' standing in these international rankings do seem to have deep roots and are not easy to shift.

Just as the ranking of countries is remarkably stable over time, we also find little change in the absolute scores. There is little sign that the UK has made much progress since 2006—but none of the other countries has really changed all that much over the same period either (apart perhaps from Germany on reading). In their detailed report of the UK's performance in 2015, John Jerrim

Figure 4.6. The UK's scores on the PISA tests of reading, maths, and science barely changed between 2006 and 2015

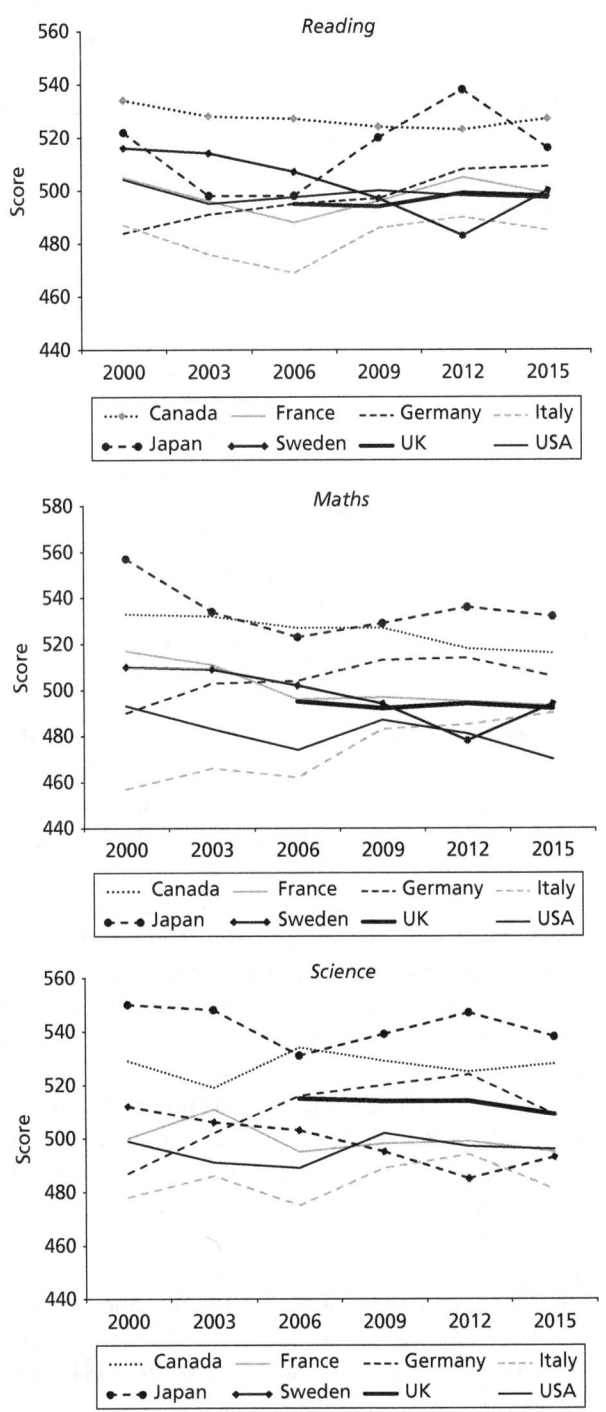

Source: OECD, Programme for International Student Assessment[29]

and Nikki Shure concluded that 'The average science, mathematics and reading scores of pupils in England have not changed since 2006.'[30] Overall, despite all the weaknesses of the individual data series, the three independent time series from Sammy Rashid and Greg Brooks on literacy, from the International Educational Association on maths and science, and from the OECD on literacy, numeracy, and science all reinforce a story of stability or at most modest progress over time.

The OECD's PISA studies also report some interesting data on the extent of inequality in test scores in each country. Just as in the examples of household income and life expectancy, the extent of inequality around the average provides important insights. In the case of education, British elites attending expensive private schools or selective grammar schools may obtain very good scores on the tests, thus pulling up the average to a respectable level. But conversely the worry is that the high performance of the elite may mask the poor performance at the other end of the distribution. Britain's average score may be respectable but the inequality around this average may be a cause for concern. This would give us a rather different perspective on the countries' educational performance from a simple comparison of average scores.

The OECD provides a measure of the extent of educational inequality in each country which is basically the same as the method used by economists to look at income inequality, and which I described in Chapter 2. In the case of income, I looked at the person or household in the middle of the distribution, who has half the population receiving a higher income and half receiving a lower income. I also looked at the income of someone at the tenth percentile, that is someone whose income was greater than that of the poorest 10 per cent but less than that of the remaining 90 per cent. And I also looked at the income of someone at the ninetieth percentile.

To carry out a similar exercise for educational inequality, one just has to arrange the students in order of their scores, arranging them from the student with the lowest score to the student with the highest test score. One can then find the median score—someone with this score will have half of the student population in his or her year scoring more highly and half scoring less highly.

One can repeat this, exactly as with income, and calculate the scores for someone at the tenth percentile and for someone at the ninetieth percentile. In Figure 4.7 I plot the three scores—tenth, median, and ninetieth percentiles. These are similar to box and whisker plots. In our case the diamond indicates the median score, and the whiskers stretch up from the score of the tenth percentile at the bottom to the score of the ninetieth percentile at the top. I have arranged the countries according to the length of the whiskers. We can regard the length of the whiskers as an indication of the extent of inequality—the longer the whiskers, the greater the inequality. So I have placed the most equal countries on the left and the most unequal on the right of each figure.

Figure 4.7. The gaps between high and low achievers were larger in the UK in 2015 than in the highest-performing countries such as Japan and Canada, but not as bad as in France[31]

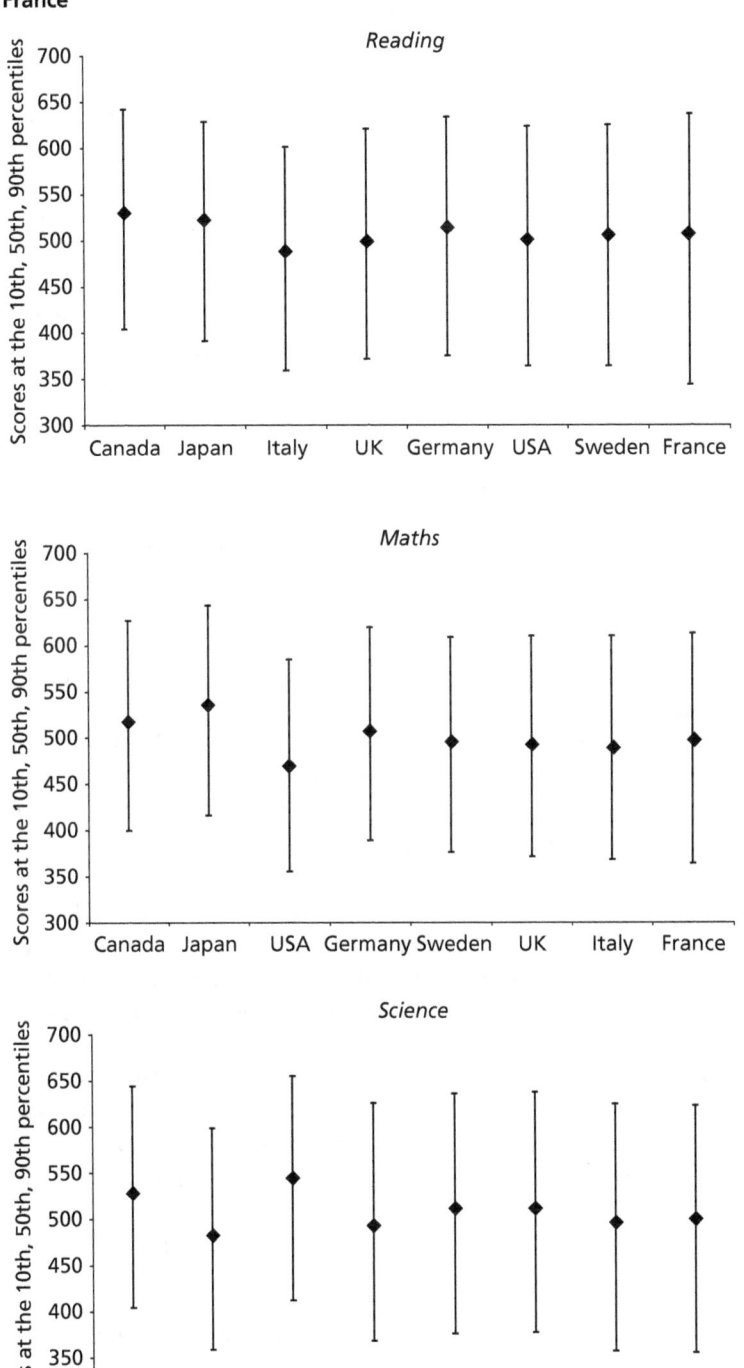

Source: OECD, *PISA 2015 Results (Volume I): Excellence and Equity in Education* (Paris: OECD Publishing, 2016), http://www.oecd-ilibrary.org/docserver/download/9816061e.pdf

The results are quite surprising. Japan and Canada, which are our two best-performing countries, also have quite low levels of educational inequality. They both have educational systems which get very good results for students at the tenth percentile as well as for the median student. It is not the case that their high ranking overall is because their educational elites perform very well—their non-elite students at the tenth percentile actually do particularly well compared with similar students in other countries. (I must emphasize that I am not using the term elite to refer to a social elite but simply in order to refer to the best-performing students, the educational elite.)

Britain, however, is by no means the most unequal of the eight peer countries. France is clearly worse while Sweden, which I had expected to be one of the most egalitarian countries, is if anything more unequal educationally than the UK. One prevalent theory in the sociology of education is that countries with selective systems of education, such as the tripartite system of grammar, technical, and modern schools which Britain had when I was growing up, and which Germany still has, will generate greater educational inequality than comprehensive systems such as Sweden and the USA have. There is not much sign of this pattern among our eight peer countries. Comprehensive Canada is indeed one of the most equal, but comprehensive Sweden looks relatively unequal.

There are also some international studies of the adult population. In some ways, these are even more informative than tests conducted at school. Schoolchildren will be under considerable pressure to perform well and will receive lots of teaching geared to improving examination performance. Possibly this can give a temporary boost to performance. Maybe it is more important what skills young people take with them from school and into the adult world. Schooling is surely intended to provide a preparation for later life.

The OECD has recently started a new international study of adult competencies (Programme for the International Assessment of Adult Competencies—PIAAC). These cover the whole of the adult population aged 16 to 64 but I will focus here on the performance of the 16 to 19 year olds since results among this age group will largely reflect how schools have been doing in the recent past. The results are pretty close to those found in the PISA and TIMSS studies. In the case of literacy, young adults in Britain are at around the same level as the USA, but behind France, Germany, and Canada, with Japan once again well in the lead. The picture is fairly similar in the case of numeracy, too, with the USA, just as in PISA, lagging behind Britain.

So we have a pretty clear picture from all three of these international studies (TIMSS, PISA, and PIAAC) that:

- Japan is top (along with other East Asian countries and territories such as Hong Kong, Singapore, and Shanghai);
- Canada does consistently well;

- England comes in the middle alongside France and Germany;
- Italy, Sweden, and the USA are more variable but on some measures come at the bottom;
- England seems better in science than in numeracy or literacy; and
- there was no major change in Britain's position, relative to the seven peer countries, since the programmes started.

Media attention tends to focus on how far Britain is behind Japan and the other Far Eastern countries. However, Japan is notorious for its 'exam hell' where there is enormous pressure on young people to obtain good results in school examinations in order to gain entry into the most prestigious universities. Indeed, so serious is exam hell that Japan has recently begun to make reforms moving in the opposite direction and trying to reduce pressure on young people. Suicide has become the most common cause of death among 14–19 year olds in Japan (although one cannot be sure that this is caused by exam hell). High educational standards may possibly come with harmful side effects for young people. Be careful what you wish for.

More detailed analysis by John Jerrim has attempted to understand East Asian success. What he finds is that East Asian students in Western countries such as Australia also outperform their peers in much the same way that East Asian countries in general outperform Western countries. This strongly suggests that there is nothing in the Western educational systems that is incompatible with educational success. John Jerrim attributes this to the high value which East Asian families place upon education, their substantial out-of-school tuition, an ethic of hard work, and a belief that anyone can succeed with effort and high aspirations for the future. He concludes:

These findings have important implications for Western policymakers attempting to catch the high-performing East Asian countries at the top of the PISA rankings. First, the experience of second-generation East Asian immigrants in Australia illustrates how high-level maths skills can be developed even within average-performing educational systems (including by children of average and low socio-economic backgrounds). Second, the attitudes and beliefs East Asian parents instil in their children make an important contribution to their high levels of academic achievement. Yet as such factors are heavily influenced by culture and home environment, they are likely to be beyond the control of schools... climbing significantly up [the PISA] rankings is unlikely to be achieved by the efforts of schools alone.[32]

I find these comments very persuasive.

The relatively low ranking of the USA is also rather intriguing given that the USA dominates world rankings of universities. I suspect that US schools do not put nearly so much pressure on 15 year olds to achieve highly at school. The USA was a pioneer in democratizing education and has a much longer history of young people staying on at school until 18, and then moving on to college. In the USA there are no high-stakes exams at all in school—there is nothing remotely like the English GCSE. The pressure starts in the USA when young people take the standardized assessment tests used for entry into high-status universities.

Canada is probably the model to aim for—I am not sure how they do it, but I would strongly recommend government to find out and see what lessons can be learned from Canada.

Did the Expansion of Education Produce Wider Social Benefits Such as a Sense of Empowerment?

Almost all of the evidence reviewed so far has taken a rather narrow, technical approach to education. It has been narrowly focussed on performance in various kinds of tests, particularly of literacy and numeracy. It is entirely possible that young people staying on at school are gaining in other less tangible respects even if they are not making as much progress at the technical aspects as might have been hoped.

In the introduction to this chapter I argued that education should not be treated solely as the handmaiden to the economy and that education can bring wider private and social benefits, for example by increasing social trust, tolerance, self-confidence, and a greater ability to engage with political authorities and hold them to account. There is pretty good evidence that higher levels of education are associated with a range of non-economic outcomes, such as greater take-up of healthy lifestyles, increased civic engagement, and higher levels of subjective well-being. It could even be the case that British education is doing a better job in these respects than it is in the narrower technical aspects measured by exams and tests.

In Figure 4.8 I explore the strength of the relationship between educational level and a range of economic and non-economic outcomes. I include two economic outcomes: whether someone is in work or not and whether (among people who receive an income) they get into the top quarter of earners. In both cases one can see very strong relationships with education: in the case of income, a graduate is just over forty points more likely to be in the top quarter of earnings than is someone with no qualifications.

What is particularly interesting is that the relationship with a sense of political efficacy is at least as strong. Our source, the British Social Attitudes Survey, asked members of the public how much they agreed or disagreed that 'sometimes politics and government seem so complicated that a person like me cannot really understand what is going on'. Only 12 per cent of people with no educational qualifications disagreed with the statement, compared with

Figure 4.8. Level of education in Britain is strongly associated both with economic and non-economic outcomes

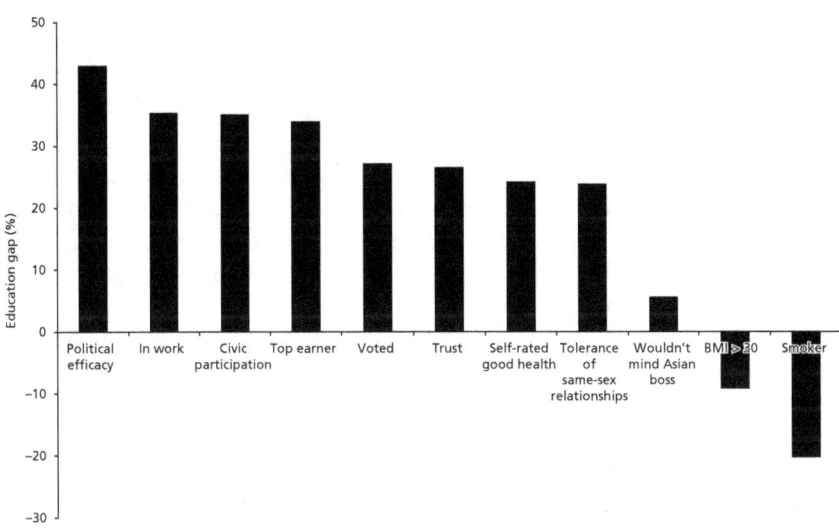

Note: gaps adjusted for age and gender[33]

Source: British Social Attitudes (2006, 2011, 2012, 2013), British Election Study (2015), Understanding Society (2014–15), Annual Population Survey (2015–16), Community Life Survey (2015–16), Health Survey for England (2014)

55 per cent of university graduates—a gap of forty-three points. Graduates therefore were much more likely to feel that they could understand politics and government. There were also significant gaps, albeit smaller ones, in the case of tolerance of same-sex relationships, of non-traditional gender roles, of ethnic prejudice, and smoking. In the case of smoking, it is the graduates who were the least likely to smoke, which is why we see a negative gap.

It is probably no accident that the strongest relationship is with a sense of political efficacy, since this is the kind of outcome where we might expect the cognitive skills developed by education to be most relevant. The connection with tolerance is somewhat weaker, and I suspect that the processes involved are different too. It is probably the case that higher education leads one to mix with a wider range of people and it is this exposure that encourages tolerance rather than anything intrinsic to the content of education.

Correlation does not of course necessarily imply causation, but John Bynner and his colleagues have used a before-and-after design to provide a more rigorous test of some relationships between education and non-economic outcomes. They showed that young people who had made greater educational progress before the age of 21 displayed improved non-economic outcomes after the age of 26.[34] This is still not proof of a causal effect, but in the absence of proper experiments (which would not be ethical or practical in this kind of field) is as persuasive as one ever gets in social science.

If increasing people's education really does improve people's civic skills, sense of political efficacy, and so on, then we would expect to find that the increasing numbers of people staying on at school and going to university, as shown in Figures 4.1 and 4.2, would be accompanied by an overall increase in feelings of political efficacy. And this is indeed what we see in Figure 4.9. In 1974, just under 25 per cent of people felt that they could understand what was going on in politics, but by 2012 (the latest year in which the question was asked) this had crept up to 31 per cent. Statistical analysis indicates that this modest increase can be satisfactorily explained by the increased educational qualifications of the population.

In the case of our other measures such as tolerance or attitudes to gender roles, the spread of education seems to be a more minor ingredient, and this is what one would expect given that they were not quite so strongly related to education in the first place.

So one can be pretty sure that education is related to quite a wide array of social outcomes, including a sense of empowerment. One can be pretty sure, too, that there has been social progress (if we agree that citizens' empowerment and tolerance are aspects of a good society in action) in the case of these social consequences of education. The spread of education is certainly not the whole story, but it is most probably a significant part.

Figure 4.9. Increasing levels of education in Britain were associated with increasing levels of political efficacy

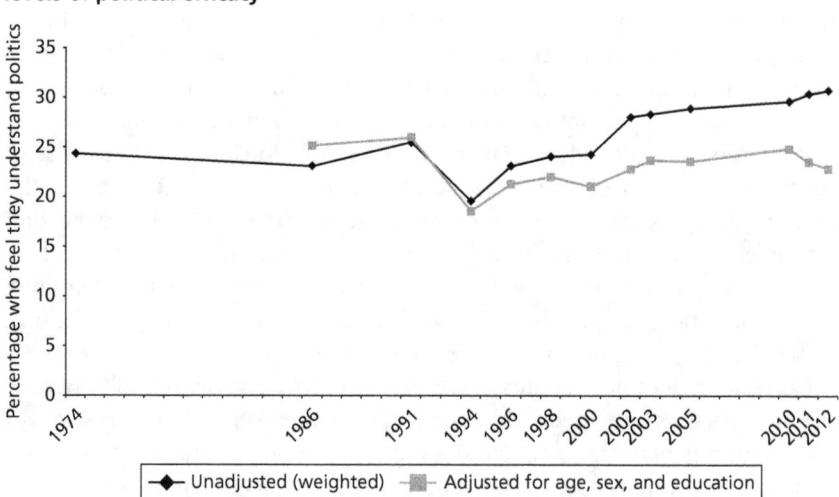

Source: Political Action Survey of Britain 1974; British Social Attitudes 1986–2012

Conclusions

So has the giant of ignorance been defeated and skills and knowledge improved? Britain has seen a host of reforms designed both to raise standards and to equalize opportunities, but how effective have these reforms been? Certainly Britain like our peer countries has seen a transformation of participation in education since the Second World War. Most strikingly, tertiary education went from being the preserve of a tiny minority of the age group in the 1950s (and largely restricted to young people who had been educated at private or grammar schools) to an opportunity that is much more widely available. The USA and Canada were early pioneers in opening access to higher education, and while Britain has not yet closed the gap with the leaders, it nonetheless compares quite favourably with European countries such as France, Germany, Italy, and Sweden (although differences in educational systems makes these comparisons somewhat suspect). Britain opted in the 1990s for a US-style system of mass higher education, just as it opted for a US model of a flexible labour market in the 1980s. Continental countries such as Germany have instead maintained quite sharp distinctions between academic university education and technical/vocational education in polytechnics.

However, unlike the US and Canadian systems, but more like European models, Britain maintained an emphasis on formal, high-stakes exams, such as GCSEs. In this respect there has been much more continuity with the 1950s educational system, although the qualifications themselves have experienced rapid evolution with GCSEs replacing O Levels which had replaced the pre-war Certificate of Education. This evolution opened access to qualifications to a much larger proportion of young people. Just as in the case of participation in higher education, Britain witnessed a huge increase in the numbers obtaining certificates such as GCSEs—from a tiny proportion of the age group in the 1950s to the great majority in the 2000s. So it makes sense to talk about the democratization of education, in the sense that educational opportunities previously available only to social and academic elites were made widely accessible to all.

While these educational qualifications are undoubtedly valuable in the labour market—young people with GCSEs have better job prospects than those without them—it is less clear whether the actual improvements in young people's skills and understanding match their acquisition of formal certificates. Some critics have suggested that standards have been dropping—that the exams have become easier to pass. There have been continuing complaints from business that young people are not adequately literate and numerate. A second, quite distinct, line of criticism is that some of the gains have been spurious as schools play the system in order to reach government targets and improve their standing in the league tables.

There is a disappointing absence of good independent evidence of the long-run changes in young people's knowledge and understanding. We cannot adjust for grade inflation in the way that economists can adjust for price inflation. And maybe we should not even try—the content of education and the exams to test young people's understanding must necessarily change over time to reflect developments in society and the labour market. There is, however, some limited independent evidence which does seem to suggest the following conclusions.

First, over the long term since the 1950s Britain saw continuing albeit modest progress on basic skills such as literacy. The rate of progress was rather glacial and contrasts with the avalanche of paper certificates. But it is still progress: there is not a shred of evidence that literacy standards of young people actually fell over this period. Maybe they did not increase as fast as is needed for young people to cope in the contemporary labour market, but they did at least rise.

Second, independent cross-national programmes of student assessment conducted by highly respected bodies such as the OECD show that Britain has more or less held its own in international rankings. Japan has always been well ahead of Britain on these tests, and Japanese young people clearly have stronger literacy, numeracy, and science understanding. Britain is also somewhat behind Canada, which has an enviable record of high achievement and low levels of educational inequality. Nevertheless, Britain compares quite favourably with France, Germany, Sweden, and the USA, and does particularly well on science. Britain seems to have been holding its own educationally in comparison with other large Western countries and there is no evidence that Britain has slipped behind as we seem to have done with health and longevity.

On the other hand, it is rather salutary that all the educational reforms which successive governments have introduced seem to have made very little difference. There has been steady but unspectacular progress, but no sign from the independent studies of the rapid progress which government statistics of educational performance portray. Perhaps the most striking conclusion to be drawn from this evidence is that the huge increase in the percentages obtaining five good GCSEs since the late 1980s is not matched by improvement in learning and skills. One should stop and wonder a bit about the effectiveness of the numerous attempts which successive governments have made over the same period to drive up standards. Britain has seen almost continual attempts to reform education, with new initiatives following one another with almost indecent haste, and yet there is little to show for it—at least as judged by independent assessment on the part of outsiders. I agree with Robert Coe that 'Education has existed in a pre-scientific world, where good measurement of anything important is rare and evaluation is done badly or not at all. It is time we established a more scientific approach.'[35]

We also need to recognize that education has many wider benefits for individuals and society than simply raising technical skills. There is plenty of evidence that people who have been through higher education not only have better chances in the labour market but also have better health and are more likely to engage in healthy lifestyles, not to be obese, and to be less likely to smoke. They are also more likely to feel that they have the skills to participate in politics (and they do in fact have higher rates of turning out to vote and joining voluntary organizations). So increasing educational participation may have a wide variety of additional benefits for individuals and society.

Some of the same kinds of problems that occur when evaluating the real changes in knowledge and understanding as opposed to nominal acquisition of certificates re-emerge when we try to assess whether the increased access to higher education has actually improved a sense of empowerment, healthy lifestyles, and the like. It is not straightforward to evaluate these claims. However, Figure 4.9 suggests that the spread of higher education may well have increased people's sense of political efficacy. Again, progress has been slow—nothing like the avalanche of credentials—but is perhaps more believable.

So my conclusion is that the giant of Ignorance is slowly being driven back in Britain, just as he is being driven back in the peer countries. While that progress may not have transformed the skills of the population as much as might have been wished, Britain is holding its own in comparison with other countries. Britain has not slipped back in the way it appears to have done with respect to life expectancy and infant mortality.

However, we also need to recognize that there may be a dark side to educational progress—what happens to those left behind without five good GCSEs to their name? I shall start to explore this in Chapter 6.

5 The Fight against Squalor

Overcrowding, Homelessness, and Affordability

with Elisabeth Garratt

Introduction

The fourth of Beveridge's giants was Squalor. The term squalor has some rather derogatory connotations, and dictionary definitions tend to include lack of care as one element of squalor.[1] I do not think that this was what Beveridge had in mind, though. In his 1944 book *Full Employment in a Free Society* he defined squalor as 'the evils of congestion, over-crowding, ill-health, bad housing, and destruction of urban and rural amenities alike'.[2] There is no suggestion here that Beveridge was blaming the victims of squalor for their plight. While I would have liked to look at all the aspects of squalor which Beveridge listed, I have not been able to find any data about long-term trends in traffic congestion or the destruction of urban and rural amenities. In this chapter, therefore, I am going to concentrate on overcrowding and bad housing.

In order to avoid derogatory overtones, I will endeavour to avoid using the term squalor as much as I can and will instead talk about overcrowding and substandard housing conditions. This still requires a judgement about what constitutes an acceptable standard of housing or an acceptable amount of space for the household, but at least we can make these judgements explicit. There are in fact government yardsticks for what constitutes acceptable standards of basic amenities and of living space—though whether these are entirely satisfactory yardsticks is another matter.

There are parallels between the notions of overcrowding and substandard housing and that of poverty. They all involve comparison with some standard or yardstick. They implicitly assume that falling below the standard has harmful consequences for those affected. And in both the cases of poverty and of housing we need to ask whether these standards have remained constant over time or whether they should be regarded as changing as social expectations change. For example, a quiet room where schoolchildren can study would not have been regarded as standard when Beveridge wrote. But in a context where all children face high-stakes exams at school, it does not seem unreasonable. So measuring the amount of substandard housing or of overcrowding is likely to involve tricky issues of what constitutes an acceptable standard, and whether that standard has stayed the same over time.

It is important to recognize that a yardstick of overcrowding or of substandard conditions need not be a purely moral judgement. There is convincing evidence that housing quality has a range of consequences for well-being—for one's physical and mental health, marital relations, care given to children, and children's education, for example.[3] A substantial body of evidence shows that falling below the normal standards is associated with poorer outcomes, even among people with similar income levels, and that well-being is responsive to improvements in housing conditions, getting better when housing conditions improve and declining when they worsen.[4] I suspect that it is also true, just as with income, that there are what economists term diminishing marginal returns. That is, an extra room for a household living in overcrowded conditions makes much more difference to well-being than an extra room for a household which already has plenty of space.

So the first question for this chapter is how much progress has Britain made in tackling the evils of overcrowding and poor housing conditions. This leads on to questions about the nature and extent of the housing crisis, which many commentators, politicians, and would-be home owners have highlighted in the years since the turn of the twenty-first century.[5] Talk of a new housing crisis suggests that progress in meeting people's housing needs must have gone into reverse. Has there been a resurgence of overcrowding or of homelessness? Do people now have less space or amenities than previous generations? Or is it more a matter of rising expectations or of declining affordability—that people are having to spend a much larger proportion of their budget on housing costs than previous generations did?

In this chapter I will first explore the quality of housing and will then turn to issues of overcrowding and homelessness. After that I will look at some of the reasons why a housing crisis may have emerged in Britain. I will focus on changing demand for housing, changing affordability, and increasing inequality in the distribution of housing. Finally, I will compare Britain's performance with that of our peer countries, although unfortunately we do not have adequate comparative data on change over time, so I shall limit myself to a brief discussion of the state of play in the twenty-first century.

Housing Quality

There was undoubtedly a housing crisis during and after the Second World War. The war had seen the destruction of many homes and an almost complete lack of house building. Added to this were legacies of poor-quality housing, lack of basic amenities, and overcrowding inherited from the pre-war period and the great depression of the early 1930s.

Improving the availability and quality of housing were therefore major objectives of post-war governments, both Labour and Conservative. Political party manifestos regularly boasted about how many houses the party had built when in office, and how many they planned to build in the next parliament. Immediately after the war there were large-scale slum clearance programmes which lasted until the 1970s.[6] Slum is another highly derogatory term, rather like squalor, but I think it was used to cover impoverished and overcrowded areas where houses lacked basic amenities, especially adequate sanitation and indoor toilets. Slum clearance was one of the most striking efforts by government to intervene in the housing market in order to improve living conditions for British people.

Some of the programmes were well intentioned but perhaps misconceived. Some large council housing estates and high-rise tower blocks subsequently became notorious for graffiti and vandalism. While the dwellings themselves were superior in terms of practical amenities like indoor toilets, the slum clearance programmes also involved the destruction of traditional communities and their replacement with rather soulless tracts. Two early classics of British sociology were *Family and Kinship in East London* and *Family and Class in a London Suburb* by Michael Young and Peter Willmott.[7] They painted a picture of densely populated traditional neighbourhoods in the east end of London, with vibrant communities based upon long-standing family and neighbourhood ties. These were replaced by less densely populated estates further out of London which, at least according to Peter Wilmott and Michael Young, lacked community spirit. Huge council estates like those of Wythenshawe in Manchester became bywords for social problems (as indeed their modern equivalents of the *banlieues* in Paris or the projects in Chicago have remained). So we must recognize that progress in formal housing terms may come at a social cost. Lack of neighbourhood amenities (jobs, shops, leisure facilities, for example) may have undermined some of the benefits of improved physical amenities like bathrooms and indoor toilets.

The Housing Act of 1949 required homes to contain the basic amenities of an indoor WC, fixed bath or shower in a bathroom, wash hand basin, sink, and hot and cold water supply. The decennial census first collected data on amenities and services in 1951, and trends in the provision of household amenities are shown in Figure 5.1. As one can see, in 1951 astonishingly high proportions lacked the basic amenities of a bath or shower and a WC. Around half of households lacked a bath or shower, while over one fifth lacked a toilet. These sound like the conditions you would expect in a third-world country, rather than one of the richest developed countries of the time. Great strides were then made in the subsequent decades. The proportion with a bath or shower climbed to nearly 80 per cent by 1971 and was close to the maximum of 100 per cent by 1991.

Figure 5.1. Provision of household amenities improved greatly between 1951 and 2015 in England and Wales

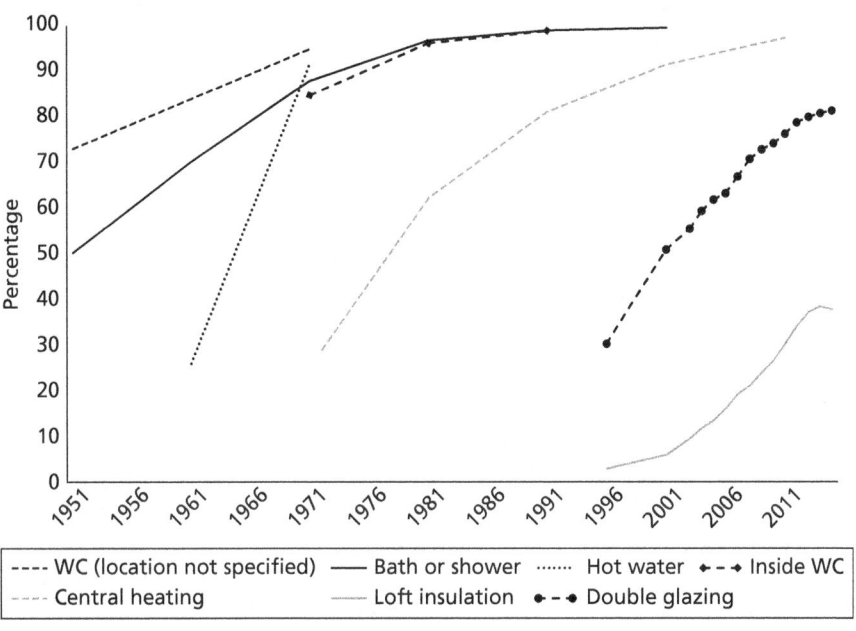

Source: WC, bath or shower, hot water from England and Wales census data (dates vary by indicator); central heating 1991–2011 from England and Wales census, 1972 and 1981 from General Household Surveys (England and Wales); double glazing and loft insulation from English Housing Survey (England only)

As coverage of these basic amenities became more or less universal, the censuses stopped collecting the data and instead collected data on additional amenities such as central heating. Central heating has a major impact on people's well-being (even after taking into account their income). Absence of central heating is associated with increased winter mortality among the over-65s,[8] and reductions in winter mortality over the past century may be due in part to improved housing and better-heated homes.[9] In turn, great strides were made, with central heating getting close to the maximum by 2011, while double glazing and loft insulation also became increasingly common. To be sure, some of these improvements reflected the extension and modernization of private-sector housing and cannot be attributed solely to the government-driven slum clearance programmes. All the same, it is an impressive story of success in tackling one aspect of the evil of bad housing.

To my knowledge, the government has never revised its statutory definition of basic amenities to include central heating and double glazing. However, in 2000 the Labour government introduced a decent homes programme as part of its wider strategy for urban regeneration and for dealing with the large backlog of repairs which had accumulated in local authority housing stock. One element of the programme was a new standard of what counted as a decent home.[10] The standard did not specify clear and precise minima in the same way that the 1949 Act had done. The criteria listed were that decent homes should:

- be in a reasonable state of repair;
- have reasonably modern facilities and services, including a reasonably modern kitchen (20 years old or less), and adequate insulation against external noise (where external noise was a problem); and
- have a reasonable degree of thermal comfort (namely effective insulation and efficient heating).

A further condition was that there had to be no risk of a serious hazard, as defined under the Housing Health and Safety Rating System.

The decent homes standard was primarily designed to ensure that the quality of social housing was improved. Statistics from the English Housing Survey suggested that in 2001 39 per cent of the social housing stock failed to meet the standard but that very considerable progress was made in subsequent years. By 2015 the figure had fallen to around 13 per cent. Returns from landlords suggested that there had been even faster progress with the proportion of non-decent homes down to a mere 3 per cent by 2015.[11] I must confess to being a little bit sceptical about the landlord returns, however. I imagine that risks of the kind of fire that engulfed Grenfell Tower with tragic loss of life in 2017 would count as a serious hazard, and that Grenfell Tower should therefore have failed the decent homes standard. Since many other tower blocks were subsequently found to have fire risks of the same kind that affected Grenfell Tower, I suspect that the figure of 3 per cent non-decent homes might be distinctly over-optimistic.

All the same, there is no reason to doubt that the quality of Britain's housing stock, admittedly starting from an abysmal level, improved greatly throughout the decades after the Beveridge Report. I am afraid that the next section of the chapter is not going to tell such a positive story about overcrowding, but we should at least recognize that the quality of housing continually improved after the war.

Overcrowding

Britain, like most developed countries, has a tripartite system of housing. There is a large private sector of owner occupiers (who tend to be older, settled, and more affluent), a private renting sector (where younger, transient, or less affluent people tend to predominate), and a social housing sector.

The owner-occupier and private renting sectors in Britain have largely been driven by market forces (with varying levels of government regulation) whereas the social housing sector—housing owned by local authorities or housing associations—has been based on need rather than on ability to pay, and is let at controlled and subsidized rents. Many social housing tenants will in fact be receiving housing benefit or other state benefits (as indeed are increasing numbers in the private renting sector, too).

As Figure 5.2 shows, however, the composition of Britain's housing stock has changed very considerably over the decades since the war. In the years immediately after the war, local authorities built a great deal of social housing and, right up until the early 1980s, the stock of social housing steadily increased—up from 2.2 million dwellings in 1951 to 5.4 million in 1981, when it peaked. Conversely, there was a decline in the stock of dwellings for private renting. After 1981, however, Margaret Thatcher's Conservative administrations started a programme of selling off social housing at subsidized prices to their tenants, without a commensurate increase in new building, so this part of the housing stock started to shrink.[12] In contrast, there was a resurgence of private renting alongside continued building for the private owner-occupier market.

The net effect of these changes was a continued, steady growth in the total housing stock, which reached 25.1 million dwellings in England and Wales in 2016. However, the shares of the three sectors were very different in 2016 from

Figure 5.2. The total housing stock in England and Wales doubled between 1951 and 2016, although the amount of social housing declined after 1981

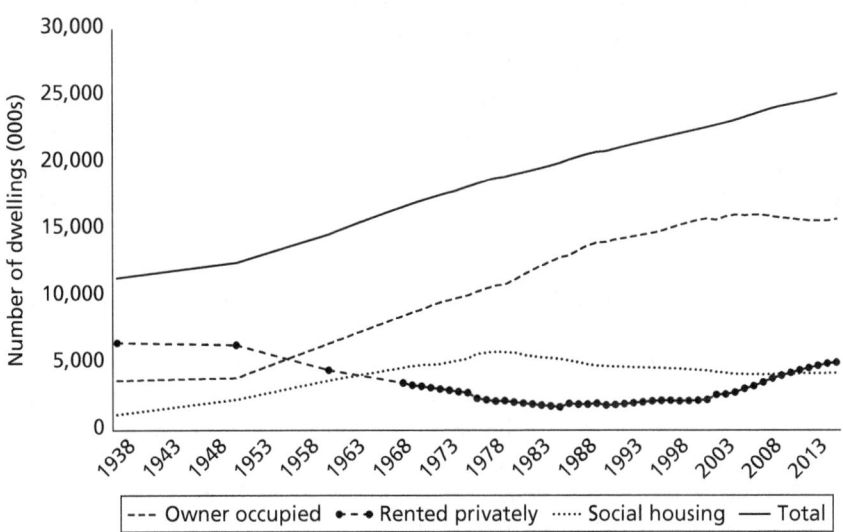

Note: the total also includes a small number of other tenures
Source: Department of the Environment, Office for National Statistics[13]

what they had been in 1981. Most crucially, the share of the social housing sector almost halved between 1981 and 2016. This means that, after 1981, an increasing proportion of the housing stock was allocated through market processes—basically on the principle of ability to pay. Conversely, a much smaller proportion was allocated on the basis of need. This was of course entirely consistent with Margaret Thatcher's vision for society: she believed in a small state based on the philosophy that government should intervene as little as possible in people's lives, instead leaving people free to choose what they spent their money on.[14] In line with this vision, her governments also deregulated the private rental sector, removing many of the restrictions that had previously been in place.[15]

I will discuss some of the implications of this shift away from social housing to a more deregulated private sector in the next section of the chapter. Nonetheless, it is clear that the overall size of the housing stock continued to grow throughout the years after 1981, with the total housing stock increasing by 31 per cent. In contrast, the population of England and Wales increased by about 13 per cent (growing from nearly 49.6 million in 1981 to 56.2 million people in 2011).[16] However, whereas the rate of growth of the housing stock exceeded population growth for much of the post-war period, the two rates of growth converged at the beginning of the twenty-first century. Since the financial crash of 2007/8 the housing stock has grown at a slower rate than the population of England. Paul Cheshire has estimated that, between 1994 and 2012, there was a shortfall of between 1.6 and 2.3 million homes compared with what was needed.[17]

Consistent with this, the number of rooms per person showed an impressive increase over the fifty years after the Second World War but appears to have flatlined after 2001 (Figure 5.3). In 1951 there was on average 1.36 rooms per person (by rooms the government statisticians included living rooms, kitchens, and bedrooms, but not bathrooms or kitchens that were too small to eat in). By 1981 this had reached 1.86, and it peaked at 2.3 rooms per person in 2001, remaining at the same level in 2011. So on this evidence, there was a major improvement in the quantity of housing. However, the absence of growth in rooms per person after 2001 is a distinctly less optimistic story than the one told by Figure 5.1 on amenities, clearly suggesting that progress had stalled.

The greatly increased number of rooms per person suggests that overcrowding should have diminished over the post-war period. Overcrowding has been a key measure of progress in housing, and has been a focus of government statisticians and policy-makers since the late nineteenth century. Back in 1885 the Royal Commission on the Housing of the Working Classes drew attention to the problem of overcrowding. Overcrowding is in essence the housing equivalent of poverty, and unsurprisingly there are similar conceptual and measurement issues with respect to overcrowding as there are with poverty.

Figure 5.3. Average rooms per person in England and Wales increased substantially between 1951 and 2001, but then plateaued

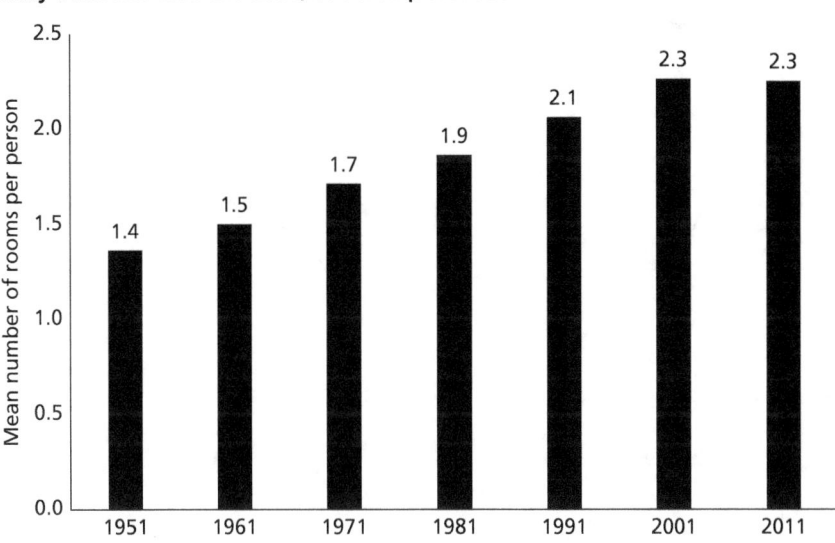

Source: decennial censuses[18]

Just as one can take a fixed subsistence measure or a changing socially acceptable measure of poverty, so one has to choose between a fixed measure of overcrowding or a changing socially acceptable measure of housing adequacy.

The government's approach has in effect been to employ a fixed measure of overcrowding, namely the bedroom standard dating from 1960. The bedroom standard has no statutory basis but remains the accepted measure of overcrowding in Britain.[19] Indeed, it was the basis for the coalition government's so-called bedroom tax (which reduced housing benefit for social housing tenants who had more bedrooms than the number specified by the bedroom standard).[20]

In essence, the bedroom standard stipulated that a household's need for bedrooms should be based on the size and composition of the household. Thus one bedroom was regarded as sufficient for a couple or lone parent. A pair of children aged under 10 get one room to share as do a pair of same-sex adolescents, or a child and adolescent of the same sex. Individual children over 10 of different sex get a single room each, as does each additional adult household member. Overcrowded households are those whose needs, as defined by these rules, exceed the number of bedrooms available.

In Figure 5.4 I show trends in overcrowding since 1960 using this bedroom standard. As we can see, on this measure overcrowding dropped sharply between 1960 and 1975 from around 11 per cent of households in 1960

Figure 5.4. Overcrowding, measured using the bedroom standard, declined sharply between 1960 and 1975 but then plateaued; overcrowding, using a relative measure, increased greatly after 1991

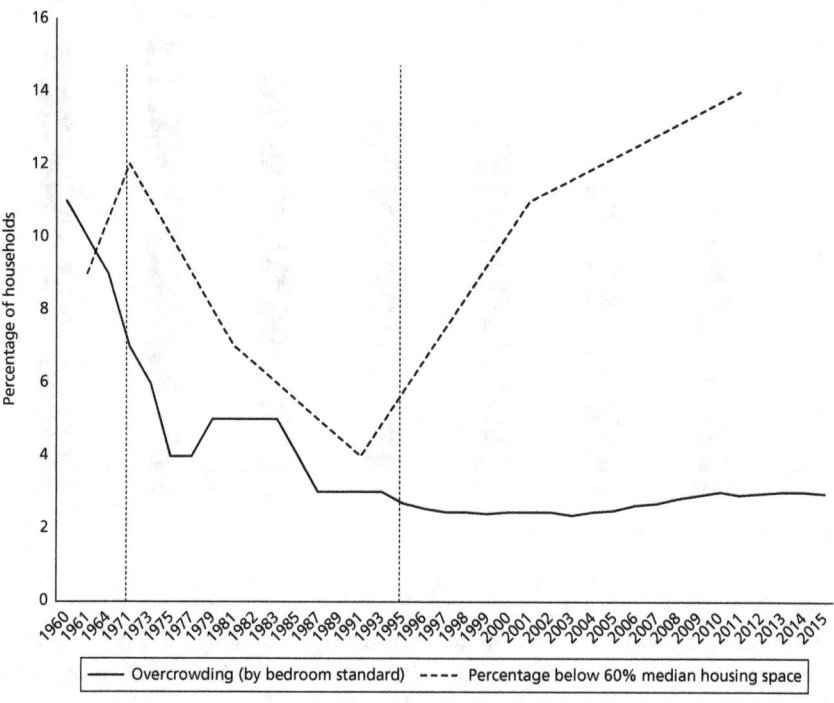

Note: the discontinuities in 1971 and 1995 apply to the measure of overcrowding using the bedroom standard[21]

Source: overcrowding (by bedroom standard): 1960–93, A. E. Holmans, *Historical Statistics of Housing in Britain*, table D.10; 1995 onwards, English Housing Survey 2015–16 results, households annex, table 1.20; relative overcrowding (percentage below 60 per cent of median housing space), B. Tunstall, 'Relative housing space inequality in England and Wales, and its recent rapid resurgence', *International Journal of Housing Policy*, 15 (2015), figure 2.[22]

down to 4 per cent in 1975. After some undulations, overcrowding then began to creep upwards again to 3 per cent in 2013–14, roughly the same level as it had been in 1987. Incidentally, Figure 5.4 tells us about the percentage of *households* that are overcrowded. It is perhaps worth pointing out that the percentage of the *population* living in overcrowded conditions will be much larger, since overcrowded households will tend to contain more people. In England, 5.6 per cent—or 2.85 million people—lived in overcrowded accommodation in 2014/15.

The story from the bedroom standard, then, is that there was basically no real reduction in overcrowding over the course of the twenty-five years after 1987. This is a remarkable lack of social progress. In effect progress on this particular criterion stalled at roughly the same time as Margaret Thatcher's programme of selling off council housing to tenants and deregulating the private rental market.

As I suggested earlier, the fixed bedroom standard of overcrowding is a bit like a subsistence measure of poverty.[23] The story is more pessimistic if one adopts a socially acceptable measure of overcrowding, analogous to the relative measures of poverty described in Chapter 2. For example, according to the bedroom standard, only one bedroom is required for each pair of children aged under 10, or for each pair of same-sex adolescents. While these standards may perhaps be appropriate when considering sleeping arrangements, they make no allowance for the space needed by children for recreation or study. Jonathan Bradshaw and his colleagues, when developing their minimum income standard (described in Chapter 2), also asked members of the public what they thought minimum standards for housing should be. Members of the public felt that, in contrast to the official standard, all children, including those of pre-school age, needed rooms of their own. Given the changes that have occurred in young people's lives, and especially the much increased emphasis on working for high-stakes exams which I described in Chapter 4, some modification to the bedroom standard would appear to be overdue.

To address the issue of changing public conceptions of what is acceptable, Becky Tunstall has put forward a measure of relative housing poverty analogous to the relative measure of income poverty described in Chapter 2. She followed exactly the same approach as economists do when measuring relative poverty. She first calculated (from census data) what the median number of rooms per person was at each census date. In 2011, for example, the median came to 1.5 rooms per person. She then calculated what percentage of the population had less than 60 per cent of this figure. This then generates a measure of relative overcrowding.

This new measure of relative housing space makes some strong assumptions, just as the relative measure of income poverty does. Thus it implicitly assumes that the public's standards of what is acceptable move in line with the overall median. It would be better if we actually had over-time data about what the public thought was acceptable, and why. But in the absence of good data about the way in which the public's conceptions change over time, Becky Tunstall's measure is the best alternative. It certainly gives us a way of thinking about housing space which takes on board the idea that standards of what constitutes a socially acceptable minimum can change over time as society changes.

As one can see from Figure 5.4, this relative measure declined steeply from 1951 to 1981, just like the bedroom standard measure. However, unlike the bedroom standard measure, the relative measure climbed over the two subsequent decades to its highest level since 1961, reaching 14 per cent of the population in 2011. In relative terms, then, Britain's overcrowding problem in 2011 had marked similarities with the post-war overcrowding problem.

Another important point is that overcrowding is sector-specific, class-specific, and area-specific. So, whether we take the fixed or the relative measure, levels of overcrowding will be very much higher in some areas or sections of society than in others. As Figure 5.5 shows, there exist clear—and unsurprising—social and economic differences in risks of experiencing overcrowding. Overcrowding disproportionately hits the poor, the unemployed, and those in routine social classes, while it is very rare among higher social classes. It is also disproportionately high in London, among younger age groups, and among couples or single parents with dependent children. As one would expect, overcrowding is also much higher among people who are renting, either in the private rental market or from local authorities and housing associations, reflecting disadvantaged groups' lack of access to owner occupation.

Some of the highest rates of all, however, are to be found among members of some of Britain's ethnic minority communities, affecting 18 per cent of people with a Pakistani or Bangladeshi background. While this may in part be due to the low incomes and larger numbers of dependent children in these communities, detailed statistical analysis suggests that this is not the whole story.

Figure 5.5. Marginal and deprived groups in England are particularly vulnerable to overcrowding, as are Londoners

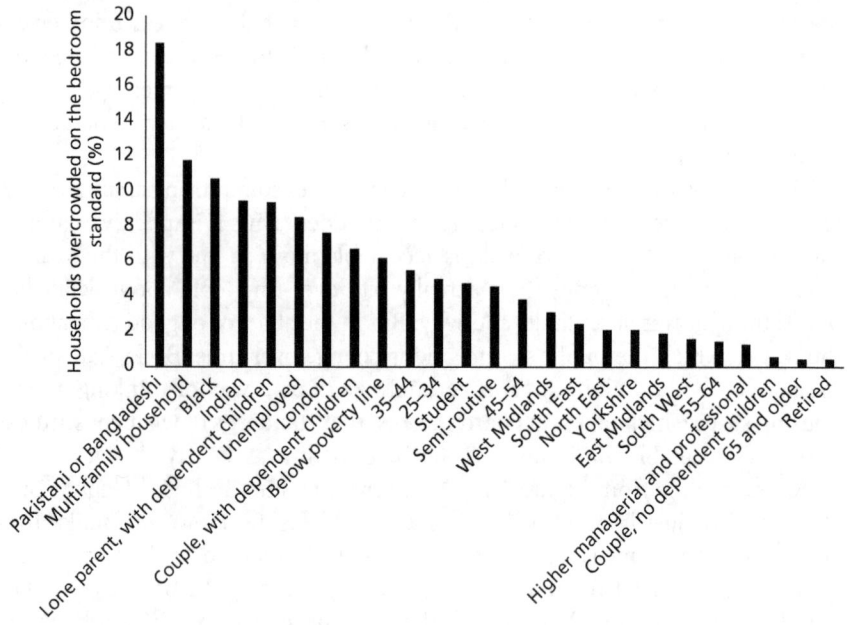

Source: English Housing Survey (pooled surveys from 2012 to 2014)

There seem to be additional reasons why members of these communities are so vulnerable to overcrowding.[24]

In short, marginal and deprived groups in British society are particularly vulnerable to problems of overcrowding—and to the negative implications of overcrowding for their health and well-being.[25] Moreover, the analysis of the English Housing Survey shows that overcrowding among most of these disadvantaged groups increased between 2003 and 2013. One also finds that the increase in overcrowding was largely confined to the social housing and private rental sectors. Among owner occupiers there was if anything a decline in overcrowding (Figure 5.6). Overcrowding among owner occupiers remained uncommon and barely changed throughout the period covered by the data. There was in contrast a marked increase in overcrowding in the social and private rental sectors. It is likely therefore that overcrowding became a greater problem for disadvantaged sections of society in the twenty-first century—with the wider social costs that this entails.

Homelessness is another criterion for assessing the potential resurgence of squalor. Homelessness will be much rarer than overcrowding, but even if the numbers are small it may be another warning sign of pressure in the housing market. To complicate matters, there are several different concepts

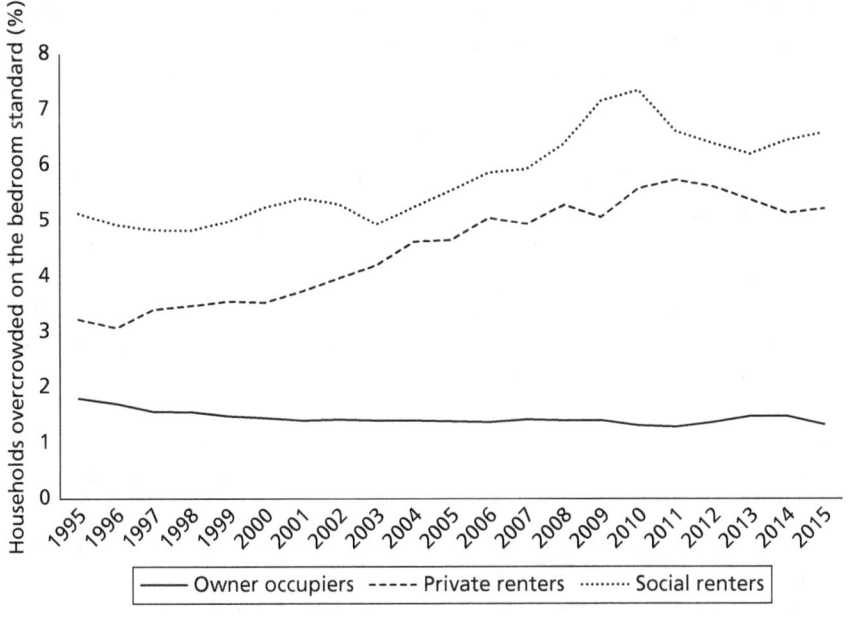

Figure 5.6. There was a slight decline in overcrowding among owner occupiers after 1995 but large increases in overcrowding among private and social renters in England

Source: English Housing Survey 2015–16, households annex table 1.20. Crown copyright (2017)

of homelessness. As A. E. Holmans has pointed out, homeless is a term of art in British government and does not have the literal meaning that you would expect (and which most other countries employ).[26] In Britain the term homeless is used to describe the situation of several (potentially) overlapping groups with somewhat different characteristics and reasons for homelessness. We can distinguish three main categories—rough sleepers, hidden homeless, and statutory homeless (people who are eligible for assistance from their local authority).

The statutory homeless will typically be placed in some kind of temporary or more permanent accommodation and so will not actually be homeless in the sense of having no roof over their heads. Rough sleepers really do not have a roof over their heads. They are people who live visibly out of doors—on the streets, in doorways, stairwells, cars or bus shelters—although they may not do so every night. Their number is estimated annually through street counts of people spotted sleeping rough on a single night. There is likely to be considerable error in these estimates, and there was also a major change in the methods employed to measure rough sleeping in 2010 (hence the apparent step change in Figure 5.7). Nevertheless, these street counts suggest considerable growth in the number of rough sleepers since 2010. The rough sleeping rate almost doubled from 3.4 to 6.5 per 100,000 between 2010 and 2016.

Moreover, high turnover means that these figures are bound to underestimate the total number of people who sleep rough at some stage of the year. An astonishing 9 per cent of young people aged 16–25 reported that they had slept rough at some point in 2014.[27] Episodes of rough sleeping are commonly interspersed with periods spent in hostels or temporary shelters, with census data identifying 21,574 people in England and Wales housed in this way in 2011. So this is not a trivial issue. Moreover, rough sleepers almost certainly include some of the most vulnerable members of society. As a Parliamentary Select Committee report on homelessness pointed out, many will have serious mental health problems; many will previously have been in local authority care—itself an indicator of extreme vulnerability; many will also be ex-offenders.[28]

Some government statistics, over a longer period of time, are also available on the statutory homeless. These are people who have been deemed eligible for assistance from their local authority because they are judged by the officials to be both unintentionally homeless and to meet criteria of priority need. Unintentional homelessness would include reasons such as eviction or the termination of a shorthold tenancy in the private sector. Priority need includes households containing children or pregnant women, people who are vulnerable due to mental or physical illness, care leavers, young people aged 16–17, and people forced to leave their homes due to violence or an emergency.

Figure 5.7 shows a rather puzzling pattern of change over time in the numbers placed by local authorities in temporary accommodation. There

Figure 5.7. The number of rough sleepers and of people in temporary accommodation rose sharply in England after 2010

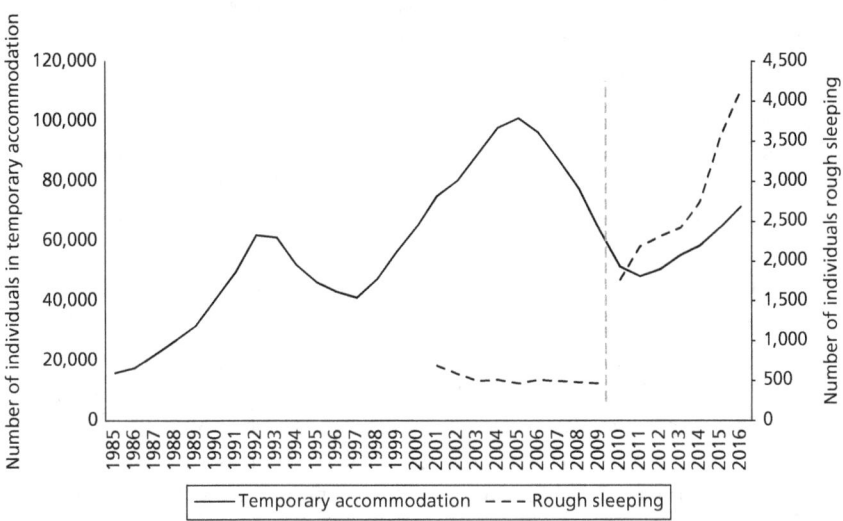

Source: rough sleepers, 2001–9, Ministry of Housing, Communities and Local Government, https://www.gov.uk/government/statistics/rough-sleeping-in-england-total-street-count-and-estimates-2010; 2010–16, MHCLG, https://www.gov.uk/government/statistics/rough-sleeping-in-england-autumn-2016. Temporary accommodation: live table 775, https://www.gov.uk/government/statistical-data-sets/live-tables-on-homelessness#statutory-homelessness-and-prevention-and-relief-live-tables

was a considerable increase up until around 2005, followed by a fall and then a resurgence. I do not think that the reasons for the fall after 2005 are well understood, but there can be little doubt about the increase since 2010. Government data on court orders by landlords for repossession also show a rise after 2010, and the National Audit Office has concluded that the ending of private-sector tenancies has overtaken all other causes to become the biggest single driver of statutory homelessness in England.[29]

Finally, the third category is that of the hidden homeless. These are homeless people who are hidden in the sense that they are not recorded by any official statistics. They could include people rather similar to the statutory homeless, but who were not deemed eligible for assistance from the local authority. They could include rough sleepers who have temporarily moved into a shelter. They could also include people who are 'sofa surfing', staying with friends or family on their floor or sofa because they have nowhere else to go. Like rough sleepers, the hidden homeless will include some of the most vulnerable members of society, although they may also include some more affluent people who have perhaps just separated from their partner and have not yet arranged alternative accommodation. It is a rather diverse group about which we know very little.

Good data on trends in the numbers of the hidden homeless simply do not exist. One recent survey, commissioned by the charity Centrepoint and conducted in 2014 among young people aged 16–25, estimated that over a quarter of a million young people were experiencing hidden homelessness on any one night. As the authors of the report concluded:

> These figures for hidden homelessness are high, and significantly higher than has been found previously. This clearly merits further research, and highlights the potential shortcomings of relying on administrative data and rough sleepers' counts for quantifying something that by its nature does not necessarily bring people into contact with those who collect the data.[30]

The data on homelessness and repossessions, despite their weaknesses, reinforce the suspicion that housing progress has gone into reverse for the most vulnerable members of society. Squalor, then, is a giant who appeared in the 1970s to have been defeated but has since made a comeback. The giant of Squalor is also quite specific in whom he attacks. The overall proportion may seem low—although it involves a large absolute number of people. But the proportion is much higher among Londoners and among vulnerable sections of the community such as the poor, the young, those who are routine or unemployed workers, and members of ethnic minority groups. For these groups overcrowding and homelessness, with their negative implications for health and well-being, can legitimately be regarded as reaching crisis levels.

Explaining the Housing Crisis: the Increasing Demand for Housing

It seems rather paradoxical, then, that I have been able to tell a positive story about major improvements in amenities and in the average number of rooms per person, and yet a negative story on overcrowding and homelessness. How can one reconcile these different findings?

One part of the answer relates to the demand for housing, which has outstripped the growth in population. Another part relates to the cost of housing—the problem of affordability. And the third relates to the distribution of housing—to increasing inequality in access to housing. I will look at each of these three in turn.

THE DEMAND FOR HOUSING

The demand for housing is driven by the number of households (and potential households) and not simply by population size. What has happened is that the number of households has grown much faster than the number of people. In 1951 there were, on official definitions of what constitutes a household, just over 13 million households in England and Wales. (In the official definition households constitute self-contained dwelling units who share meals together. It can include multiple families if they share meals or living rooms.) This had increased to over 23 million households by 2011.[31] So the number of households increased by nearly 50 per cent whereas the total population increased by only one quarter.

There were a number of reasons for this increase in the number of households. For example, there was an increasing number of widows and widowers living on their own (and, with rising life expectancy, living on their own for longer); there was an increasing rate of marital breakdown leading to couples splitting into separate households; and there was an increase in young singles forming separate households, while the rising university population created a new demand for term-time homes for students.

Moreover, the official definition of a household almost certainly understates the scale of the problem. In practice, the actual number of households formed will tend to reflect the number of homes available. What this means is that there may be many potential households who would like to set up home on their own but cannot because of the lack of housing available. These are sometimes termed *concealed* households—people currently living as part of another household, wishing to form a household of their own, but lacking the opportunity. Examples of concealed households would be recently married young couples who cannot yet afford a home of their own, or a lone parent living with family, or young singles who would like to set up on their own. Data from the English Housing Survey shows that in 2014–15, 6 per cent of all households in England (1.5 million) had one or more adults who would like to buy or rent their own home but could not afford to.[32] In this sense there is very considerable unmet demand. If each household is to have a separate dwelling—which is the taken-for-granted assumption in contemporary Britain—the increase in the housing stock needs to keep pace with the growing number of potential households, not just with the growth of population.

Historically, concealed households were prevalent during the housing shortages of the Second World War and were reduced in number following the large post-war home-building programmes. I remember that my family, during the Second World War and immediately afterwards, constituted a concealed household living in the same small flat as my grandmother. I have been told that it was a time of considerable family conflict and we moved away a few years after the war as soon as we could afford a home of our own.

My family's experience does not seem to have been unusual. Estimates suggest that the number of concealed households was particularly large during the housing shortage immediately after the war, and was still nearly 1 million households in 1951.[33] It subsequently declined progressively, falling to 165,000 in 2001. In twenty-first-century Britain, however, the undersupply of new homes and diminishing affordability of home ownership—especially for young people—means that concealed households began to increase: the proportion of concealed households in England and Wales rose from 1.2 per cent in 2001 to 1.8 per cent in 2011.[34] Moreover, these government estimates do not count one-person concealed households, so these figures will underestimate the extent of the unmet demand for housing.

Two other factors will have further increased the demand for housing. First, increasing material prosperity will have had spillover effects on the housing market. As people become richer, they want to have more space and more bedrooms, or invest in a second home (which the increase in house prices means may also be one of the best ways to invest any spare income). In economists' terminology, the demand for housing is income-elastic—as people get richer, they typically choose to spend a larger proportion of their income on housing.[35]

Second, economic growth has not been spread evenly across the country. While the supply and demand for housing may look to be in balance if we look at the country as a whole, one finds that there are major regional imbalances—which is why overcrowding is so much higher in London, for example, than in the north east or south west. Like a lot of young graduates since, I moved away from my parents' home in the declining city of Liverpool as soon as I finished university in order to take a job in London. This regional imbalance in the supply and demand for housing has become particularly marked since the 1980s with the decline of traditional manufacturing and the move to a service economy. Between 1981 and 2014, for example, the population of Liverpool declined by 10 per cent, whereas that of London expanded by almost a quarter.[36] Population growth has outstripped housing supply in London since the mid-1990s, but housing supply remains well above population growth in most of the north. So the rosy picture of increasing dwelling stock relative to population is not the case for those parts of the country where economic growth has been strongest.

In short, the demand for housing has been growing much faster than the population. The major house-building programmes in the decades immediately after the war meant that real progress was made in overcoming the wartime shortages, so that unmet need (using the criterion of concealed households) was clearly reduced. However, after the 1980s, progress in adding to the housing stock slowed while demand continued to grow, especially in areas of the country where economic growth was fastest.

INEQUALITY

As I described in Chapter 2, income inequality in Britain had been declining up until the late 1970s. It then started to widen again, and did so more rapidly than in most of Britain's peer countries. In the case of housing, as I described earlier in this chapter, the 1980s saw a move away from social housing to greater reliance on market forces. The combination of these two changes is very likely to have increased inequality in access to housing. It is therefore probable that widening income inequality has been mirrored in widening housing inequality. The combination of the greater reliance on market forces in housing and the increasing income and wealth of the most affluent is likely both to push up house prices and to put those at the top of the income distribution at the front of the queue for the available housing. It is not then just a simple matter of demand increasing. In addition, the well-off became even better off and will therefore have had increasing power in the market for housing. This is likely to have been one of the drivers for the general rise in house prices and rents.

We are fortunate that Becky Tunstall has enabled us to check this conjecture. She constructed a measure of housing inequality analogous to the measures of income inequality which I used in Chapter 2. In Figure 2.3 the population were arranged according to their position in the income distribution—starting from the poorest 10 per cent (the bottom decile), and working up to the best-off 10 per cent (the top decile). I then charted how those at the tenth percentile, the median, and the ninetieth percentile changed over time. To summarize, the real incomes of the tenth percentile grew slowly but steadily, whereas the real incomes of the ninetieth percentile grew at a much faster rate after 1980, thus leading to widening income inequality. Becky Tunstall has done the same for housing, using the ten-yearly censuses, simply replacing income with number of rooms. Figure 5.8 shows the results of her calculations for the period from 1951 to 2011.

The changes in housing inequality shown in Figure 5.8 are quite similar to the changes in income inequality shown in Figure 2.3. Thus, from 1951 to 1981 there was substantial progress both for the least well housed (the tenth percentile) and for the best housed (the ninetieth percentile). The absolute gap grew only slightly (and as a result the relative gap, as measured by the 10:90 ratio, actually narrowed somewhat). Thereafter, the improvements for the best housed continued and indeed accelerated after 1991. In contrast, there was no improvement at all for the least well housed after 1991. So this is actually a more gloomy picture than in the case of income, where at least there was continuing improvement for the poorest.

As a result inequality (measured by the 90:10 ratio) grew rapidly in the final decade of the twentieth century and the first decade of the twenty-first to a level not seen at any time in the twentieth century. As Becky Tunstall summarizes: 'while the very substantial public and private resources put into housing across the twentieth century had a big impact on average conditions, they translated very inefficiently into better conditions for the worst off'.[37]

I suspect that the increase in inequality after 1991 may actually have been even greater than Figure 5.8 indicates. Becky Tunstall's analysis will tend to

Figure 5.8. Inequality in access to housing space increased markedly after 1981 in England and Wales

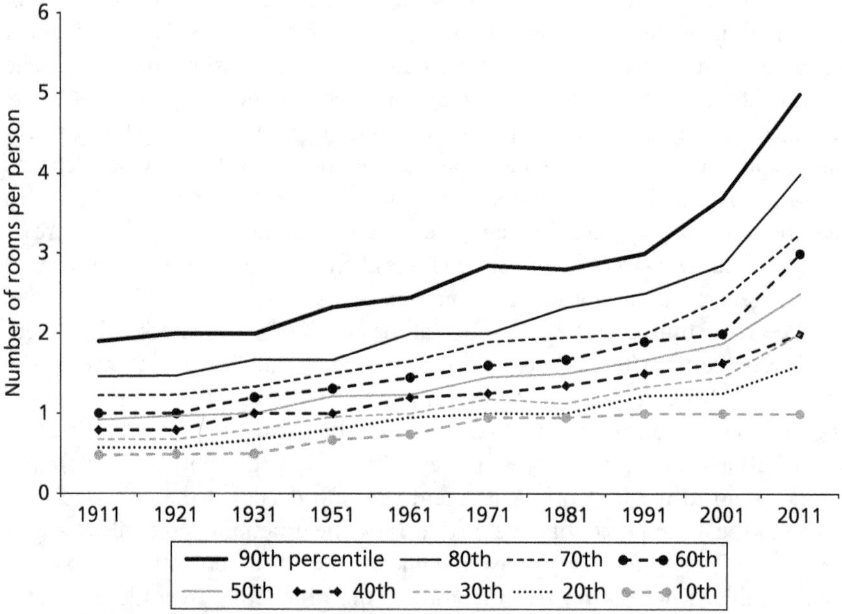

[Figure: Line graph showing number of rooms per person from 1911 to 2011, with lines for 90th, 80th, 70th, 60th, 50th, 40th, 30th, 20th, and 10th percentiles. The 90th percentile rises from about 1.9 in 1911 to about 5 in 2011, while the 10th percentile remains near 1 throughout.]

Source: B. Tunstall, 'Relative housing space inequality in England and Wales, and its recent rapid resurgence', *International Journal of Housing Policy*, 15 (2015): 105–26 (data derived from the decennial censuses). We are very grateful to Becky Tunstall for permission to reproduce this figure

underestimate inequality in housing space since the data exclude the non-household population such as homeless people and people in institutions. At the other end of the spectrum the data do not take into account the likelihood that second homes will be owned by the most affluent members of society, who most probably already have more rooms per person in their first homes. If the number of homeless people or of affluent people with second homes has been increasing, then the increase in inequality will be underestimated in Figure 5.8.

AFFORDABILITY

The imbalance between supply and demand is highlighted by the decreasing affordability of housing. There is fairly good data on house prices going back to 1977 from the Office for National Statistics. While house prices will of course be particularly relevant for people wishing to become owner occupiers, they will also have indirect effects on rents as well in the private renting market. In Figure 5.9 I show the ratio of house prices to median household income. This ratio gives an indication of the affordability of owner occupation, and I remember that, when I first bought a house back in the 1960s, the building society had rather clear rules about how much they would be prepared to lend me, based on the ratio of the house price to my annual income.

As we can see from Figure 5.9, in 1977 when the series starts, homes cost on average four times the median household income. There was a peak in 1989 when the ratio reached six (probably sparked by the 'Lawson boom' following chancellor of the exchequer Nigel Lawson's expansionist budget of 1988). There was then a second spike in 2007 when the ratio reached eight times median income. Each peak was followed by a fall, coinciding with the subsequent recession. In the twenty-first century, however, the readjustment was not as large as in the 1990s, and the house price to household income ratio remained at around seven times median household income, making home ownership almost twice as expensive as it had been in 1977 for new buyers.

To be sure, purchase price is only one aspect of affordability. The cost of servicing one's mortgage will not have increased by nearly so much. In the 1980s interest rates fluctuated around 10 per cent; from the mid-1990s they fluctuated around 5 per cent; and after the 2007/8 financial crash they were reduced to 0.5 per cent. This will have had knock-on effects on the cost of mortgages. Declining interest rates mean that housing costs (measured by

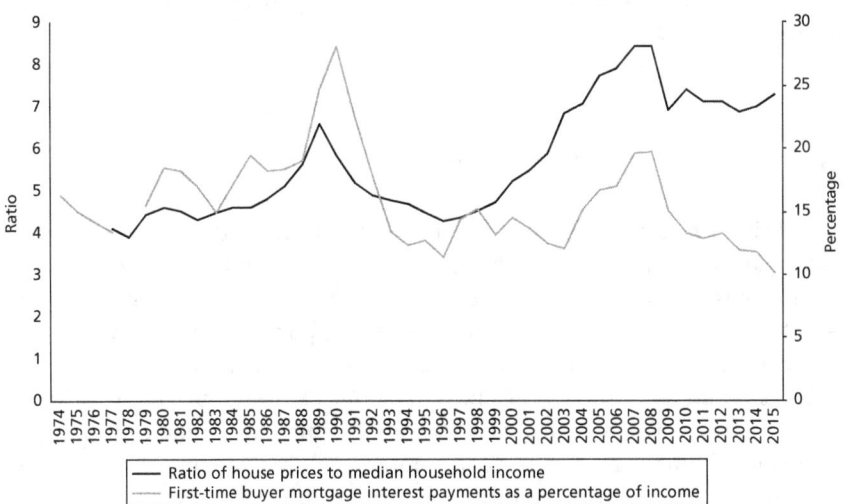

Figure 5.9. The ratio of UK house prices to household incomes doubled between 1977 and 2007, while affordability of mortgage interest payments fluctuated[38]

— Ratio of house prices to median household income
— First-time buyer mortgage interest payments as a percentage of income

Source: Income: time series of equivalized disposable income, 1977–2015/16, UK. Office for National Statistics, 'Household disposable income and inequality', table 8, https://www.ons.gov.uk/peoplepopulationandcommunity/personalandhouseholdfinances/incomeandwealth/datasets/householddisposableincomeandinequality; house prices: 1968–2014, https://www.gov.uk/government/statistical-data-sets/uk-house-price-index-data-downloads-march-2017; 2005–16/17, https:www.gov.ukgovernmentstatistical-data-sets/uk-house-price-index-data-downloads-march-2017; UK Finance.

mortgage interest payments) as a proportion of first-time buyers' income have not shown a commensurate increase to house prices.

There are also major issues of affordability within the private rental and social housing sectors. The data are rather patchy, especially in the case of private renting, and interpretation of the figures is complicated by the changing mix of accommodation as the private rental sector expanded and the social housing sector contracted after 1981. Nevertheless, the evidence is quite clear that both private and social rents rose faster than the overall rate of inflation. In his magisterial treatment of historical housing statistics, A. E. Holmans[39] showed that average weekly rents in the private sector rose in real terms from £30.50 in 1966 to £49.15 in 2000, and I suspect that the rate of increase has, if anything, increased since the turn of the century.

Drawing on Holmans' pioneering work and more recent data from the Ministry for Housing, Communities and Local Government, one can also construct long-term trends in social rents. Figure 5.10 shows that 1980 was something of a turning point. Since 1980 rents (in real terms) have more than trebled—they have increased by a factor of 3.6. To get a measure of affordability, we need to compare this with the increase in household incomes. Over the same period (from 1980 to 2015), household income for the lowest quarter of households (that is the twenty-fifth percentile) rose by a factor of only 1.7. The cost of social housing not only outstripped the general rate of inflation, it also outstripped the growth in real income among the less affluent. Declining affordability, then, has been a major issue in both the private renting and the social housing sectors.

How Does Britain Compare?

The British measures of overcrowding such as the bedroom standard are rather idiosyncratic in international terms. Other countries like France and Germany routinely use space-based measures rather than measures based on number of rooms. Space-based measures are important in their own right to counter some serious limitations of the bedroom standard, notably the size of bedrooms and other space available in the home. For example, homes where a reception room is designated as a bedroom—which is common in multiple-occupancy homes—may lack space compared with single-occupancy homes but not be considered overcrowded according to the bedroom standard. In 2011 the Greater London Authority published a new set of internal space guidelines for new builds in London and research by Malcolm Morgan and Heather Cruickshank, using this standard, found that 21 per cent of households in England in 2010 lacked sufficient space, a considerably greater percentage than suggested by the bedroom standard.[40]

Figure 5.10. Social housing rents quadrupled in England over the post-war period

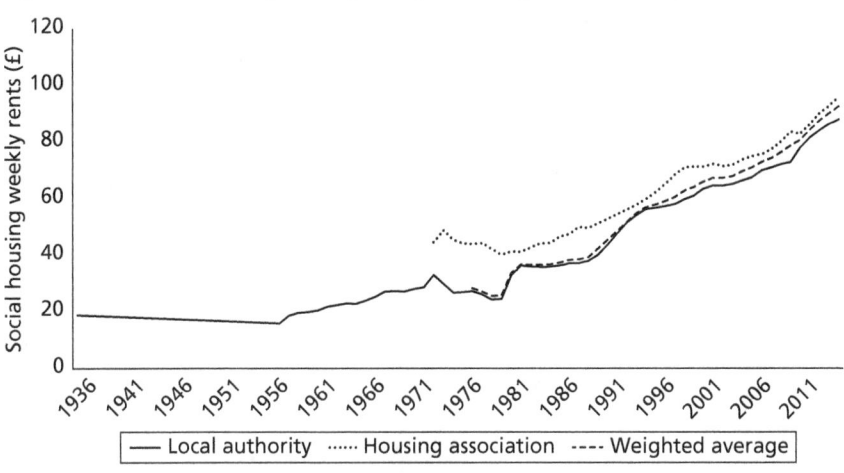

Source: A. E. Holmans, 'Historical statistics of housing in Britain', table H.7; MHCLG[41]

The physical size of homes is not monitored in Britain so we do not know whether people have more or less space than in Beveridge's day and we cannot compare British trends with those in our peer countries. However, while we cannot compare trends over time as we have done in other chapters, there are some data which allow us to compare space and overcrowding in Britain with that in European peer countries. The OECD also publishes some housing statistics covering Canada, Japan, and the USA.

Figure 5.11 shows two different measures for the five European countries: the average size of dwellings[42] and the percentage overcrowded, using a European measure of overcrowding based on room occupancy. This European measure has some similarities with the British bedroom standard but has some sensible and important differences, such as allowing each household one room in addition to the required number of bedrooms. This means that the results are not comparable to those discussed earlier in this chapter.[43]

Surprisingly, we find that neither average dwelling size nor the rate of overcrowding in Britain is all that different from those in France and Germany. I am at a loss to understand why the rate of overcrowding is so high in Italy, given its rather average size of dwellings. The results for Sweden are also something of a puzzle. The data come from well-respected and harmonized European data sources, so they should be reliable. The most likely possibility is that the extent of housing inequality is particularly high in Italy and Sweden.

I would expect that Canada and the USA would tend to have much larger home sizes than the European countries, given that they are much less densely populated countries, and there is some evidence on the size of newly built

Figure 5.11. Britain is not very different from other European countries in average housing space or in the level of overcrowding

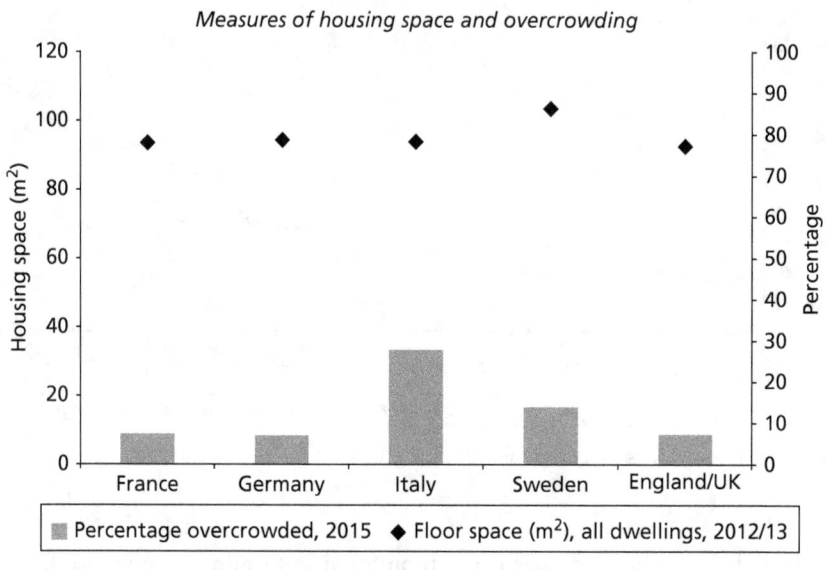

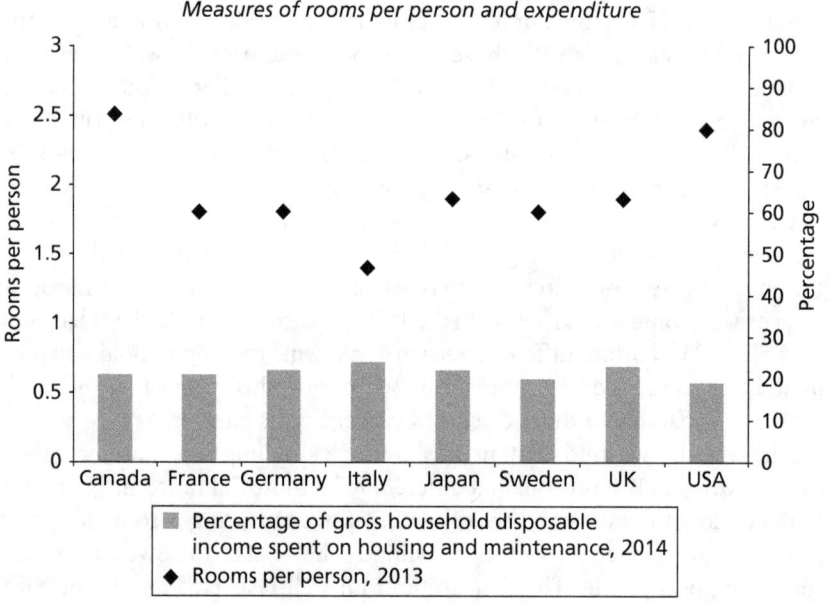

Note: statistics for dwelling size are for England

Source: floor space, all dwellings: derived from 2012/13 English Housing Survey and Eurostat 2012[44]; percentage overcrowded: EU-SILC 2016, table tessi170, http://ec.europa.eu/eurostat/web/products-datasets/-/tessi170; rooms per person and percentage of household disposable income spent on housing—OECD Better Life Index, http://www.oecdbetterlifeindex.org/topics/housing/

homes that this is indeed the case. Japan on the other hand appears to be not all that different from European countries in this respect. Incidentally, new homes in Britain seem to be considerably smaller at 76m² than the British average for the total housing stock as a whole shown in Figure 5.11 (and for those in the other European countries).[45] This may be another indication of the extent of contemporary pressures in the housing market in Britain.

The OECD figures cover rooms per person and the cost of housing—a broad concept which includes the cost of repairs and maintenance as well as heating and lighting, so very different from the measures of affordability which I used earlier in the chapter. These data confirm my expectation that Canada and the USA are, on average, better endowed with housing than the European countries. It also confirms the particular pressures experienced in Italy, where the number of rooms per person is the lowest, and also the amount spent on housing is the highest (although I should mention that the OECD uses the same European data sources that I use for the measure of overcrowding, so this is not actually an independent measure). However, the OECD data on housing expenditure do show that housing places rather greater pressure on household budgets in the UK than in peer countries other than Italy.

Overall, these data suggest that the British housing stock is not all that different in size from those of France and Germany. The size of the total housing stock will of course reflect historical patterns of building (and demolition, as during the British slum clearance programmes which often involved small terraced houses). The much smaller size of current new building in Britain may be a better guide to current pressures, especially affordability pressures, so I would not want to draw very optimistic conclusions from these international comparisons. All the same, the comparisons suggest that Britain is not alone in having a housing problem.

Conclusions

Poor housing conditions—especially overcrowding—have important implications for people's well-being and for that of family members. These negative consequences of poor housing cannot be attributed solely to the low incomes of those affected—housing conditions are an important aspect of social welfare in their own right. Beveridge was right to identify squalor as a distinct giant.

Britain made great strides in the 1950s and 1960s in tackling the post-war housing crisis. There were major building programmes both in the public and private sectors, reducing the level of overcrowding and improving amenities. Becky Tunstall has commented that 'this production of additional homes and housing space...could be rated as amongst the greatest achievements of the twentieth century economy and of twentieth century social policy in the UK'.[46]

One crucial element of this progress was the major slum clearance programme of post-war governments, the building of new towns like Milton Keynes, and investments in social housing. A. E. Holmans, the leading authority on the history of British housing, has cogently argued that state assistance was essential for the success in tackling the post-war housing crisis. His evidence suggested that the same progress could not have been made by relying purely on the market, for example through new building for private renting. Given the standards of rooms and amenities which government had set, and the cost of new building, rents could not have been set at a level which ordinary wage earners could have afforded at that time. Holmans concluded: 'beyond doubt is that the housing standards set and the facts of the level and distribution of income made large scale state assistance inevitable. Without it housing standards would not have risen as they did and sharing and crowding would not have diminished as they did.'[47] Holmans' argument may well be relevant to the current housing crisis. Since the 1980s the overall stock of housing and the quality of that stock has continued to improve. But, as this chapter has shown, progress in tackling overcrowding effectively stalled in the late 1980s, and actually became markedly worse for tenants in social housing and in the private rental sector. One is naturally inclined to wonder whether declining investment in social housing, and an increasing reliance on the private rental market ever since the 1980s, has played a role in the lack of progress in tackling the evils of crowding and homelessness. Certainly, there is good evidence that housing inequality increased after the 1980s, with the more affluent members of society continuing to improve their access to housing while those at the other end of the spectrum failed to improve their situation at all.

In some ways there are two distinct housing problems, impinging on different groups of people. Young but relatively affluent people find it more difficult than their predecessors (like myself) to buy their first home since house prices have increased so much faster than incomes. Young but less affluent people are faced with the problem of rents (both in the private and social housing sectors) which have outstripped the growth in income and as a result have become increasingly at risk of overcrowding. These risks of overcrowding impinge particularly on the most vulnerable sections of the population, who would probably not have been in a position to buy their own homes even before the increase in house prices. Affordability of house purchase, however, impinges more on younger professionals who would have been able to buy in earlier decades.

Of course, the two problems are related. But perhaps the key aspect is the shift from a mixed system with a substantial social housing sector with controlled rents up until the 1970s and a much more market-based system thereafter. This, combined with increasing income inequality, explains why increasing availability of housing relative to household numbers can also be accompanied by a housing crisis for the more vulnerable sections of the population.

The immediate post-war governments used public resources to tackle the housing crisis successfully. The decline of social housing, and the return of housing to the operation of free market forces does not seem to have been as successful in dealing with the contemporary housing crisis. Simply building more houses on the green belt, as some have suggested, is highly unlikely to solve the housing crisis on its own. A more fundamental rethink will be necessary.

6 The Fight against Idleness

Unemployment and Discouraged Workers

with Yaojun Li and Elisabeth Garratt

Introduction

Idleness has a rather pejorative connotation nowadays. It has overtones of laziness and implies that the idle person is not bothering. I am sure that this is not actually what Beveridge would have had in mind. I suspect he was thinking of the Great Depression of the 1930s when jobs simply dried up for many industrial workers leaving them with no possibility of work. It would have been *enforced* idleness that concerned Beveridge—the unemployment of people who would have preferred to work if work had been available. Indeed, Beveridge's next major piece of work, after his 1942 Report, was his 1944 book *Full Employment in a Free Society*, in which he wrote about possible ways to prevent 'Idleness enforced by mass unemployment'.[1]

In *Full Employment in a Free Society* Beveridge argued that full employment in essence involved an unemployment rate of no higher than 3 per cent, since there would always be some frictional unemployment as workers left one job and looked for another. The crucial point, in his view, was that there should be more vacancies than there were workers looking for jobs so that the time people spent between jobs was kept to a minimum. The government's role in a free society, he argued, should be to stimulate demand along the lines outlined by John Maynard Keynes in his celebrated *The General Theory of Employment, Interest and Money* (published in 1936),[2] rather than to direct labour as the wartime government had done.

Ever since the Great Depression, enforced idleness has been recognized to have wide ramifications both for the unemployed themselves and for their families. A classic ethnographic study showed the devastating social impact of mass unemployment in the Austrian town of Marienthal after the town's principal factory and main employer closed down during the Depression. A team of social scientists showed not only the poverty and material hardship which resulted but also the demoralization and the decline of community life which followed.[3] Beveridge himself was associated with a somewhat similar British study, *Men without Work*, which was conducted in six British towns in the 1930s and documented similar consequences of long-term unemployment.[4] In *Full Employment in a Free Society* he wrote that, although the purely material loss due to mass unemployment was serious, 'the main evil of unemployment is in its social and human effects upon the persons unemployed and upon the relations between citizens'.[5] He concluded 'Idleness is not the same as Want, but a separate evil, which men do not escape by having an income.'[6]

Subsequent scientific research has supported Beveridge. Unemployment does indeed have direct and immediate economic effects in the form of reduced income and lost output, but it has harmful effects over and above the loss of income involved. It affects one's longer-term economic prospects since time out of the labour market means that one's work skills are becoming rusty, while people who have kept their jobs are acquiring further job skills and experience, with major implications for their future earning power. Moreover, job loss and unemployment have a much wider range of non-economic consequences in addition to the longer-term financial implications. Job loss and unemployment affect one's psychological well-being and physical health as well as one's pocket. It is associated with increased risk of alcohol and drug problems, with increased risk of suicide and with reduced civic engagement and social participation. It also has spillover consequences for other people such as one's family, increasing for example the risks of divorce, of domestic violence, and even mental health problems for one's partner.[7] There are some tricky technical problems in demonstrating that these risks are directly caused by unemployment.[8] But my reading of the evidence suggests that we should certainly take these wider social and psychological effects of unemployment very seriously indeed. I am sure Beveridge was right to see Idleness as a serious evil in its own right and not simply as an aspect of Want.

Economists David Bell and David Blanchflower have also emphasized that unemployment when one is young, especially if it lasts for a long time, causes enduring scars rather than temporary blemishes. 'For the young, a spell of unemployment does not end with that spell; it raises the probability of being unemployed in later years and has a wage penalty. These effects are much larger than for older people.'[9] The worry is that young people, especially those with few educational qualifications, have disproportionately borne the brunt of unemployment in recent decades.

In the 1950s young people could leave school at the earliest opportunity, with no qualifications to their name, and could still expect to get reasonable jobs, for example in the shipyards or factories. The long-term decline of Britain's manufacturing industry and the growing emphasis on educational qualifications may mean that young men and women without qualifications in the twenty-first century have become increasingly at risk of unemployment. As more and more young people are acquiring qualifications, are the ones without good grades at GCSE increasingly marginalized? Has the giant of

Idleness come to pick on young people, especially young men with low qualifications, much more than he did in the past? Beveridge had argued that 'Failure to find any use for adaptable youth is one of the worst blots on the record of the period between the wars.'[10] Has youth unemployment once again become one of the worst blots on the record of contemporary governments?

We also need to think a bit about whether the giant of Idleness has changed character. The strict modern definition of unemployment from the International Labour Office defines the unemployment rate as 'the number of jobless people who want to work, are available to work and are actively seeking employment'.[11] However, long periods of unemployment or lack of suitable jobs means that increasing numbers of out-of-work people may stop seeking employment altogether, and may thus drop out of the unemployment statistics. This phenomenon of what I will term discouraged workers may be particularly prevalent among older workers who lost their manufacturing or mining jobs during the period of industrial restructuring in the 1980s and have been unable either to retrain or to move away in search of work. So I should not limit my focus in this chapter solely to unemployment as defined by government statisticians. Beveridge would certainly have wanted to include discouraged workers within his concept of Idleness.

An analogous problem, which has indeed been widely recognized in government circles, is that of young people who are neither in education, employment, nor training (often described as NEET). This again goes wider than the strict definition of unemployment, since it covers young people who maybe do not want to work, or who are not actively looking for work, as well as those who fulfil the strict International Labour Office definition. Again, there has been substantial research showing the damaging effects of being NEET on people's futures.

Before turning to these more detailed questions, I will look first at the long-term trends in unemployment, setting them in an international context. A central question for this section of the chapter is whether Margaret Thatcher's reforms of the labour market in the 1980s—reforms which aimed to make the labour market more flexible—achieved their purpose. Has Britain with its flexible labour market succeeded better than the more regulated labour markets of continental Europe in keeping unemployment closer to Beveridge's 3 per cent full employment target?

I will then move on to a more detailed examination of who is most at risk of unemployment, focussing on ethnic and gender differences as well as on youth. Has the dark side of educational progress led to greater vulnerability for young people, especially young men, who have failed to keep up in the race for educational qualifications? I will then try to supplement this with data on NEET and on discouraged workers.

Long-Run Trends in Unemployment: How Does Britain Compare?

I begin by charting unemployment trends in Britain and our seven peer countries. My central question is how Britain compares with our peer countries in protecting workers from the risks of unemployment, and whether this has changed over time. In particular, did Britain move up or down the rankings after Margaret Thatcher's reforms which deregulated the labour market in the 1980s? There were a large number of different reforms and a variety of different aims behind these reforms. Some reforms were designed to weaken the power of the trade unions to call strikes, to make work pay by reducing the relative value of unemployment benefits, to reduce government interference in the labour market (for example by abolishing wages councils), and to make self-employment more attractive (for example through the enterprise allowance scheme).[12] The overall thrust was to move Britain from the kind of highly regulated labour market typical of European countries such as France and Germany and in the direction of the much more deregulated US labour market. As a result we might expect to see Britain converging with (low) US rates of unemployment and diverging from (high) European rates.

Before turning to the actual data on long-term trends, I need to take a brief methodological digression. Basically, there are two different ways of measuring unemployment. The first relies on administrative data such as the government's records of the number of people claiming unemployment-related benefits. Administrative records like this used to be the only source of data. However, in somewhat similar fashion to education statistics, there were numerous changes over time in how unemployment was recorded. Perhaps the most important change was in 1982 when official statistics moved from measuring unemployment on the basis of the number of people *registered at employment exchanges* (the register count) to the number *claiming unemployment-related benefits* (the claimant count). This move had the effect of substantially reducing the numbers recorded as unemployed.[13] So exactly as with education and housing, there are major problems of comparability both over time and between countries if we just rely on government administrative data.[14]

The alternative method, and the one that is now generally used in developed countries for international comparisons, relies on representative sample surveys of the general population. Respondents to these surveys (in Britain the Labour Force Survey is the main one used) are asked a series of questions to determine whether they meet the International Labour Office's definition of being currently out of work, available for work, and actively seeking work. These surveys are now seen as superior to administrative data.

The OECD has constructed harmonized measures of unemployment from 1955 onwards, based on these survey measures, in order to establish what proportion of the workforce meet this formal definition of unemployment. Unfortunately, however, not all of our countries are included for the whole period because of various limitations of the data available. In the case of Britain, for example, the OECD only publishes harmonized data from 1985, whereas they publish data for the USA and Canada going back to 1955. In Figure 6.1 I have therefore added—for Britain but not for the other countries—earlier administrative data based for example on register counts.[15] This is clearly less than ideal but the margin of error is probably only a couple of percentage points.

Still, the broad outlines of the picture are clear enough. In the 1950s and 1960s, the four countries for which data are available (Canada, Japan, the UK, and the USA) had relatively low unemployment rates. These were just over Beveridge's target of 3 per cent in the cases of Canada and USA and below 3 per cent in Japan and the UK. My guess is that some of the other peer countries would have had equally low rates of unemployment at this time. For example, in the 1950s, a number of Western European countries such as France and Germany began programmes of recruiting foreign workers from outside the country in order to fill chronic labour shortages. There is no reason to doubt that there was pretty full employment immediately after the war in

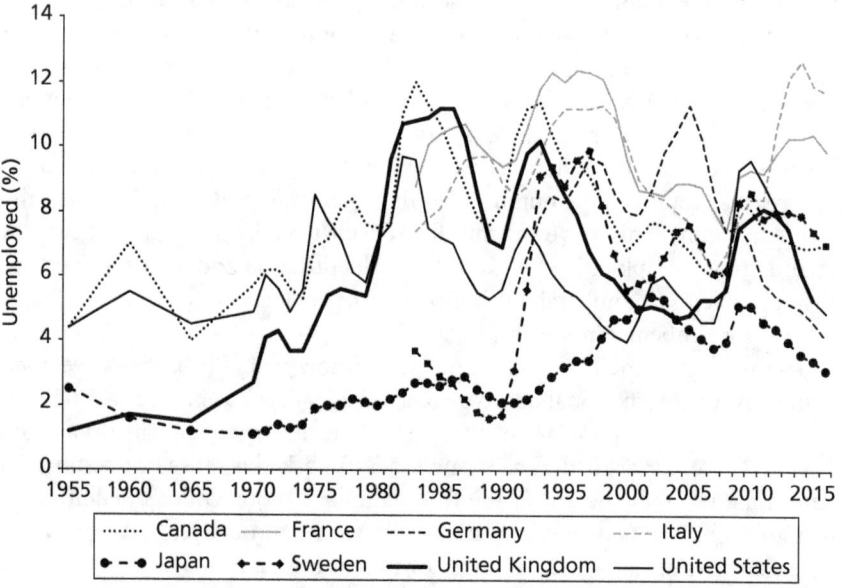

Figure 6.1. The UK's unemployment rate was relatively low in the 1950s, 1960s, and 1970s but became relatively high in the recessions of the early 1980s and early 1990s

Source: OECD harmonized unemployment rates, https://data.oecd.org/unemp/harmonized-unemployment-rate-hur.htm; register counts and modelled data for the UK 1955–82[16]

these countries, although I suspect that Italy would have been an exception and remained a country of net emigration, with more people leaving the country than entering it. Belgium, for example, recruited a large number of Italian labour migrants around this time.[17]

Unemployment rates then began to climb in the 1970s, after the oil shock of 1973/4 which pushed up the price of crude oil and led to rising inflation in many developed countries. (In a nutshell the Organization of Arab Petroleum Exporting Countries raised the price of oil and cut production.) However, unemployment remained in single figures throughout the 1970s in the four countries for which we have data, only a few points higher than it had been in the 1950s and 1960s.

Since 1980, however, it has been rather a bumpy ride, with surges in unemployment in almost all countries in the early 1980s, the early 1990s, and again after the financial crash and the great recession of 2007/8. The same global forces affected all the major economies in rather similar ways, although to slightly varying degrees.

On the other hand, it is very clear that there have been long-standing differences between countries, too. The impact of global recessions is only half the story. Thus Japan's unemployment rate remained throughout well below that of Canada or the USA—in 2015 it was still just 3.4 per cent, close to Beveridge's full employment target of 3 per cent. This is rather similar to education, where we found evidence that Japan had long been distinctive from other peer countries. In contrast, Italy had one of the highest unemployment rates of the eight countries from the earliest years for which we have harmonized data. These national differences do not appear to be new phenomena. My impression is that there are enduring institutional differences which predate, and survive, the succession of global recessions.

However, there are one or two rather interesting exceptions to this picture of stable differences between countries. The most noticeable exception is that of Sweden, a country which is often viewed as a model social democratic welfare state. Sweden did indeed use to be a model with a low unemployment rate, very similar in this respect to Japan. But this changed drastically in the 1990s, when Sweden saw its unemployment rate soar from Japanese levels to British levels and even higher. I do not claim to understand precisely why this happened, but the change coincided with a move towards a more market-oriented economy and the adoption of neoliberal, free-market policies. My interpretation is that changed political priorities account for Sweden losing its distinctively low unemployment rate and becoming a relatively high unemployment country.

What about Britain? The story is pretty clear with three distinct phases. In the first phase, which lasted up until 1980, British unemployment rates were lower than those of Canada and the USA, though not quite as low as Japan's. But then in the second phase, in every single year from 1981 to 2001, British rates of unemployment were higher than the US and Japanese rates and were among the highest of all eight countries during the two recessions of the early 1980s and early 1990s. In this second phase, a high proportion of the unemployed in Britain were long-term unemployed (that is, unemployed for twelve months or more). In 1983, for example, the proportion of the unemployed who had been out of work for twelve months or more reached 46 per cent—a considerably higher proportion than in any other peer country apart from Italy. In the third phase, since 2001, the British rate of unemployment became relatively low once again and tended to oscillate around the US rate. In this third phase the proportion who were unemployed long term also fell—in 2015 it was down to 31 per cent of the unemployed, a proportion below that of Japan, Germany, France, Italy, and Spain.[18]

It is hard to avoid the conclusion that the major change beginning in 1981 had something to do with the free-market economic policies followed by Margaret Thatcher's governments in Britain. However, the overall result of these policies seems to have been to raise the level of unemployment rather than to reduce it. Detailed analysis by the economist David Blanchflower and his colleagues suggests that the policies designed to make the British labour market more flexible did not have the intended result of reducing the rate of unemployment. Other aspects of the labour market reforms, like curbing the power of the trade unions or increasing British competitiveness, might well have been successful in achieving their goals. But the move to a flexible labour market did not achieve the goal of reducing unemployment. The economists concluded: 'The "flexibility" explanation of unemployment is wrong.' Instead 'It is the fall in demand for labour that is the culprit.'[19] Sustaining the level of demand for labour so that full employment could be achieved was of course precisely what Beveridge had been advocating in 1944.

Doubtless other economists could be found who might advance a different interpretation, but my guess is that any effects, for good or ill, of Margaret Thatcher's labour market reforms were swamped by the adverse effects of her government's monetary policy and high interest rates, designed to tackle inflation. Thousands of manual jobs in the manufacturing industry were lost during the early 1980s recession. Some might argue that this was a price worth paying in order to tackle the evil of inflation. In a famous speech in 1979 Margaret Thatcher argued that 'The evil of inflation is still with us. We are a long way from restoring honest money...We should not underestimate the enormity of the task which lies ahead. But little can be achieved without sound money. It is the bedrock of sound government.'[20] In effect, the Conservative government prioritized control of inflation over the maintenance of employment. This is not the place to get into an argument about whether or not this was the right thing to do at the time, but it is clear that Margaret Thatcher's programme, taken as a whole, did not at the time reduce unemployment but increased it.

All the same in the early twenty-first century Britain's overall unemployment rate once again compares quite well with that of peer countries—and it is not at the time of writing very much higher than the full employment target of 3 per cent. Part of the explanation for this will I suspect be found to be Britain's low interest rates, which will have kept demand for labour high. Another factor might be the rise of self-employment in Britain, which had indeed been one of Margaret Thatcher's policy objectives. Self-employment provides a potential way out for people faced with unemployment. It can be very insecure and may not generate much income, but it probably avoids some of the harmful social and psychological effects of idleness that Beveridge worried about. At all events, back in 1980 at 8.1 per cent Britain had one of the lowest self-employment rates of our eight peer countries. By 2015 this had increased to 14.9 per cent according to OECD figures, one of the highest among our peer countries.[21] It would not be unreasonable therefore to see Britain's currently low unemployment rate as in part a legacy of Margaret Thatcher's policies of making self-employment easier and more attractive in the way it was treated for tax purposes.[22]

Who Is Most Affected by Unemployment? Has This Changed over Time?

While overall levels of unemployment in Britain since 2000 have been relatively low compared with rates in most of our peer countries, the risks of unemployment strike some groups much more than others. For some people, risks of unemployment were still very high even in 2015. It has probably always been the case that the young, migrants, and the least educated were more exposed to unemployment. In the 1950s with unemployment around 3 per cent or less, the differences in risk would have been in practice very small. However, as unemployment rose—particularly in the recessions of the early 1980s and early 1990s and after the financial crash in 2007/8—inequalities in risks of unemployment will have risen, too.

An important question is whether these increases were temporary, like the recessions, or whether something more fundamental changed. The increase in income inequality which occurred in the 1980s has become a permanent new feature of the British labour market. Do we find a parallel more or less permanent increase in risks of unemployment for vulnerable groups of workers? I raised in Chapter 4 the question of the dark side of educational expansion—what happens to those left behind in the race to acquire more and better qualifications? With a growing number of highly qualified peers to compete against, one guesses that the economic prospects of the poorly qualified will have deteriorated relative to better-qualified workers.

So I shall now have a closer look at unemployment in Britain. Who is most at risk, and how have those risks changed over time? Is the giant of Idleness now more selective about whom he picks on? I will start with gender differences and then move on to differences between people with different qualification levels, ages, and ethnic backgrounds. Moreover, are these different risks compounded so that some sections of society suffer a double or treble burden?

GENDER DIFFERENCES IN UNEMPLOYMENT RATES

Britain, like most of the peer countries, saw major changes in the post-war period in the proportion of women going out to work. When I was growing up in the 1950s, it was rather rare for married women with children at home to take paid employment. Most women worked between leaving school and having their first baby, and many returned to work after their children had grown up (exactly as my mother did). But one of the major transformations of British society in the post-war period was the increased participation of mothers in the labour market (although often taking part-time jobs while their children were young).

The kinds of job that women enter have also slowly changed. In my mother's day, jobs were highly gendered—women like my mother would take jobs such as a typist or secretary which were almost totally a female preserve at the time, while there were a large number of jobs, particularly in the manufacturing, mining, and construction industries which were equally exclusively male preserves. Gender segregation is not yet a thing of the past, but it has been gradually changing alongside Britain's shift from being an industrial society to a post-industrial or service-based economy. So what have been the implications for men and women's risks of unemployment?

Figure 6.2 uses statistics from representative government surveys (not administrative data) to trace gender differentials in risks of unemployment from the early 1970s onwards.[23] (The main surveys which I draw on here only started in the 1970s, and I have not been able to find earlier administrative data which distinguish male from female unemployment rates.)

Figure 6.2 tells a striking story. In the 1970s men and women had rather similar, and fairly low, risks of unemployment.[24] This changed in the recession of the early 1980s, when male unemployment rose distinctly higher than female unemployment did. This gender differential remained evident for the following thirty years. The gender gap was particularly wide at the peak of each recession, reaching four percentage points in the recession of the early 1990s. More recently, the gap narrowed and male and female risks of unemployment more or less converged after 2012. However, I would not be surprised if the gap were to rise again during the next recession. It is probably too early to say whether the convergence of male and female unemployment rates in 2015 is the new normal.

Figure 6.2. Men experienced higher rates of unemployment than women from the 1980s onwards in Great Britain

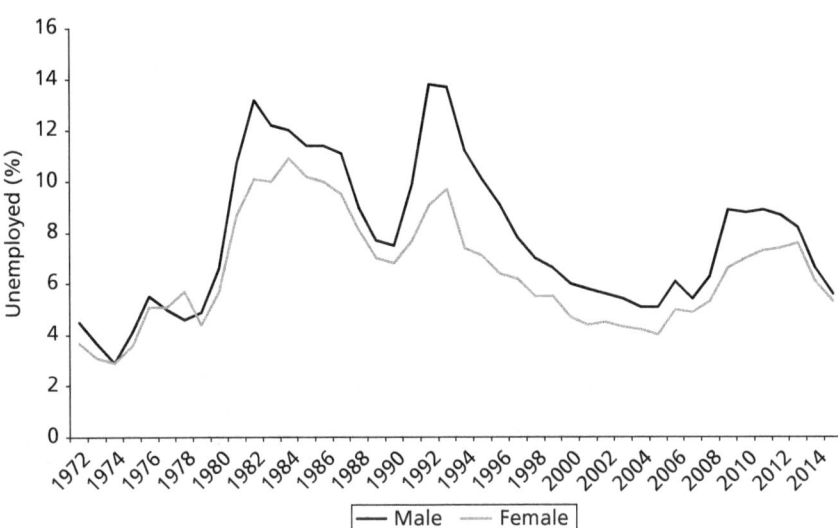

Note: samples include all economically active respondents (men aged 16–64 and women aged 16–59)
Source: pooled General Household Surveys (1972–2005) and Labour Force Surveys (1983–2015)

The natural interpretation of the 1980s shift in men's and women's relative risks of unemployment is that it reflected the changing structure of employment in the last decades of the twentieth century. There was a long-term decline of the predominantly male industries of manufacturing, shipbuilding, and the like, while increasing numbers of more female-oriented white-collar and service jobs were being created in the second half of the twentieth century.

The shift in the gender gap could also reflect in part the way in which women gradually overtook men in education, as I described in Chapter 4. Better educational qualifications reduce the risks of unemployment, since they provide access to higher-skilled and more secure employment. In contrast, unskilled work, which is predominantly all that is left for people with low qualifications, is much more precarious and brings higher risks of unemployment.[25] If men continue to lag behind women in educational qualifications, the likelihood is that they will also continue to lag behind in their chances of finding work in the contemporary service economy.

EDUCATIONAL INEQUALITIES

Higher qualifications give access to better jobs, not just ones with higher earnings but also ones with greater job security and more favourable contractual

Figure 6.3. Men and women with higher qualifications have lower risks of unemployment, with little change over time in Great Britain in their relative risks

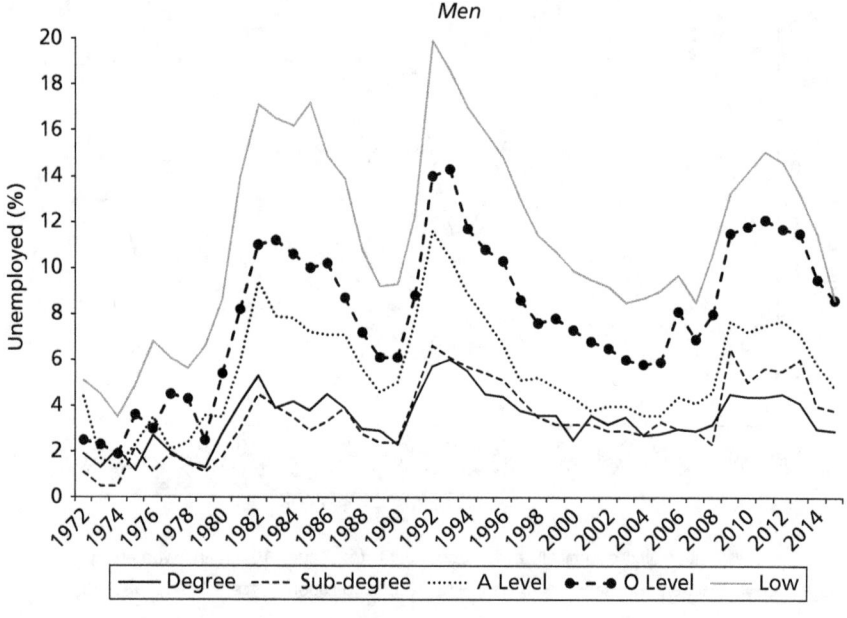

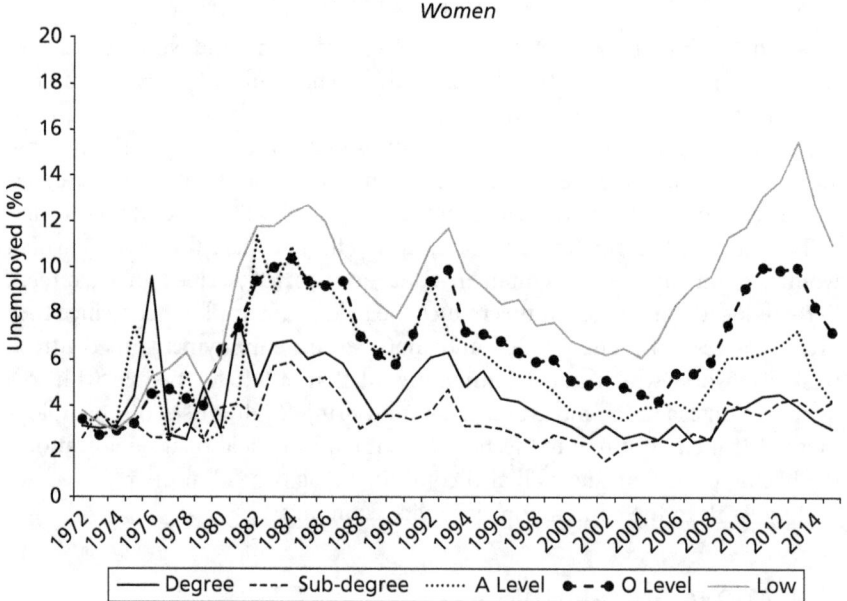

Source: pooled General Household Surveys (1972–2005) and Labour Force Surveys (1983–2015)

conditions (such as the period of notice required) and employment rights. The reason for this is that highly skilled workers are more valuable to firms, and are not so easy to replace, so firms have a greater incentive to keep them on when times become hard. The importance of educational level for risks of unemployment can clearly be seen in Figure 6.3.

Figure 6.3 shows clearly that, throughout the period covered by the data sources, the higher one's level of education, the lower one's risk of unemployment. Among both men and women graduates in 2015 the risk of unemployment was around 3 per cent, rather similar to the risk facing graduates back in the 1970s. The risks then increase steadily as one descends the educational ladder, reaching 10 per cent or more for people with no or low qualifications (that is, qualifications lower than GCSE or its equivalent).

Moreover, the vulnerability of people with low or no qualifications increases markedly during a recession. The gaps narrow when there is high demand for labour but then widen when there is a slack labour market at the height of the recession. As Figure 6.3 shows, the risks facing men with no or low qualifications were particularly large in the recessions of the early 1980s and early 1990s.

Leaving the recessions aside, has there been a long-term increase in the vulnerability of people with low qualifications? This is not an entirely straightforward question to answer, but if we compare the non-recession years of 1978, 1989, 2001, and 2015, it is hard to discern any clear long-term trends. Thus, in 1978 the gap between the best- and least-educated men was 4.1 points; in 1989 the gap was rather higher at 6.3 points; however, in 2001 the gap dropped slightly to 5.9 points; and in 2015 the gap was 5.7 points. I think it is safest to conclude that there was no discernible trend over time, at least as regards male unemployment.[26] In the case of women, the gap was considerably larger in 2015 than it had been earlier, so perhaps less-qualified women did become more vulnerable.

AGE DIFFERENTIALS

A major concern nowadays is that young people may be particularly at risk of failing to find a job and that, in Beveridge's words, 'failure to find any use for adaptable youth' has become once again one of the worst blots on Britain's record. As I remarked earlier, young people in the 1950s could leave school at the earliest opportunity, with no qualifications to their name, and could still expect to get reasonable jobs in manufacturing industry. So there is a major question as to whether the giant of Idleness has come to pick on young people, especially young men, much more than he did in the past. This is surely a fundamental social problem because of the long-term scarring effects which unemployment can have, as well as its social and psychological ramifications.

Figure 6.4 shows that young people have elevated risks of unemployment compared with older workers. Thus, among men in 2015, those aged 16–24 had almost five times the risk of unemployment as those faced by men aged 36 to 50 in mid-career. Risks of unemployment facing men or women aged 25 to 35 tend to be quite close to the risks facing older workers, so it is the young who stand out. Moreover, these age differentials are distinctly larger than the educational differentials shown in Figure 6.3.

Just as with the educational differentials, the differentials between older and younger workers tend to become larger during recessions, when young people are particularly hard hit, just as the less qualified were. However, if we compare non-recession years, it does look as though young men have become increasingly vulnerable to unemployment. In the four non-recession years of 1978, 1989, 2001, and 2015, the unemployment risks of men in mid-career remained more or less constant, but for young men they rose steadily from 8.4 per cent in 1978 to 11.2 per cent in 1989, 13.7 per cent in 2001, and 15.1 per cent in 2015. So it really does look as though the employment situation deteriorated for young men. The trend is not quite so dramatic for young women, but it too suggests that the relative vulnerability of young women deteriorated somewhat.

Perhaps even more importantly, the age and educational differentials are cumulative. For example, the risks of unemployment in 2015 were almost 9 per cent for men with qualifications below GCSE, and they were around 15 per cent for young men aged 16–24. But among men who had the misfortune to be both young *and* to have low or no qualifications, the risks rise to over 24 per cent—fifteen times the risk faced by a middle-aged male graduate (a mere 1.5 per cent in 2015). This is social inequality of a pretty extreme kind—and one that may have even more serious consequences than the purely monetary inequalities which we saw in Chapter 2.

In Figure 6.5 I restrict the analysis to people with no or low qualifications. What we can clearly see is that the age differences were distinctly greater in the last decade of the twentieth century and the first decades of the twenty-first century than they had been in the 1970s or the non-recession years in-between. If we compare the non-recession years of 1978, 1989, 2001, and 2015, we find that at the two earlier time points the difference in the unemployment risks facing younger men with no or low qualifications were ten points greater than those facing older workers with similarly low levels of education. In contrast, at the two later time points the gaps had risen to eighteen points. The picture is not quite so clear for women (as there was a rather large gap in 1978), but in 2015 the gap had reached twenty points. I think it is safe to conclude that there had been a real deterioration over time in the labour market position of younger people with low or no qualifications to their name.

Figure 6.4. Young people under 25 have higher risks of unemployment than do older people, and the differential has been increasing over time among men in Great Britain

Source: pooled General Household Surveys (1972–2005) and Labour Force Surveys (1983–2015)

Figure 6.5. Young people with low or no qualifications have greatly elevated risks of unemployment, and the differentials increased in Great Britain

Note: analysis restricted to those with no or low (below GCSE level) qualifications
Source: pooled General Household Surveys (1972–2005) and Labour Force Surveys (1983–2015)

It is not entirely clear what has driven this change but it does coincide with the great expansion in the 1990s of younger people achieving GCSE qualifications (Figure 4.4). This is consistent with the concerns that I raised earlier about the dark side of educational expansion: as more and more young people obtain qualifications, the competitive position of young people who lack qualifications becomes weaker, and their risks of unemployment become relatively worse.

To be sure, we need to recognize that the kinds of young people who lack qualifications may be rather different in the twenty-first century from what they would have been in the 1970s or earlier, when it was still common for young people to enter the labour market with no qualifications. In the twenty-first century this is much less common and the minority without qualifications may perhaps be unusual in having learning or behavioural difficulties, histories of school exclusion, or other problems which hold them back.[27] These problems in turn may reduce their chances of finding work. But all the same, lack of formal qualifications will make these young people more visible to employers in the twenty-first century, and thus perhaps make it easier for employers to reject them as unsuitable for work. In earlier days, such young people would not have been so visible—it might have been easier for them to escape unnoticed. In the twenty-first century they are much more likely to be screened out by employers.

ETHNIC DIFFERENCES

Ethnic minorities are another group of people who are vulnerable to unemployment. True, there are substantial differences between differing minority groups in their risks of unemployment, in part reflecting their different levels of education. People with Black Caribbean, Black African, and Bangladeshi or Pakistani origins have the highest risks, while Chinese and Indians have lower risks. Indeed, the risks facing the latter two groups are fairly similar to those of the white British. The question which I want to address next is whether these Black and Muslim groups have the same, better, or worse risks of unemployment compared with their white peers with similar levels of education. Do young Black men with low qualifications bear an additional burden over and above the risks that young white men experience in Britain? Do they suffer a triple rather than the double burden faced by young white men with low qualifications?

In Figure 6.6 I focus on the unemployment rates of young people (aged 16–24) with low or no qualifications so that we can roughly compare results with those shown in Figure 6.5. Because the sample sizes become rather small when one limits the analysis in this way, I combine Black Caribbeans with Black Africans to form a Black group, Pakistanis with Bangladeshis to form a predominantly Muslim group, and Indians with Chinese to form an Asian

Figure 6.6. Young Black men and women with low qualifications are even more at risk of unemployment than their white peers, especially during recessions

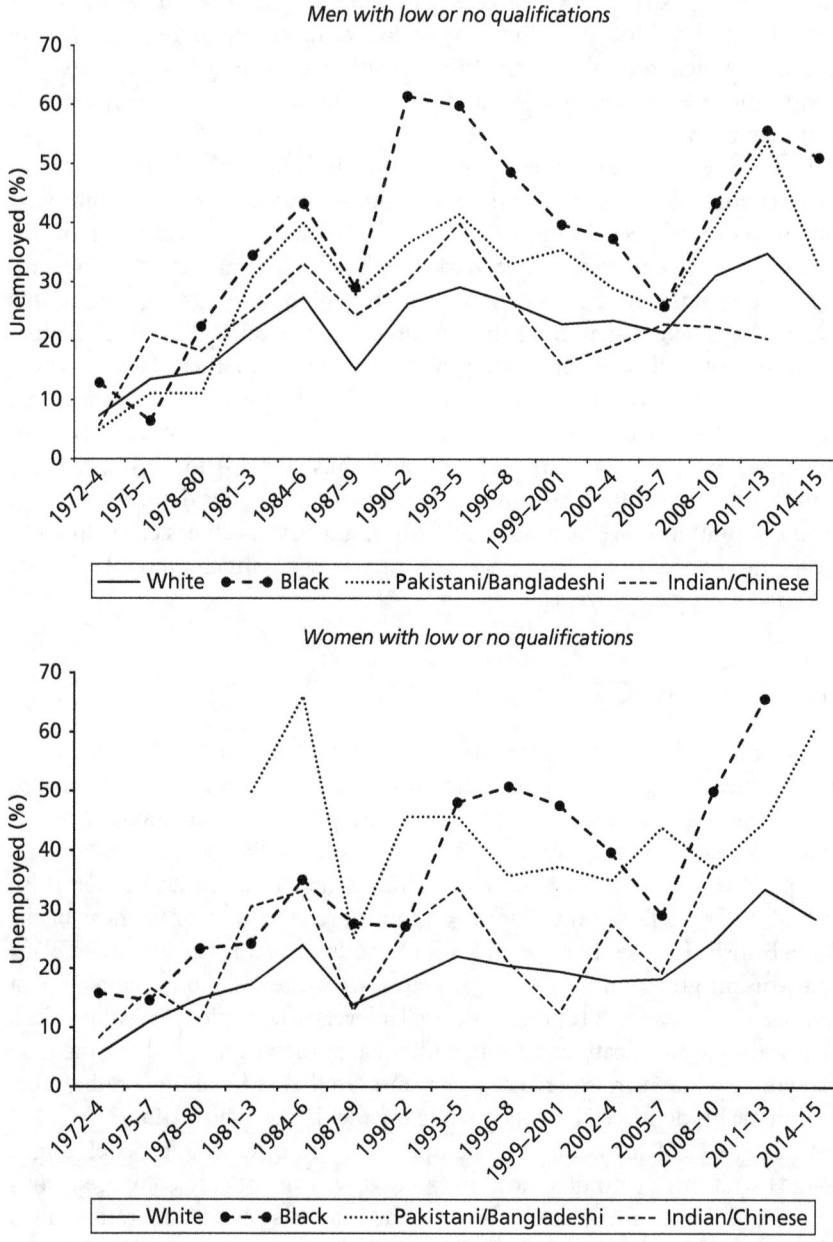

Note: analysis restricted to those with no or low (below GCSE level) qualifications and aged 16–24
Source: pooled General Household Surveys (1972–2005) and Labour Force Surveys (1983–2015)

group. I compare these three groups with the white members of the samples. I also combine three adjacent years in order to increase sample sizes and improve the reliability of the estimates. (Even with these measures taken, some cases still have rather small sample sizes and therefore in the two graphs for men and women, results are omitted if the number of people in the sample in the relevant year and ethnic group is less than ten.)

The results are a bit patchy because of the small sample sizes, but the overall picture is clear enough. What we find is that, at least in the most recent decades, there is indeed an accumulation of disadvantage affecting both the Black and the Muslim groups. In 2014/15, for example, young Black men with no or low qualifications had a 50 per cent risk of unemployment, almost double that of young white men with similar qualification levels. We can therefore speak of a treble burden which these young, less-qualified, Black or Muslim men have to carry. Young Black and Muslim women also experience this treble burden.

This accumulation of disadvantage is particularly apparent during recessions, and tends to reduce when overall unemployment rates fall (as for example in 2005–7). This strongly suggests that these groups are the most marginalized in the labour market—I suspect that they are the last to be hired and the first to be fired. As we will see in Chapter 7, racial discrimination is almost certainly a part of the explanation for this third burden.

Broadening the Measure: Discouraged Workers

The statistics on unemployment which I have reported so far in this chapter adhere to the strict definition of the unemployed as people who want to work, are available for work, and are actively seeking work. While this kind of unambiguous definition makes very good sense when attempting to make comparisons between countries or over time, it is a bit too narrow if we want to take seriously Beveridge's approach to the giant of Idleness.

The key problem with the official definition is that long periods of unemployment or lack of suitable jobs may demoralize out-of-work people. They may give up hope of finding a job—and this would not be irrational. The longer someone is out of work, the poorer their chances are of finding a job since they will have fallen behind their in-work peers in gaining skills and work experience. Employers may also question the hole in their CV. So older workers may take early retirement while young people may withdraw and look for an alternative future on the streets or in the black economy.

One specific problem, which has been widely recognized in official circles, is that of young people who are neither in education, employment, nor training. Again, there has been substantial research showing the damaging effects of being NEET on people's futures—it has been shown to lead to educational underachievement, higher risks of unemployment, a greater susceptibility to engage in crime, poor health, and feelings that life has no purpose. Low-skilled youth who become NEET find it more difficult to re-engage in employment and there is evidence that they may become trapped, leading to long-term scarring with major social and economic costs.[28]

The concept of NEET goes wider than the strict definition of unemployment, since it covers young people who maybe do not want to work, or who are not actively looking for work, in addition to those who fulfil the strict definition. In other words, it is a broader measure than unemployment in the strict sense defined by the International Labour Office. Basically, it includes all young people who are neither in work nor in some form of education or vocational training. However, it does include young people who have dependent children or other caring duties. The measure is implicitly based on the assumption that it is normal for young people to be either in education, training, or work rather than looking after the home. With the gradually rising age at which women have their first baby, this is perhaps not a silly assumption, but we do need to interpret the measure with some caution.

Another complication to be aware of when we attempt to measure the proportion who are NEET is that standard official measures (such as those used by government or the OECD) look at the proportion of the whole age group who are NEET, whereas official figures for unemployment exclude those members of the age group who are either in education or who are not looking for work. This means that we cannot directly compare NEET and unemployment figures. To make it a bit clearer what is going on, therefore, I present the figures in a different way from the usual official one. In Figure 6.7, I distinguish four categories:

(1) those still in education or training;
(2) those in work;
(3) those unemployed on the basis of the strict definition; and
(4) the remainder who do not fit into any of the first three categories (termed economically inactive in government statistics).

The latter two categories are basically the ones that make up young people who are NEET. I cumulate these four categories so that they sum up to 100 per cent, with separate charts for young men and young women.[29]

As with Figure 6.6, I combine adjacent years in order to deal with the problem of small numbers in the samples on which the results are based. As before, there will be considerable sampling error, but the broad outlines of the story are clear enough. Over the period for which we have the survey data, the proportion of young people in some form of education or training markedly increased in the 1990s, which of course is what I reported in Chapter 4. Conversely, the proportion in employment steadily fell over time, down from 58 per cent in the early 1970s to around 40 per cent in 2014/15 among young men.

What about NEET? The unemployment element of NEET naturally parallels what we saw in Figure 6.4 with peaks in the recession years of the early 1980s, early 1990s, and after the financial crash of 2007/8. However, among young men, we can also see a gradual increase in the proportions who are inactive—that is, who are neither in education or employment nor looking for work. The proportion increases from around 2 per cent at the beginning of the period to nearly 6 per cent at the end of the period (equivalent to about 50,000 young men). We cannot be sure that these are all discouraged young people. Some, for example, may be young people from affluent backgrounds who are taking gap years between school and university—although if they have gone abroad for their gap year they should not show up in the samples anyway. The data are not conclusive but they do suggest that there is a growing potential issue of young men with nothing to do.

The long-term story for young women is rather different. As we can see, much larger proportions of young women in the 1970s and 1980s were neither in education, work, nor looking for work. Almost certainly this reflects the earlier age at which women had their first child in the earlier decades. Consider, for example, women born in 1952 and who would therefore have been young adults in the first (1972–4) round of data in Figure 6.7. Twenty per cent of these young women had had their first child by their twentieth birthday, and would therefore have been rather unlikely to be studying or looking for work. In contrast, among women born in 1995, and thus becoming young adults in the final round of data, only 7 per cent had had their first child by their twentieth birthday.[30] What this in effect means is that there has been a convergence between young men and women in their rates of being NEET.

The Office for National Statistics has published its own statistics on trends in NEET, although only since 2002.[31] Their detailed figures are very similar to mine for the same period, showing that NEET peaked in 2012 and has since been declining. As in Figure 6.7, the decline since 2012 largely reflects the decline in the unemployment rate, although at some point I would expect to see an additional reduction as a result of the raising of the age (in England) during which young people have to undertake some kind of training.

As one might expect, young people with no qualifications are disproportionately likely to be NEET. Pregnancy and parenthood are also unsurprisingly associated with being outside education and the labour market.[32] An even greater risk of being NEET, however, is found among those with a disability (defined as current physical or mental health conditions which reduce one's ability to carry out day-to-day activities). Young people who have been excluded or suspended from school are more likely to be NEET, as are those who have been under supervision by a youth offending team and

Figure 6.7. The proportion of 16–24-year-old men who are neither in education, work, nor looking for work has been increasing; among 16–24-year-old women it has been decreasing

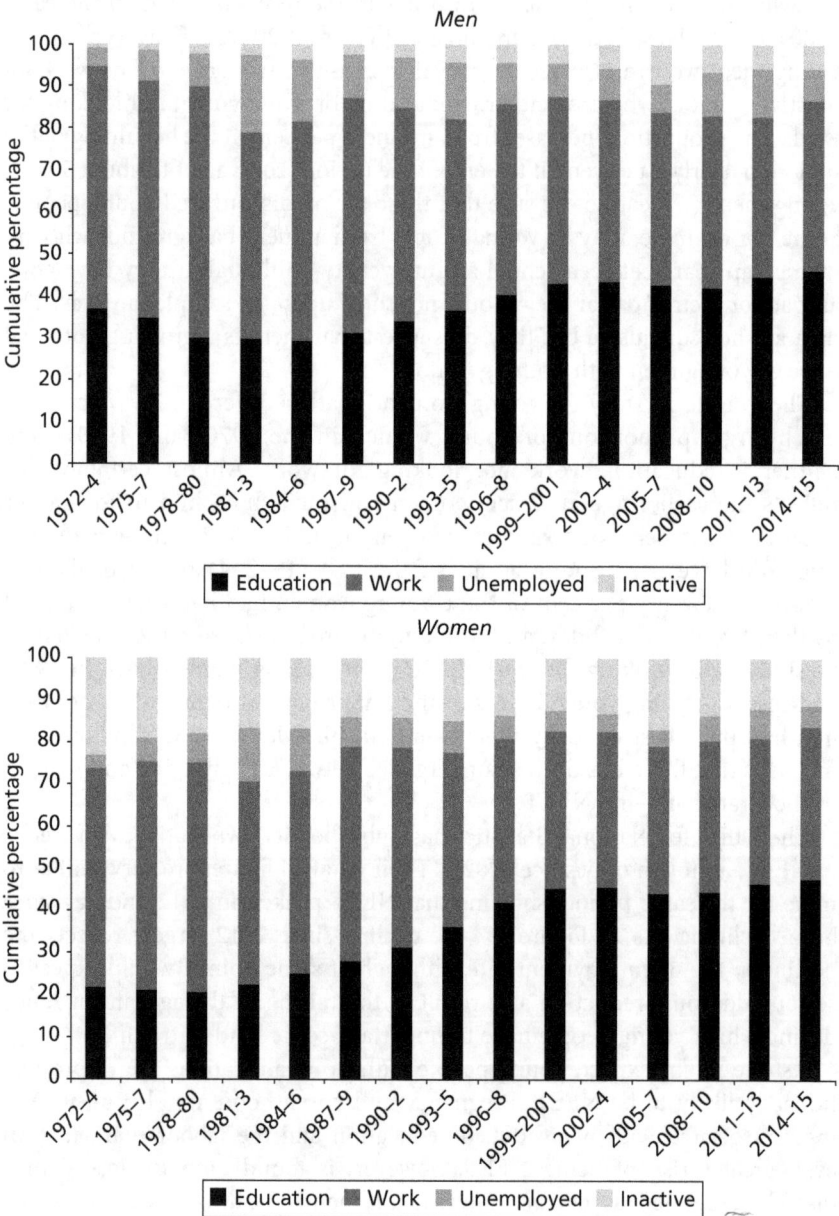

Source: pooled General Household Surveys (1972–2005) and Labour Force Surveys (1983–2015)[33]

those who have been in care. A trenchant report by the National Audit Office concluded:

> The poor life experiences of too many care leavers are a longstanding problem. Without well-targeted support their deep needs will not be met, with costly consequences both for the young people and for society. While there is a clear legal framework and an inspection regime in place, the system is not working effectively to deliver good outcomes for all care leavers. On the key measure of numbers in employment, education and training the situation has deteriorated since 2007–08.[34]

Disability, school exclusion, offending, low qualifications, experience of the care system—this is a litany of the most marginalized and vulnerable young people in British society. International comparisons also suggest that marginalization in the form of being NEET is a particular problem in Britain. Among young people under 20, Britain compares particularly unfavourably. Only Italy has a worse record. Germany in contrast has a rate of NEET less than a third of the British rate.

In Figure 6.8 I show the trends since the turn of the millennium in the proportion of young people (men and women combined) who were NEET in the eight peer countries. Italy stands out as having the poorest record—which

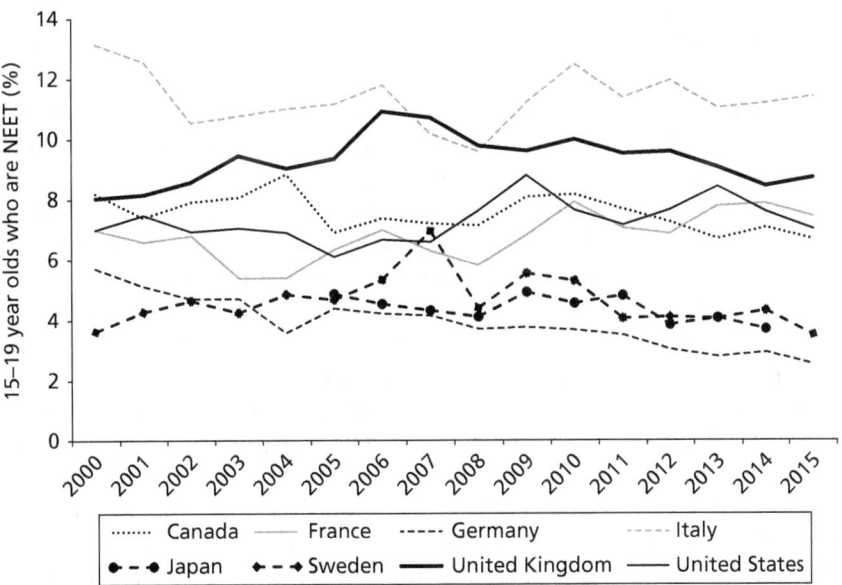

Figure 6.8. The UK had one of the highest rates of NEET among young people under 20 in the twenty-first century

Note: data for 15–19-year-old men and women

Source: OECD, 'Youth not in employment, education or training (NEET)' (2017), https://data.oecd.org/youthinac/youth-not-in-employment-education-or-training-neet.htm

echoes the high overall unemployment rate in Italy reported at the beginning of the chapter in Figure 6.1. In contrast, Germany, Sweden, and Japan have consistently had levels well below the British. Even France, with its relatively high overall unemployment rate, fares slightly better than Britain.

We can also see that most countries have experienced declining rates of NEET since 2010. British government interpretations have tended to credit the decline in Britain to the success of the government's training policies, in particular to the legislation increasing participation in education or training to ages 17 and then to 18. Figure 6.8 should, however, make one a little sceptical of this optimistic interpretation. Since rates of NEET declined in most countries, it is more likely that the explanation lies in common factors—such as the generally declining overall rate of unemployment—than to specific policy initiatives in Britain.

This is not to say that the English reforms had no value—almost certainly they were a step in the right direction. But I suspect that they will not be sufficient on their own to bring British rates of NEET down to German or Japanese levels. This brings me to an important paradox. Whereas overall British unemployment rates compare rather favourably with those in peer countries (as Figure 6.1 showed), youth unemployment and participation compares rather unfavourably.

Conclusions

Has youth unemployment once again become one of the worst blots on the record of contemporary governments? Certainly, unemployment is very bad news for those affected—especially for young people—and for the wider society. It has wide adverse consequences for well-being over and above its purely financial implications. I am sure Beveridge was right to treat it as a giant evil in its own right and to draw attention to the particular plight of young people.

In the 1970s, and probably throughout the 1950s and 1960s, too, Britain tended to have a lower overall unemployment rate than its peer countries. This changed in the 1980s and 1990s, when Britain's unemployment rate surged during the two recessions and became consistently higher than in the peer countries. However, more recently, since 2001, Britain's unemployment rate has once again become relatively low.

The theory that greater flexibility of the labour market produces a lower unemployment rate receives scant support from detailed econometric analysis. Certainly the total package of reforms which Margaret Thatcher's administrations undertook after 1979 was associated with higher, not lower, unemployment. My interpretation (and I suspect that of professional economists such as David Blanchflower) is that the focus on controlling the evil of inflation (and the associated high interest rates) in the 1980s reduced demand for labour. As the period of high interest rates came to an end, so demand recovered and unemployment fell. The policies of the European Central Bank failed to respond as effectively, and so Eurozone demand remained lower and unemployment rates in a number of European countries remained higher than in Britain.

Despite the fact that overall British unemployment rates fell, the evidence available suggests that inequalities in the risks of unemployment tended to become larger, not smaller. True, there have long been differences in who is most at risk of unemployment. A long-standing feature of most advanced economies is that the young, those with less education, and migrants or the native-born descendants of migrants have higher risks of unemployment. These groups also appear to be harder hit whenever there is a recession (as in the early 1980s, early 1990s, and after the financial crash).

These inequalities in the risks of unemployment have remained, and indeed the relative position of young men with low qualifications seems to have deteriorated after 1990. Moreover, young British men appear to be particularly at a disadvantage compared with their contemporaries in Germany, Sweden, Canada, and the USA.

I suggested earlier that this might represent the dark side of educational expansion. Many sociologists have suggested that the educational system is a kind of sorting and labelling mechanism, dividing people into the educational equivalents of sheep and goats. Moreover, this sorting and labelling takes an earlier and more visible form in Britain, with high-stakes examinations (GCSEs to be precise) taken at ages 15 or 16. For example, in countries like the USA and Canada large proportions of the age group go on to complete high school and receive their diplomas at the age of 18. In contrast, in Germany, sorting and labelling take place much earlier (around age 11 as it used to do during the tripartite system in Britain), but there is a much closer articulation between school and work with German vocational programmes having real value in the labour market.

Britain manages to fall between these two stools. After 1965 it largely moved away from the German-style selective system towards a US-style comprehensive system, but at the same time Britain retained high-stakes examinations like GCSEs from the previous system and failed to embrace the high-participation and completion rates of the US and Canadian systems. My interpretation, then, following the conclusions of Alison Wolf's influential report, is that the British system leaves many less able young people with fairly worthless qualifications. 'The staple offer for between a quarter and a third of the post-16 cohort is a diet of low-level vocational qualifications, most of which have little to no labour market value.'[35] The government has put in place reforms implementing Alison Wolf's recommendations, but it is too early to determine whether they have been sufficient to close the gap with peer countries.

Given the long-term scarring effects of unemployment, and the wider social repercussions of having large numbers of young men without work, this represents a kind of time bomb ticking away at the heart of British society—and not one for which we can put the blame on foreign extremists. It is one of our own making. To paraphrase Beveridge, failure to find any use for adaptable youth is one of the worst blots on Britain's record in the twenty-first century.

7 The Challenge of Inequality of Opportunity

Class, Gender, and Ethnic Inequalities

with Yaojun Li and Lindsay Richards

Introduction

> These are volatile and uncertain times. When more and more people feel like they are losing out, social mobility matters more than ever before. Higher social mobility can be a rallying point to prove that modern capitalist economies like our own are capable of creating better, fairer and more inclusive societies... The policies of the past have brought some progress, but many are no longer fit for purpose in our changing world. The old agenda has not delivered enough social progress. New approaches are needed if Britain is to become a fairer and more equal country. It is time for a change.

This is what Alan Milburn, the former chair of the Social Mobility Commission wrote in his foreword to the commission's report, *Time for Change: An Assessment of Government Policies on Social Mobility 1997-2017.*[1] In this chapter, I shall try to answer the question whether Britain has become a fairer and more inclusive society.

Beveridge himself did not include unfairness in his list of giants. Unfairness is also left out by contemporary treatments of social progress such as those of the Commission on the Measurement of Economic Performance and Social Progress, and by the OECD in its 'Better Life' index.[2] So let me explain why issues of fairness should be included in a book on social progress.

Alan Milburn's conception of fairness is fundamentally based on the notion of equality of opportunity—that chances for obtaining the good things in life should be equally open to all, irrespective of their gender, social background, race, or religion. This is essentially a moral notion, although one that is widely accepted in contemporary democracies. Indeed, some aspects are enshrined in law. The 2010 Equality Act, for example, prohibits discrimination (a clear infringement of the principle of equality of opportunity) on the grounds of race, gender, and a number of other 'protected characteristics'. Article 2 of the United Nations Universal Declaration of Human Rights also specifies, 'Everyone is entitled to all the rights and freedoms set forth in this Declaration, without distinction of any kind, such as race, colour, sex, language, religion, political or other opinion, national or social origin, property, birth or other status.' Progress in eliminating discrimination on these grounds is surely a legitimate criterion for assessing social progress more generally.

As well as moral objections to discrimination and inequality of opportunity, there are also practical reasons for preferring a non-discriminatory society to a discriminatory one. In essence discrimination, and inequality of opportunity more generally, are inefficient. For example, during the eighteenth and first half of the nineteenth century, it was standard practice in Britain for people from privileged backgrounds to buy commissions in the army. The practice was abolished in 1871 after an enquiry into the failings exposed during the Crimean War, which had involved such follies as the Charge of the Light Brigade.[3] The motivation was the hard-headed one to be able to compete militarily on an equal footing with our enemies rather than any moralistic concern for fairness. (The need for reform was perhaps given added impetus by the victories over Austria and France of the professional Prussian army which Bismarck had just created.) Discrimination implies the preferential treatment of less competent people from favoured backgrounds over more competent people from disfavoured backgrounds. It is therefore likely to hold an army, a business, or a country back.

Alan Milburn implicitly provides another reason for preferring a fair society over an unfair one when he raises concerns about people feeling that they are losing out. Grievances about unfair treatment are likely to reduce the legitimacy of social arrangements and of the political order. The subtext of his argument is that the increasing income inequality which Britain has experienced may undermine public confidence if there is a lack of opportunity for ordinary people to improve their own standards of living. In somewhat similar vein, I would argue that the Troubles in Northern Ireland were in part a response to the unfair treatment of the Catholic population under the Stormont regime. Social research has also suggested that unfair treatment of minorities by the police lay at the heart of the London riots of 2011 and of earlier riots such as those in Brixton in 1985.[4] Unequal treatment of minorities, therefore, can have potential implications for social order and in turn for the wider public. The experience of discrimination also has highly negative consequences for the well-being and mental health of those directly affected.[5] In this sense discrimination is directly analogous to the other deprivations on which Beveridge focussed. To the evils of Want, Disease, Ignorance, Squalor, and Idleness, I therefore wish to add the evil of Discrimination.

The 2010 Equality Act established a longlist of 'protected characteristics', namely age, disability, gender reassignment, marriage and civil partnership, pregnancy and maternity, race, religion and belief, sex, and sexual orientation.[6] A full treatment would look at all of these. Unfortunately, we do not have good data, certainly not running back over several decades, on most of them. I will therefore restrict attention in this chapter to gender, social class, and ethnic background. This is a purely pragmatic decision. It is not that I believe these to be more important in a practical or moral sense. But we really do not have good enough data on the other protected characteristics.

Some eyebrows may be raised at my inclusion of social class, which is not actually on the Equality Act's list of protected characteristics. While there is little direct evidence of discrimination against people from lower social class backgrounds, there is considerable evidence of substantial social class inequalities of opportunity. These inequalities of opportunity have been a major focus both of public concern and of government intervention. Indeed, they are at the heart of the Social Mobility Commission's work. They need to be included in any treatment of inequality of opportunity in contemporary Britain.

In the remainder of this chapter, therefore, I shall concentrate on discrimination and inequality of opportunity on the basis of social class background, ethnic background, and gender. First, however, I need to make a brief digression to explain how I define and measure discrimination and inequality of opportunity.

Some Definitional and Practical Issues

Terms like fairness and equality of opportunity are notoriously slippery. I find it helpful to distinguish between two rather different conceptions of equality of opportunity—the non-discrimination principle and the level playing field principle.

The non-discrimination principle is similar in spirit to the approach embodied in the 2010 Equality Act and the United Nations Universal Declaration of Human Rights. It holds that individuals, when being selected for a public position, should be judged solely on the basis of attributes which are relevant to performance of the position in question, and not with respect to other irrelevant criteria such as their race or gender.[7]

The non-discrimination principle is a good starting point, but it could be argued that it does not go far enough. It ignores the possibility that *prior* barriers might have prevented people from acquiring the attributes relevant for performance of the position in question.

Hence, a second and broader principle of equality of opportunity has been proposed. Economist John Roemer explains the principle as follows: 'society should do what it can to "level the playing field" among individuals who compete for positions... so that all those with relevant potential will eventually be admissible to pools of candidates competing for positions'.[8] This second conception broadens the concept by replacing the criterion of actually having the relevant attributes to having the *potential* to acquire them. By including those with potential, even if they have not had the chance to translate this potential into acquisition of the relevant qualifications and experience, we broaden considerably the reach of the concept of inequality of opportunity.

There are three main methods for measuring the extent to which these principles are satisfied in practice. First, one can use real-world field experiments to test whether the non-discrimination principle is adhered to. Field experiments are a bit like mystery shopping exercises, or restaurant reviews, where an investigator goes to a shop or restaurant incognito to see what the food or service is like. In the field experiments of discrimination, what the investigators do is to send matched applications from fictitious applicants to actual, real-life job vacancies. The applications of the two fictitious applicants indicate that they have identical work-relevant skills and experience, but the names will differ in order to indicate that the applicants come from different backgrounds. In the case of field experiments of racial discrimination, one of the applicants will have a standard British name such as Andrew Clarke while the other applicant will have a recognizably ethnic minority name such as Muhammed Kahlid or Sukjunder Singh. A large number of these paired applications will be sent out to a selection of randomly chosen vacancies and the researchers then see whether the applicants are treated equally. For example, are they equally likely to be invited for interview? Unequal treatment yields pretty conclusive evidence that the non-discrimination principle is not upheld in practice.

Britain was actually a pioneer in the use of field experiments for this purpose and has a remarkable series of field experiments testing for racial discrimination, going back to 1967. There are also similar studies in most of our peer countries. Unfortunately, however, equivalent studies investigating discrimination on the grounds of social class or gender are few and far between. I shall therefore use an alternative method which follows the same logic as the field experiment but relies on statistical analysis of survey evidence in order to carry out the matching. One of the earliest examples of this approach was a classic study by J. L. Gray and Pearl Moshinsky in 1935. They were interested in the extent of social class inequality of opportunity in gaining entry to schools such as grammar schools which prepared children for university entry. A particular concern of theirs, as of many post-war scholars and reformers, was the wastage of talent occurring when able boys and girls from less privileged homes who were unable to move on to higher education. This echoes the efficiency argument which I mentioned earlier.

The key attribute relevant for grammar school and university education was held at the time to be one's cognitive ability. Gray and Moshinsky therefore conducted a survey of young people attending schools in London and measured their social class backgrounds and cognitive ability (using the IQ tests which had recently been developed). They then compared the chances of getting into grammar school of young people who all had IQ scores of 130 or over (well above the minimum threshold for gaining entry) but who came from different social class backgrounds. What they found was that nearly all the children from professional and managerial backgrounds with these high IQs had the opportunity of higher education.[9] In contrast, only one fifth of high-ability children of unskilled wage earners had this opportunity.

As Gray and Moshinsky themselves pointed out, this gap might well be an underestimate of the full extent of inequality of opportunity: 'The inferior mean ability of the less prosperous social classes may itself arise partly from their [prior] environmental disadvantages.'[10] For example, back in the days of the 11-plus examination for entry to grammar school, many ambitious parents (like my own) would pay for private primary schooling in order to coach children for passing the exam. Children with potential for university education might therefore have missed out because their parents could not afford private primary education. The playing field did not appear to be a level one in my day.

Testing the level playing field principle is, however, rather difficult, as it is not at all clear how to measure potential. Instead, writers sympathetic to this principle tend to investigate whether there are social class, ethnic, or gender differences in gaining access to grammar schools, universities, jobs, or income. This method answers the question: do people who grow up in privileged homes have disproportionate access to privileged positions themselves? Sociologists typically interpret this kind of measure as indicating how open or closed the society is.[11] The smaller the social class differences in mobility chances, the more open the society is. Whereas the field experiments almost certainly underestimate the true extent of inequality of opportunity, this method will err in the opposite direction and tend to overestimate it. It is probably best to think of these methods as giving the upper and lower bounds.

I will start with the first method and will report the results of field experiments investigating the extent of racial discrimination in employment. I will then turn to the gender pay gap and to social class inequalities in gaining access to the advantaged occupational positions of the salariat. For these investigations I will be using survey-based methods. I will conclude by comparing Britain with peer countries with respect to racial discrimination, the gender pay gap, and social class inequalities.

Has Racial Discrimination Declined?

Racial and ethnic discrimination has been a major focus of government legislation and intervention. The 1965 Race Relations Act prohibited racial discrimination in public places. This was followed by the 1968 Race Relations Act which made it illegal to refuse housing, employment, or public services to a person on grounds of race, and the landmark 1976 Race Relations Act which prohibited both direct and indirect discrimination on the grounds of 'race, colour, nationality, ethnic and national origin' in employment and other functions. One might have hoped that this legislation would have reduced the risk of discrimination, and it is certainly true that Britain's ethnic minorities have made substantial progress in getting to university and entering the professions. But has this progress been a result of improved treatment of minorities, or does it rather reflect the efforts which minorities themselves have made to gain qualifications and succeed in British society? Britain's long history of field experiments enables us to answer this question.

Before reviewing the results of the field experiments, however, I should say a brief word about terminology. While the Acts all refer to race, few if any social scientists nowadays accept that there is any scientific basis to the concept of race. Social scientists prefer to talk about ethnic groups.[12] In Britain recent censuses have distinguished a number of distinct ethnic groups, the largest of which consist of people with Irish, Indian, Pakistani, Black Caribbean, Black African, Bangladeshi, and Chinese origins. The field experiments have basically followed the latter, ethnic approach and have compared the treatment accorded to members of different ethnic groups as identified by their or their parents' national origins.

The key measure of discrimination obtained from field experiments is the ratio of positive responses received by the white British applicant in comparison with the ethnic minority applicant. A situation of equal treatment is one where the ratio is 1:1—the two applicants are equally likely to receive a positive callback. In contrast a ratio of 2:1 indicates unequal treatment: white applicants receive twice as many positive callbacks as the ethnic minority applicant. To put this another way, a ratio of 2:1 indicates that the ethnic minority applicant has to make twice as many applications as the white applicant in order to get a positive response.

In Figure 7.1 I show the results from the main field experiments which have been carried out in Britain between 1969 and 2017.[13] The experiments differ somewhat in their precise methodology, the jobs applied for, and the state of the labour market at the time. (It is likely, for example, that discrimination will be reduced when there is a very tight labour market but will be greater when there are lots of applicants chasing a small number of jobs.) However, the studies are generally similar in focussing on young people with British citizenship, who speak and write fluent English, and who were either born in Britain or received their secondary education in Britain. The applicants are typically early in their career, and applying for middle-level positions such as office workers rather than for very senior positions or for unskilled work.

So what conclusions can we safely draw? The first panel of Figure 7.1 shows that none of the studies which included white minorities—Irish, Australian, French, Italian—found much evidence for discrimination. In all cases the ratios are close to 1:1, and are generally not statistically significant. This appears to have been as true in 1969 as in the most recent 2016/17 study.

Figure 7.1. White minorities experience little discrimination in Britain, but Black and Asian minorities continue to experience similar levels of discrimination as in the past

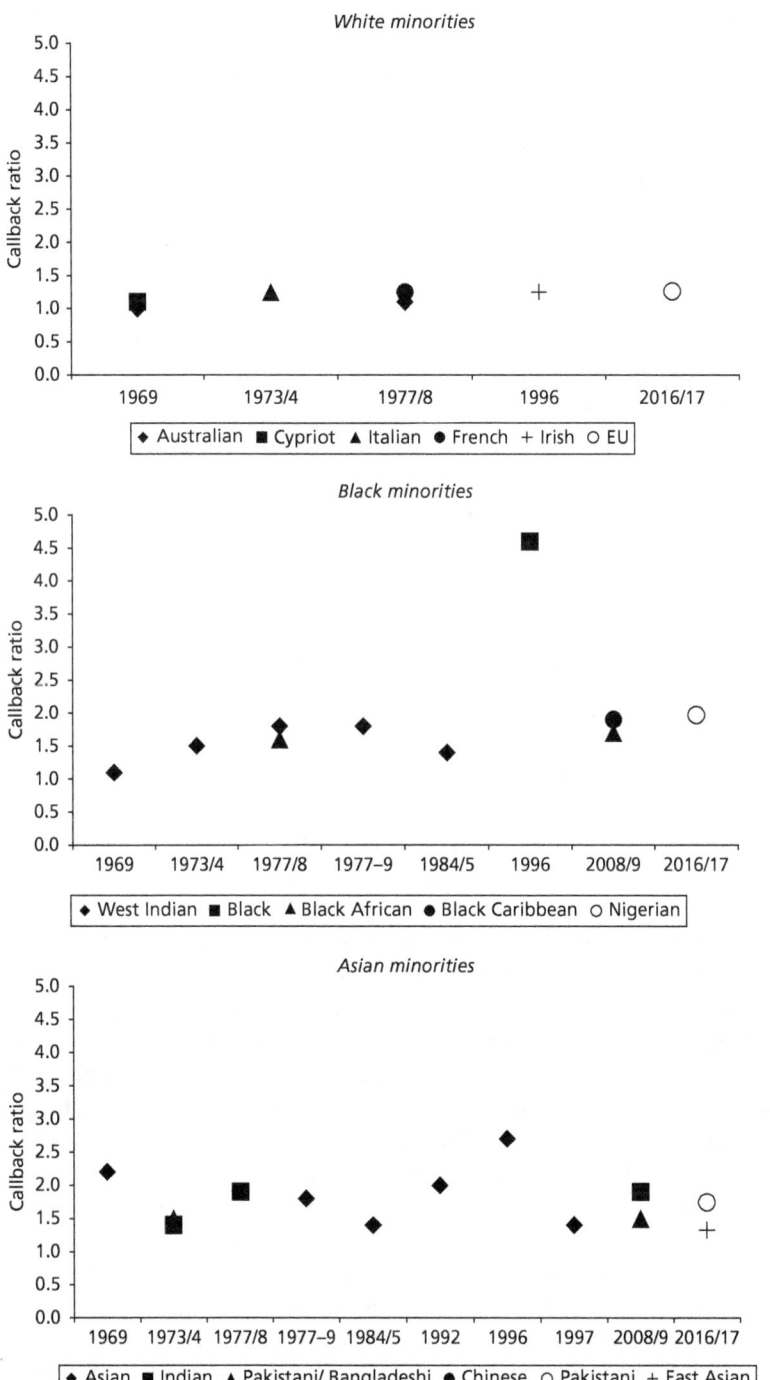

Source: based on results of field experiments conducted in 1969, 1973/4, 1977/8, 1977/9, 1984/5, 1992, 1996, 1997, 2008/9, and 2016/7[14]

In contrast, the second panel suggests that applicants with an Asian background—Indian, Pakistani, or Chinese—experienced significant discrimination throughout with ratios ranging from 1.4:1 to 2.6:1. Interestingly, there does not seem to be any consistent difference in the discrimination experienced by applicants of Chinese, Indian, or Pakistani background. My guess is that employers cannot readily distinguish between Indian and Pakistani names, and that this may account for the similarity of the results. A recent German study which was able to include photographs with the letters of application found much greater discrimination against female applicants wearing a Muslim headscarf than against identical applicants without a headscarf.[15] So I suspect that there is in fact greater discrimination against applicants who are recognizably Muslim than these studies suggest.[16] In Britain, however, unlike in Germany, it is not usual to include a photograph and so we have not been able to pursue this question in our research.

The third panel shows a rather more mixed picture for the Black, African, and Caribbean applicants. In the 1969 and 1984/5 field experiments the ratios were quite close to 1:1, although in the 1996 study the ratio reached an astonishing 4.5:1. The difficulty here is that Caribbean names are not nearly as distinctive as Asian names, and white British people have much greater difficulty in, for example, identifying Erroll or Latoya as Caribbean names than they do in recognizing Sukjunder as an Asian name.[17] So some of the variation may simply have been due to the recognizability of the particular names chosen.

Leaving these difficulties aside, Figure 7.1 clearly demonstrates that discrimination against applicants from non-European backgrounds remains a significant feature of the twenty-first century labour market. The disparities in callback rates found in the most recent studies are of the same order of magnitude as those from three or four decades earlier.

This evidence from field experiments is in line with the evidence on unemployment rates which I reported in Chapter 6. Thus, Figure 6.6 showed that unemployment rates of young ethnic minority men and women with low qualifications were consistently higher than those of their white peers from the early 1970s, with no sign of the gap narrowing over time.

So despite the various Acts of Parliament which made discrimination for jobs illegal, and despite the activities of the Commission for Racial Equality and the Equalities and Human Rights Commission, Blacks and Asians experience much the same level of discrimination as they did forty years ago. How can we explain this failure to make progress in tackling racial discrimination?

The failure to make more progress may be a consequence of the fact that the law is difficult to enforce. In effect, if someone feels that he or she has been discriminated against, the onus is on them to take the case to a tribunal, and at best the compensation awarded is rather modest, with a median award of around £7000.[18] So there is little incentive on victims to complain, and not much incentive for firms to take more active steps to avoid prosecution since prosecution is rare and the penalties are small. Moreover, many victims may simply be unaware that they have suffered discrimination in the first place. A typical rejection letter might for example simply say 'We have given your application most careful consideration but regret that you have not been selected for an interview.'[19] A real applicant would have had no way of knowing that a white applicant with exactly the same qualifications and experience had been offered an interview for the same job. Firms themselves may also be unaware of the extent of discrimination. Unless they carefully monitor the success rates of applicants from different ethnic backgrounds, they are unlikely to know how much discrimination occurs in their organization.

Other convincing evidence suggests that overt prejudice has declined in Britain in recent decades.[20] There is therefore a major contrast between the decline of racial prejudice and the stubborn persistence of discrimination in the labour market. It may be, however, that not all discrimination is the result of racist beliefs. Economists have suggested an alternative interpretation, namely that employers use the applicants' ethnicity as a guide to their likely productivity.[21] They are therefore less likely to appoint a minority applicant because they assume such applicants will be less productive (in my view a highly questionable assumption), not because of racist preferences.

Another possibility is that the discrimination against minority applicants reflects an implicit preference for people like oneself—a process known as homophily—rather than overt hostility towards others. Selection committees composed of white men will thus tend to prefer to appoint other white men, possibly because they feel that they will be more comfortable with them. I suspect that this sort of homophily is much harder to eradicate than overt racial prejudice.

Have Gender Inequalities of Opportunity Declined?

As I described in Chapter 4, girls have overtaken boys in education. Starting somewhat behind boys in the 1950s, they caught up with and then overtook boys halfway through the post-war period, and in the twenty-first century are well ahead in educational attainment (although some important differences remain—for example in the proportions studying science, technology, engineering, and mathematics). There was also a large increase in women's participation in the labour market, as more women continued to work after having children or returned to paid work after their children reached school age.

As a result of these two developments, there was a substantial increase in the proportion of higher-paid jobs in the professions, management, and administration which are held by women. In the 1960s, when I first started work, probably less than a fifth of these jobs in the higher salariat were held by women. Nowadays it is over a third—still a minority but certainly more diverse than it used to be.

However, increasing diversity does not necessarily mean that there has been increasing equality of opportunity for women. Although Alan Milburn in his foreword to the Social Mobility Commission Report used the terms fair and inclusive interchangeably, they are really rather different. The increasing supply of highly qualified women entering the labour market could increase diversity without there being any increase in equality of opportunity between men and women. From the perspective of equality of opportunity, what we are interested in is whether *equally qualified* men and women have equal chances of getting into the best jobs, and whether the gap has been narrowing over time. As with racial discrimination, there has been a series of government legislation designed to promote gender equality, most notably the Equal Pay Act of 1970, the 1975 Sex Discrimination Act, and the Employment Protection Act of 1976 (which included some provisions for maternity leave). Have these Acts been any more successful than the Race Relations Acts in promoting gender equality?

Field experiments like those on racial discrimination would be one way of investigating this. However, only a few British studies have focussed on gender discrimination, and we do not have a series of studies which would enable us to look at changes over time in levels of unequal treatment. Instead, we need to follow the second method, the one used by J. L. Gray and Pearl Moshinsky in their pre-war study of inequality of opportunity in education, using statistical analysis of survey data to look at the labour market chances of equally qualified men and women.

Heather Joshi, Gerry Makepeace, and Peter Dolton have conducted a study of exactly this sort. They used three successive surveys conducted in 1978, 1991, and 2000 to measure changes in the gender wage gap between men and women who were aged 30 or thereabouts.[22] These three surveys were part of panel studies in which people were followed up throughout their lives, collecting detailed information on the skills, qualifications, and work experience which they had acquired at different stages of their careers. The richness of the information makes these studies particularly valuable as it enabled the researchers to match people in the same way that field experiments do, and thus to ensure that they were comparing like with like.

Heather Joshi and her colleagues first calculated what they termed the crude wage gap between men and women at these three time points. They then used statistical techniques to measure how much of these gaps were due to the unequal treatment of women who had the same qualifications and experience as the men. They restricted their attention to men and women who were working full-time, as there is considerable evidence that part-time work, which is particularly common among women with young children to look after, receives much lower wages per hour than full-time work. The crude wage gap would be much larger if they had included part-time workers.[23]

As Figure 7.2 shows, the crude gender wage gap (measured in terms of hourly wages) was very substantial in 1978, with men earning 30 per cent more than women on average. This crude gap then fell substantially in 1991 to 16 per cent and then to 8 per cent in 2000. Some of this decline was due to the fact that women were becoming better qualified than men (better qualifications leading to higher wage rates) and were obtaining more work experience. So the decline in the size of the crude wage gap does not on its own tell us that women were being treated more equally.

Heather Joshi and her colleagues therefore used techniques on similar lines to those used by Gray and Moshinsky to compare the wage gaps among men and women who had the *same* qualifications and experience. (They also took account of a range of other factors such as cognitive ability.) What they found was that, in the 1978 study, around two thirds of the crude wage gap was due to unequal treatment, the other third being due to women's lower qualifications and experience. In contrast, in the 2000 study, none of the gap could be explained by women's lower qualifications and the like. Indeed, women working full time had overtaken men in their qualifications and should actually have earned more than men if their qualifications and experience were being rewarded in the same way that men's were.

Figure 7.2. The crude gender wage gap declined in Great Britain between 1978 and 2000; unequal treatment of women also declined but not as much

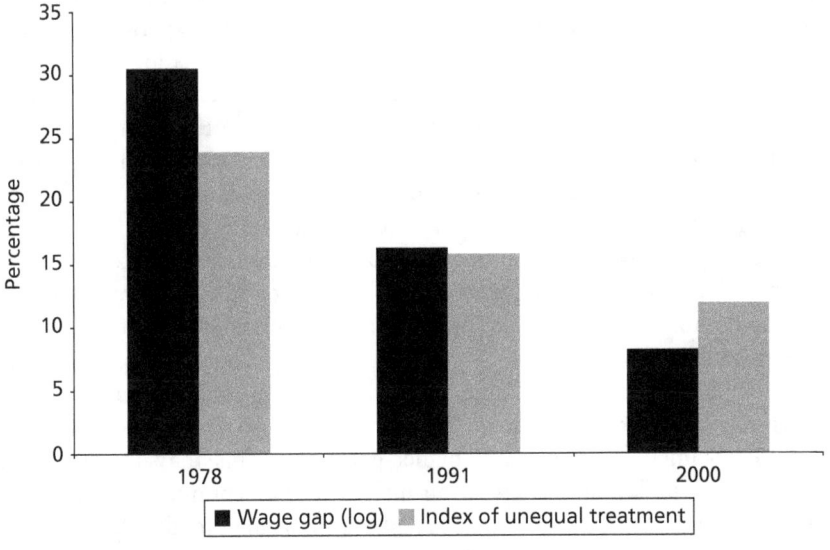

Source: National Survey of Health and Development, National Child Development Study, 1970 British Cohort Study[24]

So whereas, in 1978, the crude wage gap overestimated the extent of unequal treatment experienced by women, in 2000 the crude wage gap actually underestimated the extent of unequal treatment. Thus unequal treatment declined over this period—but the decline was much smaller than that in the crude wage gap. The index of unequal treatment calculated by Heather Joshi and her colleagues fell from 24 per cent to 12 per cent, not the fall from 30 to 8 per cent shown in the crude wage gaps.

This is certainly a more optimistic story of social progress than that told by the field experiments of racial discrimination, although it still shows a substantial degree of unequal treatment persisting at the beginning of the twenty-first century. Furthermore, Heather Joshi and her colleagues also found that the extent of unequal treatment increases as one moves to later stages in the career. Both the crude wage gaps and the extent of unequal treatment were found to be much larger around age 40 than around age 30 (where they were in turn larger than at younger ages). In other words, unequal treatment of women appears to be quite modest at the beginning of their careers but then becomes worse as they get older and move to more senior levels in the workplace—the glass ceiling. This is reflected for example in directorships of major companies. The Davis Report *Women on Boards* showed that in 2010 only 5.5 per cent of executive directorships of the FTSE 100 companies were held by women, whereas at junior levels the proportion is not far short of parity with men (5.5 per cent was however a major increase compared with 1999, when the proportion had been only 2 per cent).[25]

How can one account for these patterns and for the differences from the findings for racial discrimination? Discrimination may well be a part of the story, as in the case of race, but the main British field experiment of sex discrimination actually found a modest amount of discrimination in favour of women in mixed occupations, although there was gender discrimination in favour of men in predominantly male occupations.[26] However, this field experiment on gender discrimination, as with the field experiments on racial discrimination, focussed on early career jobs. One cannot generalize the results to later stages of the career where Heather Joshi and her colleagues' research suggests that unequal treatment of women is much greater.

Apart from discrimination, there are a number of additional reasons why women do not achieve jobs and incomes commensurate with their education. One possible reason is gender segregation of occupations—occupations that have higher proportions of women workers tending also to have lower wages. I suspect, however, that a more important factor is simply the failure to promote women to senior and higher-paid jobs. This may in part be a consequence of homophily, with all-male selection committees preferring people like themselves. It may also arise because women tend to be excluded from the networking activities of the men, which may well go on over a drink after work while women may feel obliged to get home in order to prepare the supper and put the children to bed, even if they work full time.[27] I suspect that many employers still operate family-unfriendly practices. For example, at Oxford University, seminars often take place at 5pm in the early evening, followed by dinner at high table. Women (and egalitarian men) with childcare responsibilities are in effect excluded from these networking opportunities.

On the other hand, one must recognize that the evidence provided by Heather Joshi and her colleagues does suggest quite clearly that unequal treatment of women in the labour market declined in the 1980s and 1990s. There is some evidence that the 1970 Equal Pay Act may have made a difference.[28] However, an additional ingredient may have been the declining power of the trade unions and the privatization of large parts of the public sector. These may have reduced the wage premium that men in unionized work were previously able to secure. In other words, the equalization may have partly been a result of the declining power of men rather than the improving treatment of women.

Have Social Class Inequalities of Opportunity Declined?

Many people, most notably the Social Mobility Commission, have been concerned about declining opportunities for upward social mobility in twenty-first-century Britain. I will break this down into two questions. First, has there been a declining rate of upward mobility with fewer people from lower social class backgrounds moving upwards? Second, has there been an improvement in fairness in the sense of more equal opportunities for people with the same qualifications from different social class origins? These two questions are somewhat analogous to the distinction that Heather Joshi and her colleagues made between the crude gender pay gap and the net gap due to unequal treatment of men and women.

Let me start then with the overall rate of upward social mobility. The first part of the post-war period was characterized by a considerable expansion in the size of the salariat—professional, administrative, and managerial jobs—and a gradual decline in the size of the manual working class. In essence there was a transformation of the economy from a primarily industrial one based on manufacturing industry to a postindustrial service economy. The transformation was a gradual process but the rapid change of the 1960s could never continue indefinitely at the same pace. As Figure 7.3 shows, the rate of expansion of the salariat slowed down after 1991.

It is this slowing down that provides some of the challenges which exercise the Social Mobility Commission. The increasing 'room at the top' in the first

Figure 7.3. The professional and managerial jobs of the salariat expanded in the UK while manual jobs declined between 1951 and 2011

Percentage of men in each class

	1951	1971	1991	2011
Upper salariat	4	10	15	18
Lower salariat	7	15	20	22
Intermediate classes	10 / 10 / 14	8 / 10 / 12	8 / 10 / 12	7 / 13 / 10
Working class	55	45	35	30

Note: the figures within each box represent the percentage of the working population in each class. The intermediate classes, from left to right, are the ancillary professional and administrative, the petty bourgeoisie (small employers and own account workers), and the lower supervisory and technical classes. The figures relate only to men

Source: 1951–2011 censuses[29]

decades after the war gave plenty of opportunities for upward mobility, but the slowing down since the 1990s is likely to mean that, other things being equal, the amount of upward mobility will begin to decline. To make matters worse, the earlier expansion of the salariat in the 1950s and 1960s will mean that, thirty years later in the twenty-first century, there will be more people themselves coming from salariat backgrounds, thus adding to the competition for professional and managerial jobs. As John Goldthorpe explains,

> As a result of the expansion of the salariat in the last century, increasing numbers of individuals are now *starting out in life* from more advantaged class positions... Thus, the numbers of those 'at risk' of downward mobility are steadily rising, and the number 'at risk' of upward mobility are steadily falling.[30]

To obtain estimates of the evolution of upward mobility I draw on large-scale government and academic surveys of the population.[31] I divide these samples of the population into birth cohorts. Thus in Figure 7.4 I start with a cohort born in 1939 or earlier, most of whom would have been completing their education and moving into the labour market in the immediate post-war years. Next comes my own birth cohort (born in the 1940s and completing their education in the 1960s and early 1970s), followed by younger cohorts and ending with the cohort born in the 1970s, who would have been going to university in the last decade of the twentieth century and getting established in their careers at the beginning of the twenty-first century.[32] This enables us to cover the whole post-war period.[33]

In Figure 7.4 I map the chances of people who grew up in different social class origins to reach the salariat—basically professional, managerial, and administrative work. I distinguish six class origins—higher salariat, lower salariat, routine non-manual class, petty bourgeoisie (small employers and own account workers), skilled working class (including manual foremen and higher technical workers), and the less skilled working class. (A full treatment of social mobility would look at patterns of access to all social classes, but for simplicity I restrict myself to access to the salariat, which is key for understanding upwards mobility.)

Figure 7.4 clearly shows a hierarchy with very substantial social class differences. In the earliest, pre-war birth cohort, over 60 per cent of men and women from higher salariat backgrounds made it into the salariat themselves, whereas less than 25 per cent from working-class backgrounds managed to do so. Over the next two birth cohorts, there were much improved chances of people from lower classes moving up into the salariat. But this improvement then stalled in the two most recent birth cohorts. Meanwhile people from higher salariat origins maintained throughout superior chances of occupational success. So social class inequalities in access to the salariat declined in the decades after the war but failed to maintain the same rate of improvement

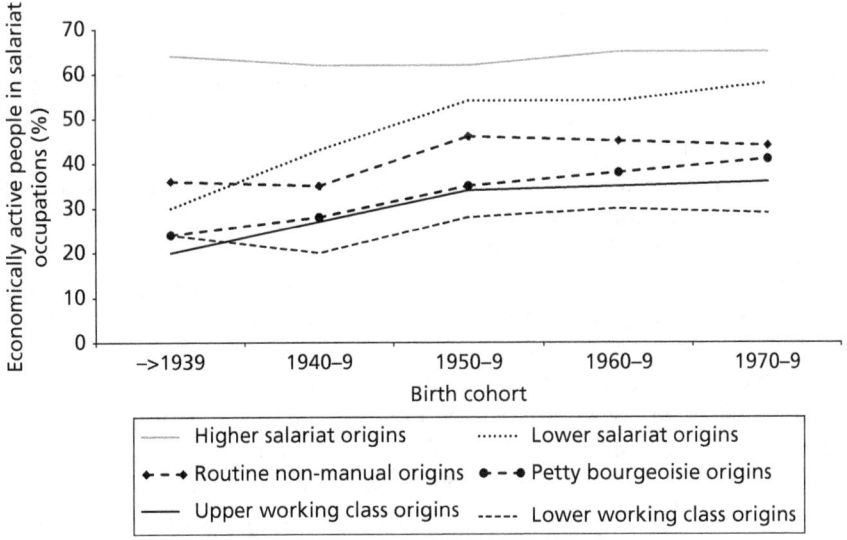

Figure 7.4. Class differences in access to the salariat declined among older birth cohorts but progress has since stalled in Great Britain

Note: samples include all economically active respondents (men aged 16–64 and women aged 16–59); the foremen/technical class is included in the upper working class

Source: General Household Survey (2005), British Household Panel Survey (2005), Labour Force Survey (2014–15), UK Household Longitudinal Study (Waves 1–3)

towards the end of the century.³⁴ More detailed analysis indicates that women from disadvantaged backgrounds started well behind men in their chances of moving upwards but gradually caught up, in effect making greater and more sustained progress than men over the post-war period.

This pattern of increasing upward mobility in the earlier birth cohorts followed by stagnation thereafter closely matches the changes in the occupational structure shown in Figure 7.3. Basically, once the increase in room at the top deriving from the expansion of the salariat began to slow, the rate of upward mobility into the salariat had to slow down too.³⁵

However, this slowing down in the volume of upward mobility does not directly tell us about trends in equality of opportunity, just as the decline in the size of the crude gender pay gap did not on its own tell us by how much unequal treatment of women had fallen. Turning, then, to equality of opportunity, one exemplary study is that conducted by Bess Bukodi and her colleagues at Oxford along the same lines as Gray and Moshinsky's original work which I cited earlier. However, whereas Gray and Moshinsky had focussed on entry to grammar schools at age 11, Bess Bukodi's team compared class inequalities in obtaining Advanced Level qualifications.³⁶ This makes perfect sense given the replacement of the pre-war selective system of education by a (largely) comprehensive system, and the key role of Advanced Level as the criterion for university entrance.

Like Gray and Moshinsky, Bess Bukodi's team used data which included measures of young people's cognitive ability at around age 10. They then investigated, among young people *all of whom had high levels of cognitive ability*, whether there were social class differences in chances of obtaining A Level, and whether these differences had declined over time. Their comparisons of three samples of young people who would have been sitting their A Levels around 1976, 1988, and 2010 confirmed enduring and substantial socio-economic differences even among young people with high cognitive skills (defined as those with scores in the top fifth of the distribution). The trend varied somewhat depending upon what precise measure of socio-economic background was used, the largest differences being linked to parental level of education. In the earliest round of data these differences amounted to thirty points; in the next round the gap had fallen to twenty-three points, but in the third round it was back up to thirty-nine points.³⁷

These gaps are not as large as the ones that Gray and Moshinsky found before the war. The studies are not really comparable, but I would not rule out the possibility class inequalities of opportunity were smaller after the war than they had been before the war.³⁸ Nevertheless, the evidence of Bess Bukodi's team strongly suggests that inequalities of opportunity in secondary education did not ameliorate over the later decades of the twentieth century and the first decade of the twenty-first. They concluded, 'The problem of "wastage of talent" remains; young people from disadvantaged backgrounds are still lacking the opportunity to fully realize their potential within the British educational system.'[39]

We can use similar methods to investigate whether social class background affects one's chances of getting advantaged professional and managerial jobs *among people who have achieved equally well in their educational careers.* While purchasing commissions in the army has long been abolished, there are enduring worries that the advantaged social classes may be able to use other more subtle resources, such as their social connections, in order to give their children a leg up in the competition against their equally qualified peers from less well-resourced backgrounds. There is certainly evidence that members of the established professions such as medicine and the law are disproportionately drawn from higher social class backgrounds.[40]

Figure 7.5, therefore, moves from education into the labour market. To keep a long story short, I look at chances of accessing the higher salariat—the higher professional and managerial occupations. (More sophisticated statistical analysis covering the full range of occupational positions confirms the story.) I then compare inequalities among people born in the different birth cohorts that were used in Figure 7.4.

Figure 7.5 shows that, for all class origins alike, the chances of getting into more privileged salariat jobs improved. However, *even among people with the same level of qualification*, those from more privileged social class backgrounds continue to have a substantial advantage over people from less privileged backgrounds. As we can see, the gaps between the most and the least privileged class origins remained remarkably constant across the four birth cohorts. In my 1940–9 cohort, the gap was eighteen points. It was virtually identical thirty years later among members of the 1970–9 cohort.

So the safest conclusion is that class inequalities of opportunity persisted unchanged throughout the post-war period. While the scale of opportunities greatly improved, with many more people going to university and many more professional and managerial jobs being created, the advantaged classes remain basically as far ahead as ever in the competition to get these jobs. They still manage to win the competition against their peers with similar qualifications and abilities.

How can the continuing advantages of the privileged classes in competition with their equally qualified peers from humbler origins be explained? It seems unlikely that it is the result of deliberate discrimination. Michelle Jackson has carried out a field experiment of discrimination in employment on the basis of social class background.[41] She sent speculative applications to large companies with the usual matched covering letters and CVs. It is pretty difficult to signal social class origins in a CV or covering letter without making the application look rather fishy. What she did was to use a range of markers to indicate whether the fictitious applicant came from an elite or non-elite background. The markers were a double-barrelled name like Edward Acheson-Gray or

Figure 7.5. Large class differences in accessing higher professional and managerial posts remain in Great Britain, even among people with the same levels of education

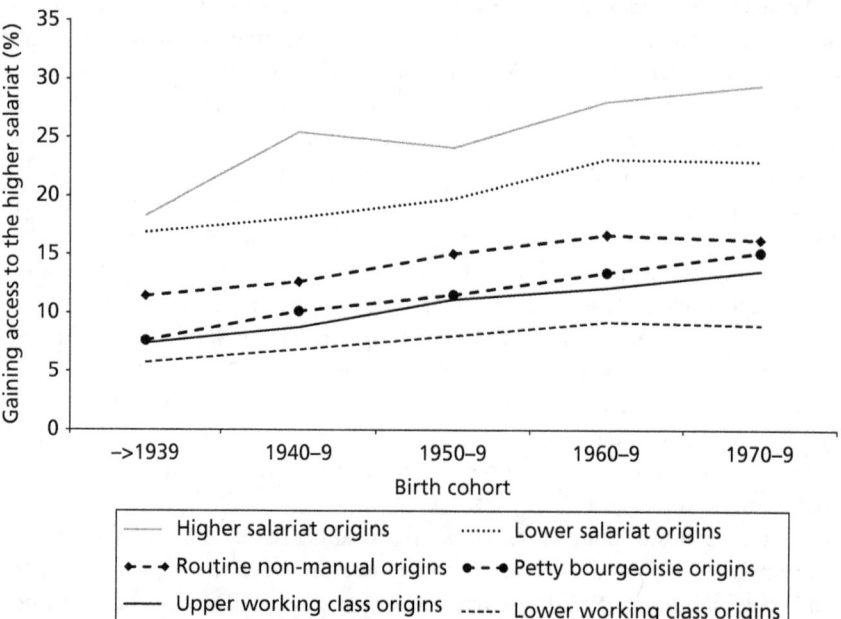

Note: the figure shows estimated percentages (average marginal effects) from different class origins in gaining access to the higher salariat among the economically active, adjusting for age, gender, ethnicity, and whether or not the respondent had a degree

Source: General Household Survey (2005), British Household Panel Survey (2005), Labour Force Survey (2014–15), UK Household Longitudinal Study (Waves 1–3)

Camilla Bevans-Brown, education at an elite independent school such as Westminster rather than a state school, and having elite rather than non-elite interests—polo, tennis, skiing, and yachting, as against snooker, football, or darts. None of these markers seemed to make any difference to one's chances of receiving a positive callback from the employer.

Michelle Jackson did however find clear evidence that employers preferred applicants from elite universities like Oxford and Cambridge compared with less elite universities. This could partly explain the findings. Our measure of university education lumps together students with good degrees, demanding subjects like maths, and top universities with those with a bare pass degree, less challenging subjects, and non-elite institutions. I suspect that part of the story is that people from elite social backgrounds use their resources and knowhow to get their children into more prestigious universities (and subjects) than parents from humbler backgrounds.

Another part of the story is likely to be that social connections can make a difference. Connections can be a source of information about possible job openings; they may lead to a helping hand for one's son or daughter's career; they could act as mentors, or they might simply provide models of successful careers, and thus provide young people with the confidence to pursue ambitious options.[42] It is very hard for government intervention to make much difference to these inequalities in knowhow and connections—hence their persistence over time.

Britain in Comparative Perspective

How does Britain compare with our peer countries in terms of inequality of opportunity? The data are not as strong as I would like, as big international bodies such as the OECD do not routinely collect and publish data on inequalities of opportunity in member states (though there are several somewhat unsatisfactory composite measures of gender inequality).[43] However, we do have results of field experiments on racial discrimination from seven of our eight countries, although there are very few on gender discrimination, and I have not been able to find any field experiments on social class discrimination in the other countries. Nor have I been able to find any comparative studies on inequality of opportunity in the classic sense of J. L. Gray and Pearl Moshinsky's work on IQ and access to educational opportunities. However, there is some recent cross-national material which enables us to compare gender wage gaps in our eight countries. And there is a huge amount of rather conflicting material on differences between the peer countries in their overall level of openness with respect to social class origins. With one or two exceptions, however, we do not have reliable data on trends over time in the different countries. I will therefore restrict myself to comparisons in the twenty-first century.

RACIAL DISCRIMINATION

Let me begin with racial discrimination, where we have field experiments in all the peer countries apart from Japan. Just as with the British studies which I reviewed in Figure 7.1, there are many technical differences in the ways in which different national teams conducted their experiments, the range of jobs they investigated, the ethnic minorities involved, and the state of the labour market at the time, so we should be very careful not to exaggerate the extent of international variation.

In Figure 7.6 I report results from a number of recent (post-2000) field experiments in the peer countries. As with the British studies shown in Figure 7.1, I report the ratio of positive callback rates received by the fictitious majority-group and minority-group applicants. The higher the ratio, the greater the discrimination.

The levels of discrimination in the peer countries against Black, African, Arab, and Middle Eastern applicants seem very similar to those I reported in Figure 7.1 against ethnic minority applicants in Britain. Only the Latinos in the USA and the Turkish in Germany appear to experience lower levels of discrimination. The low rate of discrimination in Germany against people of Turkish origin is somewhat surprising. One explanation for the German pattern is that recruitment processes in Germany are highly formalized. Germany also has a highly structured qualification system, with well-defined vocational qualifications. The British system is quite anarchic in contrast. As a result, in Germany, if you can show that you have the right technical training for the job, you should be treated fairly. However, this may not be the whole story. As I mentioned earlier, in a recent field experiment it was found that female Muslim applicants in Germany who wear a headscarf experienced very high rates of discrimination.[44] The callback ratio exceeded 4.0:1—much higher than any of the other ratios in Figure 7.6. My conclusion, therefore, is that none of the peer countries adheres to the non-discrimination principle in the way that one might have hoped. All display significant discrimination against minorities coming from non-European backgrounds.

Figure 7.6. Discrimination against ethnic minorities in most peer countries is similar to that in Britain

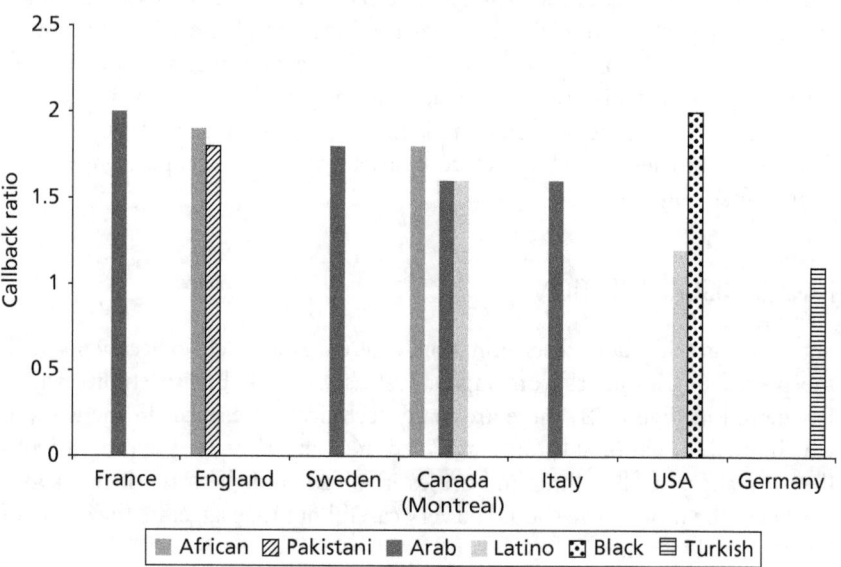

Source: Anthony Heath, Thomas Liebig, and Patrick Simon, 'Discrimination against immigrants: Measurement, incidence and policy instruments', in *International Migration Outlook 2013* (Paris: OECD, 2013), pp. 191–230[45]

GENDER PAY GAPS

Moving next to gender inequalities, there are two reasonably reliable measures that I can report drawing on the OECD's 2011 survey of adult skills (part of the OECD's Programme for the International Assessment of Adult Competencies). The survey of adult skills is a high-quality survey employing the same procedures in each country and thus giving the best basis for making rigorous cross-country comparisons. Unfortunately, the sample sizes are rather small, and so we should ignore small differences between countries.

We can use this source, first, to show the overall gender pay gap in the eight peer countries (Figure 7.7). This measure is simply the difference between men and women's median hourly earnings and is analogous to the crude gender pay gap described earlier (although it includes part-time as well as full-time workers unlike Heather Joshi's earlier measure). I supplement this with a measure of the gender gap in earnings among graduates.[46] This approximates to Heather Joshi's index of unequal treatment, although the survey of adult skills does not have the rich data available to Joshi for comparing men and women with the same skills and experience. I then set the English scores on these two measures at 100. Scores greater than 100 indicate greater gender

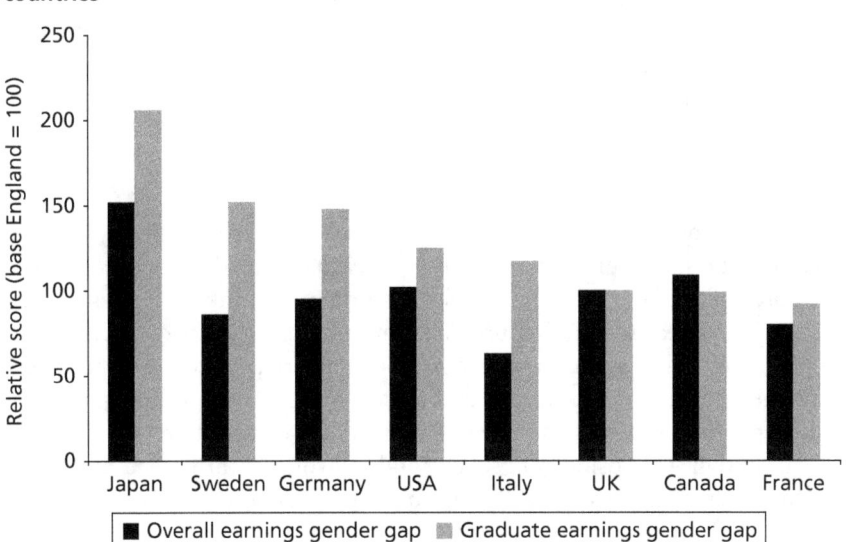

Figure 7.7. Gender inequality is much greater in Japan than in the other peer countries

Note: data are for ages 25–59. Earnings include bonuses. The data are weighted. Data for overall earnings gender equality relate to all those in work; data for graduate earnings gender equality relate to graduates only

Source: based on OECD, Adult Skills Survey 2011, public use files inequality than in England whereas scores less 100 indicate lesser inequality. In other words, the higher the score, the greater the gender inequality.

One very clear message emerges from these results—gender inequality is very much higher in Japan than in any of the other countries. This is rather salutary. Nearly all of the previous comparisons in this book have shown Japan to be a rather exemplary country with its high life expectancy, high educational attainments, and low income inequality. However, it appears to be much less progressive when it comes to gender equality, and seems much more like a traditional developing society than a modern developed democracy. Part of the explanation is that Japan used to have a marriage bar for women.[47] Thus, when a woman married or had her first child, she was expected or required to leave her job—combining work and family was not the normal option. And while the marriage bar was formally abandoned in 1985 with the Equal Employment Opportunity law, the law did not actually stipulate penalties against employers for breaking the law until the 2006 revision of the Act. I suspect that the Japanese gender gaps shown in Figure 7.7 are an enduring legacy of the marriage bar. Incidentally, Britain also had a marriage bar for many years in the civil service. The marriage bar prohibited married women from joining the civil service, and required women civil servants to resign when they became married (unless granted a waiver). It was not abolished until October 1946 for the Home Civil Service and not until 1973 for the Foreign Service.[48]

Aside from Japan, none of the other countries really stands out in terms of gender equality in earnings. France exhibits the least gender inequality, and it may be no coincidence that France is unusual in its high proportion of working women who work full time rather than part time. But Britain is not out of the ordinary.

SOCIAL CLASS INEQUALITIES

For international comparisons of social mobility, scholars typically employ measures of the openness or fluidity of each country. In essence, these measures tell us how strongly social class origins are linked to class destinations. They measure a rather broader concept than equality of opportunity; instead, they tell us about the degree of social inheritance of more and of less privileged positions in society. In effect, these measures tell us how successful are people from different social class origins in the competition to gain access to more privileged positions in society and to avoid less privileged positions.

One recent study uses the European Social Survey, probably the highest quality of all the international survey programmes, to measure the extent of social class fluidity of European countries. There are also some studies, covering all our peer countries, reporting a similar measure of income mobility—that is a measure of how strongly parents' income is linked to their children's income when they grow up. However, these data do not come from a single, harmonized international study. Instead, the income data relate to different years and were collected independently using a variety of methods. These results are therefore less reliable than the social class measures, but I decided to include them since income mobility is of considerable interest in its own right and has been highly publicized, particularly in discussions of the Great Gatsby curve.

I supplement these two measures of fluidity with a third which comes closer to the concept of equality of opportunity. This measure is constructed along the same lines as that used in Figure 7.5 for measuring social class inequality of opportunity. It therefore tells us how strongly, *among people of the same educational level*, social origins are linked to adult income. In other words, it tells us whether people from privileged backgrounds obtain higher incomes than their equally qualified peers from less privileged backgrounds. (I should point out that the only measure of social background of social origins available in the survey of adult skills is parental education, not parental social class.)

My fourth measure is of socio-economic inequalities in reading performance at school, drawing on the harmonized measures from the OECD's Programme for International Student Assessment—PISA—which I described in Chapter 4. I use this as a supplement to the measure of social class fluidity, since educational attainment is one of the main drivers of social mobility. This enables us to compare non-European countries in addition to the European ones included in the European Social Survey.

Figure 7.8 shows how the peer countries compare with each other according to these three measures. In each case, as in Figure 7.7, I have rescaled the scores setting the British scores to 100. So scores greater than 100 indicate that the country in question is more closed or sticky than Britain, while scores below 100 indicate that the country is more open or fluid. Note, however, that there are considerable margins of error around all these estimates.

As can be readily seen, the country rankings differ quite considerably depending on whether we look at income or class fluidity. However, some general patterns are evident. Canada stands out as a rather open society with all its scores well below 100. As a non-European country Canada is missing from the class fluidity study, but other evidence suggests that Canada is relatively open with respect to social class fluidity, too.[49] Sweden also appears to be fairly open on both the income measures, and other sources suggest that Sweden exhibits greater social class fluidity than Britain.[50] Possibly Japan and the USA are both slightly more open than Britain, but the differences are rather small.

France, Germany, and Italy have rather diverse scores on the different measures, on some indicators being more open than Britain and on others more closed. I hesitate to say anything definite about their level of openness. It is probably safest to regard them as middling. And what about Britain? On both of the income-based measures, Britain is the most closed of the eight countries, as

Figure 7.8. Canada and Sweden are the most open countries overall

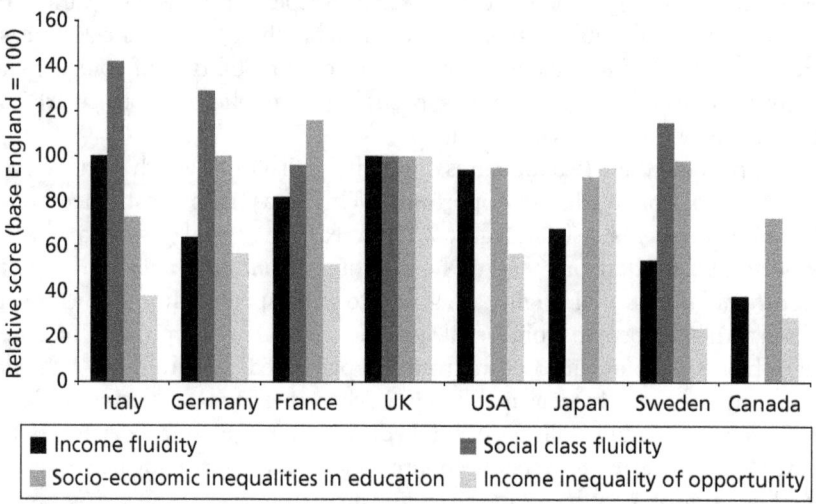

Note: data are for men only except in the case of class inequalities at school[51]

Source: European Social Survey waves 1–7, pooled (socio-economic inequalities in education), OECD Survey of Adult Skills 2011 (income inequality of opportunity), miscellaneous (income fluidity)[52]

it is on the measure of socio-economic inequality in education. The European social class mobility study, however, suggests that Britain is one of the more open European countries. So it is probably safest to regard Britain as being somewhere in the middle of the pack but certainly not as open as Canada.

How do we explain these differences? One well-publicized thesis, going under the name of the Great Gatsby curve, is that unequal societies will tend to be less mobile and closed, on the principle that 'the further the rungs are apart, the harder it is to climb the ladder'.[53] As John Ermisch and his colleagues have argued, rising inequality might be expected to have the long-term effect of reducing equality of opportunity and fluidity. 'Of all the potential consequences of rising economic inequality, none is more worrisome than the possibility that rising inequality will have the long-term effect of reducing equality of opportunity and intergenerational mobility.'[54]

On this account we would expect the most unequal of the eight peer countries, the USA, to be the most closed, and the most equal one, Japan, to be the most open. But this is not really what we see. Canada, for example, has quite a high level of income inequality (see Figure 2.2) but is clearly the most open of the eight countries. Conversely, Germany is relatively equal with respect to income, but seems quite closed on several of the indicators shown in Figure 7.8. So while there may be some truth in the thesis, it cannot be the whole story. Moreover, in order to carry out a proper test of the thesis, one should in fact investigate whether *increases* in inequality lead to *reductions* in openness over time. We need to ask whether the marked increases in inequality in Britain and the USA after 1980, and in Sweden after 1990, led to reductions in their openness. In the case of Britain, this does not appear to have been the case[55]—and I suspect it may not hold true in Sweden either. I think one needs to reserve judgement. The Great Gatsby curve is a memorable catchphrase, but we should not confuse good catchphrases with good science.

Overall, then, Britain does not come out especially well in any of these comparisons of racial, gender, or social class inequalities of opportunity. It is never the best performer—an honour that goes to Canada for class equality, to France for gender equality of opportunity, and possibly to Germany for racial parity of treatment. But, given the limitations of the data, I would hesitate to say that Britain is significantly unfairer than the other peer countries.

Conclusions

So, has Britain become a fairer and more inclusive society? The Social Mobility Commission gave a rather pessimistic answer about trends over the last twenty years, and our longer view is scarcely more optimistic. However, I think one needs to distinguish rather more carefully than Alan Milburn did between inclusiveness and fairness. Britain has become more inclusive in the sense that in the twenty-first century there are more women in universities and in salaried positions than there used to be, and the overall gender pay gap has diminished. More children from working-class backgrounds are getting GCSEs and entering university, and the same is true of young people with an ethnic minority background. So I think it would be reasonable to describe Britain as being more inclusive. Britain certainly feels different nowadays from the Britain that I grew up in.

On the other hand, I have not been able to bring forward much evidence in this chapter of increasing fairness in the sense of increasing equality of opportunity. Field experiments of racial discrimination strongly suggest that the non-discrimination principle is violated to much the same degree in 2017 as it was at the time of the first comparable field experiment nearly fifty years earlier in 1969. The data are not as robust as I would like, but they are corroborated by the kind of evidence we saw in Chapter 6 on ethnic disparities in unemployment. Similarly, the work of Bess Bukodi and her colleagues on equality of educational opportunity for young people with high ability from different social class backgrounds suggests fairness has not changed. Only in terms of the gender pay gap have I been able to report evidence of greater equality of treatment.

How can we reconcile these two different accounts? How can inclusiveness have increased but fairness have remained the same? The key point to understanding the paradox is that, over most of the post-war period, the total volume of opportunities increased—there were more places at university and more professional and managerial positions to be filled. Women, the working class, and ethnic minorities all took advantage of these new opportunities and so the composition of the universities and of the salariat class gradually changed. White men from privileged backgrounds also took advantage of the new opportunities, but because the expansion was relatively fast, and the number of people from privileged backgrounds was relatively small, there was plenty of room at the top for newcomers from non-traditional backgrounds.

Additional factors were that women increased their number of graduates faster than men did. And of course the size of the ethnic minority population also increased faster than the white British population. These two additional factors might actually have made it more difficult for white men from working-class backgrounds to achieve upward mobility into the privileged classes.

So my argument is that the supply of women, working-class, and ethnic minorities with the qualifications for entry into professional occupations increased quite fast, and so the composition of the higher salariat gradually came to change. Fairness, however, in the sense of equal opportunities for those with the requisite qualifications, changed much less. In other words, it was the increasing numbers with the requisite qualifications which was driving inclusivity rather than the improving treatment of those with those qualifications.

Moreover, on all three criteria, there is pretty convincing evidence that serious inequalities of opportunity persist. To be sure, similar inequalities of opportunity persist in all the peer countries. Britain is not alone in failing to live up to its ideals. But, compared to other countries, Britain is not especially fair in the chances it gives disadvantaged sections of society, and it is clear that some other countries, such as Canada, provide a more level playing field, and greater equality of opportunity.

8 The Challenge of Social Corrosion

National Identity, Social Divisions, and Disengagement

with Lindsay Richards

Introduction

While there has been substantial material and social progress in the years since the Beveridge Report, Britain may have lost some other strengths that were apparent when Beveridge was writing, such as a sense of solidarity and social cohesion. One worry is that growing inequality has undermined national cohesion and has returned us to the situation of two nations 'between whom there is no intercourse and no sympathy; who are as ignorant of each other's habits, thoughts, and feelings, as if they were...inhabitants of different planets' which the nineteenth-century leader of the Conservative party, Benjamin Disraeli, had condemned 170 years earlier in his novel, *Sybil, or the Two Nations*.[1]

As Richard Wilkinson and Kate Pickett cogently argued in *The Spirit Level: Why Equality Is Better for Everyone*, we may all become worse off as society becomes more unequal. They argued that inequality leads to declining social trust and social cohesion alongside rising crime and social disorder. Increasing economic inequality may thus mean that the benefits of economic progress are offset by social retreat: 'The evidence merely confirms the common intuition that inequality is divisive and socially corrosive', conclude Wilkinson and Pickett.[2] A key question for this chapter, therefore, is whether there has been progressive social corrosion, especially in the decades after 1980 when, as we saw in Chapter 2, economic inequality increased so greatly in Britain.

In addition to worries about the effects of inequality on social cohesion come worries that the increasing ethnic diversity of Britain in the post-war period, and particularly in the early twenty-first century, has placed additional strains on the social fabric and further impaired social cohesion. Some commentators worry that migrants have failed to integrate into British society.[3] Former chair of the Commission for Racial Equality, Trevor Phillips, argued that minorities were forming separate parallel communities. Britain, he claimed, was sleepwalking into segregation.[4] Louise Casey, in her 2016 report for the government on social integration, alleged that Britain's adoption of multicultural policies allowed segregated ethnic communities to lead separate lives, living according to non-Western values, and fostering extremism.[5]

A related worry is that migration may have generated a backlash among more disadvantaged sections of British society who face competition for jobs and housing from newly arrived migrants. In particular, the European Union's insistence on free movement between member states and the surge in immigration from the former communist countries of Central and Eastern Europe after they joined the Union in 2004 became a key issue fuelling opposition to membership of the European Union. The 2016 Brexit campaign and referendum highlighted these concerns and led many commentators to suggest that Britain had indeed divided into two nations or tribes with little sympathy for each other and with incompatible visions of Britain's future. Academic analysis suggested that the underlying conditions which gave rise to Brexit were the growing inequality between the winners and losers of globalization, the rapid pace of immigration, and growing distrust of the political elite on the part of those who had been left behind.[6]

Even before Brexit, former prime ministers Tony Blair, Gordon Brown, and David Cameron emphasized the need to strengthen British society in order to cope with these challenges. They particularly emphasized the importance of British values in unifying society and integrating minorities. Gordon Brown, for example, declared:

A strong sense of being British helps unite and unify us; it builds stronger social cohesion among communities...it helps us deal with issues as varied as what Britain does in Europe; to issues of managed migration and how we better integrate ethnic minorities...Like you I'm very proud of being British; proud of British values, proud of what we contribute to the world. And like you I [want] to make sure that we consider today all that we can do to build an even stronger sense of national purpose which unifies us for the years to come.[7]

Conservative prime minister David Cameron went further and argued that 'A Greater Britain doesn't just need a stronger economy—it needs a stronger society.'[8] It was not entirely clear what he meant by a stronger society, but his Big Society programme (which involved plans to give local communities more power, to encourage local people to take a more active role in their local communities, and to support co-ops, mutuals, charities, and social enterprises) suggested that his concern was to strengthen the voluntary sector, and to reverse the decline in the vibrancy of civil society.

It is not just politicians who have taken up these themes. Academics such as David Miller have emphasized the way in which a sense of national identity and shared moral commitments to fellow members of the national community can serve as a kind of social glue which can hold culturally diverse modern societies together, enabling them to function effectively. It can reduce social conflict, increase willingness to cooperate, and thereby make it easier to make provisions for the common good.[9] American political scientist Robert Putnam has emphasized the dangers of declining civic engagement for the health of democracy.[10] Indeed, David Cameron's Big Society programme seemed to be largely based on Putnam's analysis of declining social cohesion. These anxieties are not new. Paola Grenier and Karen Wright have pointed out that they were raised well over 2000 years ago by the Greek philosopher Aristotle, who warned in his study of politics that 'societies divided by economic inequality would be unable to maintain the levels of what we would now call social cohesion necessary to prevent a potentially fatal collapse into instability. [Our] research certainly supports his concern.'[11]

Before we get into the discussion of the evidence, I should say something about how I define social cohesion and what kind of evidence would be relevant for deciding whether cohesion has indeed been corroding. Metaphorically, people often write of a cohesive society as one where there is a social glue or set of bonds which holds people together—and this conception is quite closely in line with the etymology of the word cohesion. Cohesion, according to the Oxford English Dictionary, derives from the word 'cohere', which in its basic sense means to stick together, to unite or remain united in action (from the Latin *cohaerere*—to stick together). I see the heart of the concept of social cohesion as the idea that the *members of the society feel that they belong to a common national community, feel morally obliged to follow the norms of the community, and feel some responsibility for the welfare of its other members*.[12]

I also find it useful, when confronted with rather nebulous concepts, to consider what the opposite would be. Disunity and discordance are often offered in lists of antonyms as the opposite of cohesion. So we can contrast a cohesive society with a divided society or one which is falling apart—of which an extreme example might be a society in a state of civil war. One thinks of Northern Ireland during the 'Troubles' of the 1970s when it appeared to be divided into two opposing nations, with Protestants generally feeling allegiance to Britain and to the British monarchy, while many Catholics felt that they were Irish, not British, and MPs from one of the main Catholic parties, Sinn Féin, refused to take up their seats in Parliament because that involved swearing an oath of allegiance to the British monarchy.

However, I think there is also another contrast which we need to make. Conflict is not the only alternative to cohesion. One could have a situation where there is no conflict between hostile groups, but where people are simply indifferent to one another and disconnected from the national community—pursuing their own objectives without thought for others. A highly individualistic society in which there is no thought for the common good is not one that I would call cohesive. It is more like an empty shell. A classic example, as I mentioned in Chapter 5, was the Austrian town of Marienthal described by Marie Jahoda and her colleagues during the Great Depression, where mass unemployment led not to conflict but to the collapse of community life, apathy, and despair. Community spirit was destroyed. While we do not have mass unemployment in twenty-first-century Britain, we have seen evidence in previous chapters of marginalized social groups—the poor, young people with few qualifications, the homeless—who might be at risk of feeling socially detached and disengaged. Robert Putnam has advanced the thesis that one consequence of increasing ethnic diversity is declining trust and hunkering down, people keeping to themselves and opting out of community life.[13]

I will therefore begin by looking at the major cohesive or unifying forces which commentators have identified, namely a sense of national identity and commitment to a shared set of values. Do we see signs of the gradual corrosion of national identity and shared values, especially after the increase in economic inequality in the 1980s? Do we see widening social divisions in values and identities, with some groups such as the young or disadvantaged feeling increasingly marginalized? I will then turn to the divisive forces such as the social divisions that underlay the Brexit vote. Are we seeing widening social divisions dividing Britain into two opposing camps? Third, I will look at the evidence for disengagement and disconnection. Has the vibrancy and inclusiveness of civic life been declining? Is there a growing sense of disconnection from the national community? Finally, I will put Britain in a comparative context.

National Identity and British Values: the Unifying Forces

A shared sense of national identity, and a sense of belonging and attachment to that identity, can potentially be a unifying force, uniting people in a sense of being part of a single community. A shared national identity may also promote attachment to civic norms and a sense of responsibility to one's fellow citizens. To be sure, nationalism can be a source of insider/outsider distinctions, too. People who strongly identify with their own nation may feel less warmly towards outsiders who belong to a different nation (as Northern Ireland during the Troubles would suggest). Some scholars have also linked nationalistic feelings to anti-immigrant sentiments.[14] There is therefore a potential dark side to national identity, as well as a bright side.

STRENGTH OF NATIONAL PRIDE AND BELONGING

In Figure 8.1 I look at trends over time in strength of national pride and in a sense of belonging to Britain. Several relevant questions have been asked in

Figure 8.1. Pride in being British and sense of belonging to Britain do not appear to be in long-term decline

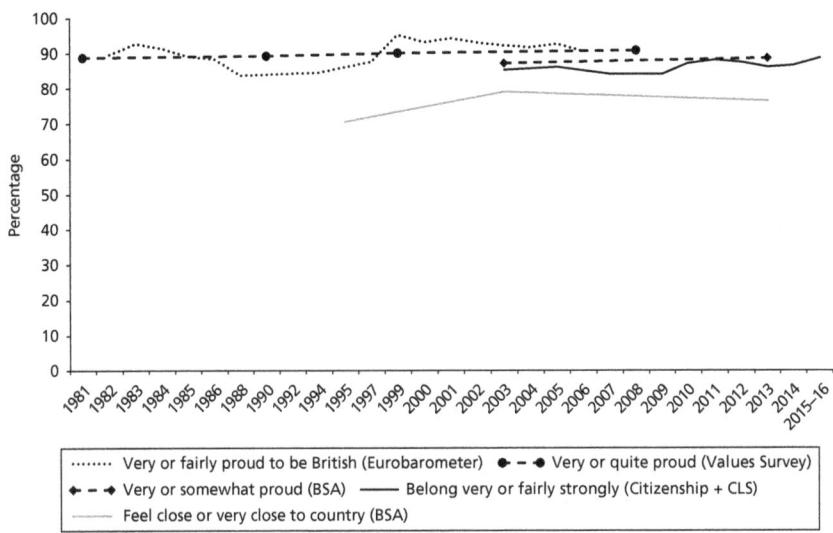

Note: territories covered vary: Eurobarometer, UK; European Values Survey, UK; British Social Attitudes, Great Britain; Citizenship Survey and Community Life Survey, England only

Source: Eurobarometer, European Values Survey, British Social Attitudes Survey (BSA), Citizenship Survey and Community Life Survey (CLS)

representative national surveys over reasonably long periods. The British Social Attitudes Surveys, the Eurobarometer, and the European Values Surveys have all asked people how proud they feel of their country; the Citizenship Survey (and its successor) asked people how strongly they feel that they belong to Britain; and the International Social Survey Programme asked people how close they feel to their country. Pride, belonging, and closeness are somewhat different aspects of attachment to one's country. You can be proud of a country's military success or sporting prowess without necessarily feeling any great responsibility to your fellow citizens. Strength of belonging to Britain is probably the ideal measure, but this measure is available only from 2002. I therefore show in Figure 8.1 all the measures available in order to get a more rounded and longer-run view.

There are clearly some differences of detail between the different measures and data sources, with feelings of national pride oscillating around 90 per cent, a strong sense of belonging to Britain hovering in the high 80s, and a feeling of closeness to Britain languishing between 70 and 80 per cent. Some of the variation is likely to arise from methodological differences between the surveys, but overall there is a rather clear picture that a sense of national belonging is high and basically stable over time.

Our earliest data point goes back only as far as 1981 and I would not rule out the possibility that a sense of national belonging was even higher in the immediate post-war decades. But I think we can be fairly sure that, in the decades after 1981, there was little if any decline in pride or national belonging. There is no sign in these data that the rise of inequality in the 1980s led to widespread corrosion of feelings of national pride or belonging.

Given the high and stable levels of pride and belonging, we would not expect to find any large differences between rich and poor or between young and old. We are unlikely to find major social divisions if 90 per cent of the population feel a sense of national pride, and this of course is what gives national identity its potential for acting as a unifying force. Nevertheless, my expectation is that more marginalized groups will have a somewhat lower sense of attachment to a Britain that has not perhaps treated them especially well.

In Figure 8.2 I focus on national pride and the extent to which there are divisions between different social groups. Following Benjamin Disraeli, I explore divisions between rich and poor (people on high and low incomes), as well as divisions between people with higher-level professional and

Figure 8.2. Social divisions in feelings of national pride have never been large and have changed little over thirty years in Great Britain

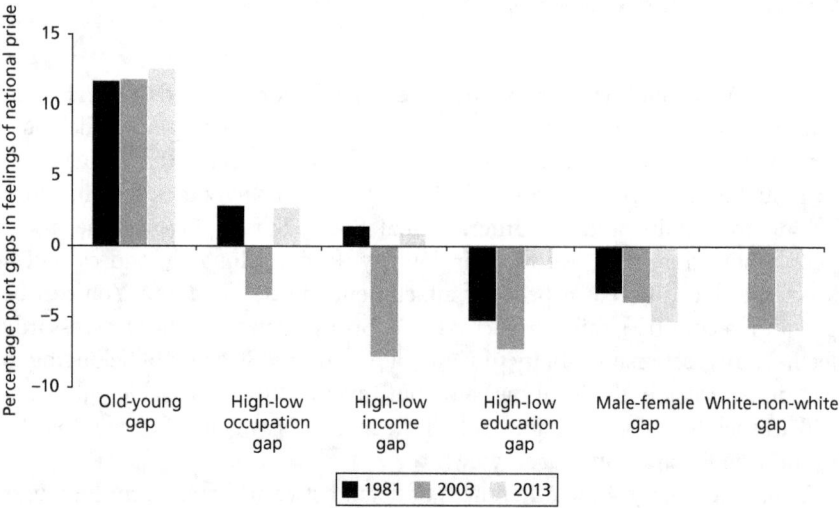

Note: high-low occupation gap is the difference between those in higher professional/management occupations and those in routine occupations. Old-young gap is the difference between the over-60s and the under-25s. The income gap is the difference between the top and bottom income quintiles. The education gap is the difference between those with a university degree and those with no qualifications. All estimates have been adjusted for age except for age, which has been adjusted for educational attainment. There was no ethnicity measure in the 1981 survey

Source: World Values Survey (1981), British Social Attitudes Surveys (2003, 2013)

managerial jobs as opposed to those in routine jobs, and between university graduates and those with low or no qualifications. The rich, the highly educated, and the professionals and managers are the groups who have done well under the existing social order.

I contrast these socio-economic differences with other possible sources of division in contemporary British society, namely ethnicity, age, and gender. These potentially cross-cut the socio-economic cleavages rather than neatly map onto them. We can think of these as horizontal axes of differentiation in contrast to the vertical axis of socio-economic position. It is true that men tend to earn more than women, that white British earn more than ethnic minorities, and that young people have greater risks of unemployment than older people. But at the same time we shall see that there are often differences between younger and older people, or between ethnic minorities and the majority, even in the absence of socio-economic differences between them.

Figure 8.2 confirms the expectation that socio-economic differences in strength of national pride will be very small and will not have changed over time. The differences between classes, educational levels, income groups, and ethnic groups are almost uniformly modest. There is no sign in these data that ethnic minorities feel detached from Britain, although in other research on young people we have found that young people with an ethnic minority background do not feel that they belong to Britain as strongly as do their white British peers.[15]

Age differences, however, are rather larger than the socio-economic divisions. Older people have a stronger sense of national pride than younger people, with a gap of just over ten percentage points, although there is no sign that the division has grown over the thirty years covered by the surveys. I have also checked this story using the measure of closeness to Britain. The gaps are somewhat larger with this alternative measure (being over fifteen percentage points in the case of age) but, just as with pride in Britain, the gaps appear to be generally stable over time.

ENGLISH, IRISH, SCOTTISH, AND WELSH IDENTITIES

However, this rather optimistic story of national unity is challenged when we distinguish the four territories of the United Kingdom. There are strong nationalist movements in Northern Ireland, Scotland, and Wales, and indeed in Scotland and Northern Ireland there are major separatist movements. In an attempt to contain these separatist movements, and to preserve the unity of the Kingdom, many powers were transferred from Westminster to the devolved administrations in Wales and Scotland following devolution referenda in 1997, and power sharing between the main Catholic and Protestant parties was introduced in Northern Ireland following the 1998 peace agreement which marked the end of the Troubles. The UK thus moved in the direction of federalism, and I remember some concerns being expressed at the time that devolution might further entrench separate Irish, Welsh, and Scottish identities in place of British ones and might hasten the break-up of the United Kingdom.

We can explore the reach of British identity in Northern Ireland, Wales, and Scotland with a question which asks people whether they feel, for example, 'Scottish not British', 'Scottish more than British', 'equally Scottish and British', 'British more than Scottish', and 'British not Scottish'. Questions along these lines have been asked in Scotland since 1992, in Wales and England since 1997, and in Northern Ireland since 2007.

Figure 8.3 shows that dual identities are predominant in all four constituent countries of the UK. In each country a majority of citizens have a dual identity, and the proportion is particularly high in England where most people think of themselves as both English and British. Indeed, it has often been said that English identity is a fuzzy one, with people making no clear distinction between Britishness and Englishness.[16] This is hardly surprising in a country where the state bank is termed the Bank of England rather than the Bank of the United Kingdom.

However, in Northern Ireland, Scotland, and to a lesser extent Wales there are substantial proportions of the public who do not accept a British identity at all, and who see themselves as exclusively Irish, Scottish, or Welsh. In Scotland, the balance is tilted towards the Scottish side whereas Northern Ireland presents a more polarized picture, with similar proportions on either side rejecting the alternative identity. Other evidence, using a slightly different formulation, suggests that over time the proportion endorsing a British identity has been declining in Northern Ireland, and we can see that the same process has been occurring in Scotland, too.[17] As Figure 8.3 shows, the proportion feeling exclusively Scottish increased rapidly during the 1990s, and the indications are that it continued to grow after devolution, albeit at a much slower pace. In Wales and England it is less clear that there has been much change over time.

The rejection of a British national identity by substantial minorities in Northern Ireland, Scotland, and Wales presents something of a challenge to the rather positive story about national pride and national belonging with which I began the chapter. This evidence certainly suggests that there are cracks in the national glue—very long-standing cracks in the case of Northern Ireland.

I doubt if these cracks in Scotland and Northern Ireland have anything much to do with the big themes of rising inequality or increasing ethnic diversity which I described in the introduction. While the cracks do not seem to be deepening quickly, they are potentially ominous for the unity of the United Kingdom. It may also be relevant that in both Scotland and Wales,

Figure 8.3. Dual identities predominate in all four territories, but substantial minorities in Wales, Scotland, and Northern Ireland reject a British identity

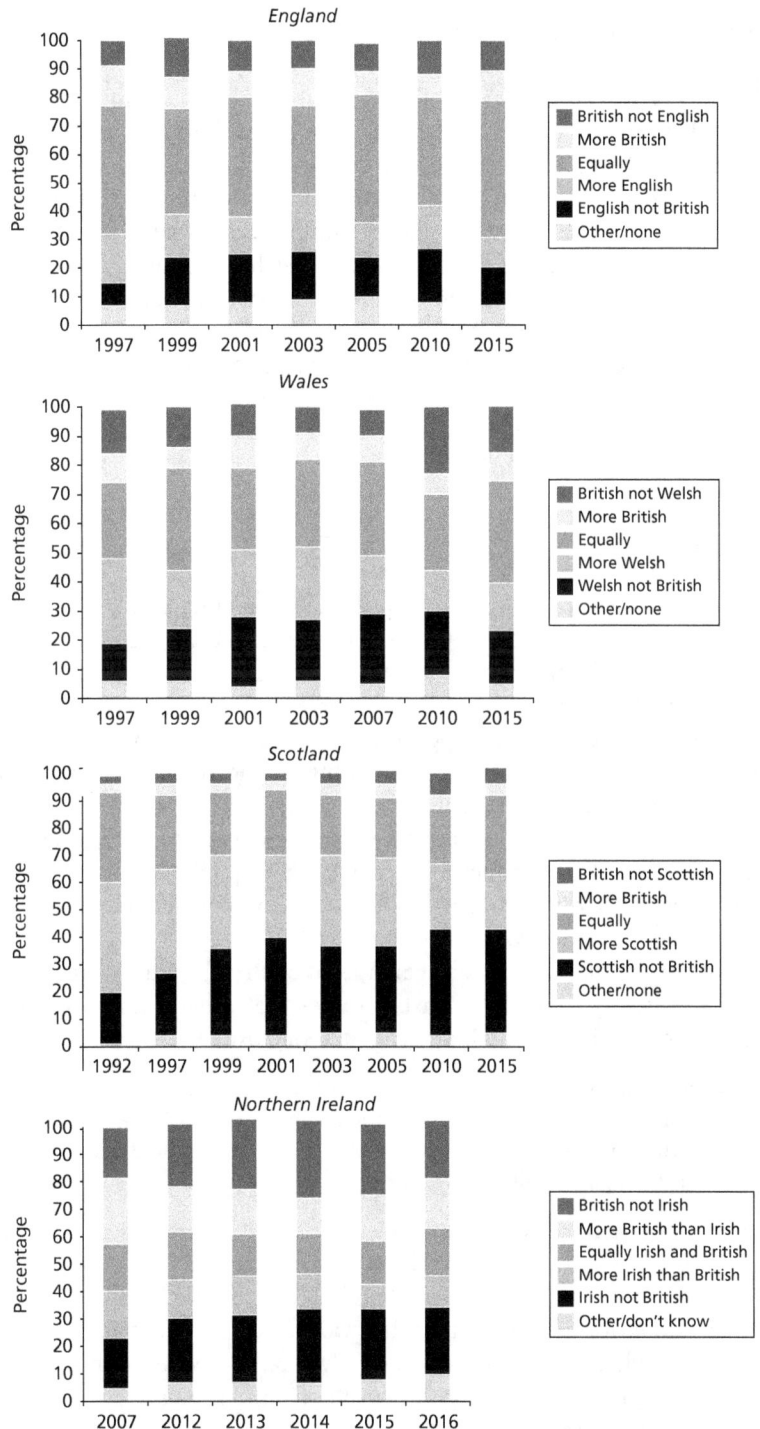

Source: England: British Election Surveys (1997, 2005, 2010, 2015) and British Social Attitudes Surveys (1999, 2001, 2003); Scotland: Scottish Election Studies (1992, 1997), Scottish Social Attitudes Surveys (1999, 2001, 2003, 2005), and British Election Surveys (2010, 2015); Wales: British Election Surveys (1997, 2010, 2015), Welsh Assembly Election Survey (1999), and Welsh Life and Times Survey (2003, 2007); Northern Ireland: Northern Ireland Life and Times Surveys (2007, 2012–16)

distinct Scottish and Welsh identities appear to be more attractive to younger people than to older generations.

Historian Linda Colley has put forward the persuasive argument that a unifying British identity was itself the creation of the shared project of Empire in the eighteenth and nineteenth centuries, a project which gave many opportunities to Scots, Welsh, and Irish and not just to the English.[18] This shared project has not had the same significance in the second half of the twentieth century since the decline of the Empire, and has little resonance for younger generations. No new common project has come to take the place of the British Empire, and there is the possibility that Brexit will be a divisive project which will further undermine a sense of shared British identity. Brexit might well deepen the cracks between the territories of the UK, and between the generations, since majorities in both Scotland and Northern Ireland and of younger people voted against Brexit.

BRITISH VALUES

British values are often held up as a possible integrating force, although the main focus of the proponents of this view has been on the integration of ethnic minorities rather than on overcoming divisions between the four territories of the UK or between young and old. For example, Dame Louise Casey's 2016 review of integration and opportunity for the prime minister stressed the importance of British values for integrating ethnic minorities into British society. She recommended attaching more weight to British values, laws and history in schools, and the introduction of a new oath for holders of public office, enshrining British values in the principles of public life.[19] Surprisingly, there has been rather little thought about the extent to which the white British majority itself is united around British values.

It is rather difficult to know what are meant by British values—and whether they are really any different from the values that other countries espouse. Former prime minister Tony Blair suggested one list:

When it comes to our essential values, the belief in democracy, the rule of law, tolerance, equal treatment for all, respect for this country and its shared heritage—then that is where we come together, it is what gives us what we hold in common; it is what gives us the right to call ourselves British.[20]

Other similar lists have been proposed, too.

Terms like belief in democracy, the rule of law, and so on are rather bland and hard to disagree with. They would probably be assented to in democracies right across the world. So I doubt if they would be able to replace the glue of shared British identity. But let us see anyway what the evidence shows, and in particular whether ethnic minorities or other disadvantaged groups deviate from or share in these values.

Unfortunately, there has been no tradition of asking about British values in survey research, so the data are very patchy indeed and I have not been able to construct any trends over time. However, I have managed to find a number of measures, in a variety of representative and authoritative national samples, such as the government's Citizenship Survey and the independent British Social Attitudes Survey. We have items on:

- support for democracy;
- responsibility to obey the law;
- the importance of understanding the reasoning of people with other opinions (an aspect of tolerance);
- the responsibility to treat all races equally (a central aspect of equal treatment for all); and
- the responsibility to treat others with fairness and respect.[21]

Not surprisingly, we find both a high level of consensus on most of the items and modest social divisions. Thus, Figure 8.4 shows that, in the twenty-first century, 97 per cent agreed that one has a responsibility to obey and respect the law, 96 per cent supported the responsibility to treat others with fairness and respect, 93 per cent supported the responsibility to treat all races equally, 90 per cent expressed support for democracy, and 84 per cent agreed that it was important to understand the reasoning behind different opinions.

I have also added two extra items on the importance of helping people in Britain and in other countries who are worse off than oneself. These do not figure on most lists of British values, but the notion of helping fellow citizens is

Figure 8.4. Support for British values is generally high, although somewhat lower in the case of tolerance and helping fellow Britons

Source: 2011 Citizenship Survey (obey the law, treat with fairness, and treat races equally, England and Wales); 2014 British Social Attitudes Survey (important to understand reasoning, to help people in Britain and to help people in the rest of the world, Great Britain); 2005 World Values Survey (support for democracy, United Kingdom)

a key feature of academic discussions of why national identity is important for society. As one can see, only 78 per cent of the British public support this idea, although the item on helping people in the rest of the world scores much worse with only 55 per cent agreeing to it. Britons do therefore make quite a sharp distinction between helping their fellow citizens and helping those who are not part of the national community.

As one would expect, social divisions are rather small in the case of the values which receive the highest levels of assent. They become somewhat wider where assent is lower. The largest gaps in values occur between university graduates and people with no qualifications. In order to save space, I simply show these educational gaps as the story is paralleled in the case of the other socio-economic measures. I also show the ethnic differences, both because these have been a particular focus of policy-makers such as Louise Casey, and because they take a slightly different form.

Figure 8.5 shows that educational divisions are minimal in the case of the items on 'obeying the law' and 'respecting others'. Divisions generally increase as we move to items which receive lower levels of assent, and are at their largest in the case of the item about helping less fortunate people in the rest of the world. For all items the university graduates are more likely to support the value than are people with no qualifications. (This may in part be because highly educated people are more likely to give politically correct responses or are more susceptible to what social psychologists term social desirability bias.)

There are two exceptions to these general patterns. First, despite its relatively low level of overall assent (78 per cent), social divisions over helping fellow Britons are markedly smaller than for some items which receive higher levels of support. This is reassuring for the thesis that British values can potentially unite the nation and encourage social cohesion. Second, and perhaps unsurprisingly, members of ethnic minorities (whose family origins will be in other parts of the world), are much more supportive of helping less well-off people in these countries. Indeed, many British ethnic minorities send substantial remittances to family members in their home countries and respond to appeals for help following disasters in their countries of origin, putting these sentiments into practice.

The overall picture on the potential unifying forces of British identity and values is therefore a rather complex and paradoxical one. On the optimistic side, the evidence suggests that feelings of national pride and belonging have held up well with no real decline over time. These feelings are also widely shared across different socio-economic strata of society, although young people do not feel quite so attached to the nation as their elders do. Similarly, the evidence on British values suggests that these are widely shared among all sections of society, including ethnic minorities, although some modest socio-economic divisions are apparent.

Figure 8.5. Social divisions in support for British values are generally small, especially for values which receive the highest levels of assent

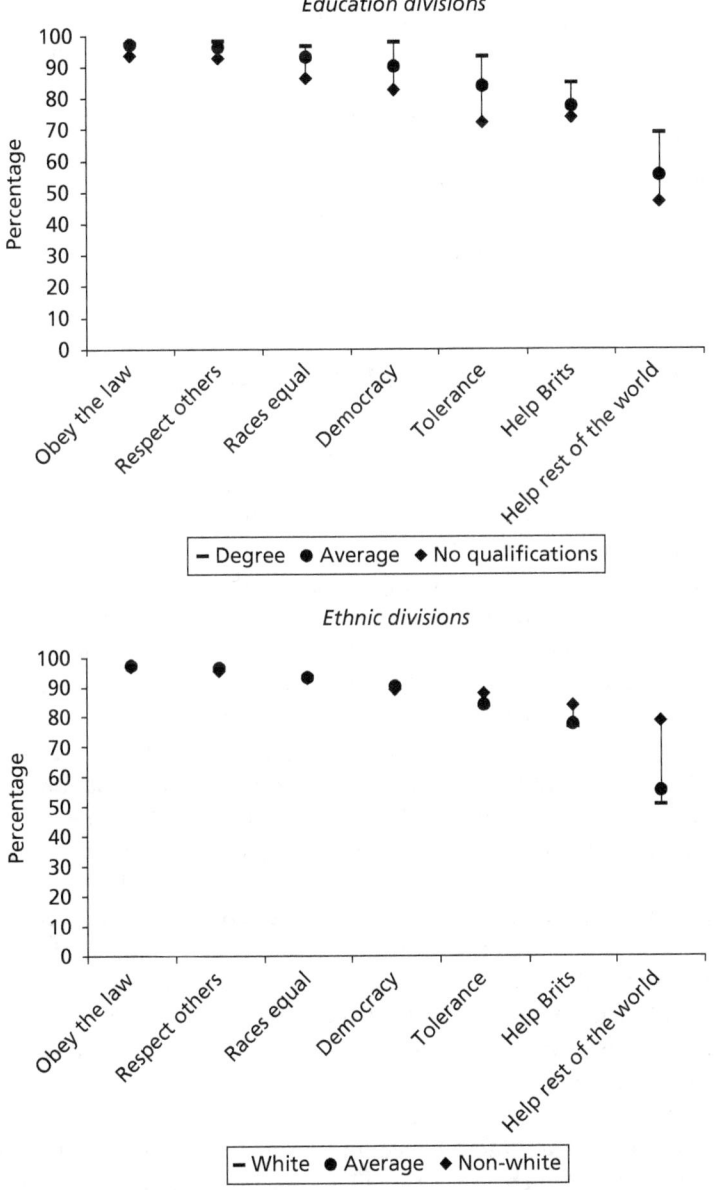

Source: 2011 Citizenship Survey (obey the law, treat with fairness, and treat races equally, England and Wales); 2014 British Social Attitudes Survey (important to understand reasoning, to help people in Britain and to help people in the rest of the world, Great Britain); 2005 World Values Survey (support for democracy, United Kingdom)

However, the evidence on the rejection of a British identity among substantial minorities of the population in Northern Ireland, Scotland, and Wales suggests a much more pessimistic picture of the extent of national unity around a shared British identity. In the case of Northern Ireland, this is a very long-standing phenomenon, whereas in the case of Scotland it is a more recent phenomenon, and not one that devolution has reversed.

One way to put this might be to say that the cohesive forces in British society do not manage to include all sections of the society equally. Some sections of society—the young, the less educated, Irish, Welsh, and Scottish nationalists—do not feel altogether included in the overarching national story. The glue is perhaps thinner and frayed around the edges.

Divisive Forces: Brexit and Other Issues

So the cohesive forces of national identity and shared values, while in some respects still looking as strong as ever, do not appeal to all sections of society equally and have acquired specific new weaknesses, too. What about the divisive forces—are these putting new strains on the (weakened) social glue?

The Brexit vote showed that opinion was split on one fundamental political issue, with 51.9 per cent (of those registered and voting) supporting exit from the European Union and 48.1 per cent voting to remain. I should, however, point out that it is wrong to say that Britain was divided down the middle: in fact, it would be more accurate to say that Britain was divided into three at the 2016 referendum, since around a third of the potential electorate either did not turn out to vote or were not even registered to vote. The official turnout was only 72.2 per cent, and this statistic takes no account of the substantial numbers (probably around 8 or 9 per cent of those eligible) who were not registered. Moreover, it tends to be younger and less affluent sections of society who are not registered.[22] The fact that between one quarter and one third of British citizens did not vote on such a fundamental political issue might also tell us something about lack of social cohesion. Scots managed much better in the 2014 Referendum on Scottish independence, when 84.6 per cent of registered electors turned out to cast a ballot. I will return to this in the next section of the chapter.

Leaving aside for the moment, then, the third of the public who did not vote at all, what is perhaps most concerning from the point of view of social cohesion is that the differences of opinion over Brexit seem to set one section of society against another. This has been characterized as a division between the winners and losers of globalization or as a division between successful groups and those left behind. To what extent, then, does it make sense to talk about two opposed nations? And how new is this phenomenon?

Britain, historically, has been divided along socio-economic lines with divisions of the sort that Disraeli would have recognized between the rich and the poor. At its crudest, social class can be seen as a contrast between the 'haves', who are in favour of preserving the status quo, and the 'have nots', who favour social change and the redistribution of income from the rich to the poor. The 'haves' are usually equated with professional and managerial workers and their families, whom I have termed the salariat; the 'have nots' are taken to be blue-collar, manual workers—the working class.[23] Class divisions of this sort formed the main basis of support for the two main political parties from the 1950s up until the 1980s, although they have since weakened.[24]

In some ways the Brexit vote can be seen as a rerun of these classic class divisions, albeit in a new guise and with some important new elements. Thus, many commentators have noted how support for Remain and for Leave ran along lines of the winners and losers of globalization. As Sara Hobolt puts it: 'the divide between winners and losers of globalization was a key driver of the [referendum] vote. Favouring British EU exit, or "Brexit", was particularly common among less-educated, poorer and older voters, and those who expressed concerns about immigration and multi-culturalism.'[25]

While academics have emphasized the role of economic inequalities in the Brexit vote, Brexit is not simply an example of new wine in old bottles. As Sara Hobolt points out, the important additional elements in Brexit, which were not present in the political and industrial conflicts of earlier decades in the same way, were those of immigration, national identity, and sovereignty. Immigration is often seen to bring economic threats to the material prosperity of poorer sections of society in the form of increased competition for jobs and housing. In addition, it may also present cultural threats to the British way of life and traditions. There is thus an important aspect of identity politics in Brexit as well as of instrumental politics. In this sense the divisions over Brexit can perhaps be related to two of the biggest social changes of the last thirty years, globalization and rising inequality on the one hand and immigration and ethnic diversity on the other. This combination potentially gives Brexit a greater divisive potential than the class conflicts of previous generations.

In Figure 8.6 I look at the magnitude of social divisions with respect to membership of the European Union (which was originally known colloquially as the Common Market). Questions on membership of the European Union and Common Market have regularly been asked in the authoritative and nationally representative British Election Surveys ever since the issue became politically salient back in the 1960s when French president General de Gaulle notoriously vetoed Britain's first and second applications to join the Common Market (in 1963 and 1967). He accused Britain of a deep-seated hostility to European construction.

Because the precise question wording varies from survey to survey[26] reflecting the changing political context, it does not make sense to chart overall levels

Figure 8.6. The same social divisions over Europe have been present for over fifty years, but their magnitude increased between 1964 and 2015

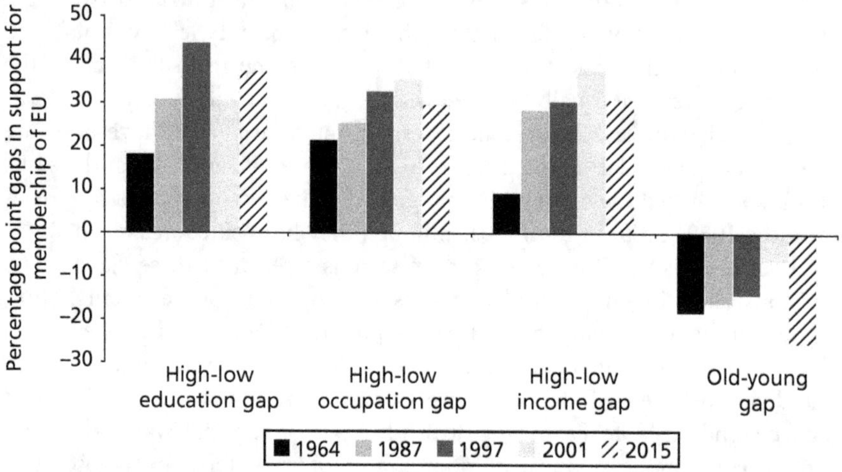

Source: British Election Surveys

of support. However, measures of the social divisions are likely to be reasonably comparable over time, and in Figure 8.6 I show the readings from 1964, 1987, 1997, 2001, and 2015 with respect to support for membership of the Common Market/European Union.

What we see is that there were quite strong socio-economic divisions on whether Britain should be a member of the Common Market even back in 1964—the 'haves', people with higher levels of education, higher occupations, and higher incomes, generally being more favourable to membership. There has also been a long-standing age division with younger people being more supportive of Europe than older generations. So there is nothing especially new about the kinds of division that scholars have recently observed in their studies of the Brexit referendum.

What is new, however, is the magnitude of these divisions, which on balance has increased over time. Surprisingly, there is no clear date at which the divisions became greater. I had expected that they might have become greater after the Maastricht Treaty of 1992, which paved the way for greater European integration (and which was strongly resisted by some Eurosceptic MPs), but the results shown in Figure 8.6 suggest that the divisions gradually widened from 1964 until the turn of the century without any clear step change.

In recent decades the educational divisions seem to be larger than the social class and income divisions, although it is hard to disentangle the separate influences of these three socio-economic measures as they overlap so considerably. Nevertheless, the rise of educational differentiation may perhaps reflect the growing importance of the more cultural concerns over Europe as opposed to the instrumental ones. There were also, as expected, quite substantial differences between older and younger citizens but much more modest differences with respect to ethnicity and gender (which I do not show in order to avoid data overload).

In the case of immigration, we have reasonably comparable questions going back to 1979.[27] Again, educational divisions dominate the story (perhaps reflecting cultural rather than economic concerns over immigration), and it is clear that they are long-standing (Figure 8.7). I guess that if comparable questions had been included in earlier surveys, we would have found similar divisions in the 1960s.

The long-standing nature of these divisions over immigration will come as no surprise to people of my age who were reading the news in the 1960s. I still recall the headlines made by Enoch Powell's 'rivers of blood' speech in which he opposed the 1968 Race Relations Bill, a bill proposing measures to protect black and minority ethnic groups from racial discrimination.[28] He was immediately sacked by the leader of the Conservative party, Edward Heath, from the Shadow Cabinet. There was also the notorious Smethwick by-election in 1965 when Labour lost a safe working-class seat to Peter Griffiths, the Conservative candidate, who was said to have used the slogan 'if you want a nigger for a neighbour, vote Labour'. There are some question marks over whether Griffiths actually used the slogan, or whether it was put about by far right groups, but Griffiths did not condemn it and defended it as 'a manifestation of popular feeling'.[29]

Figure 8.7. Divisions over immigration are long-standing, with little sign of change between 1979 and 2015

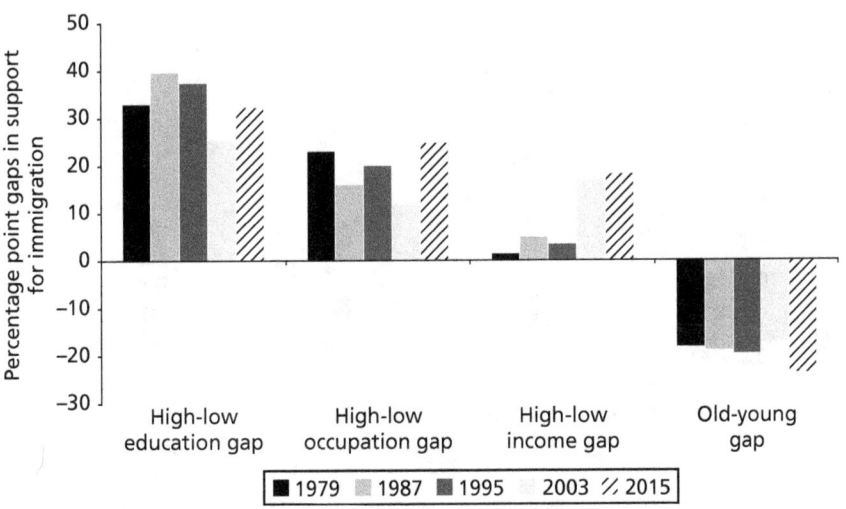

Source: British Election Surveys 1979, 1987, 2015; British Social Attitudes Surveys 1995, 2003

I should put these two issues of Europe and immigration in context by comparing them with the classic issue which divided the 'haves' from the 'have nots', namely the redistribution of income and wealth. Here we have reasonably comparable questions going back to the 1970s.[30]

Figure 8.8 is in several ways the mirror image of Figure 8.6. First, we can see that the magnitude of all the social divisions declined rather than increased over time (with the exception of the odd reading for income gap in 1974). Second, income rather than education is the strongest line of cleavage. And third, the age gap is reversed—older people have tended to be more in favour of redistribution than have younger people.

It is not surprising that income is a more important driver of attitudes towards income redistribution than is education. But I do find it surprising that divisions have tended to narrow in recent decades despite the greatly increased income inequality. My interpretation is that the magnitude of social divisions over the different issues does not simply reflect the magnitude of the objective changes in society but depends in part on the extent to which political parties and the mass media give them prominence. Thus Labour governments from 1997 to 2010 moved towards the centre of the political spectrum and did not campaign on the issue of inequality. These Labour governments broadly accepted the operation of free markets and globalization, and indeed one leading Labour modernizer and government minister, Peter Mandelson, famously stated that he was 'intensely relaxed about people

Figure 8.8. Social divisions over redistribution of income and wealth are long-standing, but their magnitude diminished between 1974 and 2014/15

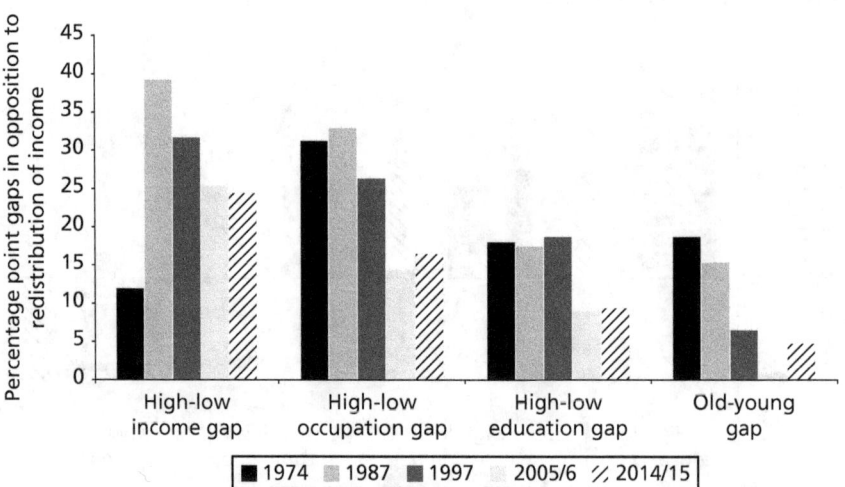

Source: British Election Surveys 1974, 1987, 1997; British Social Attitudes Surveys 2005 and 2006 pooled, and 2014 and 2015 pooled

getting filthy rich' (although he did add 'so long as they pay their taxes').[31] I think one could characterize these Labour governments, or New Labour as they were branded, as focussing more on equality of opportunity to become rich rather than on the magnitude of the inequalities themselves.

Be that as it may, the survey data do seem to suggest that social divisions over Europe have increased in magnitude, but that social divisions over redistribution have declined. It does not appear to be the case that Britain has become more divided overall. Instead, it is the issues over which Britain is divided that have changed. Thus in 1987, the survey data suggested that the income gap in attitudes towards redistribution was around forty points, slightly larger than the thirty-five point educational gap in attitudes to membership of the European Union found in 2015. Britain is indeed divided today, but on this evidence the scale of the divisions is not all that different from divisions over previous salient political issues.

Increasing Disengagement and Disconnect?

Another challenge to social cohesion may be that of declining vibrancy of civic life, declining trust in other citizens, and increasing disconnect from politics. Trust in others and active participation in collective projects has often been seen as a crucial ingredient of a cohesive society. Political scientists from Alexis de Toqueville in 1835 onwards have emphasized the importance of active participation in civic life for the health of democracy. De Toqueville visited the USA in the 1830s and was especially impressed by the active civic participation of Americans and the way in which they formed a dense network of voluntary associations. He saw this as a fundamental ingredient for successful US democracy.[32] This theme has been taken up by many subsequent scholars, most notably by US political scientist Robert Putnam. In his famous book *Bowling Alone* Putnam charted a worrying picture of declining civic engagement (measured for example by declining participation in voluntary organizations and declining turnout in elections) in the USA. He argued that one consequence of these changes was a decline in social trust.

These concerns are not about the presence or absence of conflicts over things like Brexit, redistribution, austerity, and the like, but a concern about a different kind of social malaise—people hunkering down and opting out of civic life. I think this is what former prime minister David Cameron may have had in mind when he said that 'A Greater Britain doesn't just need a stronger economy—it needs a stronger society.'

Robert Putnam brought these ideas together under the general rubric of declining social capital. He defined social capital as 'the connections among individuals—social networks and the norms of reciprocity and trustworthiness that arise from them'.[33] He (like many other scholars) argued that social capital is highly beneficial for the functioning of society, for oiling the wheels of public life, for solving collective problems and providing shared benefits for all sections of society. Analogous to physical capital, social capital is a productive resource which can bring benefits both to individuals and to communities: Putnam concluded that 'civic connections help make us healthy, wealthy and wise'.[34] He argued that social capital makes collective problems easier to resolve, as it helps to overcome the individual selfishness that can undermine shared solutions which benefit everyone. Social capital can thus result in improved social environments, such as safer neighbourhoods. Social capital can also make business and social transactions easier, since when people trust each other, there is less need to spend time and money enforcing contracts. I suspect that mutual trust and willingness to cooperate is the key ingredient of social cohesion, and is quite possibly much more important than sentiments of national pride or even shared acceptance of abstract British values.

Previous academic research on Britain has come up with contrasting assessments of the strength of social capital. Peter Hall concluded (in the late 1990s) that social capital in Britain was robust and had not shown the same kind of decline that the USA had experienced.[35] In contrast Paola Grenier and Karen Wright, a decade later, concluded from their review of the evidence that the picture was somewhat darker. They argued that, as a result of the withering of many active working-class institutions such as trade unions and mutual societies over the last two decades of the twentieth century, social capital in the sense of civic participation was increasingly concentrated among more advantaged social classes. 'The distribution of participation is not a niggling concern—it is the main story, with important implications for social trust as well.'[36]

We can now update both Hall's and Grenier and Wright's analyses. We have reasonably good data over quite a long time span on four different aspects of social disengagement. I look at two subjective measures—trust in others (as measured by the question 'Generally speaking, would you say that most people can be trusted?'), and the feeling that 'politicians don't care what people like me think', a sentiment which some scholars such as Sara Hobolt have suggested was an important source of the Brexit vote. We can think of the latter as an indicator of a political disconnect between the citizens and the political classes. (This is not generally included in lists of the indicators of social capital, but I include it for its relevance to current debates over Brexit.) I also draw on two behavioural measures which were central to Robert Putnam's conception of social capital, namely participation in voluntary associations and turnout in general elections (to which I add turnout in national referenda).

Different data sources tell slightly different stories about the trends over time—and in all four measures there seems to be considerable volatility around the trends. The most reliable evidence is on turnout in UK general elections and referenda, where we have pretty good data for every election since the war. One important caveat about the official data on turnout, however, is that the electoral register may have become increasingly inaccurate as a measure of the number of citizens who are entitled to vote. After all, if citizens increasingly feel alienated from politics and fail to register, this would undermine the value for our purposes of the standard official measure of the proportion of registered electors who cast their ballots. For this reason I also include an alternative measure of the proportion of the voting-age population who turned out to vote.

Fortunately, the two trends are not all that different, although the alternative measure gives more pessimistic readings for general election turnout in recent years. Both tell a story of large election-to-election volatility around a long-term downwards trend. There are plenty of good reasons why general election turnout might vary from one election to another—turnout will tend to increase if there is a big difference between the parties so that more is at stake, or if the election is expected to be a close one. But leaving these variations aside, it looks as though turnout fell from the high 70s in the first two decades after the war to the mid-60s in the twenty-first century—one of the larger examples of social decline that we have seen in this book, in marked contrast to all the evidence in earlier chapters on material and social progress (Figure 8.9).

Intriguingly, however, we do not find the same downwards trend when it comes to turnout for referenda, such as the 1975 and 2016 referenda on Europe and the three referenda on Scottish devolution and independence. Indeed, turnout in the Scottish Independence referendum of 2014 reached 84.6 per cent, the highest recorded for an election or referendum in the United Kingdom since the introduction of universal suffrage in 1928. So perhaps we should not be quite so pessimistic.

The data on membership of voluntary organizations is much patchier, with different sources suggesting rather different levels of membership (Figure 8.10). There does seem to be a modest downwards trend, although the earliest survey, from 1959, appears to contradict this interpretation. However, I am reluctant to put too much reliance on the single measure from 1959 as all the other data sources point to modest decline since the 1980s.

The evidence on social trust is just as patchy (Figure 8.11). Trust was at its highest back in 1959, at around 50 per cent. Since then the figure has wobbled around 40 per cent, possibly with a declining trend. It is difficult to be sure.

Any long-term trend in the extent of disconnect between citizens and politics is also hard to discern (Figure 8.12). Our different sources all ask the same question, namely whether one agrees or disagrees that 'politicians don't care what people like me think'. I show the percentage who disagreed, in other words the percentage who felt connected rather than disconnected with the political system. As we can see, the percentages vary wildly from one source to another and, in the case of the British Election Study series, from one year to

Figure 8.9. There is some evidence of slow long-term decline in general election turnout, although the changes were modest

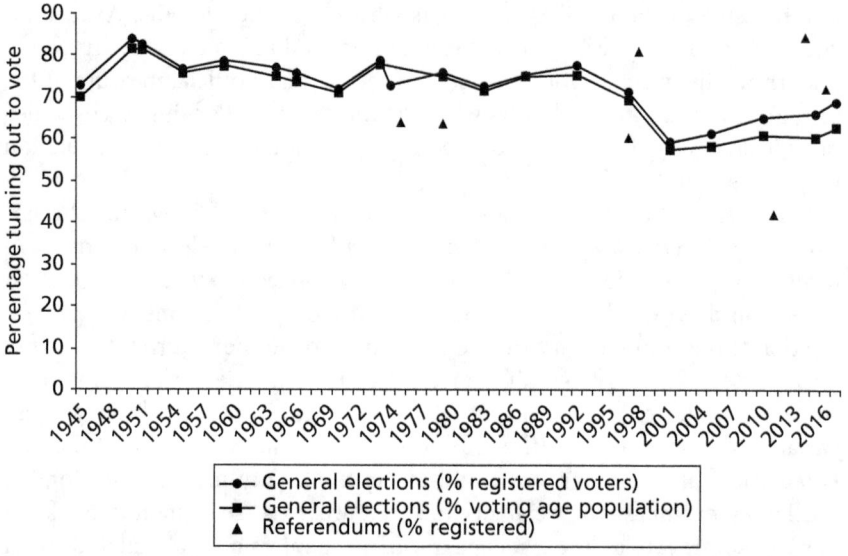

Source: House of Commons Research Papers 01/37, 01/54, 05/33, and 10/36, http://www.ukpolitical.info/Turnout45.htm; voting-age population from IDEA (not available for the 1974 elections), https://www.idea.int/data-tools/data/voter-turnout

Figure 8.10. There is some evidence of a slight long-term decline in membership of voluntary associations

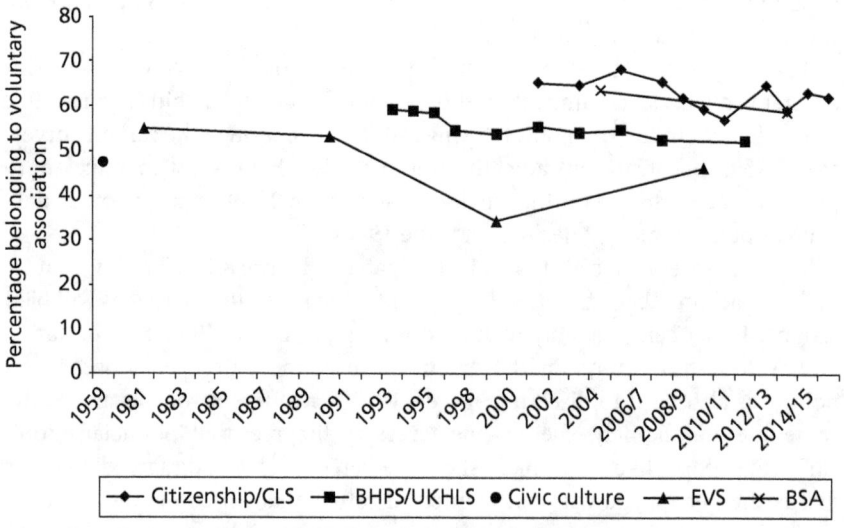

Source: Citizenship Survey and Community Life Survey (CLS) (England), British Household Panel Survey (BHPS) and UK Household Longitudinal Study (UKHLS), 1959 Civic Culture Study, European Values Surveys (EVS), British Social Attitudes Surveys (BSA)

Figure 8.11. There is perhaps some evidence of a slight long-term decline in social trust

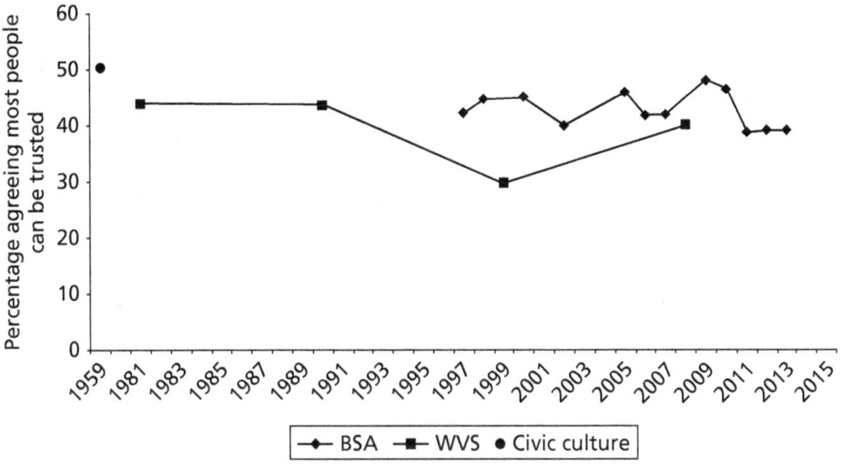

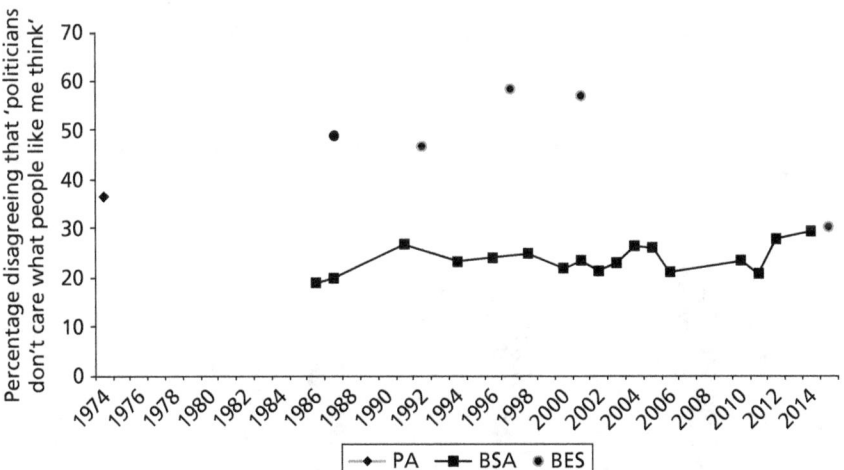

Source: British Social Attitudes Surveys (BSA), World Values Survey (WVS), 1959 Civic Culture Survey

Figure 8.12. The feeling of disconnect from politics is long-standing

Source: 1974 Political Action Survey (PA), British Social Attitudes Surveys (BSA), British Election Surveys (BES)

another. Possibly this reflects methodological variations between the sources or perhaps real but short-lived changes in the nature of politics—we cannot be sure either way.

I do not therefore feel that we can be particularly confident about the extent of the long-term trends, although most seem to be slightly downwards rather than upwards. On the other hand, I am struck by the rather low levels of trust and the high levels of disconnect with politics shown in most of the different surveys, and by the fact that low trust and high disconnect are very long-standing. Thus, even back in 1959 only half the population felt that most citizens could be trusted. Back in 1974 less than half the population felt that politicians cared what ordinary people thought. We cannot blame rising inequality in the 1980s for these pessimistic findings. Britain seems to have had an endemic problem of social and political disconnect.

These results, then, are in rather sharp contrast with the very high percentages who described themselves as proud of Britain or who assent to British values. Furthermore, Figure 8.13 shows that, in contrast with the consensus across most sections of society on national pride and British values, social divisions in civic engagement and trust are quite substantial. I focus in Figure 8.13 on divisions between the most highly and the least highly educated members of society. (Other measures of social divisions and their changes over time tell a similar story.) I compare results from early, pre-1980 studies (such as the 1959 Civic Culture study) with those conducted during the 1980s and those conducted most recently after 2010.

The main story from Figure 8.13 is that there are major socio-economic divisions both in sentiments (social trust and feelings of disconnect from politics) and behaviour (voluntary association membership and election turnout). These appear to be long-standing, with the important exception of election turnout. Social divisions appear to have become slightly greater in the case of trust and membership of voluntary organizations, although I would describe these as glacial social changes. In contrast, educational divisions in

Figure 8.13. There are long-standing educational divisions in civic engagement, plus recent ones in turnout

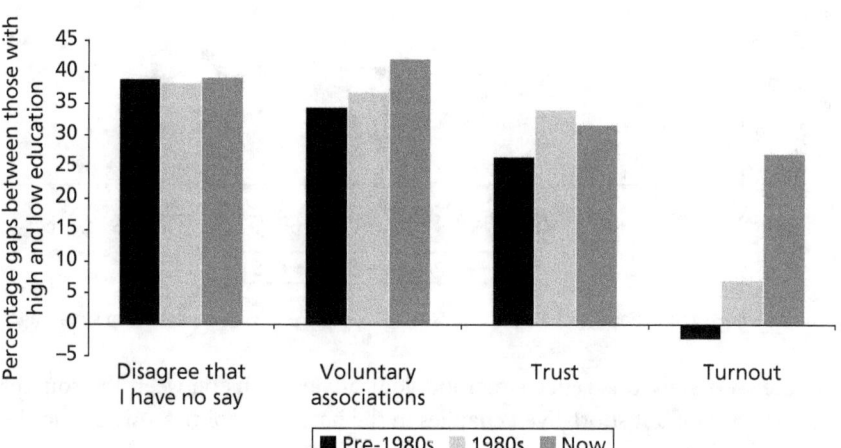

Source: UK Household Longitudinal Study Wave 3 (2012); European Values Survey (1981); Civic Culture Study (1959). The UK Household Longitudinal Study and European Values Survey include Northern Ireland; the Civic Culture Study covers Great Britain

turnout at general elections rose from basically zero to around twenty-five percentage points in the 2000s. There was also a large growth in the age divisions in turnout over the same period.

While I would not completely rule out the possibility that increasing inequality and diversity may have had some modest impact on widening social divisions with respect to trust and association membership, I think it is rather implausible that they could be responsible for the much larger changes in turnout. General theories like the increasing economic inequality of the 1980s can hardly explain why divisions in turnout increased so much more than the other divisions. Grand general theories cannot explain highly specific changes.

How might we explain the widening social divisions in election turnout? One plausible line of argument emphasizes the growing disjunction between MPs and their voters, especially on the Labour side. The proportion of Labour MPs who came from working-class backgrounds used to be quite high—the social backgrounds of Labour MPs tended to resemble those of their working-class voters, whereas the backgrounds of Conservative MPs resembled those of their middle-class voters. However, Oliver Heath has shown that the proportion of working-class Labour MPs started declining quite sharply in the 1980s as the party professionalized.[37] Labour MPs were thus no longer representative, in a socio-economic sense, of the people who had voted for them. They might also have been seen as different culturally—in their attitudes and sentiments. They were not 'one of us'.

Be this as it may, the main story from Figure 8.13 is that there have been major social divisions in the distribution of social capital ever since the late 1950s. Britain was not the harmonious and cohesive society back in the 1950s that middle-class nostalgia might suggest. Britain has long been a society where large sections of the population are socially and economically marginalized and disconnected. This is not a new problem—except in the case of turnout.

How Does Britain Compare with Peer Countries?

How does Britain compare with our peer countries in its level of social cohesion? Thinking of the general theories with which I introduced the chapter, Britain is (along with the USA) one of the most unequal societies economically, and on this theory might be expected to be relatively lacking in cohesion compared with more equal societies such as France, Germany, and Japan. Britain is not, however, especially diverse. Of our eight peer countries, Canada is much the most diverse with 39 per cent of its population having a migration background in 2013. Sweden, France, and the USA also have larger proportions of their populations with an immigration background than does the UK. The UK, with migrants and the children of migrants making up

19 per cent of its population, is around the average for OECD countries, and the only peer countries which are less diverse than Britain are Italy (9 per cent) and Japan (2 per cent).[38] My guess is that people in Britain believe that the country has received an unusually large number of migrants but, if so, they are mistaken. At any rate, on both counts we expect Japan to be more cohesive than Britain, and the USA (and perhaps Canada as well) to be less cohesive.

So what do we find? As before, I will look at the unifying forces (pride and closeness to the nation); the divisive forces (attitudes to immigration and to redistribution); and the fragmenting processes of disengagement and disconnection (trust, turnout, and government responsiveness). I draw on harmonized cross-national survey programmes where identical questions on relevant topics have been asked in all our eight peer countries (though occasionally a country may be missing). However, I do not attempt to look at trends over time, since the data are too patchy and short term to be useful.

I focus both on the levels and on the extent of inequality around the overall national level. The two tend to go together—but not always. I use box and whisker plots which enable us to put both measures on the same figure. To avoid overload, I focus on whichever social division is generally the largest in the eight countries.

THE UNIFYING FORCES

Beginning with the unifying forces, the International Social Survey Programme provides comparable measures of feelings of national pride and of closeness to one's country in seven of the eight peer countries (only missing Italy). I focus on feelings of closeness to one's country, as this is conceptually closer to the concept of social cohesion than is national pride. As in Britain, in the other countries age differences tend to be the largest and so in Figure 8.14 I plot the average levels and the magnitude of the age differences around these averages in the seven countries.

As can be seen, Japan does particularly well on closeness, whereas Britain has the lowest average score and is one of the more divided nations, with larger differences between young and old than in most other countries, apart from the USA. However, I should not exaggerate the differences—all seven countries for which we have data score pretty highly, and in all seven countries younger people feel somewhat less close to their country than do older people. On these measures, Britain is perhaps somewhat less cohesive than most of the peer countries, but it is not badly out of line.

DIVISIVE ISSUES

The issue of leaving the European Union is a rather specifically British concern, so instead I just look at divisions over immigration and redistribution. Given

Figure 8.14. There are generally high levels of closeness to one's country in peer countries, although significant age differences are apparent

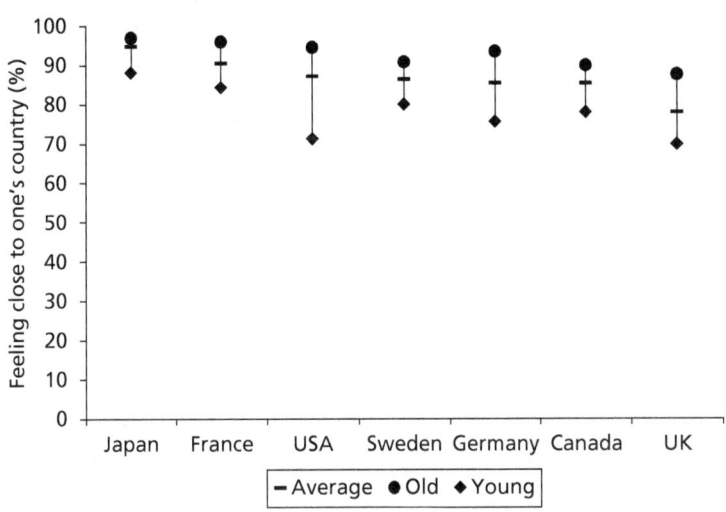

Source: International Social Survey Programme (2003 and 2013, pooled)

the focus on divisiveness, I concentrate on how large the divisions are. The actual levels of support for immigration and for redistribution are not without interest, but they are of secondary importance. I focus on educational differences in the case of immigration and income differences in the case of redistribution since these tend to be largest.[39]

As we can see from Figure 8.15, all the peer countries are more divided over these issues than they were in the case of closeness to the nation. Germany proves to be the most divided country on immigration, while Canada and the USA are the least divided. In contrast, in the case of redistribution, Sweden proves to be the most divided, with all the other countries being quite similar to each other. There does not seem to be a general pattern here, then. All the countries are divided on one or other issue (apart from Canada, for which we lack redistribution data). Britain does not look badly out of step with the other peer countries.

SOCIAL ENGAGEMENT AND DISCONNECTION

Three indicators are available for international comparisons—trust, electoral turnout, and disenchantment with politics. The trust question is basically similar to the one which I used in Figure 8.9 to examine time trends in Britain. The question on political disenchantment is worded rather differently but tackles the same underlying concept.[40] The turnout question is rather different,

Figure 8.15a. European countries generally exhibit large educational differences in support for immigration

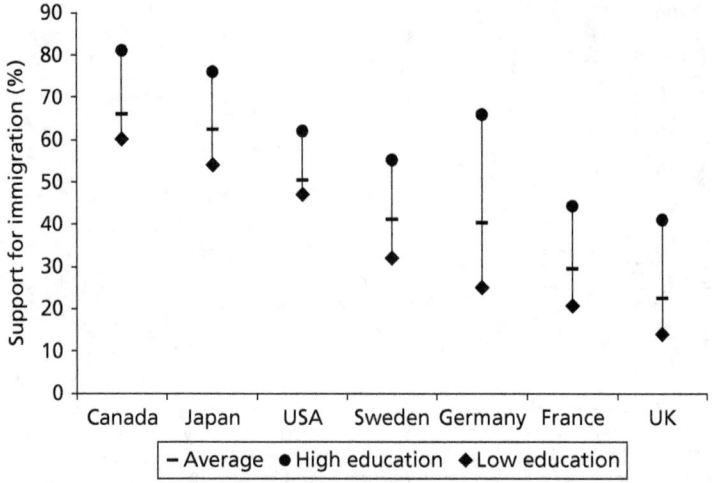

Source: International Social Survey Programme (2003 and 2013, pooled)

Figure 8.15b. There are some large income differences in support for redistribution in peer countries

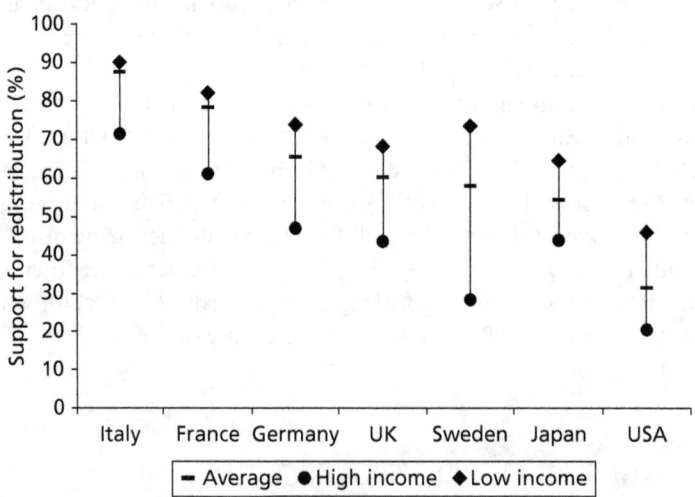

Source: International Social Survey Programme (2009)

however, in that it is derived from people's self-reports of whether they voted or not, rather than from official statistics. Self-reports are notorious for producing inflated levels of claimed turnout, so one should not take the apparent high levels of turnout too seriously. However, I have to use the self-reports as the official statistics do not allow us to calculate age or educational differences.

I look at educational divisions in the case of trust and disenchantment, but age in the case of turnout (Figures 8.16a and 8.16b, respectively). More detailed analysis indicates that, as in Britain, these tend to be the major lines of cleavage in the peer countries. In many respects the results are quite similar to the ones I reported earlier in the analysis of trends in Britain. Thus in most countries the public is not all that trusting, and there are large educational differences in levels of trust. Disenchantment with politics is also widespread (Figure 8.16c). Turnout is fairly high in most of the peer countries, although there is quite a lot of variation in the magnitude of the age divisions. The only country that really stands out is Sweden, which comes out at the top of the ranking on all three indicators.

Britain is not especially out of line in the case of trust or of political disenchantment. It does, however, have one of the lower rates of turnout (a finding which is confirmed by official statistics) and is also quite divided. Britain is certainly towards the back of the pack in this respect.[41]

Overall, then, the similarities between the countries are more striking than the differences. The British pattern of high levels of attachment to the nation, major social divisions over political issues like immigration and redistribution, and moderate levels of trust and political engagement (accompanied by major social differentiation) seems to be present in most of the other countries, too.

Figure 8.16a. Sweden shows the highest level of generalized trust

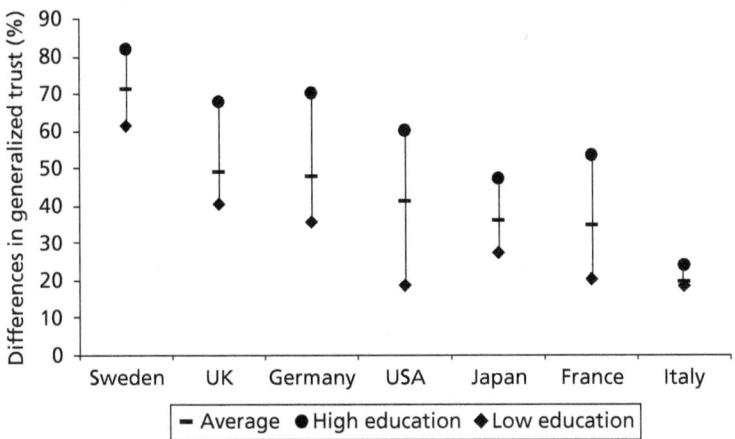

Source: International Social Survey Programme (2008 and 2014, pooled, Canada did not participate in these rounds)

Figure 8.16b. The USA is the laggard in electoral turnout

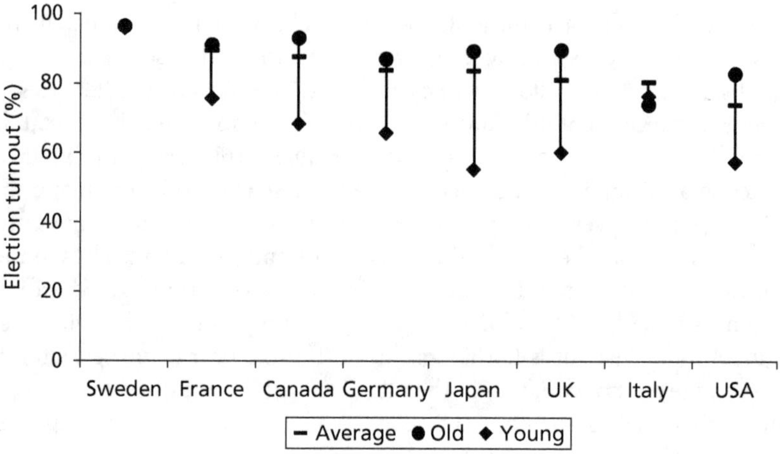

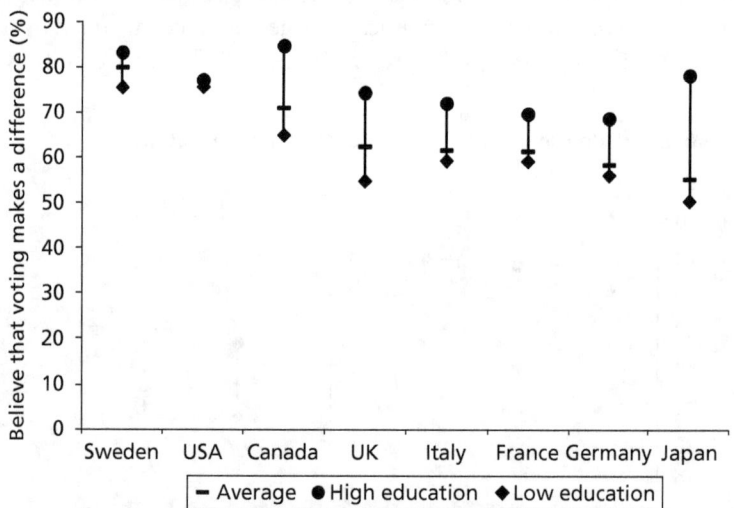

Source: Comparative Study of Electoral Systems (UK 2005 and 2015, pooled; Italy 2006, Canada 2011; France and USA 2012; Germany and Japan 2013; Sweden 2014)

Figure 8.16c. Japan is the laggard in political disenchantment

Source: Comparative Study of Electoral Systems (UK 2015; Italy 2006; Canada 2011; France and USA 2012; Germany and Japan 2013; Sweden 2014)

The ranking of the countries does, however, seem to differ across the different outcomes. Thus Japan scores best on sense of closeness to the nation, which makes sense since it is by far the most homogeneous of the eight countries. In contrast, Japan scores worst on political disconnect; this may well be linked to the fact that Japanese politics has been dominated by a single party for most of the post-war period. In contrast, Sweden scores well on all three indicators of social and political engagement, but scores worst on social divisions over redistribution of income.

This suggests that we should not regard social cohesion as a unitary phenomenon. While the data are not nearly as robust as I would like, the results are in a sense a vindication of distinguishing different aspects of cohesion from each other. As the example of Japan highlights, if we were to single out a single indicator of cohesion, such as pride or feeling of closeness to the nation, we would completely miss important sources of division and disengagement.

The results also call into question the theories that countries with higher levels of inequality and of diversity would be less cohesive. While the Japanese case suggests that one should take seriously the idea that homogeneous societies will exhibit greater feelings of national belonging, it also suggests that homogeneity on its own does little to promote unity on major social issues or promotes high levels of trust and engagement. Similarly, the US case suggests that one should take seriously the idea that economically unequal societies may also be socially and educationally divided in attitudes and sentiments (such as trust and feelings of national belonging). It also suggests, however, that inequality does not necessarily entail low absolute levels of sentiments or engagement across the board. The devil is in the detail.

The effects of inequality or diversity may therefore be specific rather than general. They may well operate on particular aspects of social cohesion rather than having positive or negative effects across the board. I am inclined to be a bit sceptical of very broad-brush theoretical claims which hold that inequality or diversity have uniformly negative effects.

Conclusions

The key question for this chapter was whether there was evidence of progressive social corrosion in the decades after the 1980s when, as we saw in Chapter 2, inequality increased so greatly in Britain and ethnic diversity increased, too. However, the data do not really support the expectation that social cohesion has been substantially corroded. Nor do the data suggest that Britain is much less cohesive than peer countries. To be sure, the picture is not uniformly positive and the major theme of the evidence is that many of

Britain's strengths and weaknesses are long-standing. Continuity is more evident than change. Thus, while social divisions over membership of the European Union are indeed much larger in the twenty-first century than they had been in the 1960s and 1970s, Britain has become less socially divided over the classic political issue of redistribution. The character of the social divisions over Brexit is thus new but the fact of being divided is not so new.

I can well remember the industrial conflict of the 1970s and 1980s and I still have on my shelf a book by Samuel Beer titled *Britain against Itself*, in which he argued that Britain had become ungovernable.[42] He argued that the source of this ungovernability was the decline of the civic culture and the rise of what he termed the new populism. Nearly forty years later, analyses of Britain's current state are not all that different from Beer's. Maybe the focus of conflict has shifted from labour relations to immigration, but the divisions in society between 'them' and 'us' are not all that new. Have we perhaps confused legitimate political disagreement with a lack of social cohesion?

The extent of continuity shown in the evidence presented in this chapter must cast considerable doubt on the grand theoretical ideas that rising social inequality and increasing ethnic diversity have been corrosive of British society. Comparisons with peer countries also suggest that Britain is not especially out of line, nor that the most unequal and diverse societies are in all respects the least cohesive. I would not claim that the evidence presented in this chapter provides a definitive test. The best kind of test would be to compare a range of comparable countries and to see whether *increases* in levels of diversity or of inequality are associated with *reductions* in social trust or other indicators of social cohesion. One of the few studies which has been conducted along these lines, comparing changes over time within the different states of the USA, found that increasing inequality was unrelated to declining levels of trust.[43]

But while I am sceptical about the value of these broad-brush theories for explaining social change in Britain, it is clear that there have been some specific changes which are in need of specific explanations. Most notably, there is evidence that turnout in general elections has declined in Britain, and that age (and other differences) in turnout have increased, too. Similarly, there is evidence of long-term increases in Scottish and Irish, rather than British, national identities within the UK, which now looks distinctly less united than it did when I was growing up.

I suspect that specific political explanations are required for these changes. In both the Scottish and Irish cases, I conjecture that nationalistic feelings may have been fuelled by perceptions that the government in Westminster was remote and relatively unconcerned about the concerns and grievances of minorities in Northern Ireland or Scotland. The fundamental issue may be that Britain's first-past-the-post electoral system, except in exceptional circumstances, gives the main political parties little incentive to worry about the concerns of numerically small groups.

Overall, on most indicators of social cohesion, Britain is not all that dissimilar from peer countries, or from its own past history. But it perhaps faces distinctive specific challenges which are rather different from those of its past or of peer countries. I fear that these challenges may be exacerbated by the Brexit referendum.

9 Progress in Tackling Beveridge's Five Giants

The Successes and Limitations of Social Reform

Social Progress and Social Reform

I started the book by asking how much progress Britain had made over the course of my lifetime in tackling Beveridge's five giants of Want, Disease, Ignorance, Squalor, and Idleness. I also asked how well Britain's progress compared with that of peer countries—Canada, France, Germany, Italy, Japan, Sweden, and the USA—and whether progress had been shared across different sections of British society. Had the giants become more selective in whom they threatened so that disadvantaged groups were left behind?

To Beveridge's five giants I added the sixth giant of unfairness or inequality of opportunity. And I also asked whether, in the pursuit of material progress, Britain might have lost some other strengths which I remember (or perhaps imagined) from my childhood—strengths of social cohesion and a sense of solidarity and belonging. Had these been undermined by rising inequality or increasing ethnic diversity?

In this concluding chapter I aim to draw together the evidence presented throughout the book and to see what answers I can provide to these questions. As I warned at the outset, there are more questions than answers. Some of my answers will be fairly robust while others are much more provisional—the data are often patchy, suspect, or contradictory. The frequent revisions to official statistics, for example, mean that they are not always a solid guide to change over time. Moreover, the operation of Goodhart's law—that once a measure becomes a target, it ceases to be a good measure—led me to be particularly sceptical about the value of official statistics on examination results for measuring progress in tackling the giant of Ignorance.

In this chapter I shall also put forward some suggestions about the possible reasons for progress, or its absence, in Britain. In particular, what can we learn from the comparisons with peer countries? Did Margaret Thatcher's reforms in the 1980s, for example, lead us to move closer to the USA and away from countries of continental Europe like Germany and Sweden with their more regulated economies and extensive welfare states?

Britain had started the post-war period with a Labour government which largely shaped Britain's economy and welfare state for the next thirty years. The 1945–50 Labour government established the National Health Service, provided free secondary education for all, nationalized industries such as coal, railways, electricity and gas, iron and steel, and the Bank of England, initiated a major programme of slum clearance and construction of social housing, introduced an extensive programme of social insurance as recommended by Beveridge, and levied high tax rates in order to pay for public services. Subsequent Labour and Conservative governments up until 1979 maintained this broad framework of a mixed economy and welfare state, although varying some of the details—most notably introducing legislation to outlaw discrimination against women and ethnic minorities and replacing the tripartite system of grammar, technical, and modern schools with comprehensive schools. For these first three decades after the war, the political economy of Britain was much closer to that of our European neighbours than to the free market model of the USA.

Margaret Thatcher's three administrations between 1979 and 1990 radically reshaped this post-war settlement and moved Britain much closer to the US model. Her administrations gradually privatized a large proportion of the public sector, notably the basic utilities of water, power, and telecoms (substantially weakening the trade unions in the process). Her administrations sold off a large proportion of the social housing stock to tenants. She deregulated the labour market and the private renting sector of housing, and introduced market forces into education and to a lesser extent into the health service. Taxes on the better-off were sharply reduced, contributing to the growth of inequality in the 1980s, while the value of several welfare benefits were reduced relative to average earnings.

Margaret Thatcher's reforms largely remained in place, or were further extended, under subsequent Conservative and Labour governments. Since the 2007/8 financial crash, austerity measures designed to balance the books further cut back public services and reduced benefit levels for some types of claimant (although hitting the young and those of working age more than pensioners). By the end of the twentieth century political economists such as Peter Hall and David Soskice described Britain as having a liberal market economy similar to those of the USA and Canada in contrast to the coordinated market economies of Germany, Sweden, and Japan.[1] Similarly, Britain's welfare arrangements were moved away from what has been termed the social democratic model of universal, publicly funded provision to a more US-style liberal model with lower benefits, extensive means testing, and greater reliance on market forces.[2]

However, my judgement is that Margaret Thatcher's reforms went much further in the economic and housing spheres than they did in the spheres of health and education. There was nothing really equivalent in either health or education to her extensive programme of privatizing public sector utilities. In the case of education, the interventions were fairly limited and, crucially, secondary education remained free and universal up to the age of 16 throughout the post-war period. Margaret Thatcher's administrations introduced measures to increase competition between schools and to reduce local authority control (for example introducing league tables, increasing parental choice, and setting up grant-maintained schools managed by central rather than by local government). But in other ways her administrations increased regulation as for example with the national curriculum and compulsory testing of schoolchildren throughout their educational careers. Moreover, fees for higher education (plus loans to help students pay for them) were only introduced much later in 1998 by Tony Blair's New Labour government. Margaret Thatcher's 1983 government had put forward similar proposals but backed down after a Conservative back-bench rebellion.[3]

Interventions in health care were even more limited under Margaret Thatcher. The NHS continued to provide universal and largely free health care (apart from charges for dental care, which had been introduced in 1951, and prescription charges, which had been introduced in 1952). The main reform was to move towards an internal market, giving family doctors the power to take control of their own budgets and to buy care under the GP fund-holding scheme.

The area of welfare where Margaret Thatcher's administrations did undertake major reforms was social insurance, which had of course been Beveridge's key concern. While the principle of social insurance itself was retained, eligibility for young people was restricted and the value of a number of benefits, such as unemployment benefits, relative to the value of real wages was sharply reduced. In the 1960s and 1970s the value of unemployment benefits in Britain had been much more generous than in the USA, but the 1980s reforms reduced the relative value of benefits bringing them much closer to those in the USA.[4] In this sense the welfare state did move much closer to the US model.

What this suggests is that the 1980s might have been something of a watershed in the case of Want, Squalor, and Idleness but less so in the case of Ignorance and Disease. Since the aims of Margaret Thatcher's reforms were to promote competition and efficiency, the crucial question therefore is whether Britain moved closer to the USA after the 1980s not only with respect to policies but also with respect to outcomes such as rates of economic growth and unemployment. I would not expect to see the same convergence with the USA, and divergence from Europe, with respect to health or education, where Margaret Thatcher's reforms had been much less radical and should not be expected to have had a major impact on Britain's trajectory.

It is perhaps also worth considering what our expectations might be in the case of inequality of opportunity and social corrosion. The 1944 Education Act had been expected to improve equality of opportunity between the social classes, and similar hopes were held out for Labour's policy of comprehensive reorganization from 1965 onwards. In contrast, subsequent reforms such as the introduction of competition between schools were intended more to drive up standards than to promote equality of opportunity. Indeed, some critics suspected that these reforms, and even more so the reintroduction of tuition fees for university education, might have the opposite effect of reducing equality of opportunity. The growth of income inequality during the 1980s was also expected to have adverse side effects on equality of opportunity and social mobility. So on balance one might expect initial progress towards equality of opportunity immediately after the war to be followed by a reversal towards the end of the century.

The growth of income inequality was also widely expected to have negative side effects on social cohesion. Other social changes, too, such as increasing immigration and ethnic diversity, were feared to bring similar negative side effects. Direct interventions designed to improve social cohesion, however, were rare. Margaret Thatcher had notoriously claimed that there was no such thing as society, although she was certainly aware of the challenges of social conflict when she entered office in the aftermath of the Winter of Discontent. On the steps of Downing Street she quoted St Francis of Assisi's words 'Where there is discord, may we bring harmony.'[5] I suspect her hope was that improved economic performance would have knock-on beneficial consequences for tackling the giant of Discord. Perhaps the most notable direct intervention to foster social cohesion, however, was David Cameron's Big Society initiative and the establishment of the National Citizen Service in 2010, but these came so late in our period that it is hard to detect their consequences for social cohesion from the data available at the time of writing.[6]

In short, then, the central question for this chapter is whether the 1980s reform package improved Britain's economic and labour market performance without entailing unwanted side effects in the form of exacerbated inequality of opportunity and social corrosion.

The difficulty of carrying out real-world experiments means that definitive explanations of social change or progress can rarely be given. A major natural experiment like Margaret Thatcher's is probably the next best thing to a rigorously controlled field experiment. As with a standard experiment, one needs to carry out before and after measurements in order to see whether the intervention made a difference, and one needs to compare results in the test case with those in a comparison group where there was no intervention. This we can do by looking at the record of social progress in Britain and in peer countries, checking whether Britain's trajectory differed from that of the peer countries after the intervention. There are bound to be a host of caveats with any natural experiment. We only have a small number of comparators—our seven peer countries—and all of these will have been undertaking their own programmes of reform. However, Britain's reform package in the 1980s was, I would argue, more radical and extensive than any undertaken at the same time in the peer countries. A comparison of Britain's trajectory with those of the seven peer countries can thus potentially provide us with pointers as to the consequences, and side effects, of the shift away from the post-war settlement towards an economy and welfare system organized more along US free market lines.

How Successful Has Britain Been in Tackling the Giants?

Before discussing the results of Margaret Thatcher's natural experiment, I will summarize my findings on Britain's record in tackling the giants. I will first look at *overall* progress in tackling the five giants—not an unreasonable approach in a democracy—before turning to the progress experienced by disadvantaged groups. I will summarize the evidence, beginning with the cases where the evidence is strongest—and therefore starting with the giant of Disease rather than with Want. After looking at overall progress, I will turn to disadvantaged groups within society and ask whether they had shared in the general progress or had slipped backwards.

The giant of Disease. The fight against the giant of Disease was largely a success. There was great progress in combatting infectious diseases, in reducing infant mortality, and in extending length of life, although progress in extending disability-free life expectancy appeared to stall after 2010.

The giant of Squalor. Great progress was made against the giant of Squalor in the decades immediately after the war. The success in tackling the immediate post-war housing crisis was one of Britain's greatest post-war welfare achievements. There was also continued progress in improving the quality of housing but progress in providing more living space stalled after 2001.

The giant of Want. There was great progress in raising material prosperity and average living standards, although progress stalled for the average person after the 2007/8 financial crash. Harold Macmillan was probably justified in boasting in 1959 that 'most of our people have never had it so good', and subsequent prime ministers such as Margaret Thatcher, when she was forced out of office by her own party in 1990, and Tony Blair when he stepped down in 2007 just before the financial crash, could justifiably have made the same boast, but David Cameron could not have made such a boast when he left office following his referendum debacle in 2016.

The giant of Idleness. There was great progress compared with the pre-war period in tackling the giant of Idleness, with full employment throughout the 1950s and well into the 1960s, contrasting with the mass unemployment of the 1930s. Thereafter, Idleness made a comeback, with very high unemployment in the recessions of the early 1980s and 1990s. However, the giant was subsequently forced on to the back foot once more, with a return towards full employment after 2010.

The giant of Unfairness. Increasing room at the top in the decades after the war provided greater opportunities for upward social mobility, but progress stalled in the twenty-first century. There were improved opportunities for women in education and in the labour market, too, and a narrowing of the gender pay gap, but no progress in reducing racial discrimination, ethnic inequalities in the labour market, or social class inequalities of opportunity.

The giant of Ignorance. There was great progress in increasing participation in upper secondary and tertiary education. Succeeding generations became much better qualified although I expressed considerable doubts in Chapter 4 as to whether the progress in securing GCSE passes was translated into similar progress in improving skills and competencies. Ignorance is the giant who appears to have been the most challenging of the five. But the giant did retreat a bit, and at least he did not advance in the way that some critics had claimed.

The giant of Discord. There was little sign of the anticipated social corrosion that I had expected to find. Back in the 1950s, Britain was probably not nearly as cohesive as I had imagined. Some new cracks in the social glue emerged but many weaknesses (and some strengths) appear to be endemic to Britain. Benjamin Disraeli's worries about the Two Nations of Britain appear never to have been fully addressed or resolved.

The typical story, then, of which the fights against Squalor, Want, and Disease are the clearest examples, is one of great initial progress in the decades immediately after the war followed by slowing down and then stalling in the twenty-first century. But I must emphasize that there are some quite important deviations from this typical story, as in the case of Idleness, as well as considerable uncertainty around the giant of Ignorance, whose position is rather obscure in the fog of battle. Reports from the frontline lack clarity and precision. I would be a very worried general if I had to rely on such poor reconnaissance reports.

To what extent does this story of substantial initial progress followed by a slowdown apply to disadvantaged groups? Perhaps the best test of whether governments have been successful in creating 'One Nation at home'[7] is whether disadvantaged groups have been catching up with the majority or have been allowed to fall by the wayside.

In the fight against Disease and mortality, disadvantaged social classes made considerable gains at first—greater indeed than those of more advantaged classes in the case of infant mortality. But this progress was not maintained and infant mortality rates among disadvantaged classes appear to have plateaued in the twenty-first century.

In the fight against Squalor, disadvantaged groups made substantial progress at first but for the most disadvantaged progress seemed to stall during the 1980s (at least with respect to living space). Overcrowding among those renting their homes in the social and private sectors clearly became worse after 1995. Homelessness, affecting the most vulnerable members of society, appears to have increased in the twenty-first century. The data are not as robust as I would wish, but significant numbers of British citizens appear to be, almost literally, falling by the wayside.

In the case of Want, I distinguished relative poverty from subsistence poverty: subsistence poverty is measured against a fixed yardstick whereas relative poverty is measured against a moving yardstick tracking average household income. Progress in tackling relative poverty came to a halt after the mid-1980s: in 2016, more people were in relative poverty than had been thirty years earlier in 1987. Furthermore, while the evidence is not nearly as strong as I would wish, the balance of the evidence suggests that progress in tackling subsistence poverty also stalled, with a rise in food insecurity after 2010.

In the case of Idleness, young people and those with low qualifications were only slightly behind their peers in the 1950s and 1960s, but they later fell well behind their better-educated peers. In 2015, their risks of unemployment were much higher than they had been in previous periods of fullish employment. Beveridge had argued that pre-war youth unemployment was one of the worst blots on Britain's record. I fear that in the twenty-first century this judgement may once again have considerable force.

In the fight against Ignorance, the evidence is mixed. Additional analyses suggest that young people from disadvantaged backgrounds actually caught up at GCSE, but fell behind in the competition for university degrees in the post-war period.[8] Overall, inequalities in education were probably somewhat lower post-war than they had been pre-war.

In the case of social cohesion, too, the evidence is rather mixed. Socio-economic inequalities in civic engagement and empowerment are long-standing and there is little evidence that disadvantaged groups fell further behind—except in the important case of electoral participation. Here it is true that young people and those with lower levels of education fell behind, with potential implications for the representativeness and legitimacy of the British political system.

So, in summary, disadvantaged sections of society made substantial gains in the first decades after the war, perhaps as in the case of infant mortality even greater gains than the overall ones. However, in the cases of Want, Idleness, and Squalor, the situation of disadvantaged groups, compared with that of their more advantaged peers, appears to have deteriorated in the twenty-first century; there are indications, for example, of increased food insecurity, overcrowding, homelessness, and youth unemployment, all of which impact most directly on the most disadvantaged sections of society. While in each particular case the evidence is not as strong as I would like, the recurring pattern is striking, with younger people, particularly those with few or no qualifications or those who have been in care, as well as the members of some (but not all) ethnic minority groups being the most vulnerable.

There appears, then, to be a pattern that, when overall progress stalls, the situation of the most disadvantaged deteriorates. Housing is a good illustration of this: in the twenty-first century, the average number of rooms per person stopped increasing but overcrowding in the social and private renting sectors actually became worse. One possible interpretation is that, where allocation is driven largely along market lines, increasing competition from the more affluent members of society will make things tougher for the less affluent if the overall supply fails to grow. In effect, distribution of opportunities becomes a zero-sum game. In contrast, where allocation is organized along non-market principles (as is predominantly the case in health and school education), absence of growth will not necessarily be accompanied by a deterioration in the position of more disadvantaged sections of society.

What Has Driven These Trends? What Light Do Comparisons with Peer Countries Shed?

In many respects, overall trends in Britain parallel trends in the peer countries. Like Britain, peer countries exhibited great progress in extending life expectancy, in increasing material prosperity, and in increasing educational participation. Peer countries were also similar to Britain in the transformation of their occupational structures, with increasing rates of upwards mobility,[9] increasing participation of women in the labour force, and narrowing gender pay gaps.[10] The increase in economic inequality after the 1980s was also apparent in most peer countries, although the changes were more dramatic in Britain than in the peer countries (Figure 2.2).

Some things also remained unchanged in peer countries just as they did in Britain. Schoolchildren's scores in maths and literacy showed glacial improvement in peer countries, with remarkable stability in countries' rankings over time. Sentiments of national belonging and trust seemed fairly stable too in peer countries just as in Britain.[11] There is also evidence that risks of racial discrimination remained constant in the USA where a time series of field experiments like the British one is available.[12]

These similarities suggest that some of the drivers of social progress, or its lack, are likely to be ones common to developed democracies—they are likely to be the results of general processes rather than of specific policy interventions. Examples of these processes include technical progress (both in health care and the economy), the shift from a manufacturing to a service economy, and globalization, all of which will have impacted on open, highly developed democracies in much the same way. Governments always like to take credit for social progress that occurs on their watch (as Harold Macmillan did) and to blame factors out of their control such as world economic conditions for failures. My view is that governments should be less inclined to take credit for shared successes, although it is fair enough to try to avoid blame for shared failures. Governments around the world do tend to copy each other's policy interventions, as many did with their austerity policies after the 2007/8 financial crash, and the European Union imposes common regulations and directives on its member states. I cannot therefore rule out political causes for shared experiences. But deviations from shared trends give stronger pointers to the success or failure of major policy interventions such as Margaret Thatcher's natural experiment in the 1980s.

So let me focus, then, on Britain's deviations from the general trends, starting with material prosperity. In 1950 Britain was an average performer. (But remember my caveat about the bench line—Sweden, for example, stayed neutral during the war and must have avoided much of the devastation that the combatants suffered). Britain then gradually slipped to the back of the pack in the 1970s, before catching up once again in the 1980s and 1990s, although Britain does not appear to have recovered quite as well as peer countries from the 2007/8 financial crash.

The consensus among economists is that the recovery was due to the free market reforms of Margaret Thatcher. The economists may well be right, although Figure 2.1 shows that the improvement in Britain's growth rate occurred some time later, in the mid-1990s. More surprisingly, I can see no evidence in Figure 2.1 that growth rates of liberal market economies such as the USA and Canada were faster than those of coordinated market economies such as Germany, Japan, and Sweden. So I am somewhat sceptical as to whether moving from one type of economy to another in itself makes much difference. It simply is not the case that the coordinated market economies as a whole grew more slowly in the first decades after the war than the liberal market economies. The problem of slow growth in the post-war decades seemed to be specific to Britain, not something intrinsic to coordinated market economies.

One should therefore perhaps consider alternative explanations for Britain's relatively poor rate of growth after the war and the improvement towards the end of the century. I wonder whether Britain's low levels of investment in research and development after the war might have been a factor in slow growth. Britain certainly allowed technical education to wither in the post-war period and the tripartite system of secondary schooling slowly transformed into a bipartite system of grammar schools and secondary modern schools. In the case of the subsequent improved rate of growth of the British economy, I wonder whether this was due to the Big Bang deregulation of the stock market in 1987, which enabled Britain's financial services sector to thrive—at least up until the financial crash of 2007/8. This was to be sure a major example of Margaret Thatcher's programme of deregulation, but I am not sure that deregulation in other sectors of the economy had similar effects on growth.

Unemployment represents another important deviation from the trajectory of peer countries (Figure 6.1). From being one of the best performers in the 1960s and 1970s, Britain became one of the worst performers in the 1980s and 1990s. Unemployment rates increased in all the peer countries at more or less the same times, but Britain experienced the biggest increase of all in the early 1980s recession. (In the early 1990s recession it was Sweden which experienced the greatest increase—and it may well be relevant that Sweden also undertook measures to liberalize the labour market around this time.)

Increased risks of unemployment, then, may well have been the downside of Margaret Thatcher's free market reforms, an important reminder that reforms may achieve one objective but have unpleasant side effects as well. Nevertheless, Britain's unemployment rate recovered in the twenty-first century. It is not entirely clear why this happened—it may have been a result of Margaret Thatcher's reforms making self-employment more attractive, or it may have been due to low interest rates, which remained at historically low levels, around 5 per cent, from the mid-1990s until the financial crash, and then became lower still. Probably both factors were important.

Housing is the third area where Margaret Thatcher's administrations made radical reforms, with the sale of council housing to their tenants at discounted prices. Unfortunately, I have not been able to find good data on trends in housing space or overcrowding for the peer countries. Nevertheless, it is striking that overcrowding showed no improvement after 1987 and that even progress in providing more space on average came to a halt after 2001. It is a plausible hypothesis that the extension of market forces in the allocation of housing is connected with the failure to overcome overcrowding.

Interpretations of these patterns are bound to be controversial. The prevalent view is that the failure to build more houses, especially affordable houses, in areas of the country where demand was greatest is the main culprit, and that the failure to build more houses was due to restrictive planning regulations (especially restrictions on building in the green belt). In essence, this explanation suggests that the solution is to deregulate and to extend the operation of market forces in the housing market. An alternative view, which was put forward most forcefully by the 2014 Redfern Report, is that increasing supply on its own would do very little to ease the housing crisis. The core of the report's argument was that falls in the incomes of typical first-time buyers had

had a bigger impact on declining levels of homeownership than constraints in the supply of new housing, and that increased building would have only a marginal effect on price levels.[13]

One also needs to remember that the problem of first-time buyers getting onto the housing ladder is somewhat different from the problems of overcrowding and homelessness which affect the most vulnerable sections of society (although they will be related). My interpretation is that the overcrowding and homelessness crises are in part unintended consequences of the declining availability and affordability of social housing for those on low incomes. However, I would not claim that this is as clear cut as the case of unemployment.

What about spheres such as education, life expectancy, equality of opportunity, and social cohesion where Margaret Thatcher's programme of free market reforms did not impact to the same extent, at least not directly? The most striking example is that of life expectancy. In 1950 Britain was one of the leaders in life expectancy and in infant mortality, alongside Sweden and the USA. Compared with other countries, Britain fell back gradually over the next fifty years from the front towards the back of the pack, although not as badly as the USA did. However, it is rather unlikely that this relative decline had much to do with reforms. The evidence suggests that it was in fact the very high levels of wartime smoking in Britain and the USA that left a legacy of excess mortality due to smoking-related cancers twenty or thirty years later.

What is particularly striking is that throughout the whole of the post-war period Britain more closely resembled Canada and the USA in health-related lifestyles than Japan or the European countries. Even though Britain had throughout a very different health-care system from that of the USA, British levels of smoking and obesity were more similar to those of North America than to those of continental Europe. In the case of health, then, it does begin to look a bit as though enduring cultural factors might be more important than the nature of the health-care system. It is conceivable that the widening inequalities in life expectancy and infant mortality which I reported in Chapter 3 might be linked in some way to the widening economic inequalities of the 1980s, but the timing of the changes does not fit at all well with this interpretation. Britain's poor record on five-year cancer survival rates raises some major questions about the organization of British health care, but I have not come across any evidence linking low cancer survival rates to the internal market-oriented reforms of the NHS.

Education is another sphere where enduring cultural differences are clearly important, with Britain lagging some way behind Japan both in the very earliest international comparison of educational performance and in the most recent. As John Jerrim has pointed out, children of East Asian descent also score very highly when they attend schools in the average-performing educational system of Australia (and my research indicates that the same holds true of children with an East Asian background in Britain, Canada, Sweden, and the USA).[14] Culture and home environment seem to be key. It is also striking that the stream of educational reforms in Britain, from comprehensive reorganization to the more recent introduction of academies and free schools, seems to have had very little impact on educational performance, at least as measured by rigorous independent international studies such as those conducted by the OECD.

Why were reforms apparently so ineffective in education whereas in the cases of material prosperity, housing, and unemployment they appear to have had major impacts (if not always the intended impacts)? Part of the explanation is likely to be that, as in the case of the NHS, the reform agenda left intact the principle of universal provision of health care, free at the point of access. Similarly, access to education (until late in the period with the introduction of fees for university education) was not subject to the operation of market forces in the way that increasingly held true in the case of housing from the 1980s onwards. There has always been a highly influential private sector in British education but there were no major attempts to increase the scope of the private sector in secondary education (and very limited attempts in tertiary education).[15]

In the cases of inequality of opportunity and social corrosion, major reform programmes were not directly attempted in the post-war period. Here my expectation was that one might find indirect consequences of Margaret Thatcher's reform programme, with increasing economic inequality leading to reduced equality of opportunity and to reduced social cohesion. The evidence from Britain does not really support this expectation, however, with inequality of opportunity in education and the labour market changing little throughout the post-war period. Unfortunately, I was unable to provide good long-term evidence on inequality of opportunity or social corrosion in other countries, so it might be wisest to return a 'not proven' verdict. True, rates of upwards mobility declined towards the end of the period, but this probably should be attributed to the fact that the size of the professional and managerial class was not expanding as fast as it had been in earlier decades. Social divisions over Europe grew larger, but other social divisions appeared to decline. In neither case is it safe to conclude that increased economic inequality had adverse side effects on social relations.

It may well be that, with better and more up-to-date data than that currently available to me, the hypothesis that increasing inequality has deleterious effects on inequality of opportunity and social cohesion will be confirmed. However, there are some theoretical reasons too for reserving judgement. With respect to inequality of opportunity I suspect that, in contemporary Britain, culture and home environment play a more important role than do purely material resources.[16] Greater material resources may give improved access to better-quality state and private schools, but the evidence is that the quality of school one attends is much less important (perhaps only a tenth as important) as the nature of the home environment. This contrasts with the case of housing, where material resources provide direct access to larger and better-quality houses.

So I would certainly not want to argue that increasing material inequality has no impact on other aspects of social progress. My argument, rather, is that the impacts of economic inequality are likely to be the most immediate and direct on commodities such as housing which are predominantly allocated through the market nowadays. In the cases of health and education, the impacts are likely to be more indirect and muted.

In the case of social cohesion and corrosion, too, it seems that some of the biggest challenges are not material ones but cultural and political ones. Scottish nationalism, for example, is unlikely to have much to do with increasing economic inequality, for example, while social divisions in trust, feelings of efficacy, and political objectives all precede the 1980s increase in economic inequality.

Challenges for the Future

The overall story which the evidence supports is in many ways an encouraging one of continuing social progress, or in the cases of equality of opportunity and social cohesion a story of little long-term change. Following the principle that the best guide to the future is the recent past, I would anticipate that future decades will exhibit continuing progress in extending length of life (though perhaps less progress with respect to disability-free life expectancy), in raising median real household income, in increasing educational participation, and, much more modestly, in increasing skills and capacities. There may also be continued progress in narrowing gender gaps, although the past evidence is less optimistic about future prospects of narrowing social class and ethnic gaps. In all these respects I expect Britain to remain fairly similar to peer countries, just as it has in the past.

In contrast, the bumpy ride which unemployment has travelled in the past makes me very uncertain about future prospects for tackling the giant of Idleness. The evidence does not allow us to be confident that the low unemployment rates at the time of writing will be sustained in the longer term. As a rule of thumb, I would suggest that, the greater have been Britain's past deviations from the trajectories of peer countries, the less confident one should be about extrapolating past trends into the future. My concern is that unpredictable political changes of direction, perhaps as a consequence of Brexit, could change Britain's trajectory, just as it was changed in the 1980s by Margaret Thatcher's revolution.

The same applies to some extent to material prosperity, where we have seen unpredictable changes of trajectory in the past. While it would be very surprising if economic growth were to come to a long-term halt, the uncertainty around Brexit, and the political decisions which future governments might choose, makes it hazardous to predict whether Britain will keep up with peer countries or fall behind.

On the other hand, recent trends suggest that there may be social regress rather than progress for the most vulnerable and disadvantaged sections of society. Rather than progress, the evidence on balance indicates that, in the twenty-first century, life has been getting worse not better for some groups. The evidence is not nearly as robust as one would wish, but we need to take very seriously the likelihood that poverty and food insecurity, overcrowding and homelessness, obesity, and youth unemployment (for those with low qualifications) have been deteriorating and will continue to deteriorate. The worry is that Britain may be moving on a trajectory which will take it closer to the USA's exceptionally high rates of poverty and exceptionally low life expectancy (as benchmarked against the performance of peer countries).

These are relatively recent new challenges—and some of them could potentially be linked to what are hopefully temporary issues such as the austerity measures which different governments have pursued with varying vigour and success since the financial crash of 2007/8. On the other hand, the roots of these problems appear to go back earlier than the financial crash. The challenge for future governments will be to develop a new Beveridge plan for tackling these giant evils and to emulate the successes of the 1945–50 Labour government in achieving social progress for all sections of society.

ENDNOTES

Chapter 1

1. William H. Beveridge, *Social Insurance and Allied Services: Report by Sir William Beveridge* (Beveridge Report), Cmd. 6404 (London: HMSO, 1942), paragraph 3.
2. Ibid., paragraph 8.
3. Speech at Bedford, 20 July 1957, cited in Antony Kay (ed.), *The Oxford Dictionary of Political Quotations* (Oxford: Oxford University Press, 1996), p. 244.
4. *The Conservative Party Manifesto 2015: Strong Leadership, a Clear Economic Plan, a Brighter More Secure Future* (promoted by Alan Mabbutt on behalf of the Conservative party, both at 4 Matthew Parker Street, London, SW1H 9HQ), https://www.conservatives.com/manifesto.
5. In 2017 the Conservative party manifesto even talked about the five giant challenges that faced Britain. The list was however somewhat different from Beveridge's and included some of the newer challenges which I tackle in this book. The five challenges were the need for a strong economy, Brexit and a changing world, enduring social divisions, an ageing society, and fast-changing technology. See *The Conservative and Unionist Party Manifesto 2017: Forward, Together: Our Plan for a Stronger Britain and a Prosperous Future* (promoted by Alan Mabbutt on behalf of the Conservative party, both at 4 Matthew Parker Street, London, SW1H 9HQ).
6. William H. Beveridge, *Full Employment in a Free Society* (London: George Allen & Unwin, 1944), paragraph 35.
7. Anthony B. Atkinson, *Inequality: What Can Be Done?* (Cambridge, MA: Harvard University Press, 2015).
8. Social Mobility Commission, *Time for Change: An Assessment of Government Policies on Social Mobility 1997–2017* (London: Social Mobility Commission, 2017), p. 1, https://www.gov.uk/government/publications/social-mobility-policies-between-1997-and-2017-time-for-change.
9. Richard Wilkinson and Kate Pickett, *The Spirit Level: Why Equality Is Better for Everyone* (London: Allen Lane, 2009), p. 195. Wilkinson and Pickett's arguments have not however gone unchallenged. See, for example, the review by David Runciman, 'How messy it all is', *London Review of Books*, 31 (22 October 2009): 3–6.
10. Benjamin Disraeli, *Sybil; or, the Two Nations* (London: Henry Colburn, 1845).
11. What Margaret Thatcher actually said was: 'I think we've been through a period where too many people have been given to understand that if they have a problem, it's the government's job to cope with it: "I have a problem, I'll get a grant." "I'm homeless, the government must house me." They're casting their problem on society. And, you know, there is no such thing as society. There are individual men and women, and there are families. And no government can do anything except through people, and people must look to themselves first. It's our duty to look after ourselves and then, also to look after our neighbour. People have got the entitlements too much in mind, without the obligations. There's no such thing as entitlement, unless someone has first met an obligation.' *Woman's Own* (31 October 1987).

12. Alexis de Tocqueville, *De la démocratie en Amérique* (Paris: Librairie de Charles Gosselin, 1835).
13. Robert D. Putnam, *Bowling Alone: The Collapse and Revival of American Community* (New York: Simon & Schuster, 2000), p. 20.
14. William H. Beveridge, *Voluntary Action: A Report on Methods of Social Advance* (London: George Allen & Unwin, 1948), p. 9.
15. See, for example, A. M. Carr-Saunders, D. Caradog Jones, and C. A. Moser, *A Survey of Social Conditions in England and Wales as Illustrated by Statistics* (Oxford: Clarendon Press, 1958), chapter 2, table 2.6. This volume provides a valuable contemporary guide to the social conditions in England and Wales when I was growing up, and in some respects is a precursor to the current book.
16. Sara B. Hobolt, 'The Brexit vote: A divided nation, a divided continent', *European Journal of Social Policy* 23 (2016): 1259–77; Matthew Goodwin and Oliver Heath, 'Brexit vote explained: Poverty, low skills and lack of opportunities' (Joseph Rowntree Foundation, 2016), https://www.jrf.org.uk/report/brexit-vote-explained-poverty-low-skills-and-lack-opportunities.
17. Gordon Brown, speech on Britishness at the Commonwealth Club, London (27 February 2007), http://gu.com/p/qeay/sbl.
18. The Organisation for Economic Co-operation and Development's (OECD) 'Better Life' index also has a longer list than I am able to cover. It includes Beveridge's five giants in the form of housing, income, education, and health but also adds community, environment, civic engagement, life satisfaction, safety, and work-life balance. I cover community and civic engagement in my discussion of social cohesion. I am surprised, however, that the OECD list does not include either discrimination or inequality of opportunity. See OECD, *How's Life? 2015: Measuring Well-Being* (Paris: OECD Publishing, 2015), DOI: 10.1787/how_life-2015-en.
19. There is an extensive literature on the different conceptualizations of well-being and the various drivers of those concepts. Studies such as the British Household Panel Study and the German Socio-Economic Panel have provided robust evidence that health and unemployment, for example, have substantial effects on well-being by examining change over time within the same individuals. There are other important drivers of well-being, too, but many of these are more individual and personal than the policy areas that were central to Beveridge's vision of a better society. Examples include personality traits such as extraversion or neuroticism, the degree to which one's social networks can offer emotional support, but also demographic factors outside the scope of policy such as age and marital status. For an overview of this area of research see E. Diener, E. M. Suh, R. E. Lucas, and H. L. Smith, 'Subjective well-being: Three decades of progress', *Psychological Bulletin*, 125 (1999): 276–302.
20. The World Happiness Report 2013 (appendix B) compares effect sizes from a multivariate model on happiness and suggests that being in poor health has a far larger (negative) effect than (the effect in the opposite direction of) having a 30 per cent rise in income. See John F. Helliwell, Richard Layard, and Jeffrey Sachs, *World Happiness Report 2013*, http://unsdsn.org/resources/publications/world-happiness-report-2013.
21. John Bynner, Thomas Schuller, and Leon Feinstein, 'Wider benefits of education: Skills, higher education and civic engagement', *Zeitschrift für Pädogogik*, 49 (2003): S341–61.

22. See, for example, M. Shaw, 'Housing and public health', *Annual Review of Public Health*, 25 (2004): 397–418; T. Leventhal and S. Newman, 'Housing and child development', *Children and Youth Services Review*, 32 (2010): 1165–74; W. J. Fisk, Q. Lei-Gomez, and M. J. Mendell, 'Meta-analyses of the associations of respiratory health effects with dampness and mold in homes', *Indoor Air*, 17 (2007): 284–96; S. Angel and B. Bittschi, Housing deprivation and health: A European comparison (2013), http://www.gesis.org/fileadmin/upload/dienstleistung/daten/amtl_mikrodaten/europ_microdata/Abstracts_2013/Angel_Bittschi.pdf; O. P. Galpin, C. J. Whitaker, and A. J. Dubiel, 'Helicobacter pylori infection and overcrowding in childhood', *The Lancet*, 339 (1992): 619; C. D. Solari and R. D. Mare, 'Housing crowding effects on children's wellbeing', *Social Science Research*, 41 (2012): 464–76; M. Barnes, S. Butt, and W. Tomaszewski, 'The duration of bad housing and children's well-being in Britain', *Housing Studies*, 26 (2011): 155–76; D. Goux and E. Maurin, 'The effect of overcrowded housing on children's performance at school', *Journal of Public Economics*, 89 (2005): 797–819.

23. D. J Pevalin, M. P. Taylor, and J. Todd, 'The dynamics of unhealthy housing in the UK: A panel data analysis', *Housing Studies*, 23 (2008): 679–95; Alex Marsh, David Gordon, Pauline Heslop, and Christina Pantazis, 'Housing deprivation and health: A longitudinal analysis', *Housing Studies*, 15 (2000): 411–28.

24. G. Waddell and K. Burton, 'Is work good for your health and well-being?' Report commissioned by the Department for Work and Pensions (2006), https://www.gov.uk/government/uploads/system/uploads/attachment_data/file/214326/hwwb-is-work-good-for-you.pdf; J. Gulliford, D. Shannon, T. Taskila, D. Wilkins, M. Tod, and S. Bevan, 'Sick of being unemployed: The health issues of out of work men and how support services are failing to address them', Work Foundation, Lancaster University online report, https://www.menshealthforum.org.uk/sick-being-unemployed; A. Björklund, 'Unemployment and mental health: Some evidence from panel data', *Journal of Human Resources*, 20 (1985): 469–83; Morton O. Schapiro and Dennis A. Ahlburg, 'Suicide: The ultimate cost of unemployment', *Journal of Post Keynesian Economics*, 5 (1982): 276–80; D. Anderberg, H. Rainer, J. Wadsworth, and T. Wilson, 'Unemployment and domestic violence: Theory and evidence', *The Economic Journal*, 126 (2015): 1947–79; J. Marcus, 'The effect of unemployment on the mental health of spouses: Evidence from plant closures in Germany', *Journal of Health Economics*, 32 (2013): 546–58.

25. The estimates in Figure 1.1 are based on the UK Longitudinal Panel Study. A multivariate analysis which estimates the net effects of each giant in a model including all five shows very similar results, with the net effects only slightly smaller than the gross effects shown in Figure 1.1. The one exception is that the effect of education becomes non-significant. It may of course be the case that education has indirect effects on life satisfaction, for example as a result of its effects on income and health.

26. Saffron Karlsen and James Y. Nazroo, 'Relation between racial discrimination, social class and health among ethnic minority groups', *American Journal of Public Health*, 92 (2002): 624–31; Stephanie Wallace, James Y. Nazroo, and Laia Bécares, 'Cumulative effect of racial discrimination on the mental health of ethnic minorities in the United Kingdom', *American Journal of Public Health*, 106 (2016): 1294–300.

27. Heather J. Smith, Thomas F. Pettigrew, Gina M. Pippin, and Silvana Bialosiewicz, 'Relative deprivation: A theoretical and meta-analytic review', *Personality and Social Psychology Review*, 16 (2011): 203–32; Juta Kawalerowicz and Michael Biggs, 'Anarchy in the UK:

Economic deprivation, social disorganization, and political grievances in the London riot of 2011', *Social Forces*, 94 (2015): 673–98.

28. Joseph E. Stiglitz, Amartya Sen, and Jean-Paul Fitoussi, *Report by the Commission on the Measurement of Economic Performance and Social Progress* (2009), http://ec.europa.eu/eurostat/documents/118025/118123/Fitoussi+Commission+report.

29. The Commission argued that a multidimensional definition of well-being should be used and identified the following key dimensions that should be taken into account: 'i. Material living standards (income, consumption and wealth); ii. Health; iii. Education; iv. Personal activities including work; v. Political voice and governance; vi. Social connections and relationships; vii. Environment (present and future conditions); viii. Insecurity, of an economic as well as a physical nature. All these dimensions shape people's well-being, and yet many of them are missed by conventional income measures' (Executive Summary, p. 29). I would put it much more strongly and argue that all of them apart from the first are missed by conventional income measures.

30. Canada, France, Germany, Italy, Japan, Sweden, the UK, and the USA are all classified as having very high human development, according to UNDP's Human Development Index (HDI). The HDI is a summary measure (the geometric mean of normalized indices) of average achievement in three key dimensions of human development: life expectancy at birth, educational participation, and per capita gross national income, http://hdr.undp.org/en/composite/HDI. All apart from Sweden are relatively large established democracies with populations over 35 million in 2010. Other large democracies which were also classified as having very high human development included Spain, Australia, and South Korea. I excluded Spain as on many indicators it resembles Italy (which is also closer to the UK in size). Spain incidentally did not become a democracy until 1975. I excluded Australia as on many indicators it resembles Canada, which is again closer to the UK in size. And I excluded South Korea as in many ways it resembles Japan, and less data are available for South Korea.

31. Christopher Jencks, Marshall Smith, Henry Acland, Mary Jo Bane, David Cohen, Herbert Gintis, Barbara Heyns, and Stephan Michelson, *Inequality: A Reassessment of the Effect of Family and Schooling in America* (New York: Basic Books, 1972), p. 15.

32. Kenneth Mahood, *Why Are There More Questions than Answers Grandad?* (Seattle, WA: Bradbury Press, 1974).

Chapter 2

1. Sir William Beveridge, *Social Insurance and Allied Services: Report by Sir William Beveridge*, Cmnd 6404 (London: HMSO, 1942), paragraph 8.

2. B. Seebohm Rowntree and G. R. Lavers, *Poverty and the Welfare State: A Third Social Survey of York* (London: Longmans Green, 1951).

3. A. M. Carr-Saunders, D. Caradog Jones, and C. A. Moser, *A Survey of Social Conditions in England and Wales* (Oxford: Clarendon Press, 1958), footnote 26.

4. Ibid., p. 203.

5. David G. Blanchflower and Richard B. Freeman, 'Did the Thatcher reforms change British labour market performance?' CEP/NIESR Conference: Is the British Labour Market Different? NBER Working Paper 4384 (June 1993). A. B. Atkinson and John Micklewright, 'Turning the screw: Benefits for the unemployed 1979–1988', in *The Economics of Social Security*, edited by Andrew Dilnot and Ian Walker (Oxford: Oxford University Press, 1989).

6. For a more detailed analysis of changes in welfare policy after 2010, see Ruth Lupton with Tania Burchardt and others, 'The coalition's social policy record: Policy, spending and outcomes 2010–2015', Social Policy in a Cold Climate, Research Report 4 (LSE, Centre for Analysis of Social Exclusion, 2015).
7. Rachel Loopstra, Aaron Reeves, David Taylor-Robinson, Ben Barr, Martin McKee, and David Stuckler, 'Austerity, sanctions, and the rise of food banks in the UK', *British Medical Journal* (2015), 350: h1775.
8. GDP can be determined in three ways, all of which should, in principle, give the same result. They are the production (or output or value-added) approach, the income approach, and the expenditure approach. The data presented in this chapter use the expenditure approach. Using the expenditure approach GDP is the sum of consumption, investment, government spending, and net exports.
9. Adjusting for inflation is fairly straightforward, although it becomes less straightforward the longer the time span. Adjusting for purchasing power in different countries is much more challenging. There is a consensus among economists about the best method of doing this, but there is no independent way of checking whether the consensus works. See, for example, the discussion by Simon Johnson, William Larson, Chris Papageorgiou, and Arvind Subramanian, 'Is newer better? Penn World Table Revisions and their impact on growth estimates', *Journal of Monetary Economics*, 60 (2013): 255–74.
10. Derived from Robert C. Feenstra, Robert Inklaar, and Marcel P. Timmer, 'The next generation of the Penn World Table', *American Economic Review*, 105 (2015): 3150–82.
11. https://data.worldbank.org/indicator/NY.GDP.PCAP.PP.CD.
12. See the Maddison-Project, http://www.ggdc.net/maddison/maddison-project/home.htm, 2013 version and J. Bolt and J. L. van Zanden, 'The Maddison Project: Collaborative research on historical national accounts', *The Economic History Review*, 67 (2014): 627–51.
13. See, for example, Joseph E. Stiglitz, Amartya Sen, and John-Paul Fitoussi, *Report by the Commission on the Measurement of Economic Performance and Social Progress* (2009), http://www.communityindicators.net/system/publication_pdfs/9/original/Stiglitz_Sen_Fitoussi_2009.pdf?1323961027.
14. Corrado Gini, 'Variabilità e mutabilità: contributo allo studio delle distribuzione e delle relazioni statistiche', Studi Economico-Giuridici della Facoltà di Giurisprudenza della Regia Università di Cagliari 3, part 2 (1912).
15. This is something of a simplification. In small populations the maximum value of the Gini index will not be 1, but will approach 1 as population size increases. Values greater than 1 are also possible if we take account of debt.
16. Jonathan Cribb, 'Income inequality in the UK', https://www.ifs.org.uk/docs/ER_JC_2013.pdf.
17. For the period since 1980 see the Incomes across the Distribution Database of the Institute for New Economic Thinking at the Oxford Martin School, http://www.inet.ox.ac.uk/projects/view/176.
18. These figures are presented in Chris Bellfield, Jonathan Cribb, Andrew Hood, and Robert Joyce, 'Living standards, poverty and inequality in the UK: 2016' (London: Institute for Fiscal Studies, 2015), table 3.1, https://www.ifs.org.uk/publications/8371.

Bellfield and his colleagues also point out that the rules for adjusting for family size and composition mean that the annual income required to be at a given point in the distribution is different for different household types: for example, a single individual with no children would be at the ninetieth percentile if he or she had a net income of £33,000.

19. While it may look, from the way the lines fan out, that inequality has continued to increase, we should be careful before drawing this conclusion. The absolute differences in real terms got wider—there is indeed a bigger material gulf between the rich and the not-so-rich than there used to be. Thus in 1990 the gap between a household at the ninetieth percentile and the median was £365 per week. By 2010 it had grown to £455 per week. This kind of absolute gap may well be highly relevant to the debate about whether Britain is once again dividing into two nations. However, this is not the way in which inequality is usually defined in economics. The economist will rightly point out that the ratio of tenth to ninetieth percentiles increased sharply between 1980 and 1990 but has since remained more or less constant.
20. The source of these findings is the Incomes across the Distribution Database of the Institute for New Economic Thinking at the Oxford Martin School, http://www.inet.ox.ac.uk/projects/view/176.
21. Office for National Statistics data show that the population of England and Wales rose from 46,104,548 in 1961 to 56,075,900 in 2011. This is a growth of 24 per cent. In contrast, the number of households rose from 14,640,897 in 1961 to 23,366,000 in 2011. This is a growth of 60 per cent. ONS, 2011 census: Population and household estimates for England and Wales (March 2011), http://www.ons.gov.uk/peoplepopulationandcommunity/populationandmigration/populationestimates/bulletins/2011censuspopulationandhouseholdestimatesforenglandandwales/2012-07-16.
22. For this reason, economists tend to calculate poverty rates both before and after taking account of housing costs.
23. Mike Brewer, Ben Etheridge, and Cormac O'Dea, 'Why are households that report the lowest income so well off?' *The Economic Journal*, 127 (2017): F24–49.
24. Marii Paskov, 'Have we become more indebted?' CSI Briefing Note 16 (November 2015), http://csi.nuff.ox.ac.uk/wp-content/uploads/2015/11/CSI-16-Have-we-become-more-indebted.pdf.
25. For further details see Marii Paskov, 'Have we become more indebted?'.
26. Chris Bellfield, Jonathan Cribb, Andrew Hood, and Robert Joyce, *Living Standards, Poverty and Inequality in the UK: 2016* (London: Institute for Fiscal Studies, 2015), p. 58, https://www.ifs.org.uk/uploads/publications/comms/R117.pdf.
27. This notion of a subsistence level of poverty should not be confused with economists' concept of absolute poverty. This concept does take a fixed baseline, but is not based on the criterion of subsistence. Closer to the notion of subsistence is the measure of material deprivation which has been recently developed by the Institute for Fiscal Studies. See Chris Bellfield, Jonathan Cribb, Andrew Hood, and Robert Joyce, *Living Standards, Poverty and Inequality in the UK: 2016* (London: Institute for Fiscal Studies, 2015), figure 5.5, https://www.ifs.org.uk/publications/8371.
28. Sir William Beveridge, *Social Insurance and Allied Services: Report by Sir William Beveridge*, Cmnd 6404 (London: HMSO, 1942), paragraph 11.
29. B. Seebohm Rowntree, *Poverty: A Study of Town Life* (London: Macmillan and Co. 1901), p. 86.
30. Ibid., p. 87.
31. B. Seebohm Rowntree and G. R. Lavers, *Poverty and the Welfare State: A Third Social Survey of York* (London: Longmans Green, 1951), p. 39.
32. Jonathan Bradshaw, Sue Middleton, Abigail Davis, Nina Oldfield, Noel Smith, Linda Cusworth, and Julie Williams, *A Minimum Income Standard for Britain: What People Think* (York: Joseph Rowntree Foundation, 2008), p. 3.

33. Ibid., p. 14.
34. Jaqueline Scott and Elizabeth Clery, 'Gender roles', in *British Social Attitudes: The 30th Report*, edited by Alison Park and others (London: NatCen Social Research, 2013), http://www.bsa-30.natcen.ac.uk.
35. Chris Bellfield, Jonathan Cribb, Andrew Hood, and Robert Joyce, *Living Standards, Poverty and Inequality in the UK: 2016* (London: Institute for Fiscal Studies, 2015), table B1, https://www.ifs.org.uk/publications/8371.
36. In 2015, the poverty rate after taxes and transfers (poverty line 60 per cent of the median) was 14.5 in France, 15.3 in Germany (2014), 17.0 in Sweden, 17.9 in the UK, 19.8 in Italy (2014), 21.0 in Canada, 21.9 in Japan (2012), and 23.6 in the USA, http://stats.oecd.org/Index.aspx?DataSetCode=BLI.
37. However, there is evidence that some items that were considered necessities in the 1999 Breadline Britain Survey were no longer judged as such in 2012, although we do not know whether the changes occurred before or after the 2008 financial crash. Necessities were identified as items rated as necessary by 50 per cent or more respondents to a national representative survey. The items listed below were all considered necessities in 1999 but not in 2012. For adults: having friends or family round for a meal or drink at least once a month; presents for family or friends once a year; having a small amount of money to spend each week on yourself (not your family); replacing worn-out clothes with new (not second-hand) clothes. For children: having friends round for tea or a snack once a fortnight. See Stewart Lansley and Joanna Mack, *Breadline Britain: The Rise of Mass Poverty* (London: Oneworld, 2015).
38. Suzanne Fitzpatrick, Glen Bramley, Filip Sosenko, and others, *Destitution in the UK* (York: Joseph Rowntree Foundation, 2015).
39. To check that the reason for going without these essential items was that they could not afford them the researchers asked respondents if this was the reason; checked that their income was below the standard relative poverty line (i.e. 60 per cent of median income after housing costs for the relevant household size); and checked that they had no or negligible savings.
40. The Office for National Statistics estimated the population to be 65,110,000 at mid-2015, http://www.ons.gov.uk/peoplepopulationandcommunity/populationandmigration/populationestimates.
41. The researchers also considered benefit sanctions and the proportion of migrants without access to state benefits, but these are rather indirect indicators.
42. Suzanne Fitzpatrick, Glen Bramley, Filip Sosenko, and others, *Destitution in the UK* (York: Joseph Rowntree Foundation, 2015), p. 3.
43. For further details see Elisabeth Garratt, 'Food insecurity and foodbank use', CSI Briefing note 28 (November 2016), http://csi.nuff.ox.ac.uk/wp-content/uploads/2016/11/CSI-28-Food-insecurity-revised.pdf. Note that the survey data come from the English Longitudinal Study of Aging, which covers only those people aged 50 and over. In the government's 2016 Food and You Survey 8 per cent of respondents were found to live in food-insecure households—meaning that the eating patterns of one or more household members were interrupted and food intake reduced at times during the year because the household lacked money for food. An earlier government survey in 2004, the Low Income Diet and Nutrition Survey, had found a similar level of food insecurity, but this survey was restricted to low-income (bottom 15 per cent) households, who are known to be more at risk of food insecurity. These two sources therefore also suggest that food insecurity had increased.

44. Nicholas R. V. Jones, Annalijn I. Conklin, Marc Suhrcke, and Pablo Monsivais, 'The growing price gap between more and less healthy foods: Analysis of a novel longitudinal UK dataset', *PLoS ONE*, 9 (2014): e109343.
45. Rachel Griffith, Martin O'Connell, and Kate Smith, 'Food expenditure and nutritional quality over the Great Recession' (London: Institute for Fiscal Studies, 2013), https://www.ifs.org.uk/publications/6919.
46. DEFRA, *Family Food 2012* (London: DEFRA, 2013).
47. http://www.hscic.gov.uk/catalogue/PUB14568/prov-mont-hes-admi-outp-ae-April%202014-toi-rep.pdf.
48. David Taylor-Robinson, E. Rougeaux, Dominic Harrison, Margaret Whitehead, and Ben Barr, 'The rise of food poverty in the UK', *British Medical Journal*, 347 (2013): f7157.
49. Office for National Statistics, 'Percentage term low birthweight live births by ethnic group, 2006 to 2012 and 2014 to 2015, England and Wales', https://www.ons.gov.uk/peoplepopulationandcommunity/birthsdeathsandmarriages/deaths/adhocs/006681percentagetermlowbirthweightlivebirthsbyethnicgroup2006to2012and2014to2015englandandwales.
50. Michael Goldacre, N. Hall, and D. Yeates, 'Hospitalisation for children with rickets in England: A historical perspective', *The Lancet*, 383 (15 February 2014).
51. Episode-based rates (hospital discharges) for England, 1968–2011: between 1968 and 1985 the data were a one in ten sample of all NHS hospital discharges (excluding day cases), then termed the Hospital In-Patient Enquiry, and they were scaled to 100 per cent by multiplying each number of annual admissions for rickets by ten. There were no national data for 1986–90. Between 1990 and 2011, the Hospital Episode Statistics included day cases (patients admitted to hospital who did not stay overnight) and inpatients.
52. Chris Bellfield, Jonathan Cribb, Andrew Hood, and Robert Joyce, *Living Standards, Poverty and Inequality in the UK: 2016* (London: Institute for Fiscal Studies, 2015), figure 5.5, https://www.ifs.org.uk/publications/8371. The measure of material deprivation used by Bellfield and his colleagues is based on questions asked in the Family Resources Survey. Unfortunately, the questions were changed in 2010, introducing some uncertainty into the measurement of trends over time. The measure appears to be something of a hybrid between the subsistence and socially acceptable measures of material deprivation described in the text above.

Chapter 3

1. Ray Fitzpatrick and Tarani Chandola, 'Health', in *Twentieth-Century British Social Trends*, edited by A. H. Halsey with Josephine Webb (Basingstoke: Macmillan, 2000), pp. 94–127.
2. Anne Case and Angus Deaton have shown that, in the USA, mortality among mid-life white non-Hispanic men and women actually increased between 1999 and 2013, whereas in peer countries such as Canada, France, Germany, Sweden, and the UK mortality among this age group continued to decline. Anne Case and Angus Deaton, 'Rising morbidity and mortality in midlife among white non-Hispanic Americans in the 21st century', *Proceedings of the National Academy of Sciences*, 112 (2015): 15078–83.
3. E. B. Crimmins, S. H. Preston, and B. Cohen (eds), *Explaining Divergent Levels of Longevity in High-Income Countries*. Panel on understanding divergent trends in longevity in high-income countries, National Research Council of the National Academies (Washington, DC: National Academies Press, 2011).
4. Ibid., p. 141.

5. The difference between this improvement over time and that shown in Figure 3.1 is of course because of the great progress made in reducing child and infant mortality.
6. Life tables, principal projection, United Kingdom, Office for National Statistics, https://www.ons.gov.uk/peoplepopulationandcommunity/birthsdeathsandmarriages/lifeexpectancies/datasets/lifetablesprincipalprojectionunitedkingdom.
7. Disability-free life expectancy (DFLE) estimates the average number of years spent by individuals free from limiting persistent illness or disability based upon a self-rated assessment. Unlike life expectancies, DFLE relies on survey data. For the estimates from 2000–2 to 2009–11, the General Lifestyle Survey of the Office for National Statistics was used for estimates for England, Wales, and Scotland; for Northern Ireland the Continuous Household Survey was used for 2009 data and the Health Survey Northern Ireland (HSNI) was used for 2010–11 data. The Office for National Statistics revised the data sources used for DFLE, and more recent DFLE estimates rely on the Annual Population Survey (APS) for measures of disability prevalence. For the estimates from 2009–11 to 2013–15, DFLE estimates using the APS are reported in official statistics. Surveys are combined over three-year periods to generate large sample sizes for computing DFLE as three-year rolling averages. These survey data are used to factor in the age-specific disability prevalence rates into life expectancy calculations for a period, and assume that age-specific mortality and age-specific disability prevalence rates of that period continue into the future. These data sources include information on private households as well as communal residences such as student dormitories and NHS accommodations. Other institutionalized populations are not included in these estimates.
8. The gender gap in disability-free lifespans varies significantly across the UK's constituent countries, with Scotland showing the biggest gap (around 3.5 years in 2009–11) between men and women while the gap in England, Wales, and Northern Ireland is considerably smaller (less than two years).
9. The Office for National Statistics changed the survey used to estimate disability from the General Lifestyle Survey to the (larger) Annual Population Survey.
10. Jacques Vallin and France Meslé, 'Convergences and divergences in mortality: A new approach of health transition', *Demographic Research*, S2.2 (2004): 11–44.
11. Clare Griffiths and Anita Brock, 'Twentieth-century mortality trends in England and Wales', *Health Statistics Quarterly*, 18 (2003): 5–16.
12. M. P. Coleman and others, 'Cancer survival in Australia, Canada, Denmark, Norway, Sweden, and the UK, 1995–2007 (the International Cancer Benchmarking Partnership): An analysis of population-based cancer registry data', *The Lancet*, 377, no. 9760 (2011): 127–38. M. Abdel-Rahman and others, 'What if cancer survival in Britain were the same as in Europe: How many deaths are avoidable?' *British Journal of Cancer*, 101 (2009): S115–S124.
13. Roger Williams and others, 'Addressing liver disease in the UK: A blueprint for attaining excellence in health care and reducing premature mortality from lifestyle issues of excess consumption of alcohol, obesity, and viral hepatitis', *The Lancet* 384 (2014): 1953–97.
14. Richard Doll and A. Bradford Hill. 'Smoking and carcinoma of the lung', *British Medical Journal*, 2, no. 4682 (1950): 739–48.
15. Richard Doll and A. Bradford Hill. 'The mortality of doctors in relation to their smoking habits: A preliminary report', *British Medical Journal*, 1, no. 4877 (1954): 1451–5. A review of the reception of the findings is provided by Virginia Berridge, 'The policy response to the smoking and lung cancer connections in the 1950s and 1960s', *Historical Journal*, 49 (2006): 1185–209.

16. Richard Doll, R. Peto, J. Burnham, and I. Sutherland, 'Mortality in relation to smoking: 50 years' observations on male British doctors', *British Medical Journal*, 328 (2004): 1519.
17. International Smoking Statistics, Web edition. © Barbara Forey, Jan Hamling, John Hamling, Alison Thornton, Peter Lee, 2006–2016. Comparisons between countries, table vi, http://www.pnlee.co.uk/ISS3.htm.
18. Computational method from Samuel H. Preston, Dana A. Glei, and John R. Wilmoth, 'A new method for estimating smoking-attributable mortality in high-income countries', *International Journal of Epidemiology*, 39, no. 2 (2010): 430–8.
19. These calculations draw on a counterfactual exercise that involves deleting the contributions of smoking-related deaths, particularly lung cancer deaths for which the effects of smoking are most clear, from the mortality statistics of a year and computing what life expectancy would have been. The method used is described in Samuel H. Preston, Dana A. Glei, and John R. Wilmoth, 'A new method for estimating smoking-attributable mortality in high-income countries', *International Journal of Epidemiology*, 39, no. 2 (2010): 430–8.
20. Clare Griffiths and Anita Brock, 'Twentieth-century mortality trends in England and Wales', *Health Statistics Quarterly*, 18 (2003): 12.
21. E. B. Crimmins, S. H. Preston, and B. Cohen (eds), *Explaining Divergent Levels of Longevity in High-Income Countries*. Panel on understanding divergent trends in longevity in high-income countries, National Research Council of the National Academies (Washington, DC: National Academies Press, 2011), p. 47.
22. Kevin R. Fontaine, David T. Redden, Chenxi Wang, Andrew O. Westfall, and David B. Allison, 'Years of life lost due to obesity', *Journal of the American Medical Association*, 289 (2003): 187–93.
23. K. Backholer, E. Wong, R. Freak-Poli, H. L. Walls, and A. Peeters, 'Increasing body weight and risk of limitations in activities of daily living: A systematic review and meta-analysis', *Obesity Reviews*, 13 (2012): 456–68.
24. Helen L. Walls, Kathryn Backholer, Joseph Poietto, and John J. McNeil, 'Review article: Obesity and trends in life expectancy', *Journal of Obesity* (2012): article ID 107989.
25. E. B. Crimmins, S. H. Preston, and B. Cohen (eds), *Explaining Divergent Levels of Longevity in High-Income Countries*. Panel on understanding divergent trends in longevity in high-income countries, National Research Council of the National Academies (Washington, DC: National Academies Press, 2011), figure 3.2.
26. Non-Communicable Disease Risk Factor Collaboration, 'Trends in adult body-mass index in 200 countries from 1975 to 2014: A pooled analysis of 1698 population-based measurement studies with 19.2 million participants', *The Lancet*, 387 (2016): 1377–96, http://thelancet.com/cms/attachment/2056387469/2061341461/mmc1.pdf.
27. Ibid., p. 58.
28. The best data on physical activity come from the Health Survey for England, which reports on the proportion of people meeting physical activity recommendations between 1997 and 2012. The Health Survey for England finds progressive increases in meeting these guidelines among men and women, although a far higher proportion of men fulfil these recommendations.
29. Census data show no change in cycle commuting and a small decrease in walking to work between 2001 and 2011. This pattern of no change conceals some variation, where cycling in some locations (inner London and Manchester included) became more prevalent. This pattern of stability is slightly puzzling in light of rising use of the 'cycle to work' scheme,

which suggests that intentions to cycle commute are not being matched by changing commuting behaviours.
30. Lars Bo Andersen and others, 'Active commuting is beneficial for health', *British Medical Journal*, 357 (2017): j1740.
31. E. B. Crimmins, S. H. Preston, and B. Cohen (eds), *Explaining Divergent Levels of Longevity in High-Income Countries*. Panel on understanding divergent trends in longevity in high-income countries, National Research Council of the National Academies (Washington, DC: National Academies Press, 2011), pp. 65–6.
32. Ministerie van Verkeer en Waterstaat, Fietsberaad. *Cycling in the Netherlands 2009*, section 1.2, http://www.fietsberaad.nl/library/repository/bestanden/CyclingintheNetherlands2009.pdf.
33. Bicycle: Department for Transport, table TRA0401, https://www.gov.uk/government/statistical-data-sets/tra04-pedal-cycle-traffic. Cars/taxis: Department for Transport, table TRA0101, https://www.gov.uk/government/statistical-data-sets/tra01-traffic-by-road-class-and-region-miles.
34. J. Rehm, 'The risks associated with alcohol use and alcoholism', *Alcohol Research and Health*, 34 (2011): 135–43.
35. M. Ramstedt, 'Per capita alcohol consumption and liver cirrhosis mortality in 14 European countries', *Addiction*, 96 (2001): S19–S34. W. C. Kerr, K. M. Fillmore, and P. Marvy, 'Beverage-specific alcohol consumption and cirrhosis mortality in a group of English-speaking beer-drinking countries', *Addiction*, 95 (2000): 339–46.
36. Affordability is defined with respect to adjusted household disposable income and alcohol prices (indexed to 1980), such that higher index values indicate lower affordability.
37. Health and Social Care Information Centre, Statistics on Alcohol, England (London: HSCIC, 2015).
38. ONS, 'Alcohol-related deaths in the United Kingdom: Registered in 2014', *Office for National Statistics Statistical Bulletin* (2 February 2016), https://www.ons.gov.uk/peoplepopulationandcommunity/healthandsocialcare/causesofdeath/bulletins/alcoholrelateddeathsintheunitedkingdom/registeredin2014.
39. OECD/EU, 'Alcohol consumption among adults', in *Health at a Glance: Europe 2016—State of Health in the EU Cycle* (Paris: OECD Publishing, 2016).
40. Johan P. Mackenbach and others, 'Socioeconomic inequalities in health in 22 European countries', *New England Journal of Medicine*, 358 (2008): 2468–81.
41. Michael Marmot, *The Health Gap: The Challenge of an Unequal World* (London: Bloomsbury, 2015).
42. Richard Wilkinson and Kate Pickett, *The Spirit Level: Why Equality Is Better for Everyone* (London: Penguin Books, 2010).
43. The data are taken from table 4.3 of Roderick Floud, Robert W. Fogel, Bernard Harris, and Sok Chul Hong, *The Changing Body: Health, Nutrition, and Human Development in the Western World since 1700* (Cambridge: Cambridge University Press, 2011).
44. Office for National Statistics, 'Trend in life expectancy at birth and at age 65 by socio-economic position based on the National Statistics Socio-Economic Classification, England and Wales: 1982–1986 to 2007–2011' (2015), figures 5 and 8, https://www.ons.gov.uk/peoplepopulationandcommunity/birthsdeathsandmarriages/lifeexpectancies/bulletins/trendinlifeexpectancyatbirthandatage65bysocioeconomicpositionbasedonthenationalstatisticssocioeconomicclassificationenglandandwales/2015-10-21#detailed-methods-measurement-of-inequality-using-the-slope-and-relative-index-of-inequality.

45. Ray Fitzpatrick and Tarani Chandola, 'Health', in *Twentieth-Century British Social Trends*, edited by A. H. Halsey (Basingstoke: Macmillan, 2000), pp. 94–127. Michael Marmot and others, *Fair Society, Healthy Lives: The Marmot Review* (London: Marmot Review, 2010), figure 2.1, p. 44, www.ucl.ac.uk/marmotreview.
46. For a review of the possible explanations for widening health inequalities, see Johan P. Mackenbach, 'The persistence of health inequalities in modern welfare states: The explanation of a paradox', *Social Science and Medicine*, 75 (2012): 761–9.
47. Philippe Autier and Mathieu Boniol, 'Caution needed for country-specific cancer survival', *The Lancet*, 377, no. 9760 (8–14 January 2011): 99–101.
48. M. V. Williams and K. J. Drinkwater, 'Geographical variation in radiotherapy services across the UK in 2007 and the effect of deprivation', *Clinical Oncology*, 21, no. 6 (2009): 431–40; B. Rachet and others, 'Socioeconomic inequalities in cancer survival in England after the NHS cancer plan', *British Journal of Cancer*, 103, no. 4 (2010): 446–53.
49. Department of Health, *The NHS Cancer Plan* (London: Department of Health, 2000).
50. Bernard Rachet and others, 'Population-based cancer survival trends in England and Wales up to 2007: An assessment of the NHS cancer plan for England', *The Lancet Oncology*, 10, no. 4 (2009): 351–69.
51. Economist Intelligence Unit, *The NHS: How Does It Compare?* (London: EIU, 2015), http://www.eiu.com/Handlers/WhitepaperHandler.ashx?fi=NHS-Report-2015.
52. Total health-care expenditure in the UK increased progressively between 2000 and 2013. In constant prices, however, spending flattened out after 2009, and when measured as a share of GDP, decreased slightly between 2009 and 2013, although this might reflect changing GDP as much or more than changing health-care spending.

Chapter 4

1. James Callaghan, 'A rational debate based on the facts', speech given at Ruskin College, Oxford (18 October 1976), http://www.educationengland.org.uk/documents/speeches/1976ruskin.html

    More recently, the close link envisaged by government between education and the economy was symbolized by the fact that the 2010 coalition government moved further and higher education away from the Department for Children, Schools and Families to the responsibility of the Department for Business, Innovation and Skills (although it has subsequently been moved back to the renamed Department for Education).
2. An excellent review of the wider benefits of education and of the evidence suggesting that the effects may be causal is provided by John Bynner, Thomas Schuller, and Leon Feinstein, 'Wider benefits of education: Skills, higher education and civic engagement', *Zeitschrift für Pädogogik*, 49 (2003): S341–61.
3. Tim Dyson, 'Growing regional variation: Demographic change and its implications', in *Diversity and Change in Modern India: Economic Social and Political Approaches*, edited by Anthony F. Heath and Roger Jeffery (Oxford: Oxford University Press/British Academy, 2010), pp. 19–46.
4. For more details, see, for example, United Nations Development Programme Human Development Report 2016, http://hdr.undp.org/en/2016-report. The index was revised in 2010 and there is also a version which adjusts for inequality.

5. Committee on Higher Education, *Higher Education: Report of the Committee Appointed by the Prime Minister under the Chairmanship of Lord Robbins 1961-63*, Cmnd. 2154 (London: HMSO, 1963).
6. Labour's manifesto for the 2001 General Election stated that 'It is time for an historic commitment to open higher education to half of all young people before they are 30' (p. 20), http://www.politicsresources.net/area/uk/e01/man/lab/ENG1.pdf.
7. For an overview of the issues involved in assessing changing educational standards over time, see Harvey Goldstein and Anthony Heath (eds), *Educational Standards* (Oxford: Oxford University Press/British Academy, 2000).
8. In England (although not in Northern Ireland, Wales, or Scotland since education is a devolved responsibility), 'You can leave school on the last Friday in June if you'll be 16 by the end of the summer holidays. You must then do one of the following until you're 18:
   - stay in full-time education, for example at a college
   - start an apprenticeship or traineeship
   - spend 20 hours or more a week working or volunteering, while in part-time education or training.'

   https://www.gov.uk/know-when-you-can-leave-school.
9. For a detailed account of the differences between the educational systems of England, Wales, Northern Ireland, and Scotland, see David Raffe, Karen Brannen, Linda Croxford, and Chris Martin, 'Comparing England, Scotland, Wales and Northern Ireland: The case for "home internationals" in comparative research', *Comparative Education*, 35 (1999): 9-25.
10. Lindsay Paterson and Christina Ianelli, 'Social class and educational attainment: A comparative study of England, Wales, and Scotland', *Sociology of Education*, 80 (2007): 330-58.
11. For 1946/7 till 1960/1 the figures are for pupils leaving maintained secondary schools in England and Wales at age 16 or older as a proportion of all school leavers in that year (that is, the denominator are those leaving in a given year). For 1961 to 1979 the figures are for pupils in the United Kingdom at all schools (including private schools) who were aged 16 on 1 January. For 1980 to 1995 the figures are for all full-time and sandwich students (including those both at school and in further education) aged 16 on 31 August in the United Kingdom. For 1997-9 the figures are for England and Wales, not the UK. From 2001 to 2005 the figures revert to being for the UK (but the gender breakdown is not reported in the education statistics in all years). From 2009 to 2011 the figures relate to England only (covering all those in full-time education at the *end* of the year).
12. Another approach is to use surveys of the adult population which included questions on when the respondent left full-time schooling. We can break this down by year of birth, although there are problems in recall here.
13. So why didn't the figures increase to 100 per cent? I am not sure of the answer but I think it was probably that young people could leave school as soon as they reached the age of 16, so young people whose birthdays were during the summer holidays did not need to return to school after their sixteenth birthday. I suspect that another reason was that many young people were leaving school but continuing their education in further education colleges— these were not included in the statistics until 1980.
14. Paul Willis, *Learning to Labour: How Working Class Kids Get Working Class Jobs* (Farnborough: Saxon House, 1977).
15. My main reservation about the Barro-Lee dataset is that the estimates sometimes show very large and implausible jumps in the percentages from one period to another. This is

particularly noticeable in the case of Canada. This may be due to uneven coverage of the censuses available to Barro and Lee, and to the limitations of their techniques for trying to plug the gaps. There are a number of alternatives which cover shorter periods and do not distinguish specific age groups, just covering the whole of the adult population. The OECD also publishes estimates in its publication *Education at a Glance*, but unfortunately there is missing data for most of our peer countries. I suspect that this means that the OECD did not feel that the national statistics for the missing countries (which include the UK) were strictly comparable.

16. Robert Barro and Jong-Wha Lee, 'A new data set of educational attainment in the world, 1950–2010', *Journal of Development Economics*, 104 (2013): 184–98.
17. In 2014 the published statistics excluded some vocational qualifications and followed other recommendations of the Wolf Report. They also showed only passes taken at the first attempt. In subsequent years further changes were made, moving to numerical scores instead of the previous alphabetical ones, and showing pass rates at the so-called English Baccalaureate rather than the numbers obtaining five or more GCSEs.
18. From 1961 to 1973/4, the figures are for the percentage of school leavers (all schools) in England and Wales obtaining five or more GCE or O Level passes (excluding CSE grade 1 and O level passes awarded on A Level papers). From 1974/5 the figures are for five or more passes at grades A to C (new grading system). From 1976/7 they include grade 1 passes at CSE. From 1988 they refer to five or more passes at GCSE (grades A to C). From 2000/1 the figures are for five or more passes at GCSE grades A*–C, for pupils in their last year of compulsory education in England, Wales, and Northern Ireland. In 1997 additional qualifications such as GNVQ were added as 'equivalents' to a GCSE pass, and from 2004 a wider range of qualifications were allowed to be equivalents.
19. By comparing pupils' scores in the YELLIS ability test with their GCSE results within a period of approximately twenty years, Robert Coe found a general increase in results which ranged from 0.2 (Science) to 0.8 (Maths) of a GCSE grade.
20. The original formulation by Goodhart was: 'As soon as the government attempts to regulate any particular set of financial assets, these become unreliable as indicators of economic trends.' This is because investors try to anticipate what the effect of the regulation will be, and invest so as to benefit from it. While it originated in the context of market responses, the law has profound implications for the selection of high-level targets in organizations. C. A. E. Goodhart, 'Problems of monetary management: The UK experience', *Papers in Monetary Economics* (London: Reserve Bank of Australia, 1975).
21. Alison Wolf, *Review of Vocational Education: The Wolf Report*, DFE-00031-2011 (London: Department for Business, Innovation and Skills and Department for Education, 2011), https://www.gov.uk/government/publications/review-of-vocational-education-the-wolf-report.
22. Details from Sammy Rashid and Greg Brooks, 'The levels of attainment in literacy and numeracy of 13- to 19-year-olds in England, 1948–2009: Research report', National Research and Development Centre for Adult Literacy and Numeracy (London: Institute for Education, 2010), http://dera.ioe.ac.uk/21953/1/doc_4690.pdf. See also Bryan Rogers, 'The trend of reading standards re-assessed', *Educational Research*, 26 (1984): 153–6.
23. K. B. Start and B. K. Wells, *The Trend of Reading Standards* (Slough: NFER, 1972).
24. Robert Coe, 'Improving education: The triumph of hope over experience', www.cem.org/attachments/publications/ImprovingEducation2013.pdf. See also Robert Coe, 'Changes in standards at GCSE and A-Level: Evidence from ALIS and YELLIS', Report for the ONS,

CEM Centre, Durham University (2007), www.cem.org/attachments/ONS report on changes at GCSE and A-level.pdf.

25. The IEA also conducted some additional studies of maths and science among different age groups, but I focus on the ones for the 13 and 14 year olds.

26. In the case of the 1964 and 1980 results I ranked countries according to the metrics provided by FIMS and SIMS80, and also maintained the gaps between the countries' scores proportional to those in the original metrics. I then assigned the top and bottom countries in 1964 and 1980 to levels identical to the average scores of those countries in the subsequent TIMSS studies. The absolute levels are thus arbitrary and cannot be used to infer anything about trends over time between 1964 and 1996.

27. Thorsten Husén (ed.), *International Study of Achievement in Mathematics: A Comparison of Twelve Countries* (Vols 1–2) (Stockholm: Almqvist and Wiksell, 1967); Ian Westbury and Kenneth Travers, *Second International Mathematics Study* (Urbana, IL: University of Illinois, 1990), http://www4.gu.se/compeat/SIMS/Design/Westbury_Travers.pdf; Ina V. S. Mullis, Michael O. Martin, Pierre Foy, and Martin Hooper, *TIMSS 2015 International Results in Mathematics* and Michael O. Martin, Ina V. S. Mullis, Pierre Foy, and Martin Hooper, *TIMSS 2015 International Results in Science*, retrieved from Boston College, TIMSS and PIRLS International Study Center website, http://timssandpirls.bc.edu/timss2015/international-results, copyright © 2013 International Association for the Evaluation of Educational Achievement (IEA). Publisher: TIMSS and PIRLS International Study Center, Lynch School of Education, Boston College. Reproduced with permission.

28. John Jerrim, 'England's "plummeting" PISA test scores between 2000 and 2009: Is the performance of our secondary school pupils really in relative decline?' DoQSS Working Paper No 11-09 (London: Institute of Education, University of London, 2011).

29. OECD, *Excellence and Equity in Education, PISA 2015 Results* (Volume 1) (Paris: OECD Publishing, 2016), http://www.oecd-ilibrary.org/docserver/download/9816061e.pdf.

30. John Jerrim and Nikki Shure, 'Achievement of 15-Year Olds in England: PISA 2015 National Report' (London: Department for Education, December 2016), p. 4, https://www.gov.uk/government/uploads/system/uploads/attachment_data/file/574925/PISA-2015_England_Report.pdf.

31. For a more detailed discussion see John Jerrim and Nikki Shure, 'Achievement of 15 year olds in England: PISA 2015 National Report', https://www.gov.uk/government/uploads/system/uploads/attachment_data/file/574925/PISA-2015_England_Report.pdf.

32. John Jerrim, 'Why Do East Asian children Perform so Well in PISA? An Investigation of Western-Born Children of East Asian Descent' (London: Institute of Education, 2014), p. 20, https://johnjerrim.files.wordpress.com/2013/07/australia_asia_paper.pdf.

33. The gaps shown in Figure 4.8 are adjusted for age and gender, using a multivariate statistical model. This is done in order to take account of the fact that, because of the expansion of education over time, younger people tend to have higher levels of education than older people. Similarly, women tend to have higher educational levels than men. We therefore want to avoid confounding differences due to age or gender with differences due to educational level.

34. The outcomes which John Bynner and colleagues looked at were: malaise (twenty-four-item psychological test designed to measure 'depressive mood'); general health (four-point scale—poor, fair, good, excellent); smoking (smokes regularly, never smokes); voting (voted in last general election, did not vote); interested in politics (very, fairly, not at all interested); and attitude scales of political cynicism, racism, gender equality, and work ethic.

See John Bynner, Thomas Schuller, and Leon Feinstein, 'Wider benefits of education: Skills, higher education and civic engagement', *Zeitschrift für Pädagogik*, 49 (2003), S341-60. See also John Bynner, Steve McIntosh, Anna Vignoles, Lorraine Dearden, Howard Reed, and John Van Reenen, 'Improving adult basic skills: Benefits to the individual and to society', DfEE Research Report No 251 (2001).

35. Robert Coe, 'Improving education: The triumph of hope over experience', www.cem.org/attachments/publications/ImprovingEducation2013.pdf.

Chapter 5

1. The 1944 edition of the Shorter Oxford English Dictionary defined squalor as 'The state or condition of being physically squalid; a combination of misery and dirt'. In turn squalid was defined as 'Naturally foul and repulsive because of the presence of slime, mud etc., and the absence of all cultivation or care... Wretched, miserable, morally repulsive or degraded'.

2. William H. Beveridge, *Full Employment in a Free Society* (London: George Allen and Unwin, 1944), paragraph 36.

3. M. Shaw, 'Housing and public health', *Annual Review of Public Health*, 25 (2004): 397–418; W. J. Fisk, Q. Lei-Gomez, and M. J. Mendell, 'Meta-analyses of the associations of respiratory health effects with dampness and mold in homes', *Indoor Air*, 17 (2007), 284–96; O. P. Galpin, C. J. Whitaker, and A. J. Dubiel, 'Helicobacter pylori infection and overcrowding in childhood', *The Lancet*, 339 (1992): 619; C. D. Solari and R. D. Mare, 'Housing crowding effects on children's wellbeing', *Social Science Research*, 41 (2012): 464–76; N. Britten, J. M. Davies, and J. R. Colley, 'Early respiratory experience and subsequent cough and peak expiratory flow rate in 36 year old men and women', *BMJ* 294 (1987): 1317–20; S. L. Mann, M. E. Wadsworth, and J. R. Colley, 'Accumulation of factors influencing respiratory illness in members of a national birth cohort and their offspring', *Journal of Epidemiology and Community Health*, 46 (1992): 286–92; M. Barnes, S. Butt, and W. Tomaszewski, 'The duration of bad housing and children's well-being in Britain', *Housing Studies*, 26 (2011): 155–76; D. Goux and E. Maurin, 'The effect of overcrowded housing on children's performance at school', *Journal of Public Economics*, 89 (2005): 797–819.

4. D. J. Pevalin, M. P. Taylor, and J. Todd,'The dynamics of unhealthy housing in the UK: A panel data analysis', *Housing Studies*, 23 (2008): 679–95; Alex Marsh, David Gordon, Pauline Heslop, and Christina Pantazis, 'Housing deprivation and health: A longitudinal analysis', *Housing Studies*, 15 (2000), 411–28.

5. Shelter, *What Is the Housing Crisis?* (London: Shelter, 2017), http://england.shelter.org.uk/campaigns_/why_we_campaign/the_housing_crisis.

6. A. E. Holmans, *Historical Statistics of Housing in Britain* (Cambridge: Cambridge Centre for Housing and Planning Research, 2005), p. 477, http://www.cchpr.landecon.cam.ac.uk/Projects/Start-Year/2005/Other-Publications/Historical-Statistics-of-Housing-in-Britain.

7. Michael Young and Peter Willmott, *Family and Kinship in East London* (London: Routledge and Kegan Paul, 1957); Peter Willmott and Michael Young, *Family and Class in a London Suburb* (London: Routledge and Kegan Paul, 1960).

8. P. Aylin, S. Morris, J. Wakefield, A. Grossinho, L. Jarup, and P. Elliott, 'Temperature, housing, deprivation and their relationship to excess winter mortality in Great Britain, 1986–1996', *International Journal of Epidemiology*, 30 (2001): 1100–8.

9. C. Carson, S. Hajat, B. Armstrong, and P. Wilkinson, 'Declining vulnerability to temperature-related mortality in London over the 20th century', *American Journal of Epidemiology*, 164 (2006): 77–84.
10. DCLG, 'A decent home: Definition and guidance for implementation, June 2006 update' (London: DCLG, 2006), https://www.gov.uk/government/uploads/system/uploads/attachment_data/file/7812/138355.pdf.
11. See DCLG, Statistical Data Return (2017), Homes and Communities Agency, table 119. The National Audit Office has published a report on the programme's progress up to 2009, and has also attempted to explain the discrepancy between the survey and local authority returns. See National Audit Office, 'The decent homes programme', HC 212, Session 2009–2010 (London: National Audit Office, January 2010).
12. Whereas in the first part of the period the majority of the social housing stock consisted of local authority housing stock, subsequently the balance shifted towards housing association stock. Within England local authority rented homes decreased from 28 per cent to just 7 per cent between 1981 and 2011, a reduction of 3.4 million homes. Despite a rise in housing association rented homes from 2 per cent in 1981 to 10 per cent in 2014, an increase of 2 million homes, over this period, the growth of housing association stock was inadequate to compensate for the loss of local authority homes, leaving a shortfall of nearly 1.5 million homes. See A. E. Holmans, *Historical Statistics of Housing in Britain* (Cambridge: Cambridge Centre for Housing and Planning Research, 2005), table N 12.
13. 1938, 1951, 1961: A. H. Halsey, *Twentieth-Century British Social Trends*, table 14.12 (based on statistics from the Department of the Environment); data for England, 1969–2016 taken from Office for National Statistics live tables for dwelling stock, table 104; data for Wales, 1969–2000 taken from Office for National Statistics live table 106, 2001–16 taken from Welsh Government, http://gov.wales/docs/statistics/2017/170427-dwelling-stock-estimates-2015-16-en.pdf.
14. John Campbell, *Margaret Thatcher. Volume 1: The Grocer's Daughter* (London: Jonathan Cape, 2000).
15. Rent control was introduced during the First World War to avoid landlords profiteering at a time when demand outstripped supply. Rent controls were lessened in the 1950s and 1960s in an attempt to increase investment in the private rented sector. Controls on new lettings were removed completely in 1989. See http://researchbriefings.parliament.uk/ResearchBriefing/Summary/SN06747.
16. There was also an increase in the number of vacant dwellings. Data from the 2011 census reveal that over 1 million—or 4.4 per cent of dwellings in England and Wales—had no usual residents. This would include holiday homes and second homes as well as empty properties in declining areas such as former mining villages. Data from earlier censuses suggest that the proportion of vacant homes was much smaller in the 1950s and 1960s (around 2.5 per cent). The growth in the size of the total stock shown in Figure 5.2 is therefore somewhat over-optimistic, but even if we strip out the increasing number of vacant dwellings, we still find that the stock of housing increased much more than the size of the population.
17. Paul Cheshire, 'Turning houses into gold: The failure of British planning', *Centrepiece* (Spring 2014), http://blogs.lse.ac.uk/politicsandpolicy/turning-houses-into-gold-the-failure-of-British-planning
18. Census figures from 1951 to 1991 reported in A. H. Halsey, *Twentieth-Century British Social Trends*, table 14.10. Figures from 2001 and 2011 calculated from census data on rooms per household and household size, downloaded from nomis, https://www.nomisweb.co.uk/.

19. One statutory measure of overcrowding, established in the 1935 Housing Act, related the number of members of the household to the number of rooms. Thus, the permitted number for one room was two persons, for two rooms it was three people, and for three rooms it was five people. Children under 10 years of age were only counted as half a person, and children under 1 year counted as zero. (So this is rather like the equivalization that measures of household income use.) These were statutory minima, designed to tackle the problem of overcrowding in the private rental sector, and local authorities were given the power to prosecute landlords who broke these permitted numbers. There were attempts in the early 2000s to designate the bedroom standard as a statutory measure. These attracted some support but were never subject to legislation. The 2010 coalition and the 2015 Conservative government subsequently took a different approach to addressing overcrowding through measures aimed at reallocating existing social housing stock and the introduction of the controversial spare room subsidy.
20. In practice there are some small differences between the bedroom standard and the criteria used by the Department for Work and Pensions for assessing the under-occupancy penalty. The two key differences are that the department considers an adult to be anyone aged 16 and over, and that a property is defined to be under-occupied if it has one or more spare bedrooms. In contrast, the bedroom standard definition of under-occupation is two or more spare bedrooms.
21. Data for overcrowding using the bedroom standard from 1960 and 1964 relate to England and Wales, data from 1971 to 1993 relate to Britain, data from 1995–6 to 2015–16 relate to England. Data from 1995–6 onwards are based on three-year averages, up to and including the labelled date.
22. For details of the relative measure see Becky Tunstall, 'Relative housing space inequality in England and Wales, and its recent rapid resurgence', *International Journal of Housing Policy*, 15 (2015): 105–26. The measures are based on data from the decennial censuses.
23. Moreover, it is not at all clear how the bedroom standard was arrived at in 1960. I doubt if it was based on any scientific evidence of the relationship between bedroom occupancy and ill health or children's educational progress. It probably reflected the assumptions of the officials who came up with the measure. Some critics considered it inadequate even at the time when it was introduced in government surveys, and it was never considered a standard to aspire to. See, for example, P. G. Gray and R. Russell, *The Housing Situation in 1960* (London: Central Office of Information, 1962).
24. These figures are based on a three-year average from 2011 to 2013. More recent data from 2014/15 is not used because these data contain a limited set of demographic variables. These ethnic variations also reflect differences between the ages and incomes of ethnic groups: overcrowding is 8.8 percentage points more prevalent among Pakistani or Bangladeshi than white households, after income, and 11.5 percentage points higher after accounting for age.
25. Census data from 2011 further confirm these patterns of overcrowding: two thirds of overcrowded households contained dependent children (68 per cent) despite accounting for only 29 per cent of households overall. Overcrowding was most common in London, affecting 11.3 per cent of households, partly reflecting the higher population density and greater proportion of rented properties in the capital. There are also the expected ethnic variations, with higher levels of overcrowding among Asian (16.6 per cent) and Black (16.4 per cent) households than households headed by a white person (3.3 per cent, or 681,072).
26. A. E. Holmans, *Historical Statistics of Housing in Britain* (Cambridge: Cambridge Centre for Housing and Planning Research, 2005), p. 465.

27. A. Clarke, 'The prevalence of rough sleeping and sofa surfing amongst young people in the UK', *Social Inclusion*, 4 (2016): 60–72.
28. Communities and Local Government Committee, 'Homelessness: Third report of session 2016–17' (London: HC 40, 2017).
29. National Audit Office, 'Homelessness', HC 308 (London: NAO, 2017).
30. Anna Clarke, Gemma Burgess, Sam Morris, and Chihiro Udagawa, 'Estimating the scale of youth homelessness in the UK: Final report' (Cambridge: Cambridge Centre for Housing and Planning Research, 2015), p. 42, http://www.cchpr.landecon.cam.ac.uk/news/Estimating-scale-youth-homelessness-UK.
31. Office for National Statistics, *2011 Census: Population and Household Estimates for England and Wales* (March 2011), http://www.ons.gov.uk/peoplepopulationandcommunity/populationandmigration/populationestimates/bulletins/2011censuspopulationandhousehold \estimatesforenglandandwales/2012-07-16.
32. DCLG, 'English housing survey: First time buyers and potential home owners report, 2014–15', https://www.gov.uk/government/statistics/english-housing-survey-2014-to-2015-first-time-buyers-and-potential-home-owners-report.
33. A. E. Holmans, *Historical Statistics of Housing in Britain* (Cambridge: Cambridge Centre for Housing and Planning Research, 2005), table N.14.
34. Figures from 1991 are from census table 29, based on a 10 per cent sample; 2001 and 2011 figures from http://webarchive.nationalarchives.gov.uk/20160105160709/http://www.ons.gov.uk/ons/dcp171776_350282.pdf.
35. The Redfern Review no longer appears to be available online. However, a summary by David Kingman can be found at http://www.if.org.uk/2016/11/23/redfern-review-argues-housing-crisis-is-caused-by-falling-wages-rather-than-housing-supply/.
36. National Infrastructure Commission, *The Impact of Population Change and Demography on Future Infrastructure Demand* (London: National Infrastructure Commission, 2016), https://www.gov.uk/government/publications/the-impact-of-population-change-and-demography-on-future-infrastructure-demand.
37. B. Tunstall, 'Relative housing space inequality in England and Wales, and its recent rapid resurgence', *International Journal of Housing Policy*, 15 (2015), p. 115.
38. Thanks to Nathan Thomas at the Office for National Statistics for providing the data and methodology specifications.
39. A. E. Holmans, *Historical Statistics of Housing in Britain* (Cambridge: Cambridge Centre for Housing and Planning Research, 2005), table H.15.
40. Malcolm Morgan and Heather Cruickshank, 'Quantifying the extent of space shortages: English dwellings', *Building Research and Information*, 42 (2014): 710–24.
41. DCLG, live tables on rents, lettings, and tenancies, https://www.gov.uk/government/statistical-data-sets/live-tables-on-rents-lettings-and-tenancies.
42. The measure of dwelling size does not take into account differences between the countries in household size. However, the average number of people per household is roughly comparable between countries. Average household sizes are 2.0 in Sweden, 2.1 in Germany, 2.2 in France, and 2.3 in the UK and Italy, http://ec.europa.eu/eurostat/statistics-explained/index.php/File:Average_household_size,_2014_(average_number_of_persons_in_private_households).png.

43. Briefly, the British bedroom standard requires separate bedrooms for children aged over 10 of different sex, while the EU-SILC uses an older threshold of 12 years. While the EU-SILC requires single adults over 18 to have their own bedroom, the British standard only requires adults over 21 to have a bedroom. The EU-SILC also requires one room for the household in addition to their bedroom standard, so presents a broader measure of household space. The two standards are likely to correspond fairly closely overall, but might show discrepancies for certain households.
44. Eurostat did not include the results for the UK in their statistics because of the very low response rate. However, the results from the English Housing Survey are likely to be broadly comparable.
45. Malcolm Morgan and Heather Cruickshank, 'Quantifying the extent of space shortages: English dwellings', *Building Research and Information*, 42 (2014), figure 1.
46. B. Tunstall, 'Relative housing space inequality in England and Wales, and its recent rapid resurgence', *International Journal of Housing Policy*, 15 (2015), p. 119.
47. A. E. Holmans, *Historical Statistics of Housing in Britain* (Cambridge: Cambridge Centre for Housing and Planning Research, 2005), p. 461.

Chapter 6

1. William H. Beveridge, *Full Employment in a Free Society* (London: George Allen and Unwin, 1944), p. 38, paragraph 50.
2. John Maynard Keynes, *The General Theory of Employment, Interest and Money* (London: Macmillan, 1936).
3. Marie Jahoda, Paul F. Lazarsfeld, and Hans Zeisel, *Marienthal: The Sociography of an Unemployed Community* (London: Tavistock, 1972 [1933]).
4. Pilgrim Trust, *Men without Work* (Cambridge: Cambridge University Press, 1938).
5. William H. Beveridge, *Full Employment in a Free Society* (London: George Allen and Unwin, 1944), p. 28, paragraph 29.
6. Ibid., paragraph 8.
7. Gordon Waddell and A. Kim Burton, 'Is work good for your health and well-being?' Report commissioned by the Department for Work and Pensions (London: Stationery Office, 2006), https://www.gov.uk/government/uploads/system/uploads/attachment_data/file/214326/hwwb-is-work-good-for-you.pdf; Anders Björklund, 'Unemployment and mental health: Some evidence from panel data', *Journal of Human Resources*, 20 (1985): 469–83; Tom Clemens, Paul Boyle, and Frank Popham, 'Unemployment, mortality and the problem of health related selection: Evidence from the Scottish and England and Wales (ONS) Longitudinal Studies', *Health Statistics Quarterly*, 43 (2009): 7–13; Morton O. Schapiro and Dennis A. Ahlburg, 'Suicide: The ultimate cost of unemployment', *Journal of Post Keynesian Economics*, 5 (1982): 276–80; Ben Barr and others, 'Suicides associated with the 2008–10 economic recession in England: Time trend analysis', *British Medical Journal*, 354 (2012): e5142; Dan Anderberg, Helmut Rainer, Jonathan Wadsworth, and Tanya Wilson, 'Unemployment and domestic violence: Theory and evidence', *The Economic Journal*, 126 (2016): 1947–79; Dongxu Wu and Zhongmin Wu, 'Crime, inequality and unemployment in England and Wales', *Applied Economics*, 44 (2012): 3765–75; Jan Marcus, 'The effect of unemployment on the mental health of

spouses: Evidence from plant closures in Germany', *Journal of Health Economics*, 32 (2013): 546–58.
8. For a review of these issues, see Jennie E. Brand, 'The far-reaching impact of job loss and unemployment', *Annual Review of Sociology*, 41 (2015): 359–75.
9. David N. F. Bell and David G. Blanchflower, 'Young people and the Great Recession', *Oxford Review of Economic Policy*, 27 (2011): 241–67.
10. William H. Beveridge, *Full Employment in a Free Society* (London: George Allen and Unwin, 1944), p. 72, paragraph 89.
11. International Labour Organization, 'Resolutions concerning economically active population, employment, unemployment and underemployment adopted by the 13th International Conference of Labour Statisticians' (October 1982), paragraph 10, http://www.ilo.org/public/english/bureau/stat/res/index.htm.
12. David G. Blanchflower and Richard B. Freeman, 'Did the Thatcher reforms change British labour market performance?' NBER Working Paper 4384 (June 1993); Anthony B. Atkinson and J. Micklewright, 'Turning the screw: Benefits for the unemployed 1979–1988' in *The Economics of Social Security*, edited by Andrew Dilnot and Ian Walker (Oxford: Oxford University Press, 1989).
13. Yorgos Vournas, 'Official statistics and the manipulation of conceptual and technical instruments: Implications for research on social security', *Radical Statistics*, 72 (1999), http://www.radstats.org.uk/no072/article4.htm.
14. Other important differences in the way unemployment was counted are: 1913–47, excluding 1919, unemployment rates are expressed as a percentage of the insured unemployed to all insured persons; 1948–68: the unemployment rate is expressed as the number of people registered as unemployed at employment exchanges and associated offices as a percentage of the total of those unemployed plus the number of employees in employment; 1969–71: the unemployment rate is expressed as the number of registered unemployed as a percentage of the total of employees and unemployed; 1972–82: the unemployment rate is expressed as the number of registered unemployed aged 18 and over as a percentage of the workforce (that is, of employees in employment, the self-employed, the unemployed, HM Forces, and people on work-related government training programmes); 1983–April 1998: the unemployment rate is expressed as the number of persons aged 18 and over claiming unemployment-related benefits as a percentage of the workforce.
15. For 1955–70 I use the register counts provided by James Denman and Paul McDonald, 'Unemployment statistics from 1881 to the present day', *Labour Market Trends*, 104 (1996): 5–18. For 1971–82 I use the historical time series provided by the Office for National Statistics. The methods employed are described by Craig Lindsay, 'Employment and unemployment estimates for 1971 to 1991', *Labour Market Trends*, 113 (2005): 15–20. They are the result of complex modelling drawing on the claimant count data.
16. UK 1955–70: register counts reported in J. Denman and P. McDonald, 'Unemployment statistics from 1881 to the present day', *Labour Market Trends*, 104 (1996): 5–18.

    UK 1971–82: modelled figures reported in Office for National Statistics, 'Time series data: Unemployment rate (aged 16 and over, seasonally adjusted)', https://www.ons.gov.uk/employmentandlabourmarket/peoplenotinwork/unemployment/timeseries/mgsx.
17. For accounts of the history of immigration to the main Western countries after the Second World War see the chapters in Anthony F. Heath and Sin Yi Cheung (eds), *Unequal Chances: Ethnic Minorities in Western Labour Markets* (Oxford: Oxford University Press, 2007).

18. https://data.oecd.org/unemp/long-term-unemployment-rate.htm.
19. David N. F. Bell and David G. Blanchflower, 'Youth unemployment: Déjà vu?' Stirling Economics Discussion Paper 2010-14 (January 2010), pp. 12-13, https://dspace.stir.ac.uk/bitstream/1893/2117/1/SEDP-2010-04-Bell-Blanchflower%5B1%5D.pdf.
20. Margaret Thatcher, *The Downing Street Years* (London: HarperCollins, 1993), p. 36.
21. https://data.oecd.org/emp/self-employment-rate.htm. The only peer country with a higher rate of self-employment in 2015 was Italy (24.7 per cent). Italy had had an even higher rate of self-employment in 1980, so in fact had been moving in the opposite direction.
22. David G. Blanchflower and Richard B. Freeman, 'Did the Thatcher reforms change British labour market performance?' CEP/NIESR Conference: Is the British Labour Market Different? NBER Working Paper #4384 (June 1993). This contains a detailed discussion of the effects of Margaret Thatcher's labour market reforms on self-employment.
23. I should point out that the official source which I used for the 1971-82 period in Figure 6.1 shows that women had a lower unemployment rate than men in the 1970s. However, I am not sure that I trust this finding since it is based on claimant count data and on the assumption that the association between claimant rates and International Labour Organization unemployment in the 1980s was the same as that in the 1970s.
24. Statistics prepared by the Office for National Statistics show that women actually had a higher unemployment rate than men in the 1970s. However, to obtain their estimates for the 1970s the ONS statisticians did not directly draw on the General Household Survey as we have done but instead adjusted administrative data in order to make it comparable to later survey-based definitions. I am somewhat sceptical of their modelling techniques and prefer the results shown in Figure 6.2 which stick close to the actual data. For further details see Craig Lindsay and Paul Doyle, 'Experimental consistent time series of historical labour force survey data', *Labour Market Trends*, 111 (2003): 467-75.
25. Ghazala Azmat, Maia Guell, and Alan Manning, 'Gender gaps in unemployment rates in OECD countries', *Journal of Labour Economics*, 24 (2006): 1-37.
26. An alternative measure is to look at the ratio rather than the percentage point gap. The male low:high education ratio was 3.7 in 1978, falling to 3.2 in 1989, 2.6 in 2001, and 3.0 in 2015. The trend over time is less clear for women, with both percentage point gap and ratio being higher in 2015 than previously. The female low:high education ratio was 2.5 in 1978, 2.5 in 1989, 2.5 in 2001, but 3.7 in 2015.
27. In technical language, young people without qualifications may be negatively selected in the twenty-first century to a greater extent than they had been before the great credentialization of the 1990s. We may not therefore be comparing like with like over time.
28. See David N. F. Bell and David G. Blanchflower, 'Youth unemployment: Déjà vu?' Stirling Economics Discussion Paper 2010-14 (January 2010), and the references cited therein, and National Audit Office, '16- to 18-year-old participation in education and training', HC 624 (3 September 2014), https://www.nao.org.uk/report/16-to-18-year-old-participation-in-education-and-training/.
29. The government's definition of NEET differs somewhat from my approach, since it excludes those people who were unemployed but who were also engaged in some form of education or training. However, the patterns shown in Figure 6.7 do not differ in any material way from those shown by government statistics. See Andrew Powell, 'NEET: Young people not in education, employment or training', House of Commons Library, Briefing paper SN06705 (2017), http://researchbriefings.files.parliament.uk/documents/SN06705/SN06705.pdf.

30. Office for National Statistics, 'Childbearing for women born in different years, England and Wales: 2014', statistical bulletin (10 November 2015), https://www.ons.gov.uk/people populationandcommunity/birthsdeathsandmarriages/conceptionandfertilityrates/bulletins/ childbearingforwomenbornindifferentyearsenglandandwales/2015-11-10.
31. The Department for Education has also published a series extending back to 1994, primarily using administrative data. This shows a somewhat different pattern over time from the Office for National Statistics figures, with no sign of a peak after the 2007/8 crash (which I find rather surprising). See Department for Education, 'Participation in education, training and employment: 2016' (London: DfE: 2017), https://www.gov.uk/government/uploads/ system/uploads/attachment_data/file/622347/SFR29_2017_Technical_Document.pdf.
32. House of Commons Library, 'NEET: Young people not in education, employment or training', Briefing paper number SN 0765 (6 April 2016).
33. The proportion of students in the Labour Force Survey 1983 is much smaller than in Labour Force Survey 1984 or in General Household Survey 1983, and therefore the data for Labour Force Survey 1983 are not used here.
34. National Audit Office, 'Care leavers' transition to adulthood', HC 269 (17 July 2015), https:// www.nao.org.uk/wp-content/uploads/2015/07/Care-leavers-transition-to-adulthood.pdf.
35. Alison Wolf, 'Review of vocational education: The Wolf Report', DFE-00031-2011, p. 7, https://www.gov.uk/government/publications/review-of-vocational-education-the-wolf-report.

Chapter 7

1. Social Mobility Commission, *Time for Change: An Assessment of Government Policies on Social Mobility 1997–2017* (London: Social Mobility Commission, 2017), p. 1, https://www. gov.uk/government/publications/social-mobility-policies-between-1997-and-2017-time-for-change.
2. Joseph E. Stiglitz, Amartya Sen, and Jean-Paul Fitoussi, *Report by the Commission on the Measurement of Economic Performance and Social Progress* (2009), http://www.com munityindicators.net/system/publication_pdfs/9/original/Stiglitz_Sen_Fitoussi_2009.pdf? 1323961027; OECD, *Measuring Well-Being and Progress: Well-Being Research*, http://www. oecd.org/statistics/measuring-well-being-and-progress.htm#publications.
3. The abolition of purchase of commissions was one of the Cardwell reforms, undertaken in 1871. See http://www.victorianweb.org/history/armyrefs.html.
4. Lord Scarman, *The Brixton Disorders, 10–12th April 1981* (London: HMSO, 1981); Gareth Morrell, Sara Scott, Di McNeish, and Stephen Webster, *The August Riots in England: Understanding the Involvement of Young People*, prepared for the Cabinet Office (London: NatCen, 2011); Juta Kawalerowicz and Michael Biggs, 'Anarchy in the UK: Economic deprivation, social disorganization, and political grievances in the London riot of 2011', *Social Forces*, 94 (2015): 673–98.
5. Kamaldeep Bhui, Stephen Stansfeld, Kwame McKenzie, Saffron Karlsen, James Nazroo, and Scott Weich, 'Racial/ethnic discrimination and common mental disorders among workers: Findings from the EMPIRIC study of ethnic minority groups in the United Kingdom', *American Journal of Public Health*, 95 (2005): 496–501.
6. The full list of nine protected characteristics is age, disability, gender reassignment, marriage and civil partnership, pregnancy and maternity, race, religion and belief, sex, and sexual orientation. Remarkably, social class background is not on the list.

7. John E. Roemer, *Equality of Opportunity* (Cambridge, MA: Harvard University Press, 1998), p. 1.
8. Ibid., p. 1.
9. By opportunity for higher education Gray and Moshinsky meant attending grammar and private schools. They excluded central and senior elementary schools, and technical schools maintained by the local educational authority which did not prepare students for university.
10. J. L. Gray and Pearl Moshinsky, 'Ability and opportunity in English education', *Sociological Review*, 27 (1935): 113–62.
11. In order to deal with the problem that there have been considerable changes over time in the absolute quantity of places at university or positions in the salariat, sociologists typically use measures such as odds ratios to measure trends in the openness of society. Odds ratios measure the relative chances of people from different backgrounds achieving advantaged positions and avoiding disadvantaged ones. They have some useful mathematical properties; for example their value is not constrained by the absolute numbers of positions available.
12. Ethnic groups have been defined by Max Weber, one of the founding fathers of sociology, 'as those human groups that entertain a subjective belief in their common descent because of similarities of physical type or of customs or both, or because of memories of colonization and migration'. See Max Weber, 'Ethnic groups', in G. Roth and C. Wittich (eds), *Economy and Society: An Outline of Interpretive Sociology*, Vol. 1, Part II (Berkeley, CA: University of California Press, 1978 [1922]), p. 389.
13. I have excluded the very first field experiment by W. W. Daniel, *Racial Discrimination in England* (London: Penguin, 1968), as it only looked at firms which had been accused of discrimination—in other words it did not cover a representative sample of firms. I have also excluded two studies, by M. Noon, 'Racial discrimination in speculative application: Evidence from the UK's top 100 firms', *Human Resource Management Journal*, 3 (1993): 35–47 and by K. Hoque and M. Noon, 'Racial discrimination in speculative applications: New optimism six years on?' *Human Resource Management Journal*, 9 (1999): 71–82, since the fictitious applicants were not applying for actual job vacancies but simply asking for information.
14. 1969: Roger Jowell and Patricia Prescott-Clarke, 'Racial discrimination and white-collar workers in Britain', *Race and Class*, 11 (1970): 397–417.

    1973/4: Neil McIntosh and David J. Smith, *The Extent of Racial Discrimination* (London: PEP, 1974).

    1977/8: Michael Firth, 'Racial discrimination in the British labor market', *Industrial and Labor Relations Review*, 34 (1981): 265–72.

    1977–9: James Hubbuck and Simon Carter, *Half a Chance? A Report on Job Discrimination against Young Blacks in Nottingham* (London: Commission for Racial Equality, 1980).

    1984/5: Colin Brown and Paul Gay, *Racial Discrimination: 17 Years after the Act* (London: Policy Studies Institute, 1985).

    1992: Aneez Esmail and Sam Everington, 'Racial discrimination against doctors from ethnic minorities', *British Medical Journal*, 306 (1993): 691ff.

    1996: Commission for Racial Equality, *We Regret to Inform You: Testing for Racial Discrimination in Youth Employment in the North of England and Scotland* (London: Commission for Racial Equality, 1997).

    1997: Aneez Esmail and Sam Everington, 'Asian doctors are still being discriminated against', *British Medical Journal*, 314 (1997): 1619.

2008/9: Martin Wood, Jon Hales, Susan Purdon, Tanya Sejersen, and Oliver Hayllar, *A Test for Racial Discrimination in Recruitment Practice in British Cities*. (London: Department for Work and Pensions, 2009).

2016/17: Valentina de Stasio and Anthony Heath, 'Discrimination in Britain: First results from the GEMM project', CSI briefing paper.

15. Doris Weichselbaumer, 'Discrimination against migrants wearing headscarves', Institute for the Study of Labour, Discussion Paper No. 10217 (Bonn: IZA, 2016), http://ftp.iza.org/dp10217.pdf.

16. A recent study of Muslim applicants has been conducted in Britain by Abubaker and Bagley. Mahmoud Abubaker and Christopher Adam Bagley, 'Methodology of correspondence testing for employment discrimination involving ethnic minority applications: Dutch and English case studies of Muslim applicants for employment', *Social Sciences*, 6 (2017): 112, http://www.mdpi.com/2076-0760/6/4/112/htm.

17. Martin Wood and his colleagues show that Caribbean names are not especially distinctive from traditional British names, and this may explain the couple of studies where there appear to be low rates of discrimination against Caribbeans. See Martin Wood, Jon Hales, Susan Purdon, Tanya Sejersen, and Oliver Hayllar, *A Test for Racial Discrimination in Recruitment Practice in British Cities*, Department for Work and Pensions Research Report 607 (London: DWP, 2009).

18. Anthony Heath, Thomas Liebig, and Patrick Simon, 'Discrimination against immigrants: Measurement, incidence and policy instruments', in *OECD International Migration Outlook 2013* (Paris: OECD, 2013), pp. 191–230.

19. James Hubbuck and Simon Carter, *Half a Chance? A Report on Job Discrimination against Young Blacks in Nottingham* (London: Commission for Racial Equality, 1980), p. 17.

20. Robert Ford, 'Is racial prejudice declining in Britain?', *British Journal of Sociology*, 59 (2008): 609–36; Ingrid Storm, Maria Sobolewska, and Robert Ford, 'Is ethnic prejudice declining in Britain? Change in social distance attitudes among ethnic majority and minority Britons', *British Journal of Sociology*, 68 (2017): 410–34.

21. Kenneth Y. Arrow, 'The theory of discrimination', *Discrimination in Labor Markets*, 3 (1973): 3–33.

22. Heather Joshi, Gerry Makepeace, and Peter Dolton, 'More or less unequal? Evidence on the pay of men and women from the British birth cohort studies', *Gender, Work and Organization*, 14 (2007): 37–55.

23. See, for example, Heather Joshi, 'Gender and pay: Some more equal than others', in Anthony F. Heath, John Ermisch, and Duncan Gallie (eds), *Understanding Social Change* (Oxford: Oxford University Press for the British Academy, 2005), pp. 151–86; Monica Costa Dias, William Elming, and Robert Joyce, 'The gender wage gap', IFS Briefing note BN186 (2016), https://www.ifs.org.uk/uploads/publications/bns/bn186.pdf.

24. Based on results published in Heather Joshi, Gerry Makepeace, and Peter Dolton, 'More or less unequal? Evidence on the pay of men and women from the British Birth Cohort Studies', table 3, reproduced with permission from Wiley and Copyright Clearance Center via Rightslink, License Number 4270130568581.

25. Lord Davies, 'Women on boards', table 1, https://www.gov.uk/government/uploads/system/uploads/attachment_data/file/31480/11-745-women-on-boards.pdf.

26. Peter A. Riach and Judith Rich, 'An experimental investigation of sexual discrimination in hiring in the English labor market'. *B. E. Journal of Economic Analysis and Policy*, 6 (2006): article 1.
27. Z. Macdonald and M. Shields, 'The impact of alcohol use on occupational attainment in England', *Economica*, 68 (2001): 427–54.
28. Simon Deakin, Sarah Fraser Butlin, Colin McLaughlin, and Aleksandra Polanska, 'Are litigation and collective bargaining complements or substitutes for achieving gender equality? A study of the British Equal Pay Act', *Cambridge Journal of Economics*, 39 (2015): 381–403.
29. Reproduced from John H. Goldthorpe, 'Social class mobility in modern Britain: Changing structure, constant process', *Journal of the British Academy*, 4 (2016): 89–111, with permission from the author and the British Academy.
30. John H. Goldthorpe, 'Social class mobility in modern Britain: Changing structure, constant process', *Journal of the British Academy*, 4 (2017): 89–111, p. 96.
31. The Social Mobility Commission Report, for example, uses administrative data for the most part. However, the only proxy for social origins which is available in these data is whether the child receives free school meals. This is simply a binary measure, relating in essence to the income of the household rather than its social class. It is in effect a measure of poverty. We use the Labour Force Survey for 2014 and 2015 (the third quarter) and the first three waves of the UK Longitudinal Household Study, including the British Household Panel Survey 'rolled over' in Wave 2 of the UK Longitudinal Household Study. The most important reason for using these data sources is that they permit parental and respondents' class and ethnicity to be coded in a consistent way.
32. The data also include respondents born in the 1980s, but I drop members of this birth cohort since they would have been relatively young at the time of our surveys and would have had less time to progress in their careers than the members of earlier birth cohorts.
33. I should mention that there are some important limitations to this cohort approach to measuring change. Because of differential mortality (and emigration), the sample of people born in the earlier decades and remaining in the Labour Force Survey and UK Longitudinal Household Study in 2009–15 will be a biased subset of those born in the decade in question. There will also be some lifecycle processes which need to be taken into account.
34. If we use methods based on odds ratios, as mentioned above in note 11, we find that relative fluidity has barely changed across these birth cohorts.
35. Across the five birth cohorts the rate of upward mobility into the salariat was 40 per cent in the oldest birth cohort followed by 43, 45, and 43 per cent in the next three cohorts, before dropping to 38 per cent in the youngest birth cohort.
36. Erzsébet Bukodi, Mollie Bourne, and Bastian Betthaeuser, 'Wastage of talent? Social origins, cognitive ability and educational attainment in Britain', *Advances in Life Course Research* (2017). The three studies used are the National Child Development study (the 1958 birth cohort), the British Cohort Study (the 1970 birth cohort) and the Avon Longitudinal Study of Parents and Children (the 1991/2 birth cohort). The measure of A Levels is that of achieving at least two A Levels or NVQ 4 equivalents. Bukodi and her colleagues use a relative measure of parental education. First, parental education is coded to one of seven ordered categories (ranging from the highest where both parents have degree-level qualifications to the lowest where neither parent has any qualification). Second, the proportion of parents whose level of qualification is below their own within the cumulative distribution for their child's cohort is calculated. This measure is then rescaled to take values within the range 0–1.

37. Ibid., figure 3, threshold 3.
38. Richard Breen, Ruud Luijkx, Walter Müller, and Reinhard Pollak, 'Non-persistent inequality in educational attainment: Evidence from eight European countries', *American Journal of Sociology*, 114 (2009): 1475–521.
39. Erzsébet Bukodi, Mollie Bourne, and Bastian Betthaeuser, 'Wastage of talent? Social origins, cognitive ability and educational attainment in Britain', *Advances in Life Course Research* (2017), p. 1.
40. Panel on Fair Access to the Professions, 'Unleashing aspiration: The final report of the panel on fair access to the professions, 2009'; Daniel Laurison and Sam Friedman, 'The class pay gap in Britain's higher professional and managerial occupations', *American Sociological Review*, 81 (2016): 668–95.
41. Michelle Jackson, 'Disadvantaged through discrimination? The role of employers in social stratification', *British Journal of Sociology*, 60 (2009): 669–92.
42. The direct evidence in support of the idea that social connections increase social mobility is limited. Self-reported help from parents did not have a strong effect in a recent study by Alexi Gugushvili and his colleagues, although parents who directly employ their children may protect those with low education from ending up in routine jobs (Alexi Gugushvili, Erzsébet Bukodi, and John H. Goldthorpe, 'The direct effect of social origins on social mobility chances: "Glass floors" and "Glass ceilings" in Britain', *European Sociological Review*, 33 (2017): 305–16). General evidence linking social connections to the probability of finding a job is more robust. Nan Lin and Mary Dumin showed how high-status connections are more valuable than low-status ones for accessing higher-status positions (Nan Lin and Mary Dumin, 'Access to occupations through social ties', *Social Networks*, 8 (1986): 365–85). Effects may also be indirect through education. Erin Horvat and her colleagues, for example, found that high-class parents use their networks (e.g. parent-teacher associations) to intervene in their children's schooling. Social ties were drawn upon, for instance, to contest placement decisions, teacher selection, and even the curriculum (Erin M. Horvat, Elliot B. Weininger, and Annette Lareau, 'From social ties to social capital: Class differences in the relations between schools and parent networks', *American Educational Research Journal*, 40 (2003): 319–51). Fiona Devine has also presented qualitative evidence on how parents get their children good jobs (Fiona Devine, *Class Practices: How Parents Help Their Children Get Good Jobs* (Cambridge: Cambridge University Press, 2004)).
43. For example, the United Nations Development Programme's Gender Empowerment Measure, the World Economic Forum's Global Gender Gap Index, and the European Institute for Gender Equality's Gender Equality Index.
44. Doris Weichselbaumer, 'Discrimination against migrants wearing headscarves', Institute for the Study of Labour, Discussion Paper No. 10217 (Bonn: IZA, 2016).
45. http://dx.doi.org/10.1787/migr_outlook-2013-en. The sources which Heath, Liebig, and Simon draw upon are:

    Canada: P. Eid, *Mesurer la discrimination à l'embauche subie par les minorités racisées: résultats d'un 'testing' mené dans le grand Montréal* (Quebec: Commission des droits de la personne et des droits de la jeunesse, 2012).

    England: Valentina de Stasio and Anthony Heath, 'Discrimination in Britain: First results from the GEMM project', CSI briefing paper, in preparation.

    France: E. Cediey and F. Foroni, 'Discrimination in access to employment on grounds of foreign origin in France', ILO International Migration Papers, No. 85E (2008), ILO, Geneva.

Germany: L. Kaas and C. Manger, 'Ethnic discrimination in Germany's labour market: A field experiment', *German Economic Review*, 13 (2012): 1–20.

Italy: E. Allasino, E. Reyneri, A. Venturini, and G. Zincone, 'Labour market discrimination against migrant workers in Italy', *ILO International Migration Papers*, No. 67 (Geneva: ILO, 2006).

Sweden: Bursell, M., 'What's in a name? A field experiment test for the existence of ethnic discrimination in the hiring process', *Working Paper Series*, No. 7 (Stockholm: Linnaeus Center for Integration Studies, 2007).

USA: M. Bertrand and S. Mullainathan, 'Are Emily and Greg more employable than Lakisha and Jamal? A field experiment on labor market discrimination', *American Economic Review*, 95 (2004): 991–1013.

46. For some of the countries, the PIAAC dataset gives income banded in deciles. I have therefore used the percentages in each decile to calculate the net difference index between graduate men and women's earnings. For the net difference index, see Stanley Lieberson, 'Rank-sum comparisons between groups', *Sociological Methodology*, 7 (1976): 276–91.

47. Linda N. Edwards, 'Equal employment opportunity in Japan: A view from the West', *ILR Review*, 41 (1988): 240–50; Kunihiro Kimura, 'Sex-based discrimination trends in Japan, 1965–2005: The gender wage gap and the marriage bar', in Miguel Angel Centeno and Katherine S. Newman, *Discrimination in an Unequal World* (New York: Oxford University Press, 2010), pp. 156–71.

48. 'Women in the UK civil service: History', http://www.civilservant.org.uk/women-history.html.

49. M. Yaish and R. Andersen, 'Social mobility in 20 modern societies: The role of economic and political context', *Social Science Research*, 41 (2012): 527–38.

50. Richard Breen and Ruud Luijkx, 'Social mobility in Europe between 1970 and 2000', in Richard Breen (ed.), *Social Mobility in Europe* (Oxford: Oxford University Press, 2004), figure 3.3 and accompanying text.

51. Technical details are as follows:

Income inequality of opportunity. Measure: difference in log income (adjusted for age and immigration status) between those with at least one parent who attained tertiary and neither parent attained upper secondary, controlling for respondent's educational level.

Income fluidity. Measure: intergenerational elasticity between father and son earnings.

Social class fluidity. Measure: global log odds ratio (7 by 7 class matrix).

Social-economic inequalities in education. OECD, *Overcoming Social Background, Equity in Learning Opportunities and Outcomes* (Volume II, 2010), figure II.3.2, http://www.oecd/education/pisa-2009-results-overcoming-social-background.

52. The published sources are as follows:

Income inequality of opportunity. J. Jerrim and L. Macmillan, 'Income inequality, intergenerational mobility, and the Great Gatsby curve: Is education the key?' *Social Forces*, 94 (2015): 5056–533, table 2.

Income fluidity. Miles Corak, 'Inequality from generation to generation: The United States in comparison', IZA discussion paper no. 9929 (2016), figure 1, http://ftp.iza.org/dp9929.pdf.

Social class fluidity. Erzsebet Bukodi, Marii Paskov, and Brian Nolan, 'Intergenerational class mobility in Europe: A new account and an old story', INET Oxford Working Paper no. 2017-03, figure 4.

Socio-economic inequalities in education. Measure: the slope of the socio-economic gradient (score point difference associated with one unit increase in the PISA index of economic, social, and cultural status).

53. Alan B. Krueger, 'The rise and consequences of inequality in the United States', speech at the Centre for American Progress, 12 January 2012, https://cdn.americanprogress.org/wp-content/uploads/events/2012/01/pdf/krueger.pdf.
54. John Ermisch, Markus Jantti, and Timothy Smeeding, *Inequality from Childhood to Adulthood: A Cross-National Perspective on the Transmission of Advantage* (New York: Russell Sage Foundation, 2012), p. 3.
55. There is a very large and contentious debate among scholars about trends over time in the openness of British society. Economists have found evidence of declining income mobility over time, while sociologists have either found no change over time in social class mobility or have found a slight increase in openness. For recent reviews of the debate see John H. Goldthorpe, 'Understanding—and misunderstanding—social mobility in Britain: The entry of the economists, the confusion of politicians and the limits of educational policy', *Journal of Social Policy*, 42 (2013): 431–50; Joanne Blanden, Paul Gregg, and Lindsey Macmillan, 'Intergenerational persistence in income and social class: The effect of within-group inequality', *Journal of the Royal Statistical Society*, Series A, 176 (2013): 1–23.

Chapter 8

1. Benjamin Disraeli, *Sybil, or The Two Nations* (London: Henry Colburn, 1845).
2. Richard Wilkinson and Kate Pickett, *The Spirit Level: Why Equality Is Better for Everyone* (London: Allen Lane, 2009).
3. See, for example, David Goodhart, *The British Dream: Successes and Failures of Post-War Immigration* (London: Atlantic Books, 2013); Social Integration Commission, 'Social integration: A wake-up call' (2014), http://socialintegrationcommission.org/a-wake-up-call-social-integration-commission.pdf.
4. Trevor Phillips, speech at the Manchester Council for Community Relations, 22 September, 2005.
5. Dame Louise Casey, 'The Casey review: A review into opportunity and integration' (London: DCLG, 2016), https://www.gov.uk/government/uploads/system/uploads/attachment_data/file/575973/The_Casey_Review_Report.pdf.
6. Sara B. Hobolt, 'The Brexit vote: A divided nation, a divided continent', *European Journal of Social Policy*, 23 (2016): 1259–77; Matthew Goodwin and Oliver Heath, *Brexit Vote Explained: Poverty, Low Skills and Lack of Opportunities* (York: Joseph Rowntree Foundation, 2016), https://www.jrf.org.uk/report/brexit-vote-explained-poverty-low-skills-and-lack-opportunities.
7. Brown, Gordon, speech on Britishness at the Commonwealth Club, London, 27 February 2007, http://gu.com/p/qeay/sbl.
8. David Cameron, speech to the Conservative party conference, 7 October 2015.
9. David Miller, *On Nationality* (Oxford: Clarendon Press, 1995); David Miller and Sundas Ali, 'Testing the national identity argument', *European Political Science Review*, 6 (2013): 237–59.
10. Robert D. Putnam, *Bowling Alone: The Collapse and Revival of American Community* (New York: Simon and Schuster, 2000).
11. Paola Grenier and Karen Wright, 'Social capital in Britain: Exploring the Hall paradox', *Policy Studies*, 27 (2006): 27–53, p. 50.
12. On somewhat similar lines the OECD defines a cohesive society as one which 'works towards the well-being of all its members, fights exclusion and marginalisation, creates a sense of

belonging, promotes trust, and offers its members the opportunity of upward social mobility', although I find the inclusion of upward social mobility in the definition rather idiosyncratic. See OECD Development Centre, *Perspectives on Global Development, 2012: Social Cohesion in a Shifting World* (Paris: OECD, 2012), http://www.oecd.org/site/devpgd2012/49067954.pdf.

13. Robert D. Putnam, '*E Pluribus Unum*: Diversity and community in the twenty-first century', 2006 Johan Skytte Prize Lecture, *Scandinavian Political Studies*, 30 (2007): 137–74.
14. Anthony F. Heath and James R. Tilley 'British national identity and attitudes towards immigration', *International Journal on Multicultural Societies*, 7 (2005): 119–32.
15. Anthony F. Heath, Konstanze Jacob, and Lindsay Richards, 'Young people in transition: The national identity of minority youth', in Frank Kalter, Janne Jonsson, Frank van Tubergen, and Anthony F. Heath (eds), *Growing Up in Diverse Societies: The Integration of the Children of Immigrants in England, Germany, the Netherlands, and Sweden* (Oxford: Oxford University Press, forthcoming).
16. Robin Cohen, 'Fuzzy frontiers of identity: The British case', *Social Identities*, 1 (1995): 35–62.
17. John Curtice, Paula Devine, and Rachel Ormston, 'Devolution: Identities and constitutional preferences across the UK', in Alison Park, Caroline Bryson, Elizabeth Clery, John Curtice, and Miranda Phillips (eds), *British Social Attitudes 30: 2013 edition* (London: NatCen, 2013), http://www.bsa.natcen.ac.uk/media/38458/bsa30_devolution_final.pdf.
18. Linda Colley, *Britons: Forging the Nation, 1707–1837* (New Haven, CT: Yale University Press, 2005).
19. Dame Louise Casey, 'The Casey review: A review into opportunity and integration' (London: DCLG, 2016), recommendations 4 and 12, pp. 17–18.
20. Tony Blair, speech delivered at Downing Street, 8 December 2006.
21. The question wording of each item was as follows:

    Citizenship Survey: On this card are things which some people feel should be the responsibilities of every person living in the UK. Which, if any, do you feel should be the responsibilities of everyone living in the UK?...To respect the law, to treat others with fairness and respect, to treat all races equally.

    World Values Survey: I'm going to describe various types of political systems and ask what you think about each as a way of governing this country. For each one, would you say it is a very good, fairly good, fairly bad, or very bad way of governing this country? Having a democratic political system ('very good' and 'fairly good' responses combined).

    British Social Attitudes Survey: There are different opinions as to what it takes to be a good citizen. As far as you are concerned personally on a scale of 1 to 7, where 1 is not at all important and 7 is very important, how important is it...to try to understand the reasoning of people with other opinions, to help people in Britain who are worse off than yourself, to help people in the rest of the world who are worse off than yourself? (scores greater than 4 combined).

22. The Electoral Commission, *The Completeness and Accuracy of Electoral Registers in Great Britain* (London: Electoral Commission, 2010), https://www.electoralcommission.org.uk/__data/assets/pdf_file/0018/87111/The-completeness-and-accuracy-of-electoral-registers-in-Great-Britain.pdf.
23. Anthony F. Heath, Roger M. Jowell, and John K. Curtice, *How Britain Votes* (Oxford: Pergamon Press, 1985), p. 13.

24. Geoffrey Evans and James Tilley, *The New Politics of Class: The Political Exclusion of the British Working Class* (Oxford: Oxford University Press, 2017).
25. Sara B. Hobolt, 'The Brexit vote: A divided nation, a divided continent', *European Journal of Social Policy* 23 (2016), p. 1259.
26. The detailed question wordings were as follows:

    BES 1964: If the question of going into the Common Market comes up again, do you think that Britain should go in or stay out, or don't you have an opinion on that? ('No opinion' responses included in the denominator.)

    BES 1987: Britain should continue to be a member of the EEC—the Common Market—or should it withdraw?

    BES 1997: Do you think Britain should continue to be a member of the European Union or should it withdraw? ('Don't know' responses included in the denominator.)

    2001: Overall, do you approve or disapprove of Britain's membership in the European Union? ('Approve' and 'strongly approve' responses combined.)

    BES 2015: Overall, do you approve or disapprove of Britain's membership in the European Union? ('Approve' and 'strongly approve' responses combined.)

27. The detailed question wordings of the questions used in Figure 8.7 are as follows:

    BES 1979: Do you think that too many immigrants have been let into this country, or not? ('Don't know' responses included in the denominator.)

    BES 1987: Do you agree that... Immigration has gone too far? ('Disagree' and 'strongly disagree' responses combined.)

    BSA 1995, 2003: Do you think the number of immigrants to Britain nowadays should be increased a lot, increased a little, remain the same as it is, reduced a little, or reduced a lot? ('Increased a lot' and 'increased a little' responses combined.)

    BES 2015: Do you think that too many immigrants have been let into this country, or not? ('Don't know' responses included in the denominator.)

28. Powell did not in fact use the phrase 'rivers of blood'. What he did say was: 'As I look ahead, I am filled with foreboding; like the Roman, I seem to see "the River Tiber foaming with much blood"', speech to a Conservative Association meeting in Birmingham, 20 April 1968. Here Powell is quoting the Roman poet Virgil's (mythical) account in the *Aeneid* of the founding of Rome by Aeneas, a refugee from the sack of Troy. The relevance of the story of Aeneas to ethnic conflict in Britain is opaque.
29. *Guardian*, 15 October 2014, https://www.theguardian.com/world/2014/oct/15/britains-most-racist-election-smethwick-50-years-on.
30. The detailed wordings of the questions were as follows:

    BES 1974: How important is it that the government should... Redistribute income and wealth in favour of ordinary working people? ('Very important' and 'important' responses combined.)

    BES 1987, 1997: How much do you agree that... Income and wealth should be redistributed towards ordinary working people? ('Disagree' and 'strongly disagree' responses combined.)

    British Social Attitudes Surveys: How much do you agree or disagree that... government should redistribute income from the better off to those who are less well off? (Disagree and strongly disagree responses combined.)

31. Peter Mandelson apparently denies ever making the quote.
32. Alexis de Tocqueville, *De la démocratie en Amérique* (Paris: Librairie de Charles Gosselin, 1835).

33. Robert D. Putnam, *Bowling Alone: The Collapse and Revival of American Community* (New York: Simon and Schuster, 2000), p. 19.
34. Ibid., p. 287.
35. Peter A. Hall, 'Social capital in Britain', *British Journal of Political Science*, 29 (1999): 417–61.
36. Paola Grenier and Karen Wright, 'Social capital in Britain: Exploring the Hall paradox', *Policy Studies*, 27 (2006): 27–53.
37. Oliver Heath, 'Policy representation, social representation and class voting in Britain', *British Journal of Political Science*, 45 (2015): 173–93.
38. OECD/European Union, *Indicators of Immigrant Integration 2015: Settling in* (Paris: OECD Publishing, 2015), figure 1.1. The OECD figures include native-born with two foreign-born parents, native-born with mixed background, foreign-born who arrived as children, and foreign-born who arrived as adults.
39. Question wording for the immigration question was: 'Do you think the number of immigrants to Britain nowadays should be increased a lot, increased a little, remain the same as it is, reduced a little or reduced a lot?' (I combine the 'increased a lot' and 'increased a little' responses.) For the redistribution question it was: 'To what extent do you agree or disagree...[that]...It is the responsibility of the government to reduce the differences in income between people with high incomes and those with low incomes?' (I combine the 'agree' and 'strongly agree' responses.)
40. Trust: the International Social Survey Programme question has four response options— 'always trusted', 'usually trust', 'usually can't be too careful', 'almost always can't be too careful'. Government responsiveness: the question wording is 'Some people say that no matter who people vote for, it won't make any difference to what happens. Others say that who people vote for can make a big difference to what happens. Using the scale on this card (where 1 means that voting won't make any difference to what happens and 5 means that voting can make a big difference), where would you place yourself?' For trust and government responsiveness, estimates are adjusted for age.
41. Data on turnout among the voting-age population, based on official figures, indicate that election turnout in the UK in 2017 was lower than that in the most recent elections in Canada, France, Germany, Sweden, and Italy but was slightly higher than that in Japan and the USA, http://www.idea.int/data-tools/. Figures relate to 2017 in the UK and France, 2016 in the USA, 2015 in Canada, 2014 in Japan and Sweden, and 2013 in Italy and Germany.
42. Samuel H. Beer, *Britain against Itself: The Political Contradictions of Collectivism* (London: Faber and Faber, 1982).
43. Malcolm Fairbrother and Isaac W. Martin, 'Does inequality erode social trust? Results from multilevel models of US states and counties', *Social Science Research*, 42 (2013): 347–60. However, in a second paper based on data from the World Values Surveys for a large number of Western and non-Western countries, Fairbrother did find modest support for the hypothesis that increasing inequality erodes trust. Malcolm Fairbrother, 'Two multilevel modelling techniques for analyzing comparative longitudinal survey datasets', *Political Science Research and Methods*, 2 (2014): 119–40.

Chapter 9

1. Peter A. Hall and David Soskice, *Varieties of Capitalism: The Institutional Foundations of Comparative Advantage* (Oxford: Oxford University Press, 2001).
2. Gøsta Esping-Andersen, *The Three Worlds of Welfare Capitalism* (Princeton, NJ: Princeton University Press, 1990).

3. Fees for higher education were in fact abolished in 1962 and reintroduced in 1998 by Tony Blair's Labour government, http://www.historyandpolicy.org/policy-papers/papers/university-fees-in-historical-perspective.
4. OECD, 'Tax-benefit models', www.oecd.org/els/social/workincentives.
5. http://www.margaretthatcher.org/document/104078.
6. Early evaluations of the National Citizens Service have shown positive effects on the young people who have participated, but the numbers participating are relatively small as a proportion of the age group and so the impact on overall levels of social cohesion will be modest. See National Audit Office, 'National Citizen Service', HC 916 (January 2017).
7. A claim made in the 1959 Conservative party manifesto, http://www.conservativemanifesto.com/1959/1959-conservative-manifesto.shtml.
8. This is based on special analyses undertaken by Yaojun Li. See Yaojun Li and Anthony Heath, 'Class inequalities in educational attainment', CSI working paper, in preparation. See also Anthony Heath and Alice Sullivan, 'The democratisation of upper secondary education?' *Oxford Review of Education*, 37 (2011): 123–38. Somewhat similar results have been reported by the Social Mobility Commission, although the commission found that disadvantaged young people had been increasing their access to university. This is a case where Goodhart's law might well apply, as universities are under pressure from the regulator to improve access for these groups. See Social Mobility Commission, *Time for Change: An Assessment of Government Policies on Social Mobility 1997–2017* (London: Social Mobility Commission, 2017), https://www.gov.uk/government/publications/social-mobility-policies-between-1997-and-2017-time-for-change.
9. Richard Breen (ed.), *Social Mobility in Europe* (Oxford: Oxford University Press, 2004), chapter 3.
10. OECD data cover only the years since 2000 and look only at the crude gender pay gap, http://stats.oecd.org/index.aspx?queryid=54751.
11. See International Social Survey Programme, http://www.issp.org/about-issp/. The data cover only the period from 1995 to 2013, however. Longer-term trends are less certain.
12. Lincoln Quillian, Devah Pager, Ole Hexel, and Arnfinn H. Midtbøen, 'Meta-analysis of field experiments shows no change in racial discrimination in hiring over time', *Proceedings of the National Academy of Sciences*, 114 (2017): 10870–5.
13. The Redfern Review no longer appears to be available online. However, in his blog on the Redfern Review (posted 23 November 2016), David Kingman of the Intergenerational Foundation stated that: 'The Review's most eye-catching finding was that falls in the incomes of typical first-time buyers (whom they define as people aged 28 to 40) had a more significant impact on declining levels of homeownership than constraints in the supply of new housing. They found that between 2002 and 2014, the incomes of people in the younger age group fell by 10% relative to those of people who were over 40, severely weakening their buying power. The Review found that this was accompanied by tightening access to first-time buyer mortgages for people in the same age group, which was one of the other main drivers of falling homeownership', http://www.if.org.uk/2016/11/23/redfern-review-argues-housing-crisis-is-caused-by-falling-wages-rather-than-housing-supply/.
14. Anthony Heath and Catherine Rothon, 'Ethnic penalties and premia at the end of lower secondary education', in *Unequal Attainments: Ethnic Educational Inequalities in Ten Western Countries*, edited by Anthony Heath and Yaël Brinbaum (Oxford: Oxford University Press/British Academy, 2014), pp. 63–93.

15. The assisted places scheme, introduced by the Conservative government in 1980, might be regarded as an exception, but in many ways the scheme was simply a reversion to the previous direct grant system, which had operated between 1945 and 1976, rather than a new extension of access to private education. The assisted places scheme was discontinued by Labour in 1997.
16. For example, Bess Bukodi's work, cited in Chapter 7, shows that parental education has become a more important driver of success at A Level than social class.

INDEX

Abitur 69
Administrative data 15, 19, 31, 58, 65, 68, 71, 117
  see also Goodhart's law
Adult Skills Survey (PIAAC) 159, 161, 162
Age differences in
  attitudes to immigration 179
  attitudes to membership of the EU 180
  attitudes to redistribution 182
  birth of first child 133
  feelings of closeness to one's country 190
  national pride 170-1
  unemployment 125
Alcohol
  affordability 50-1
  consumption 44, 50-2
  international comparisons of consumption 52
  trends 50-2
Alzheimer's disease *see* dementias
American National Research Council panel 37, 38
Annual Population Survey 41, 83
Aristotle 167
Atkinson, Anthony 4, 17
Attitudes to immigration 179, 181, 192
Attitudes to membership of the EU 180
Attitudes to redistribution 182, 192
Austerity measures 14, 33, 211
Australia 81

baccalauréat 69
Bank of England 22
Barro, Robert 68
Barro-Lee dataset 68
Basic amenities *see* housing conditions
Bedroom standard 95-7
Beer, Samuel 196
Bell, David 115
Better Life Index *see* OECD
Beveridge, William 2, 3, 4, 6, 7, 8, 10, 12, 13, 23, 24, 34, 61, 88, 114, 115, 116, 125, 198-211
Beveridge Report *see* Social Insurance and Allied Services, report
Big Society programme 167, 201

Black Caribbean and African
  experience of discrimination 145-7, 158
  experience of overcrowding 98
  risks of unemployment 129-31
  see also ethnic differences
Blair MP, Tony 8, 166, 174
Blanchflower, David 115, 120
Body mass index (BMI) 47, 83
Bowling Alone 6, 183
Bradshaw, Jonathan 25, 26, 97
Brexit 8, 166, 178-9, 211
Brexit Referendum 178
Britain Against Itself 196
British Beer and Pub Association 50, 51
British Cohort Study 1970 149
British Election Survey 83, 173, 179-80, 181, 182, 187
British Household Panel Study 23, 153, 156, 186
British identity 171-4
British Medical Journal 30, 45
British Social Attitudes Survey 82, 83, 84, 169, 170, 173, 175, 177, 181, 182, 186, 187
British values 8, 166, 174-8
Brooks, Greg 72, 73, 74
Brown MP, Gordon 8, 166
Bukodi, Bess 154, 163
Bynner, John 83

Callaghan MP, James 61
Cameron MP, David 6, 8, 166, 201
Canada 11
  see also peer countries
Cancer
  breast 42, 43
  lung 33, 42, 43, 45
  survival rates 57-8
Care-leavers and risks of NEET 135
Casey, Louise 166
Casey Report 166, 174
Causal evidence 9, 33, 45, 83, 84, 115, 201, 206
Census, decennial 90, 91, 95, 97, 100, 105, 106, 144, 152
Centrepoint 102
Chandola, Tarani 56
Charges for healthcare 56

Cheshire, Paul 94
Citizenship Survey 169, 175, 177, 186
Civic community 6, 166
Civic Culture Survey 1959 186, 187, 188
Civic participation 83, 115, 185–9
Claimant count (of unemployment) 117
Classification of occupations 53, 54
Coe, Robert 73, 86
Colley, Linda 174
Commission for Racial Equality (CRE) 146, 165
Commission on the Measurement of Economic Performance and Social Progress 11, 139
Community Life Survey 83, 169, 186
Community spirit 90, 114, 168
Comparative Study of Electoral Systems 194
Comprehensive system of education 62, 80
Cribb, Jonathan 18, 19, 27
Crime and disorder 9
Cross-national comparisons *see* peer countries
Cruickshank, Heather 108
Culture
   role in educational attainment 81, 208–9
   role in health 53, 56, 208
Curriculum and Qualifications Authority 72
Cycling 49

Davis Report 150
De Gaulle, General 179
Death rates from diseases 42–6, 51
Debt
   secured 22
   trends in 23
   unsecured 22–3
Debt to income ratio 22–3
Decent homes standard 91–2
Defence of the Realm Act 1914 50
Dementias 42, 44
Deming, J. Edwards 8
Democracy in America 66
Democratization of education 81
Department for Education statistics 65, 66, 70
Department of the Environment statistics 93
Department for Transport statistics 49
Depression, the Great 90, 114, 168
Deregulation 15, 97, 117, 120, 136, 207, 229
Destitution 28–9, 33
Devolution 171–2
Diminishing marginal returns 53, 89
Disability-free life expectancy 41–2, 47, 221
Disconnect from politics 185–9
   see also political efficacy

Discord, the giant of 201, 203
   see also social cohesion
Discouraged workers 116
Discrimination
   effects on well-being 10, 140
   field experiments 142
   international comparisons 158
   legislation 139, 143, 181
   Muslim discrimination 158
   racial discrimination 143–7, 157–8, 203, 205
   sex discrimination 148, 150
   social class discrimination 15
   trends 143–7
Disease
   cerebrovascular 42
   infectious 34
   ischaemic heart 42, 43
   liver 44, 50
   of affluence 34, 44
   the giant of 2, 9, 34–60, 202
   see also dementias, cancer
Disengagement 183–9
Disraeli MP, Benjamin 6, 165
Diversity
   and social cohesion 195, 196
   ethnic 165, 168, 179, 189
   gender 148
Doll, Richard 45
Dolton, Peter 148
Dose-dependence 47

East Asian educational success 81, 208
Education
   and capabilities 62
   and empowerment 62
   and healthy lifestyles 62
   and the labour market 61
   democratization of 81
   reforms 72, 86, 200, 208–9
   systems 62, 80
   see also comprehensive system, tripartite system
Educational differences in
   attitudes to immigration 181, 192
   attitudes to membership of the EU 180
   attitudes to redistribution 182, 192
   British values 176–8
   civic engagement 188
   economic outcomes 82–3
   life satisfaction 11
   national pride 170
   non-economic outcomes 82–3, 228
   risks of unemployment 123–5

trust 188, 193
turnout 188
voluntary association membership 188
Education Act 1944 2, 3, 62
Educational participation 9, 64–9
Educational progress, dark side 87, 116, 121, 137
Educational standards 9, 63, 74
Employment Protection Act 1976 148
English Housing Survey 91, 96, 98, 103, 110
English identity 171–4
English Longitudinal Study of Ageing 30
Environment 9
Equal Pay Act 1970 148, 151
Equal treatment, measures of 144, 149
Equality Act 2010 139, 140
Equality of opportunity 3, 4–5, 139
Equity 60
  see also fairness
Ermisch, John 162
Ethnic differences in
  British values 176–8
  national pride 170
  overcrowding 98
  rickets 31
  segregation 166
  unemployment 129–31
  see also diversity, ethnic
Ethnicity 236
Exercise 37, 48
Eurobarometer 169
European Social Survey 160, 162
European Values Survey 169, 186, 188
European Union
  attitudes to membership of 179–80
Eurostat 23, 110
Evaluation
  of educational reforms 71, 86
  of effects of education 83, 87
Examinations
  11 plus 63
  Abitur 69
  baccalauréat 69
  GCE A level 63, 154
  GCE Ordinary Level 63, 69, 70
  GCSE 69, 70
  High-stakes 69, 81, 85, 88, 97, 137
  School Certificate 69
Expectations, changing 88, 89
Experiments
  and causal evidence 84
  field 142, 143–7
  natural 201, 206

Fairness 5, 60, 139, 140, 141, 148, 163–4
Family and Class in a London Suburb 90
Family and Kinship in East London 90
Family Expenditure Survey 19, 27
Family Resources Survey 19, 27
FareShare 29, 30
Financial crash of 2007/8 14, 16, 22, 27, 33, 94, 107, 119, 121, 133, 199, 202, 206, 207
First International Mathematics Study (FIMS) 74–5
Fisher, R.A. 45
Fitzpatrick, Ray 56
Flexible labour market see deregulation
Floud, Roderick 53
Focus groups 25
Food
  banks 29
  insecurity 29–31, 219
  nutritional quality 24, 29
  parcels 30
France 11
  see also peer countries
Free school meals as a measure of social class 238
Full Employment in a Free Society 4, 7, 88, 114, 115
Full employment 114, 121

Garratt, Elisabeth 30
GDP per head
  definition of 15
  international comparisons 15
  limitations of 17
  measures of 217
  trends in 15, 36
Gender differences in
  disability-free life expectancy 41–2
  diseases 43
  educational participation 66–7, 70–1
  life expectancy 41–2, 55
  modal age at death 40
  national pride 170
  obesity 48
  occupational segregation 150
  opportunity 147
  smoking-related mortality 46
  unemployment 122–31
  upwards mobility 154
  wages 148–51
General Household Survey 91, 123, 124, 127, 128, 130, 134, 153, 156
General Lifestyle Survey 41
General Register Office 53

Germany 11
  see also peer countries
Giants, the Five 2–4, 7, 8, 9, 11, 198–211
Gini coefficient 17
Gini, Corrado 17
Global Burden of Disease Study 42
Globalization 18, 166, 179
Goldacre, Michael 30, 31
Goldthorpe, John 152
Goodhart, Charles 71
Goodhart's law 71, 72, 73, 198, 226, 245
Grade inflation 71, 72, 86
Gray, J. L. 142, 143, 149, 154
Great Gatsby curve 161–2
Grenfell Tower fire 92
Grenier, Paola 167, 184
Griffiths MP, Peter 181

Hall, Nick 31
Hall, Peter 184, 199
Health
  differences in life satisfaction 11
  self-rated 83
  see also disease, life expectancy
Health Survey for England 83
Healthcare
  expenditure 58, 224
  systems 37, 38, 56
Healthy lifestyles 10, 37, 44–52
Heath, Anthony 158
Heath MP, Edward 181
Heath, Oliver 189
Hidden homeless 100
Higher education
  expansion 62
  participation 67
Higher Education Statistics Agency 67
Hill, Austin Bradford 45
Hobolt, Sarah 179, 184
Holmans, A.E. 96, 100, 108, 112
Homelessness
  definitions of 99–100
  hidden 100
  statutory 100
  trends in 99–102
Homophily 147
Hospital admissions
  alcohol-related 51
  malnutrition-related 30
House prices, ratio to household income 107
House-building 3, 111
Households
  concealed 103–4
  debt 22–3
  definition of 103
  dual career 18
  growth in number 103
  income 19–21
  increasing number of 21
  median income 19–21, 27
Housing
  affordability of 106–8
  cost of mortgage interest payments 107
  demand for 102–4
  inequality of 104–6
  space 108–11
  trends in stock 93
Housing Act 1949 90
Housing conditions
  and amenities 90–1
  and well-being 89
  quality 88
  see also overcrowding
Housing crisis
  after Second World War 89–90, 103
  in twenty-first century 89, 102–13, 208
Housing Health and Safety Rating System 92
Human Development Index (HDI) 62, 64, 216
Human Mortality Database 36, 46

Idleness, the giant of 2, 9, 114–38, 203
Ignorance, the giant of 2, 9, 61–87, 203
Income tax rates 18
Income differences in
  attitudes to immigration 181
  attitudes to membership of the EU 180
  attitudes to redistribution 182
  life satisfaction 11
  national pride 170–1
  mobility 161–3
Indebtedness 22
  see also debt
Inequality
  and Brexit vote 179
  and social cohesion 165, 195, 196, 201, 209
  effects of 35, 53, 165, 209
  evil of 4
  international comparisons 17
  measurement of 17, 78, 105, 218
  of housing space 96, 104–6
  of income 4–5, 17–18, 19–21, 56
  of opportunity 140–64, 200–1
  of social progress 204
  of test scores 78–9
  socioeconomic 37, 38, 52–6
  trends 17

Infant mortality *see* mortality
Inflation, evil of 120, 135
Institute for Fiscal Studies 23, 32
International Educational Association for the Evaluation of Educational Achievement 74, 76
International Labour Office 116, 117, 132
International Social Survey Programme 191, 193
Irish identity 171–4
Italy 11
  see also peer countries

Jackson, Michelle 155, 156
Jahoda, Marie 168
Japan 11
  see also peer countries
Jencks, Christopher 12
Jerrim, John 76, 77, 81, 208
Joad, Professor 24
Joseph Rowntree Foundation 28
Joshi, Heather 148, 150

Key Stage 3 72
Keynes, John Maynard 114

Labour Force Survey 117, 123, 124, 127, 128, 130, 134, 153, 156
Labour market
  conditions 66
  reforms 116, 117, 120, 199
League tables 71, 85
Learning to Labour 66
Lee, Yong-Wha 68
Level playing field principle 141, 143
Liebig, Thomas 158
Life expectancy
  international comparisons 35–8
  trends 35–8, 41–2, 55
  see also disability-free life expectancy
Life satisfaction 10, 11
  see also well-being
Literacy
  adult 80
  international comparisons 73–4, 76–8, 80, 81
  trends in 72–3, 86

Maastricht Treaty 1992 180
Macmillan MP, Harold 3, 10
Makepeace, Gerry 148
Malnutrition, hospital admissions 30
Mandelson MP, Peter 182
Marienthal 114, 167

Marginalized groups 99, 115, 131, 135, 168, 170, 189, 204–5
Market economy
  coordinated 199, 206
  liberal 199, 206
Market forces
  in housing 94, 112–13, 207
  in education 209
Marmot, Michael 52
Marmot Review 56
Marriage bar 160
Material deprivation 23, 32, 220
Material prosperity
  and health 37, 44, 60
  as a measure of social progress 9
  international comparisons 14–16
  spillover effects on the housing market 104
  trends 14–23, 202, 206, 211
Maths performance
  international comparisons 74–80
  trends in 75
Median 17, 20, 78
Men Without Work 114
Mental health 133
Milburn MP, Alan 5, 139, 163
Miller, David 166
Minimum income standard 25–6
Minimum school-leaving age, *see* school-leaving age
Ministry of Housing, Communities and Local Government (MHCLG, formerly DCLG) 101, 108
Modal age at death 40
Morelli, Salvatore 17
Morgan, Malcolm 108
Mortality
  adult 40
  from different diseases 42–4
  infant 38–9, 53
  smoking-related 46
Moshinsky, Pearl 142, 143, 149, 154
Muslims
  risks of unemployment 131
  discrimination against 146, 158

National Audit Office 101, 135
National Child Development Study 149
National Citizen Service 201
National Health Service (NHS) 34, 56–8, 60
National identity 8, 166, 168–71
National pride and belonging
  international comparisons 190–1
  trends in 168–71

National Statistics Socio-Economic Classification 54
National Survey of Health and Development 149
NEET (not in Education, Employment or Training)
  definition of 132, 235
  effects of 132
  international comparisons 135-6
  trends in 133-4
Non-discrimination principle 141
Northern Ireland identities 171-4
Northern Ireland Life and Times Survey 173
Non-voting 178
  see also turnout

Obesity
  educational differences 83
  international comparisons 46-8
  trends in 46-8, 83
Occupational differences in
  attitudes to immigration 181
  attitudes to membership of the EU 180
  attitudes to redistribution 182
  national pride 170-1
Occupational structure, changes in 123, 151-2
Ofsted 72
OECD Better Life Index 110, 139, 214
OECD Health Statistics 57
Office for National Statistics 22, 23, 40, 42, 50, 54, 67, 93, 106, 107, 133, 135
Office for National Statistics Longitudinal Study 55
Official statistics see administrative data
One nation at home 3, 6, 203
  see also two nations
Organization for Economic Co-operation and Development (OECD) 23, 52, 57, 64, 76, 77, 79, 80, 111, 117, 118
Our World in Data 15, 39, 54
Overcrowding
  bedroom standard 95, 96, 97, 98, 108, 109, 230
  European measure 109, 232
  Greater London Authority internal space guidelines 108
  in different housing sectors 99
  international comparisons 109-11
  parallels with poverty 88, 94
  risks of 98
  space-based measures 108-11
  statutory measure 230
  trends 96, 99
Owner occupation 92-3

Paskov, Marii 22, 23
Peer countries
  choice of 11-12
  comparisons of alcohol consumption 52
  comparisons of breast cancer survival rates 57
  comparisons of closeness to one's country 190-2, 205
  comparisons of cycling and exercise 49
  comparisons of educational standards 73-8
  comparisons of educational inequality 78-80
  comparisons of ethnic diversity 189-90
  comparisons of GDP per head 14-16, 206
  comparisons of gender earnings gaps 159, 205
  comparisons of healthcare expenditure 58
  comparisons of household income 21
  comparisons of housing space and expenditure 109-10
  comparisons of income inequality 17-18
  comparisons of infant mortality 39
  comparisons of life expectancy 35-8
  comparisons of NEET 135
  comparisons of obesity 47-8
  comparisons of political disconnect 194
  comparisons of relative poverty 27
  comparisons of racial discrimination 157-8, 205
  comparisons of smoking 45
  comparisons of social fluidity and mobility 161-2, 205
  comparisons of support for immigration 192
  comparisons of support for redistribution 192
  comparisons of university graduation 68-9
  comparisons of trust 193, 205
  comparisons of turnout 194
  comparisons of unemployment rates 117-21, 207
Phillips, Trevor 165
Pickett, Kate 5, 6, 165
Political Action Survey 1974 84, 187
Political efficacy 82-4
Polytechnics 67
Populism 196
Poverty 24
Poverty
  definitions of 24
  international comparisons 27
  measurement of 22, 218, 219

parallels with overcrowding 88
trends 27-31
see also destitution, material deprivation, relative poverty, socially acceptable standard of living, subsistence level of living
Powell MP, Enoch 181, 243
Prescription charges 56
Pride, national 8
Private sector
  renting 92-3, 108
  schools 66
Programme for International Student Assessment (PISA) 76-81, 161-2
Programme for the International Assessment of Adult Competencies (PIAAC) 80, 159, 240
  see also Adult Skills Survey
Protected characteristics 140
Purchase of commissions 140
Putnam, Robert 6, 167, 168, 183, 184

Quality of life 34-5, 44

Race Relations Acts 143
Racial prejudice, trends in 147
Rashid, Sammy 72, 73
Recessions 14, 16, 107, 118, 119, 125, 126, 133, 207
Redistribution of income and wealth, attitudes to 182
Redfern Review 207, 231, 245
Register count (of unemployment) 117, 118
Registration of deaths 35
Relative deprivation 10
Relative housing poverty 96-7
Relative poverty
  definition 26
  international comparisons 27
  measurement 219
  trends 27
Response rates 76
Rickets 30-1
Riots 140
Robbins report 62
Roemer, John 141
Roser, Max 15, 39, 54
Rough sleeping 100-2
Rowntree, Joseph 28
Rowntree, Seebohm 13, 24, 25, 26, 28
Royal Commission on the Housing of the Working Classes 1885 94
Russia 36-7

School exclusion 133
School improvement 73
Schooling, participation after minimum leaving age 65, 66
School-leaving age 62, 63, 64, 133, 136, 225
Science performance, international trends in 74-5
Scotland 65, 69
Scottish Election Survey 173
Scottish Independence Referendum 178, 185
Scottish Social Attitudes Survey 173
Scottish identity 171-4
Second International Mathematics Study (SIMS80) 75
Self-harm 44
Sex Discrimination Act 1975 148
Shure, Nikki 78
Simon, Patrick 158
Slum clearance 3, 90, 112
Smoking 37, 45-6, 83, 208
Social capital 7, 183-4, 189
Social class differences in
  attitudes 182
  entry to the salariat 153
  fluidity 160, 236, 241
  healthy lifestyles 52
  infant mortality 53-4
  life expectancy 53-6
  opportunities 151-7
  political support 179
  see also occupational differences
Social cohesion 4-7, 165-97, 200-1, 242
Social desirability bias 50
Social housing 92-3, 108
Social insurance 2, 13, 200
Social Insurance and Allied Services, report (the Beveridge Report) 2, 12, 13
Social integration 37, 44
Social mobility *see* social class
Social Mobility Commission 5
Social progress
  Commission on Measurement 11, 139
  concept 7, 8-9
  indicators 9-11, 35, 60, 64, 84, 94, 140, 216
  trends 198-211
Social surveys *see* Surveys
Social trust *see* Trust 183-7
Socially acceptable
  standard of living 25-6, 32
  housing space 97
Soskice, David 199
Squalor, the giant of 2, 9, 88-113, 202
Stevenson, T.H.C. 53, 56, 60
Stroke *see* disease, cerebrovascular

Subsistence level of living 24, 26, 32
Suicide 81, 115, 232, 233
Survey data
  limitations of 76
  representative samples 19, 41, 68, 117, 152
  Rowntree's surveys of York 24-5, 28, 33
Sweden 11
  see also peer countries
Sybil: or, the Two Nations 6, 165

Technical progress 18, 39, 59, 206
Thatcher MP, Margaret 6, 15, 32, 120
  reform programme of 16, 32, 116, 120, 136, 199-220
  speech on discord 201
  speech on evil of inflation 120
  speech on society 201, 213
  vision 94
The General Theory of Employment, Interest and Money 114
The Spirit Level 5, 165
Trends in International Mathematics and Science Study (TIMSS) 75, 80
Time for Change 5, 139
Tobacco
  companies 33, 45
  smoking 45
Tolerance 83
Toqueville, Alexis de 6, 183
Tripartite system
  of education 1, 62, 63, 80, 207
  of housing 92
Trussell Trust 29, 30
Trust
  international differences in 193, 205
  trends in 83, 183-7
Tunstall, Becky 96, 97, 105, 106, 111
Turnout 8, 185-9
Two nations 6, 8, 165, 166, 203, 218

UK Longitudinal Household Survey (also known as Understanding Society) 11, 83, 153, 156, 186, 188
Unemployment 9, 10, 114-38
  definition 116
  international comparisons 117-19
  long-term 114-15, 120
  measurement 117, 233, 234
  scarring effects of 125
  social and psychological effects 115
  trends 117-21
  youth 116, 125-9

Unfairness, the giant of 203
  see also discrimination, fairness, inequality of opportunity
United Nations Development Programme (UNDP) 62
United Nations Universal Declaration of Human Rights 139, 141
University
  enrolments 67, 69
  graduation 68-9
USA 11
  see also peer countries

Vehicle miles
  by bicycle 49
  by car or taxi 49
Vocational qualifications 137
Voluntary Action 7
Voluntary associations 6, 7, 185-9
  see also civic participation
Voting *see* turnout

Wage gap *see* gender differences
Want, the giant of 2, 9, 13-33, 202
Welfare arrangements
  liberal 199
  models 12, 199
  policy 13, 18
  reforms 13, 15-16, 32
  social democratic 199
  state 2, 13, 15, 199
Well-being 9, 10, 89, 115, 140, 214, 216
Welsh identity 171-4
Welsh Assembly Election Survey 173
Welsh Life and Times Survey 173
Why are there more questions than answers, Grandad? 12
Wiertz, Dingeman 67
Wilkinson, Richard 5, 6, 165
Willis, Paul 66
Willmott, Peter 90
Wolf, Alison 71, 137
Women
  employment 18, 21, 25
  participation in the labour market 147
Women on Boards 150
World Health Organization 36, 46
World Values Survey 170, 175, 177, 187
Wright, Karen 167, 184

Yeates, David 31
Young, Michael 90

The manufacturer's authorised representative in the EU for product safety is Oxford University Press España S.A. of el Parque Empresarial San Fernando de Henares, Avenida de Castilla, 2 – 28830 Madrid (www.oup.es/en or product.safety@oup.com). OUP España S.A. also acts as importer into Spain of products made by the manufacturer.

www.ingramcontent.com/pod-product-compliance
Lightning Source LLC
LaVergne TN
LVHW051917060526
838200LV00004B/189